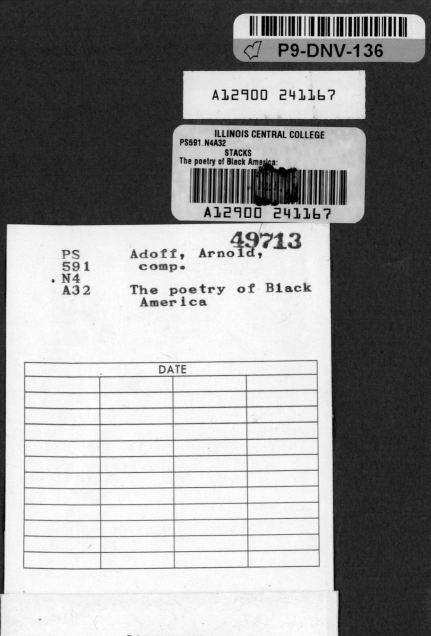

DATE		

THE POETRY OF
BLACK AMERICA

Anthology of the 20th Century

BY ARNOLD ADOFF

anthologies

BLACK ON BLACK
Commentaries by Negro Americans

BLACK OUT LOUD
An Anthology of Modern Poems by Black Americans

BROTHERS AND SISTERS
Modern Stories by Black Americans

CITY IN ALL DIRECTIONS
An Anthology of Modern Poems

I AM THE DARKER BROTHER
An Anthology of Modern Poems by Negro Americans

IT IS THE POEM SINGING INTO YOUR EYES
Anthology of New Young Poets

biography

MALCOLM X

picture book

MA nDA LA

THE POETRY OF
BLACK AMERICA
Anthology of the 20th Century

Edited by
ARNOLD ADOFF, *comp.*

Introduction by
Gwendolyn Brooks

Harper & Row, Publishers
New York, Evanston,
San Francisco, London

Acknowledgments

The 7 pages following constitute an extension of this copyright page.

Nanina Alba: "Be Daedalus" and "For Malcolm X" reprinted by permission of A. Ruben Alba.

Lewis Alexander: "Dream Song" and "Nocturne Varial" reprinted by permission of Anna Thompson. "Enchantment" from *The New Negro*, edited by Alain Locke and published by Atheneum Publishers, Inc. "Negro Woman" from *Caroling Dusk*, edited by Countee Cullen (Harper & Row). Copyright 1927 by Harper & Row, Publishers, Inc.; renewed 1955 by Ida M. Cullen. Reprinted by permission of the publisher and Anna Thompson.

Samuel Allen (Paul Vesey): "Dylan, Who Is Dead," "If the Stars Should Fall," "A Moment Please," "The Staircase," and "To Satch" reprinted by permission of Samuel Allen.

Johari Amini: "positives" and "to a poet i knew" from *Let's Go Some Where* by Johari Amini (Third World Press, Chicago, 1970). "signals" from *Black Essence*, 2nd edition (Third World Press, Chicago, 1972). All reprinted by permission of Johari M. Amini.

S. E. Anderson: "Junglegrave," "The Sound of Afroamerican History Chapt I," and "The Sound of Afroamerican History Chapt II" reprinted by permission of S. E. Anderson.

Russell Atkins: "It's Here In The," "Narrative," "Night and a Distant Church," and "On the Fine Arts Garden, Cleveland" reprinted by permission of Russell Atkins.

Imamu Amiri Baraka (LeRoi Jones): "Bumi," "Legacy," "leroy," "Letter to E. Franklin Frazier," "SOS," and "W.W." from *Black Magic Poetry 1961–1967*; copyright © 1969 by LeRoi Jones. Reprinted by permission of the publisher, the Bobbs-Merrill Company, Inc. British Commonwealth reprint rights granted by the Ronald Hobbs Literary Agency. "Each Morning," "Preface to a Twenty Volume Suicide Note," and "Way Out West" copyright © 1961 by LeRoi Jones. Reprinted from *Preface to a Twenty Volume Suicide Note* by LeRoi Jones (Totem Corinth Books, New York). Used with permission of the Ronald Hobbs Literary Agency. "A Guerrilla Handbook" from *The Dead Lecturer* by LeRoi Jones (Evergreen). "The Invention of Comics" from *The Dead Lecturer* by LeRoi Jones (Evergreen); copyright © 1964 by LeRoi Jones. "A Poem for Black Hearts" from *Negro Digest*, September 1965; copyright © 1965 by LeRoi Jones. All three reprinted by permission of the Sterling Lord Agency, Inc. "Study Peace" from *The Journal of Black Poetry*, Vol. 1, No. 10, 1968. Copyright © 1968 by LeRoi Jones. Reprinted by permission of the author and the Ronald Hobbs Literary Agency. "We Own the Night" copyright © 1968 by LeRoi Jones. Reprinted by permission of the Sterling Lord Agency, Inc., from *Black Fire*, edited by LeRoi Jones and Larry Neal (William Morrow & Co.).

Gerald W. Barrax: "Black Narcissus" reprinted by permission of Gerald W. Barrax. "Efficiency Apartment," "For Malcolm: After Mecca," "Fourth Dance Poem," "To a Woman Who Wants Darkness and Time," and "Your Eyes Have Their Silence" from *Another Kind of Rain* by Gerald W. Barrax (University of Pittsburgh Press). Copyright © 1970 by the University of Pittsburgh Press, and reprinted with their permission.

Lerone Bennett, Jr.: "And Was Not Improved" and "Blues and Bitterness" reprinted by permission of Lerone Bennett, Jr.

Lebert Bethune: "Blue Tanganyika," "Bwagamoyo," "Harlem Freeze Frame," and "A Juju of My Own" copyright © 1968 by Lebert Bethune. Reprinted from *Black Fire*, edited by LeRoi Jones and Larry Neal (William Morrow & Co.). Used with permission of the author and the Ronald Hobbs Literary Agency.

Arna Bontemps: "A Black Man Talks of Reaping," "Close Your Eyes!," "The Day-Breakers," "The Return," and "Southern Mansion" copyright © 1963 by Arna Bontemps. Reprinted by permission of Harold Ober Associates Incorporated.

William Stanley Braithwaite: "Golden Moonrise" and "In a Grave-Yard" reprinted by permission of Coward, McCann & Geoghegan, Inc., from *Selected Poems* by William Stanley Braithwaite (Coward-McCann). Copyright 1948 by William Stanley Braithwaite.

Gwendolyn Brooks: "The Bean Eaters," "Strong Men, Riding Horses," and "We Real Cool" copyright © 1959 by Gwendolyn Brooks. "The Blackstone Rangers" and "The Sermon on the Warpland" copyright © 1968 by Gwendolyn Brooks Blakely. "Bronzeville Man with a Belt in the Back," "The Chicago *Defender* Sends a Man to Little Rock," "The Egg Boiler," and "The Last Quatrain of the Ballad of Emmett Till" copyright © 1960 by Gwendolyn Brooks. "Malcolm X" and "from: Two Dedications" copyright © 1967 by Gwendolyn Brooks Blakely. "Medgar Evers" copyright © 1964 by Gwendolyn Brooks Blakely. "The Old-Marrieds" and "A Song in the Front Yard" copyright 1945 by Gwendolyn Brooks Blakely. "The Second Sermon on the Warpland" copyright © 1968 by Gwendolyn Brooks Blakely. All from *The World of Gwendolyn Brooks* by Gwendolyn Brooks (Harper & Row). All reprinted by permission of Harper & Row, Publishers, Inc. "Martin Luther King, Jr." and "Riot" from *Riot* by Gwendolyn Brooks (Broadside Press). Copyright © 1970 by Gwendolyn Brooks Blakely. Both reprinted by permission of Broadside Press.

Sterling A. Brown: "After Winter," "Foreclosure," "Old Lem," "An Old Woman Remembers," "Remembering Nat Turner," "Sister Lou," "Southern Road," "Strange Legacies," and "Strong Men" reprinted by permission of Sterling A. Brown.

F. J. Bryant, Jr.: "Cathexis" reprinted by permission of F. J. Bryant, Jr.

John Henrik Clarke: "Determination" and "Sing Me a New Song" from the book *Rebellion and Rhyme*; copyright 1948 by John Henrik Clarke, and used with the author's permission.

Carole Gregory Clemmons: "I'm Just a Stranger Here, Heaven Is My Home" and "Spring" published by permission of Carole Gregory Clemmons. "Love from My Father" and "Migration" from *Nine Black Poets*, edited by R. Baird Shuman (Moore). Reprinted by permission of Moore Publishing Company.

Lucille Clifton: "For deLawd," "Good Times," "Miss Rosie," "My Mama Moved Among the Days," and "Those Boys That Ran Together" from *Good Times* by Lucille Clifton (Random House). Copyright © 1969 by Lucille Clifton. Reprinted by permission of Random House, Inc. "listen children" and "to Bobby Seale" copyright © 1972 by Lucille Clifton. Reprinted from *Good News About the Earth* by Lucille Clifton (Random House) by permission of Random House, Inc., and Curtis Brown, Ltd.

Charlie Cobb: " 'Containing Communism,' " "For Sammy Younge," "Nation," and "To Vietnam" from *Every Where Is Yours* by Charlie Cobb (Third World Press). Reprinted by permission of Third World Press, Chicago, Illinois.

Conyus: "he's doing natural life" and "upon leaving the parole board hearing" reprinted by permission of Conyus. Copyright © 1970 by Conyus. "san francisco county jail cell b-6," "six ten sixty-nine," and "untitled requiem for tomorrow" published by permission of Conyus.

Charles Cooper: "Dreams," "Honky," and "Rubin" from *Nine Black Poets*, edited by R. Baird Shuman (Moore). Reprinted by permission of Moore Publishing Company.

Sam Cornish: "A Black Man," "Death of Dr. King," and "Panther" from *Generations* by Sam Cornish (Beacon Press). Copyright © 1968, 1969, 1970, and 1971 by Sam Cornish. Reprinted by permission of Beacon Press. "Frederick Douglass," "Montgomery," and "One Eyed Black Man in Nebraska" reprinted by permission of Hill and Wang, a division of Farrar, Straus & Giroux, Inc., from *Natural Process*, edited by Ted Wilentz and Tom Weatherly (Hill and Wang). Copyright © 1970 by Hill and Wang, Inc. "The River" reprinted by permission of Sam Cornish. "To a Single Shadow Without Pity" from *The New Black Poetry*, edited by Clarence Major (International Publishers). Reprinted by permission of International Publishers, Inc.

Jayne Cortez: "For Real," "Initiation," and "Lead" reprinted by permission of Jayne Cortez.

Joseph Seaman Cotter, Jr.: "And What Shall You Say?" and "Sonnet to Negro Soldiers" from *An Anthology of Verse by American Negroes*, edited by Newman I. White and Walter C. Jackson (Moore). Reprinted by permission of Moore Publishing Company.

Stanley Crouch: "Albert Ayler: Eulogy for a Decomposed Saxophone Player" copyright © 1971 Stanley Crouch. Originally appeared in *Black World*, August 1971. "No New Music" copyright © August 1969 by *Negro Digest*. "Riding Across John Lee's Finger" copyright © September 1968 by *Negro Digest*. All reprinted by permission of *Black World*. "Blackie Thinks of His Brothers" copyright © 1968 by Stanley Crouch. Reprinted from *Black Fire*, edited by LeRoi Jones and Larry Neal (William Morrow & Co., New York, N.Y.). Used with permission of the author and the Ronald Hobbs Literary Agency.

Victor Hernandez Cruz: "CARMEN," "The Electric Cop," and "The Story of the Zeros" reprinted by permission of Victor Hernandez Cruz. "Energy" and "spirits" from *Snaps* by Victor Hernandez Cruz (Random House). Copyright © 1968, 1969 by Victor Hernandez Cruz. Reprinted by permission of Random House, Inc.

Countee Cullen: "Black Majesty" from *On These I Stand* by Countee Cullen (Harper & Row); copyright 1929 by Harper & Row, Publishers, Inc.; renewed 1957 by Ida M. Cullen. "Brown Boy to Brown Girl" and "In Memory of Colonel Charles Young" from *Color* by Countee Cullen (Harper & Row); copyright 1925 by Harper & Row, Publishers, Inc.; renewed 1953 by Ida M. Cullen. "For a Mouthy Woman," "Heritage," "Incident," "Saturday's Child," "Tableau," and "Yet Do I Marvel" from *On These I Stand* by Countee Cullen (Harper & Row); copyright 1925 by Harper & Row, Publishers, Inc.; renewed 1953 by Ida M. Cullen. "Four Epitaphs" and "From the Dark Tower" from *On These I Stand* by Countee Cullen (Harper & Row); copyright 1927 by Harper & Row, Publishers, Inc.; renewed 1955 by Ida M. Cullen. "Scottsboro, Too, Is Worth Its Song" from *On These I Stand* by Countee Cullen (Harper & Row); copyright 1935 by Harper & Row, Publishers, Inc.; renewed 1963 by Ida M. Cullen. All reprinted by permission of Harper & Row, Publishers.

Ray Garfield Dandridge: "Zalka Peetruza"

from *An Anthology of Verse by American Negroes,* edited by Newman I. White and Walter C. Jackson (Moore). Reprinted by permission of Moore Publishing Company.

Margaret Danner: "Best Loved of Africa," "The Elevator Man Adheres to Form," "Far From Africa: Four Poems," and "Sadie's Playhouse" reprinted by permission of Margaret Danner.

Frank Marshall Davis: "Flowers of Darkness," "Four Glimpses of Night," "Giles Johnson, Ph.D.," "I Sing No New Songs," "Robert Whitmore," and "Snapshots of the Cotton South" reprinted by permission of Frank Marshall Davis.

Djangatolum (Lloyd M. Corbin, Jr.): "Ali" and "Dedication to the Final Confrontation" reprinted by permission of Lloyd M. Corbin, Jr.

Owen Dodson: "I Break the Sky," Part VII from "Poems for My Brother Kenneth," and "Sorrow Is the Only Faithful One" reprinted with the permission of Farrar, Straus & Giroux, Inc., from *Powerful Long Ladder* by Owen Dodson (Farrar, Straus). Copyright 1946 by Owen Dodson. "Mary Passed This Morning" and "Yardbird's Skull" reprinted by permission of Owen Dodson.

William Edward Burghardt Du Bois: "The Song of the Smoke" reprinted by permission of *Freedomways* magazine. From Vol. 5, No. 1, 1965. Published at 799 Broadway, New York City.

Alfred A. Duckett: "Sonnet" reprinted by permission of Alfred Duckett.

Henry Dumas: "America," "Black Star Line," "Black Trumpeter," "Buffalo," and "knock on wood" reprinted by permission of Eugene Redmond and Loretta Dumas.

Paul Laurence Dunbar: "Frederick Douglass," "The Paradox," "Sympathy," "We Wear the Mask," and "When Malindy Sings" reprinted by permission of Dodd, Mead & Company, Inc., from *The Complete Poems of Paul Laurence Dunbar* (Dodd, Mead).

Ray Durem: "Award," "Friends," "I Know I'm Not Sufficiently Obscure," "Problem in Social Geometry—The Inverted Square!," and "Vet's Rehabilitation" reprinted by permission of Dorothy Durem.

Ebon (Dooley): "The Easter Bunny Blues Or All I Want For Xmas Is The Loop," "The Prophet's Warning or Shoot to Kill," and "Query" from *Revolution* by Ebon Dooley (Third World Press). Reprinted by permission of Third World Press.

James A. Emanuel: "Church Burning: Mississippi," "Emmett Till," "Get Up, Blues," "Old Black Men Say," and "The Treehouse" reprinted by permission of Broadside Press. "Emmett Till" copyright © 1963 by The New York Times Co.

Mari Evans: ". . . And the Old Women Gathered," "Black jam for dr. negro," "into blackness softly," "The Rebel," "To Mother and Steve," and "Vive Noir!" from *I Am a Black Woman* (William Morrow & Co., 1970). Reprinted by permission of the author.

Sarah Webster Fabio: "Black Man's Feast" and "Evil Is No Black Thing" reprinted by permission of Sarah Webster Fabio. All rights reserved.

Julia Fields: "Alabama" and "Poems: Birmingham 1962–1964" reprinted by permission of Julia Fields.

Calvin Forbes: "Lullaby for Ann-Lucian" and "Reading Walt Whitman" reprinted by permission of Calvin Forbes.

Carol Freeman: "Christmas morning i" and "i saw them lynch" copyright © 1968 by Carol Freeman. Reprinted from *Black Fire,* edited by LeRoi Jones and Larry Neal (William Morrow & Co., N.Y., N.Y.). Used with permission of the author and the Ronald Hobbs Literary Agency.

Hoyt W. Fuller: "Lost Moment" reprinted by permission of Hoyt W. Fuller. "Seravezza" reprinted by permission of Hoyt W. Fuller and *Black World.*

Carl Gardner: "The Dead Man Dragged from the Sea" reprinted by permission of Carl Gardner. "Reflections" from *New Negro Poets: USA,* edited by Langston Hughes (Indiana University Press). Reprinted by permission of Indiana University Press.

Zack Gilbert: "For Angela" from *Black World,* June 1971. Copyright © June 1971 by *Black World.* Reprinted by permission. "For Stephen Dixon," "My Own Hallelujahs," and "When I Heard Dat White Man Say" from *My Own Hallelujahs* by Zack Gilbert (Third World Press). Copyright © 1971 by Zack Gilbert. Reprinted by permission of Third World Press, Chicago, Illinois.

Nikki Giovanni: "Dreams," "Knoxville, Tennessee," "My Poem," "Nikki-Rosa," "Poem of Angela Yvonne Davis," "The True Import of Present Dialogue, Black vs. Negro," and "Word Poem" reprinted by permission of Nikki Giovanni. "Poem for Aretha," "Poem for Flora," and "12 Gates to the City" from *Re: Creation* by Nikki Giovanni. Copyright © 1970 by Nikki Giovanni. Reprinted by permission of Broadside Press and Nikki Giovanni.

D. L. Graham: "Soul," "tony get the boys," and "the west ridge is menthol-cool" reprinted by permission of Earl J. Hooks.

Richard E. Grant: "Broken Heart, Broken Machine" reprinted by permission of Richard E. Grant.

Angelina Weld Grimké: "Tenebris," "A Winter Twilight," and "Your Hands" from *Caroling Dusk,* edited by Countee Cullen (Harper & Row). Copyright 1927 by Harper & Row, Publishers, Inc.; renewed 1955 by Ida M. Cullen. Reprinted by permission of the publishers.

Michael S. Harper: "Barricades," "Deathwatch," and "Effendi" from *Dear John Dear Coltrane* by Michael S. Harper (University of Pittsburgh Press). Copyright © 1970 by the University of Pittsburgh Press, and reprinted with their permission. "Blue Ruth: America," "Come Back Blues," "Here Where Coltrane Is," "Martin's Blues," "Newsletter from My Mother:," and "Photographs: A Vision of Massacre" reprinted by permission of Michael S. Harper.

William J. Harris: "For Bill Hawkins, a Black Militant" and "A Grandfather Poem" reprinted by permission of William J. Harris. "Practical Concerns" published by permission of William J. Harris. "We Live in a Cage" reprinted by permission of the author and Hill and Wang, a division of Farrar, Straus & Giroux, Inc., from *Natural Process*, edited by Ted Wilentz and Tom Weatherly (Hill and Wang). Copyright © 1970 by Hill and Wang, Inc. "Why Would I Want" from *Nine Black Poets*, edited by R. Baird Shuman (Moore). Reprinted by permission of Moore Publishing Company and William J. Harris.

De Leon Harrison: "A Collage for Richard Davis: Two Short Forms," "The Room," "The Seed of Nimrod," "some days/out walking above," and "Yellow" reprinted by permission of De Leon Harrison.

Walter Everette Hawkins: "The Death of Justice" and "A Spade Is Just a Spade" from *An Anthology of Verse by American Negroes*, edited by Newman I. White and Walter C. Jackson (Moore). Reprinted by permission of Moore Publishing Company.

Robert Hayden: "Aunt Jemima of the Ocean Waves" and "El-Hajj Malik El-Shabazz" from *Words in the Mourning Time* by Robert Hayden (October House). Copyright © 1970 by Robert Hayden. "Bahá'u'lláh in the Garden of Ridwan," "A Ballad of Remembrance," "Frederick Douglass," "Homage to the Empress of the Blues," "Middle Passage," "Mourning Poem for the Queen of Sunday," "O Daedalus, Fly Away Home," "Runagate Runagate," "Those Winter Sundays," " 'Summertime and the Living . . .,' " and "The Whipping" from *Selected Poems* by Robert Hayden (October House). Copyright © 1966 by Robert Hayden. All reprinted by permission of October House, Inc.

Donald Jeffrey Hayes: "Appoggiatura" reprinted by permission of Donald Jeffrey Hayes.

David Henderson: "Do Nothing Till You Hear from Me," "Keep on Pushing," "The Louisiana Weekly #4," "Walk with De Mayor of Harlem," and "white people" from *De Mayor of Harlem* by David Henderson (E. P. Dutton & Co., Inc.). Copyright © 1965, 1967, 1969, 1970 by David Henderson. Reprinted by permission of E. P. Dutton & Co., Inc., and Robert Lantz-Candida Donadio Literary Agency. "They Are Killing All the Young Men" from *Felix of the Silent Forest* (Poets Press, New York and San Francisco, 1967). Copyright © 1967 by David Henderson. Copyright (revised version) © 1971. Copyright © 1964, 1967, 1971 by David Henderson, and reprinted with his permission.

Calvin C. Hernton: "D Blues" and "The Patient: Rockland County Sanitarium" copyright © 1971 by Calvin C. Hernton. Reprinted by permission of Calvin C. Hernton and Quincy Troupe. "Fall Down" reprinted by permission of Calvin C. Hernton. "Jitterbugging in the Streets" copyright © 1968 by Calvin Hernton. Reprinted from *Black Fire*, edited by LeRoi Jones and Larry Neal (William Morrow & Co., New York, N.Y.). Used with permission of the author and the Ronald Hobbs Literary Agency.

Leslie Pinckney Hill: "So Quietly" reprinted by permission of Hermione Hill Logan.

M. Carl Holman: "And on This Shore," "Notes for a Movie Script," and "Picnic: The Liberated" reprinted by permission of M. Carl Holman.

Frank Horne: "Kid Stuff" copyright 1953 by Frank Horne. "Notes Found Near a Suicide" copyright 1926 by Frank Horne. "On Seeing Two Brown Boys in a Catholic Church" copyright 1932 by Frank Horne. "Resurrection" copyright 1955 by Frank Horne. All reprinted by permission of Frank Horne.

Langston Hughes: "Christ in Alabama" reprinted from *The Panther and the Lash* by Langston Hughes (Knopf) by permission of Alfred A. Knopf, Inc., and Harold Ober Associates Incorporated. Copyright 1932 by Langston Hughes. "Cross," "Dream Variation," "I, Too, Sing America," and "The Negro Speaks of Rivers" reprinted from *Selected Poems* by Langston Hughes (Knopf) by permission of the publisher. Copyright 1926 by Alfred A. Knopf, Inc., and renewed 1954 by Langston Hughes. "Cultural Exchange" reprinted from *The Panther and the Lash* by Langston Hughes (Knopf) by permission of Alfred A. Knopf, Inc., and Harold Ober Associates Incorporated. Copyright © 1961 by Langston Hughes. "Death in Yorkville," "Freedom," "Militant," "October 16: The Raid," "Prime," and "Special Bulletin" from *The Panther and the Lash* by Langston Hughes (Knopf). Copyright © 1967 by Arna Bontemps and George Houston Bass. Reprinted by permission of Alfred A. Knopf, Inc., and Harold Ober Associates Incorporated. "Dream Deferred" and "Motto" reprinted from *The Panther and the Lash* by Langston Hughes (Knopf) by permission of Alfred A. Knopf, Inc., and Harold Ober Associates Incorporated. Copyright 1951 by Langston Hughes. "Juke Box Love Song" from *Montage of a Dream Deferred* by Langston Hughes (Holt, Rinehart & Winston). Copyright 1951 by Langston Hughes. Reprinted by permission of Harold Ober Associates Incorporated. "Song for a Dark Girl" reprinted from *Selected Poems* by Langston Hughes (Knopf) by permission of the publisher. Copyright 1927 by Alfred A. Knopf, Inc., and renewed 1955 by Langston Hughes.

Mae Jackson: "The Blues Today," "For Some Poets," "i remember . . . ," "i used to wrap my white doll up in," and "January 3, 1970" reprinted by permission of Mae Jackson. "reincarnation" copyright © September 1970 by *Black World*. Reprinted by permission.

Lance Jeffers: "Grief Streams Down My Chest," "How High the Moon," and "On Listening to the Spirituals" reprinted by permission of Lance Jeffers. "My Blackness Is the Beauty of This Land" from *My Blackness Is the Beauty of This Land* by Lance Jeffers (Broadside Press). Reprinted by permission of Broadside Press.

Ted Joans: "Its Curtains" and "Scenery" reprinted by permission of Hill and Wang, a division of Farrar, Straus & Giroux, Inc., from *Black Pow-Wow* by Ted Joans (Hill and Wang). Published in Great Britain by Calder and Boyars Ltd., London. Copyright © 1969 by Ted Joans. "The Protective Grigri" reprinted by permission of Hill and Wang, a division of Farrar, Straus & Giroux, Inc., from *Afrodisia* by Ted Joans (Hill and Wang). Copyright © 1970 by Ted Joans.

Fenton Johnson: "Aunt Jane Allen" from *Golden Slippers*, compiled by Arna Bontemps

(Harper & Row). Copyright 1941 by Harper & Row, Publishers, Inc. Reprinted by permission of the publisher.

Fred Johnson: "Arabesque" and "Fire, Hair, Meat and Bone" reprinted by permission of Fred Johnson.

Georgia Douglas Johnson: "The Suppliant" from *Caroling Dusk*, edited by Countee Cullen (Harper & Row). Copyright 1927 by Harper & Row, Publishers, Inc.: renewed 1955 by Ida M. Cullen. Reprinted by permission of the publishers.

Helene Johnson: "Poem" from *Caroling Dusk*, edited by Countee Cullen (Harper & Row). Copyright 1927 by Harper & Row, Publishers, Inc.; renewed 1955 by Ida M. Cullen. Reprinted by permission of the publisher.

James Weldon Johnson: "The Creation" and "Go Down Death" from *God's Trombones* by James Weldon Johnson (Viking). Copyright 1927 by The Viking Press, Inc., renewed 1955 by Grace Nail Johnson. "The Glory of the Day Was in Her Face" and "O Black and Unknown Bards" from *Saint Peter Relates an Incident* by James Weldon Johnson (Viking). Copyright 1939 by James Weldon Johnson, © renewed 1958 by Grace Nail Johnson. All reprinted by permission of The Viking Press, Inc.

Joe Johnson: "If I Ride This Train" and "Judeebug's Country" reprinted by permission of Joe Johnson.

June Jordan: "All the World Moved," "In Memoriam: Martin Luther King, Jr.," "The New Pietà: For the Mothers and Children of Detroit," and "Uncle Bull-boy" from the book *Some Changes* by June Jordan. Copyright © 1967, 1971 by June Meyer Jordan. Published by E. P. Dutton & Co., Inc., and used with their permission.

Norman Jordan: "August 2," "Black Warrior," and "July 31," reprinted by permission of Norman Jordan. "Feeding the Lions" from *The New Black Poetry*, edited by Clarence Major (International Publishers). Reprinted by permission of International Publishers, Inc.

Bob Kaufman: "African Dream," "Blues Note," "I Have Folded My Sorrows," "Mingus," "Patriotic Ode on the Fourteenth Anniversary of the Persecution of Charlie Chaplin," "To My Son Parker, Asleep in the Next Room," and "Walking Parker Home" from *Solitudes Crowded with Loneliness* by Bob Kaufman (New Directions). Copyright © 1959, 1960, 1961, 1965 by Bob Kaufman. Reprinted by permission of New Directions Publishing Corporation. "Falling" from *Golden Sardine* by Bob Kaufman (City Lights Books). Copyright © 1967 by Bob Kaufman. Reprinted by permission of City Lights Books.

Keorapetse Kgositsile: "For Eusi, Ayi Kwei & Gwen Brooks" and "My Name Is Afrika" from *My Name Is Afrika* by Keorapetse Kgositsile (Doubleday). Copyright © 1971 by Keorapetse Kgositsile. Reprinted by permission of Doubleday & Company, Inc., and Keorapetse Kgositsile. "Ivory Masks in Orbit," "Origins," and "Spirits Unchained" from *Spirits Unchained* by Keorapetse Kgositsile (Broadside Press). Reprinted by permission of Broadside Press.

Etheridge Knight: "Cell Song," "He Sees Through Stone," "The Idea of Ancestry," "It Was a Funky Deal," "Portrait of Malcolm X," "The Sun Came," and "To Dinah Washington" from *Poems from Prison* by Etheridge Knight (Broadside Press). "For Black Poets Who Think of Suicide" from *Black Poetry*, edited by Dudley Randall (Broadside Press). All reprinted by permission of Broadside Press.

Don L. Lee: "Assassination" and "But He Was Cool" from *Don't Cry, Scream* by Don L. Lee (Broadside Press). "AWARENESS" and "Wake-Up Niggers" from *Think Black* by Don L. Lee (Broadside Press). "Change-Up," "One Sided Shoot-Out," "A Poem for a Poet," and "We Walk the Way of the New World" from *We Walk the Way of the New World* by Don L. Lee (Broadside Press). "Positives: For Sterling Plumpp" from *Directionscore* by Don L. Lee (Broadside Press). All reprinted by permission of Broadside Press.

Julius Lester: "From: In the Time of Revolution" from *In a Time of Revolution*, edited by Walter Lowenfels (Random House). "On the Birth of My Son, Malcolm Coltrane" from *Soulscript*, edited by June Jordan (Doubleday). "Us" from *The Writing on the Wall*, edited by Walter Lowenfels (Doubleday). All copyright © 1967 by Julius Lester. All reprinted by permission of the author and the Ronald Hobbs Literary Agency.

Angelo Lewis: "America Bleeds" and "Clear" first published in *Motive* magazine, November 1970. Reprinted by permission of Angelo Lewis.

Elouise Loftin: "Virginia," "Weeksville Women," and "Woman" published by permission of Elouise Loftin.

Pearl Cleage Lomax: "Glimpse" reprinted by permission of Pearl Cleage Lomax.

Doughtry Long: "Ginger Bread Mama," "#4," and "One Time Henry Dreamed the Number" reprinted by permission of Broadside Press. "Negro Dreams" reprinted by permission of Dudley Randall and Doughtry Long.

Audre Lorde: "And What About the Children," "Father Son and Holy Ghost," "Father, the Year Is Fallen," "Suffer the Children," and "Summer Oracle" reprinted by permission of Audre Lorde. "Coal," "Now that I Am Forever with Child," "Rites of Passage," and "What My Child Learns of the Sea" published by permission of Audre Lorde.

Felipe Luciano: "You're Nothing But a Spanish Colored Kid" copyright © 1972 by Random House, Inc. Reprinted by permission of the Sterling Lord Agency, Inc.

K. Curtis Lyle: "Lacrimas or There Is a Need to Scream" copyright © 1972 by K. Curtis Lyle. "Sometimes I Go to Camarillo & Sit in the Lounge" copyright © 1970 by K. Curtis Lyle. Both reprinted by permission of K. Curtis Lyle. "Songs For the Cisco Kid / or singing" and "Songs For the Cisco Kid / or singing for the face" published by permission of K. Curtis Lyle.

Charles Lynch: "If We Cannot Live as People" and "Memo" reprinted by permission of Charles H. Lynch.

L. V. Mack: "Biafra" and "Death Songs" reprinted by permission of Hill and Wang, a division of Farrar, Straus & Giroux, Inc., from *Natural Process*, edited by Ted Wilentz and Tom Weatherly (Hill and Wang). Copyright © 1970 by Hill and Wang, Inc.

Naomi Long Madgett: "Black Woman" and "Simple" published by permission of Naomi Long Madgett. "Her Story" and "Mortality" from *Star by Star* by Naomi Long Madgett (Harlo, Detroit, 1965, 1970). Reprinted by permission of Naomi Long Madgett.

Barbara Mahone: "colors for mama," "a poem for positive thinkers," and "sugarfields" from *Sugarfields* by Barbara Mahone (distributed by Broadside Press). Copyright © 1970 by Barbara Mahone. Reprinted by permission of Barbara D. Mahone.

Clarence Major: "Blind Old Woman," "The Design," "Swallow the Lake," and "Vietnam" copyright © 1970 by Clarence Major. Reprinted from *Swallow the Lake* by Clarence Major (Wesleyan University Press) by permission of Wesleyan University Press. "Vietnam #4" copyright © 1967 by Clarence Major. Reprinted by permission of Clarence Major.

Herbert Martin: "Antigone I" and "Antigone VI" copyright by Herbert Woodward Martin. Reprinted by permission of Herbert Woodward Martin. "Lines" and "A Negro Soldier's Viet Nam Diary" published by permission of Herbert Woodward Martin.

Lawrence McGaugh: "To Children," "Two Mornings," and "Young Training" reprinted by permission of Lawrence McGaugh.

Claude McKay: "After the Winter," "America," "If We Must Die," "In Bondage," "The Lynching," "Outcast," "St. Isaac's Church, Petrograd," "To the White Fiends," "The Tropics in New York," and "The White House" from *Selected Poems of Claude McKay.* Copyright 1953 by Bookman Associates. Reprinted by permission of Twayne Publishers, Inc.

Adam David Miller: "Crack in the Wall Holds Flowers" reprinted by permission of Adam David Miller. "The Hungry Black Child" from *Dices or Black Bones*, edited by Adam David Miller (Houghton Mifflin). Reprinted by permission of Houghton Mifflin Company.

Wayne Moreland: "Sunday Morning" reprinted by permission of Wayne Moreland.

Pauli Murray: "Death of a Friend," "For Mack C. Parker," and "Harlem Riot, 1943" copyright © 1970 by Pauli Murray. "Mr. Roosevelt Regrets" copyright 1943 by Pauli Murray. "Without Name" copyright 1948 by Pauli Murray. All reprinted from *Dark Testament* (Silvermine) by permission of Silvermine Publishers, Inc., and the copyright owner.

Alice Dunbar Nelson: "Sonnet" from *Caroling Dusk*, edited by Countee Cullen (Harper & Row). Copyright 1927 by Harper & Row, Publishers; renewed 1955 by Ida M. Cullen. Reprinted by permission of the publisher.

Effie Lee Newsome: "Morning Light (The Dew-Drier)" reprinted by permission of Effie Lee Newsome.

Gloria C. Oden: "The Carousel," "Man White, Brown Girl and All That Jazz," "Review from Staten Island," and "The Riven Quarry" reprinted by permission of Gloria C. Oden.

Myron O'Higgins: "Two Lean Cats . . .," "Vaticide," and "Young Poet" reprinted by permission of Myron O'Higgins.

Raymond R. Patterson: "At That Moment," "Birmingham 1963," "Black All Day," "I've Got a Home in That Rock," "Letter in Winter," "Night-Piece," "When I Awoke," and "You Are the Brave" reprinted with permission from *26 Ways of Looking at a Black Man* by Raymond R. Patterson. (An *Award* book published by Universal-Award House, Inc.) Copyright © 1969 by Raymond R. Patterson.

Rob Penny: "and we conquered," "be cool, baby," "i remember how she sang," and "the real people loves one another" copyright © 1970 by Oduduwa Productions, Inc. Reprinted by permission of Rob Penny.

Julianne Perry: "no dawns" and "to L." published by permission of Julianne Perry.

Oliver Pitcher: "The Pale Blue Casket" and "Salute" reprinted by permission of Oliver Pitcher.

Sterling Plumpp: "Beyond the Nigger" from *Portable Soul* by Sterling Plumpp (Third World Press). Copyright © 1969 by Sterling D. Plumpp. "Half Black, Half Blacker," "I Told Jesus," and "The Living Truth" from *Half Black, Half Blacker* by Sterling Plumpp (Third World Press). Copyright © 1970 by Sterling Plumpp. All reprinted by permission of Third World Press.

Quandra Prettyman: "The Mood," "Still Life: Lady with Birds," and "When Mahalia Sings" reprinted by permission of Quandra Prettyman Stadler. "Photograph" published by permission of Quandra Prettyman Stadler.

Norman Henry Pritchard II: "Aswelay," "Gyre's Galax," "Love," "Self," and "#" reprinted by permission of Norman Henry Pritchard II.

Dudley Randall: "Black Magic" reprinted by permission of Dudley Randall. "The Intellectuals," "Legacy: My South," "Memorial Wreath," "On Getting a Natural," "The Profile on the Pillow," "Roses and Revolution," and "The Southern Road" reprinted by permission of Broadside Press.

Lennox Raphael: "Mike 65" reprinted by permission of Hill and Wang, a division of Farrar, Straus & Giroux, Inc., from *Natural Process*, edited by Ted Wilentz and Tom Weatherly (Hill and Wang). Copyright © 1970 by Hill and Wang, Inc.

Eugene Redmond: "Definition of Nature" and "Gods in Vietnam" reprinted by permission of Eugene B. Redmond.

Ishmael Reed: "beware: do not read this poem," "The Feral Pioneers," "The Gangster's Death," "I Am a Cowboy in the Boat of Ra," "Instructions to a Princess," "Rain Rain on the Splintered Girl," and "Sermonette" reprinted by permission of Ishmael Reed.

Conrad Kent Rivers: "Four Sheets to the Wind," "If Blood Is Black Then Spirit Neglects My Unborn Son," "On the Death of William Edward Burghardt Du Bois by African Moonlight and Forgotten Shores," "Prelude," "The Still Voice of Harlem," "To Richard Wright,"

"The Train Runs Late to Harlem," and "Watts" reprinted by permission of Cora Rivers.

Ed Roberson: "blue horses," "mayday," "poll," "seventh son," and "from: when thy king is a boy" from *When Thy King Is a Boy* by Ed Roberson (University of Pittsburgh Press). Copyright © 1970 by the University of Pittsburgh Press, and reprinted with their permission. "if the black frog will not ring" and "othello jones dresses for dinner" reprinted by permission of Ed Roberson. "if the black frog will not ring" from *New Directions in Prose and Poetry, #22,* copyright © 1970 by New Directions Publishing Corporation.

Carolyn M. Rodgers: "Jesus Was Crucified Or: It Must Be Deep," "Me, in Kulu Se & Karma," "Newark, for Now," and "U Name This One" reprinted by permission of Carolyn M. Rodgers. "We Dance Like Ella Riffs" reprinted by permission of Hill and Wang, a division of Farrar, Straus & Giroux, Inc., from *Natural Process,* edited by Ted Wilentz and Tom Weatherly (Hill and Wang). Copyright © 1970 by Hill and Wang, Inc.

Primus St. John: "Benign Neglect / Mississippi, 1970," "Elephant Rock," "Lynching and Burning," "The Morning Star," and "Tyson's Corner" published by permission of Primus St. John.

Sonia Sanchez: "definition for blk/children," "homecoming," "hospital/poem," "now poem. for us.," "poem," "poem at thirty," "right on: white america," and "to all sisters" reprinted by permission of Sonia Sanchez.

Alvin Saxon (Ojenke): "Black Power" and "Watts" from *The Ashes,* edited by Budd Schulberg (World). Copyright © 1967 by Budd Schulberg. Reprinted by arrangement with The New American Library, Inc., New York, N.Y. "A Poem for Integration" reprinted from *The Antioch Review,* Vol. XXVII, No. 3, by permission of the editors and the author.

Welton Smith: "The Beast Section" and "Interlude" copyright © 1968 by Welton Smith. Reprinted from *Black Fire,* edited by LeRoi Jones and Larry Neal (William Morrow & Co., New York, N.Y.). Used with permission of the author and the Ronald Hobbs Literary Agency. "Strategies" from *The New Black Poetry,* edited by Clarence Major (International Publishers). Reprinted by permission of International Publishers Co., Inc.

A. B. Spellman: "For My Unborn & Wretched Children," "in orangeburg my brothers did," "john coltrane / an impartial review," "tomorrow the heroes," "when black people are," and "zapata and the landlord" reprinted by permission of A. B. Spellman.

Anne Spencer: "Lady, Lady" and "Letter to My Sister" reprinted by permission of Anne Spencer.

Sun Ra: "Nothing Is" copyright © 1968 by Sun Ra. Reprinted from *Black Fire,* edited by LeRoi Jones and Larry Neal (William Morrow & Co., New York, N.Y.). Used with permission of the author and the Ronald Hobbs Literary Agency. "The Plane: Earth" and "Primary Lesson: The Second Class Citizens" reprinted by permission of Sun Ra.

Lorenzo Thomas: "Onion Bucket" and "The Subway Witnesses" copyright © 1968 by Lorenzo Thomas. Reprinted by permission of Lorenzo Thomas.

Richard W. Thomas: "Amen" copyright © 1968 by Richard Thomas. Reprinted from *Black Fire,* edited by LeRoi Jones and Larry Neal (William Morrow & Co., New York, N.Y.). Used with permission of the author and the Ronald Hobbs Literary Agency. "Life After Death," "Martyrdom," "Riots and Rituals," "To the New Annex to the Detroit County Jail," and "The Worker" from *Nine Black Poets,* edited by R. Baird Shuman (Moore). Reprinted by permission of Moore Publishing Company.

James W. Thompson: "The Yellow Bird" copyright © James W. Thompson 1961, 1970, from *First Fire* by James W. Thompson (Paul Breman Ltd., London). "You Are Alms" copyright © James W. Thompson 1966, 1967, 1970, from *Transatlantic Review #24, Negro Digest* November 1967, Fire Publications broadside in limited edition of 100 hand-numbered copies. Both reprinted by permission of James W. Thompson.

Larry Thompson: "Black Is Best" reprinted by permission of Larry E. Thompson.

Melvin B. Tolson: "African China" reprinted by permission of Ruth S. Tolson. "PSI" and "The Sea-Turtle and the Shark" from *Harlem Gallery* by Melvin B. Tolson (Twayne). Copyright © 1965 by Twayne Publishers, Inc. Reprinted by permission of the publisher.

Jean Toomer: "Beehive," "Georgia Dusk," "Reapers," and "Song of the Son" reprinted from *Cane* by Jean Toomer by permission of Liveright, Publishers, New York. Copyright ® 1951 by Jean Toomer. "Brown River, Smile," "Five Vignettes," and "The Lost Dancer" reprinted by permission of Marjorie C. Toomer.

Askia Muhammad Touré: "Floodtide," "JuJu," and "Tauhid" reprinted by permission of Askia Muhammad Touré.

Quincy Troupe: "Dirge" copyright © 1968 by Quincy Troupe. "In Texas Grass" copyright © 1969 by Quincy Troupe. "A Sense of Coolness" copyright © 1970 by Quincy Troupe. "Poem for Friends" copyright © 1970 by New Directions Publishing Corporation. All reprinted by permission of Quincy Troupe. "For Malcolm Who Walks in the Eyes of Our Children" published by permission of Quincy Troupe.

Alice Walker: "In These Dissenting Times" originally appeared in *Black World,* November 1970; reprinted by permission of *Black World.* Copyright © 1971 by Alice Walker. Reprinted from her volume *Revolutionary Petunias* by permission of Harcourt Brace Jovanovich, Inc., and the Julian Bach Literary Agency. "From: Once" from *Once,* copyright © 1968 by Alice Walker (Harcourt, Brace & World). Reprinted by permission of Harcourt Brace Jovanovich, Inc., and International Famous Agency.

Margaret Walker: "Birmingham," "For Malcolm X," "Girl Held Without Bail," and "October Journey" reprinted by permission of Margaret Walker Alexander. "Childhood," "For My People," "Lineage," and "We Have Been Believers" from *For My People* by Margaret Walker (Yale University Press). Copyright 1942 by Yale University Press and reprinted with their permission.

Tom Weatherly: "arroyo" reprinted by permission of Hill and Wang, a division of Farrar, Straus & Giroux, Inc., from *Natural Process*, edited by Ted Wilentz and Tom Weatherly. Copyright © 1970 by Hill and Wang, Inc. The sixteen lines from "Autobiography" in the biographical sketch are from *Maumau American Cantos* by Tom Weatherly (Corinth). Reprinted by permission of Tom Weatherly. "Canto 4," "Canto 5," "Canto 7," "first monday scottsboro alabama," and "imperial thumbprint" reprinted from *Maumau American Cantos* by Tom Weatherly (Corinth). Reprinted by permission of Corinth Books.

Ron Welburn: "Avoidances," "Cecil County," and "Eulogy for Populations" reprinted by permission of Ron Welburn.

Joseph White: "Black Is a Soul" reprinted by permission of Joseph White.

August Wilson: "Theme One: The Variations" reprinted by permission of August Wilson.

Bruce McM. Wright: "The African Affair" reprinted by permission of Bruce McM. Wright.

Jay Wright: "Death As History" from *The Homecoming Singer* by Jay Wright (Corinth). Copyright © 1971 by Jay Wright. Reprinted by permission of Corinth Books. "The Homecoming Singer," "An Invitation to Madison County," and "Wednesday Night Prayer Meeting" reprinted by permission of Hill and Wang, a division of Farrar, Straus & Giroux, Inc., from *Natural Process*, edited by Ted Wilentz and Tom Weatherly. Copyright © 1970 by Hill and Wang, Inc.

Richard Wright: "Between the World and Me" from *White Man, Listen!* by Richard Wright (Doubleday). Copyright 1935 by *Partisan Review*; reprinted by permission of Paul R. Reynolds, Inc., 599 Fifth Avenue, New York, N.Y. 10017. Copyright © 1957 by Richard Wright; reprinted by permission of Doubleday & Company, Inc. "Hokku Poems" and "I Have Seen Black Hands" copyright by Richard Wright; reprinted by permission of Paul R. Reynolds, Inc., 599 Fifth Avenue, New York, N.Y. 10017.

Sarah E. Wright: "To Some Millions Who Survive Joseph E. Mander, Senior" and "Until They Have Stopped" from *Give Me a Child*, copyright 1955 by Sarah E. Wright and Lucy Smith. Reprinted by permission of International Famous Agency, Inc.

Al Young: "A Dance for Militant Dilettantes," "Dance of the Infidels," "The Dancer," "For Poets," and "Myself When I Am Real" copyright © 1969 by Al Young. "Kiss," "The Move Continuing," and "Yes, the Secret Mind Whispers" copyright © 1971 by Al Young. "Loneliness" from *New Directions in Prose and Poetry, #22*. Copyright © 1970 by New Directions Publishing Corporation. All reprinted by permission of the author.

THANKS

In a project that has taken three years, it is impossible to thank all of the hundreds who gave encouragement, assistance, and love. Flyers telling about the anthology were sent around the country by editors, poets, teachers, and librarians. Announcements appeared in periodicals and newspapers, and were posted on workshop and library walls, or passed around by hand. Libraries in New York, in Ohio, and on half a dozen college campuses provided information and material. Bookstores invariably turned up some out-of-print volume that proved valuable.

In Yellow Springs, Joe Cali, and his superb staff at the Antioch College Library. Ray Price and Sue Beth Fair of the Antioch Community Bookstore, and their staff. Dorothy Scott, and the staff of *The Antioch Review*. Virginia Hamilton.

In New York, the Schomburg Collection, other branch collections of the New York Public Library, dedicated librarians. The private library and encouragement of John and Quandra Stadler. Nikki Giovanni, Charles Lynch, Ron Welburn, and many others. Benny Andrews.

A special thanks to editors such as John Henrik Clarke, Hoyt Fuller, Dudley Randall, E. F. Bickerstaff. Dozens of poets who wrote and called and sent information about themselves and their colleagues.

Finally, the people at Harper & Row, and their commitment to fine literature and the truth.

Dedication:

For the black men and women
in cages of steel and snow

For the memory of heroes and victims
under the ground too soon

For my children, Leigh and Jaime,
and their sisters and brothers

Direction:

This book is a weapon
of power and love

Use it to stand free
and take control

Preface

Use the Words To Raise the Children
Singing with Their Power

I came to the words from the music. Twenty years ago in Birdland and other clubs around New York. Listening to Parker and Bud Powell and Lester Young. Mingus. Max Roach. Dozens of names. Some bright and shining still. Others as worn in memory as their records on my shelves. Old records reminding me of when, like Lester, I leaped in. Into the music and the line of history continuing beyond the music. To go back and study. To go on ahead for the long ride. To listen. Music and musicians. Words. Poems and poets. History of a people. Power and grace. Love.

Langston Hughes was my first poet beyond that neighborhood of culture and race that surrounded my childhood. Beyond my white on white for white education. It seems now that Langston was waiting there as I wandered through the books with a tune in my head and a notebook of my own poems. Open and young to a singing line of words. Langston's poems were in the books and his Simple stories were in the newspapers. He was down on Bleecker Street with a production of *Simply Heavenly*. Later on at the Village Vanguard on Sunday afternoons, actually alive and reading his poems with Mingus and music. Talking warmly around a small table.

The Poetry of Black America is as comprehensive a collection of Black American poetry as I could assemble. Not as white "critic" or "expert" or sunshine soldier. But as dealer, pushing together as large a chunk of life, of history, of the finest poems as I could gather. To let them stand in their line from Du Bois and Dunbar to Angelo Lewis, Elouise Loftin, and Julianne Perry. And the 150 stops along the way. Poets. Black poets. Men and women from towns and cities and crossroads settlements. Life and scratching out a life. All the years of putting it down for themselves and for their children and the children now. Holding it together. Holding a people together. Working on the craft of poetry and the craft of survival.

The poem is most fragile. It can be blown away with a closing of the eyes. Yet it can hold a grown man for some time. Can be steel-strong. Can be a dangerous thing. Has to be held and listened to. Kept close and loved. Allowed to sing beyond its time on the page. To sing in the memory.

This anthology presents a big chunk of a long line of superb craft and vision. It shows the diversity, the depth of Black American poetry up to its "second renaissance" of today's fine young poets. There are over six hundred poems. In making my selections, I have been able to put aside all considerations but the quality of the work. I have been able to attempt to balance and show the range of many of the major poets of our time. Point a few directions for the future. But there are limits to any range, and three thousand poems could not be put in the book.

I leaped in at Langston in the middle and found I would have to move. Back from Hughes to Countee Cullen and Dunbar and before. Beyond to Gwendolyn Brooks and Mari Evans and Sam Allen. A. B. Spellman and Ishmael Reed. Don Lee. Sonia Sanchez. Nikki Giovanni. The hundreds of young poets growing their words in the blood-rich land. Making poems from the nights of sudden death. The nights and days of sunny love.

As a teacher I had students who wanted life in those dusty classrooms. They wanted pictures of themselves inside themselves. I began to bring some in. I was the dealer. The pusher of the poems and stories. Plays and paintings. Jazz and Blues. And my students began to push on me. To deal their sounds and write their poems. And I was made to become serious about myself. To get my head together and attempt to go beyond the classrooms and students and schools. To go beyond the racist textbooks and anthologies that were on the shelves and in the bookstores.

I had been a poet and a teacher. Now I was also an anthologist. And an editor. But I didn't work for a publisher. I worked for the poems. I took a long look and found that I was jumping in again in the middle of a line. A long Black line from W. S. Braithwaite and James Weldon Johnson, to Cullen and Hughes and Arna Bontemps. It has been just five years since *I Am the Darker Brother* was published in 1968. There have been fine collections by Imamu Baraka (LeRoi Jones) and Larry Neal, Clarence Major, Adam David Miller, Dudley Randall, and many others. *The Poetry of Black America* is only one more stop. The line continues.

There are dozens of poets whose work is not represented. There will be other anthologies of Black American poetry. Other chunks to add. Poems to push.

There is much work to be done. We are putting it down, putting it together. And at these moments it is all subtly changing. We must be at the cutting edge of that change. We must help to create that change. We must try for the finest music and meaning. And the bravest uses for our work.

I remember Mrs. Anthony would come to visit her son each summer. Up to Ohio from Kentucky until she was ninety and became ill. Each year she would arrive with her Bible and *The Complete Poems of Paul Laurence Dunbar*. Both books bound black. Binding Black. Feeding her memory to create visions for the young. Continuing in that long line that is the history and future of a people.

All power. All power to the poets. Strong for the people. Rise with shouts of love louder than the bullets. Use the words. Use the words to raise the children singing with their power. Strong for the people. No silent death.

ARNOLD ADOFF
Yellow Springs, Ohio, 1973

Contents

Introduction

Anaïs Nin, whose uses of language I consider mint-fumed, intent, and delightful, on a television panel bristled delicately when a black asked what recourse to injustice, and the relics of injustice, the ghettoite may enjoy. Miss Nin, who had already brightly eschewed both bitterness and violence, proceeded to offer her own remedies. For she, too, had once been "poor." The salves, it seems, were literary. *She read a lot, and wrote.*

Astonishing and reprehensible as such unawareness may be, it is nevertheless interesting that many blacks in the "ghetto" (these days the "ghetto" is often called Hometown) are reading and writing, with publication in mind and in view. Today large numbers of the blackness-oriented have been moved, at one time or another, to express their new excitement by writing poetry. There is a growing inquisitiveness about mechanics, about writing tools and writing methods: a maturing concern for *words* and their black potential. Many blacks, those who want to create one poem only, *and* those who want to create poetry the rest of their lives, are asking for help. Their questions are poignant. *How* do I make words work for me? Are there ways, is there *any* way, to make English words speak blackly? Are there forms already that, with a little tampering, will encase blackness properly, or must we blacks create forms of our own? If we must create forms of our own, how shall we go about this work? Is *length* helpful—should blacks write epics? Or will blacks find that they need to forge poems "bullet"-size (with bullet-precision)?

Some young blacks believe tricks should be avoided, believe that blackness, by contemporary black definition, is straightforward and substantial, clean-lined, even spare. Others, who may have begun their careers with columns of expletives (kill the honky kill the honky kill the honky, etc.), have curled their way into such degrees of super-subtlety, or outright obscurity, as must confound some of those "Negroes" they mercilessly attacked—in 1967, 1968, and part of 1969—for inhabiting ivory towers and chanting "Art for art's sake" at the borders of whitetown.

This writing and this concern are the products of stormy resentments, intensified anger, fed by amazed observation and voracious reading. The books earnestly read are not *Moby Dick, Ulysses,* and *Finnegans Wake,* not *Evangeline, The Waste Land,* and Hart Crane's *The Bridge*—although many of the poets here have exposed themselves to such—but *The Autobiography of Malcolm X,* Frantz Fanon's *The Wretched of the Earth,* Lerone Bennett's *Confrontation: Black and White* and *The Challenge of Blackness,* Margaret Walker's *For My People,* W. E. B. Du Bois's *Autobiography* and *The Souls of Black Folk,* the principles of Elijah Muhammad, the hard cautions of Baraka, and The Quotable Karenga.

In a *Phylon* essay, in 1950, I spoke of the black poet—in that different dispensation I called him the *Negro* poet—as having distinctive "advantages. Ready-made subjects—which he may twist as he wills. Great drives. And that inspiriting emotion, like tied hysteria, found only in the general territory of great drives."

Some things in that essay I would change today. But the opening paragraph is still appropriate.

And appropriate, still, is my old—and informed—conviction that "many a Gentile poet, longing for a moving, authoritative and humane subject, longing almost for major indignities because he knows that such make the pen run wild, longing to be 'carried away,' envies him these."

The Arnold Adoff collection opens with such elder heralds and songmakers as James Weldon Johnson, W. E. B. Du Bois, Paul Laurence Dunbar, Angelina Weld Grimké. And those readers who always want a fair sprinkling of "established" stars, no matter how many electric new ones may be part of the gift, will be happy. But what surprises, of a less-anthologized nature, are available for them. Seldom anthologized are the poems of Frank Marshall Davis, Owen Dodson, Hoyt Fuller, Sun Ra, Ted Joans (and we regret the absence of his popular "The .38"). Many applauders of black poetry have never heard of the searching New York poet Raymond Patterson, or of the carefully rich technics of Audre Lorde and Keorapetse W. Kgositsile. Johari Amini, A. B. Spellman, and Clarence Major are chiefly known and loved in their own circles. Etheridge Knight, one of the most distinguished notes of the new call, is here, but strange and regrettable is the omission of his prime poem, "Hard Rock Returns to Prison from the Hospital for the Criminal Insane." You would *expect* to find Don L. Lee, the early stimulus for so many of the younger poets here included, but seldom to be seen outside their own books are new-time molder Charlie Cobb (now living in Dar-es-Salaam), Barbara Mahone, Sterling Plumpp, Charles Lynch, Stanley Crouch, and Carole Gregory Clemmons (see the remarkable "Love from My Father"), all of whom are welcome. Where is Carole's husband, François Clemmons, who is writing pertinent and sensitive lyrics? Sonia Sanchez is represented, but in view of her standing and following, her contribution should be twice as long as it is. Well, always, in these collections, along with our exultings we are doomed to mourn certain absences. Here we are sorry not to find the excellent and long-celebrated Washington poet May Miller. We are sorry not to find Walter Bradford, Ronda Davis, Arthur Pfister, Sharon Scott, David (Amus) Moore, Jackie Earley.

But always remember the extending self-solace of poet-publisher-anthologist-fatherfigure and platform-provider Dudley Randall. In the introduction to his recent *The Black Poets* he said, ". . . Each book is valuable for its discoveries, and its omissions are compensated for by the inclusions of other anthologies."

Arnold Adoff is only human. He has done what must have been a bewildering job of ardent research, and he must have suffered as often as he rejoiced along the way. He has given us impressive variety. He has given us the hot, broad blockbuster, and he has given us the precious precious passage that reminds us of Leroy Anderson's "Jazz Pizzicato": picky-clean, spare; unencumbered; tightly, tinily dizzy.

GWENDOLYN BROOKS
Chicago   August, 1972

WILLIAM EDWARD BURGHARDT DU BOIS (1868–1963)

The Song of the Smoke

I am the smoke king,
I am black.
I am swinging in the sky.
I am ringing worlds on high:
I am the thought of the throbbing mills,
I am the soul of the soul toil kills,
I am the ripple of trading rills,

Up I'm curling from the sod,
I am whirling home to God.
I am the smoke king,
I am black.

I am the smoke king,
I am black.
I am wreathing broken hearts,
I am sheathing devils' darts;
Dark inspiration of iron times,
Wedding the toil of toiling climes
Shedding the blood of bloodless crimes,

Down I lower in the blue,
Up I tower toward the true,
I am the smoke king,
I am black.

I am the smoke king,
I am black.

I am darkening with song,
I am hearkening to wrong;
I will be black as blackness can,
The blacker the mantle the mightier the man,
My purpl'ing midnights no day dawn may ban.

I am carving God in night,
I am painting hell in white.
I am the smoke king,
I am black.

I am the smoke king,
I am black.

I am cursing ruddy morn,
I am nursing hearts unborn;
Souls unto me are as mists in the night,
I whiten my blackmen, I beckon my white,
What's the hue of a hide to a man in his might!
Hail, then, grilly, grimy hands,

Sweet Christ, pity toiling lands!
Hail to the smoke king,
Hail to the black!

JAMES WELDON JOHNSON (1871–1938)

O Black and Unknown Bards

O black and unknown bards of long ago,
How came your lips to touch the sacred fire?
How, in your darkness, did you come to know
The power and beauty of the minstrel's lyre?
Who first from midst his bonds lifted his eyes?
Who first from out the still watch, lone and long,
Feeling the ancient faith of prophets rise
Within his dark-kept soul, burst into song?

Heart of what slave poured out such melody
As "Steal away to Jesus"? On its strains
His spirit must have nightly floated free,
Though still about his hands he felt his chains.
Who heard great "Jordan roll"? Whose starward eye
Saw chariot "swing low"? And who was he
That breathed that comforting, melodic sigh,
"Nobody knows de trouble I see"?

What merely living clod, what captive thing,
Could up toward God through all its darkness grope,
And find within its deadened heart to sing
These songs of sorrow, love and faith, and hope?
How did it catch that subtle undertone,
That note in music heard not with the ears?
How sound the elusive reed so seldom blown,
Which stirs the soul or melts the heart to tears.

Not that great German master in his dream
Of harmonies that thundered amongst the stars
At the creation, ever heard a theme
Nobler than "Go down, Moses." Mark its bars
How like a mighty trumpet-call they stir
The blood. Such are the notes that men have sung
Going to valorous deeds; such tones there were
That helped make history when Time was young.

There is a wide, wide wonder in it all,
That from degraded rest and servile toil
The fiery spirit of the seer should call
These simple children of the sun and soil.
O black slave singers, gone, forgot, unfamed,
You—you alone, of all the long, long line
Of those who've sung untaught, unknown, unnamed,
Have stretched out upward, seeking the divine.

You sang not deeds of heroes or of kings;
No chant of bloody war, no exulting paean
Of arms-won triumphs; but your humble strings
You touched in chord with music empyrean.
You sang far better than you knew; the songs
That for your listeners' hungry hearts sufficed
Still live,—but more than this to you belongs:
You sang a race from wood and stone to Christ.

The Creation

A Negro Sermon

And God stepped out on space,
And He looked around and said,
*"I'm lonely
I'll make me a world."*

And as far as the eye of God could see
Darkness covered everything,
Blacker than a hundred midnights
Down in a cypress swamp.

Then God smiled,
And the light broke,
And the darkness rolled up on one side,
And the light stood shining on the other,
And God said, *"That's good!"*

Then God reached out and took the light in His hands,
And God rolled the light around in His hands
Until He made the sun;
And He set that sun a-blazing in the heavens.
And the light that was left from making the sun
God gathered it up in a shining ball
And flung it against the darkness,
Spangling the night with the moon and stars.
Then down between
The darkness and the light
He hurled the world;
And God said, *"That's good."*

Then God Himself stepped down—
And the sun was on His right hand
And the moon was on His left;
The stars were clustered about His head,
And the earth was under His feet.
And God walked, and where He trod
His footsteps hollowed the valleys out
And bulged the mountains up.

Then He stopped and looked, and saw
That the earth was hot and barren.
So God stepped over to the edge of the world
And He spat out the seven seas;
He batted His eyes, and the lightnings flashed;
He clapped His hands, and the thunders rolled;
And the waters above the earth came down,
The cooling waters came down.

Then the green grass sprouted,
And the little red flowers blossomed,
The pine tree pointed his finger to the sky,
And the oak spread out his arms,
And the lakes cuddled down in the hollows of the ground,
And the rivers ran to the sea;
And God smiled again,
And the rainbow appeared,
And curled itself around His shoulder.

Then God raised His arm and He waved His hand,
Over the sea and over the land,
And He said, *"Bring forth. Bring forth."*
And quicker than God could drop His hand
Fishes and fowls
And beasts and birds
Swam the rivers and the seas,

Roamed the forests and the woods,
And split the air with their wings.
And God said, *"That's good."*

Then God walked around,
And God looked around
On all that He had made.
He looked at His sun,
And He looked at His moon,
And He looked at His little stars;
He looked on His world,
With all its living things,
And God said, *"I'm lonely still."*

Then God sat down
On the side of a hill where He could think;
By a deep, wide river He sat down;
With His head in His hands,
God thought and thought,
Till He thought, *"I'll make me a man."*

Up from the bed of a river
God scooped the clay;
And by the bank of the river
He kneeled Him down;
And there the great God Almighty
Who lit the sun and fixed it in the sky,
Who flung the stars to the most far corner of the night,
Who rounded the earth in the middle of His hand;
This Great God,
Like a mammy bending over her baby,
Kneeled down in the dust
Toiling over a lump of clay
Till He shaped it in His own image;

Then into it He blew the breath of life,
And man became a living soul.
Amen. Amen.

The Glory of the Day Was in Her Face

The glory of the day was in her face,
The beauty of the night was in her eyes.
And over all her loveliness, the grace
Of Morning blushing in the early skies.

And in her voice, the calling of the dove;
Like music of a sweet, melodious part.
And in her smile, the breaking light of love;
And all the gentle virtues in her heart.

And now the glorious day, the beauteous night,
The birds that signal to their mates at dawn,
To my dull ears, to my tear-blinded sight
Are one with all the dead, since she is gone.

Go Down Death

A Funeral Sermon

Weep not, weep not,
She is not dead;
She's resting in the bosom of Jesus.
Heart-broken husband—weep no more;
Grief-stricken son—weep no more;
She's only just gone home.

Day before yesterday morning,
God was looking down from his great, high heaven,
Looking down on all his children,
And his eye fell on Sister Caroline,
Tossing on her bed of pain.
And God's big heart was touched with pity,
With the everlasting pity.

And God sat back on his throne,
And he commanded that tall, bright angel standing at his right hand:
Call me Death!
And that tall, bright angel cried in a voice
That broke like a clap of thunder:
Call Death!—Call Death!
And the echo sounded down the streets of heaven
Till it reached away back to that shadowy place,
Where Death waits with his pale, white horses.

And Death heard the summons,
And he leaped on his fastest horse,
Pale as a sheet in the moonlight.
Up the golden street Death galloped,
And the hoof of his horse struck fire from the gold,
But they didn't make no sound.
Up Death rode to the Great White Throne,
And waited for God's command.

And God said: Go down, Death, go down,
Go down to Savannah, Georgia,
Down in Yamacraw,
And find Sister Caroline.
She's borne the burden and heat of the day,
She's labored long in my vineyard,
And she's tired—
She's weary—
Go down, Death, and bring her to me.

And Death didn't say a word,
But he loosed the reins on his pale, white horse,
And he clamped the spurs to his bloodless sides,
And out and down he rode,
Through heaven's pearly gates,
Past suns and moons and stars;
On Death rode,
And the foam from his horse was like a comet in the sky;
On Death rode,
Leaving the lightning's flash behind;
Straight on down he came.

While we were watching round her bed,
She turned her eyes and looked away,
She saw what we couldn't see;
She saw Old Death. She saw Old Death.
Coming like a falling star.
But Death didn't frighten Sister Caroline;
He looked to her like a welcome friend.
And she whispered to us: I'm going home,
And she smiled and closed her eyes.

And Death took her up like a baby,
And she lay in his icy arms,
But she didn't feel no chill.
And Death began to ride again—
Up beyond the evening star,
Out beyond the morning star,
Into the glittering light of glory,
On to the Great White Throne.
And there he laid Sister Caroline
On the loving breast of Jesus.

And Jesus took his own hand and wiped away her tears,
And he smoothed the furrows from her face,
And the angels sang a little song,
And Jesus rocked her in his arms,
And kept a-saying: Take your rest,
Take your rest, take your rest.

Weep not—weep not,
She is not dead;
She's resting in the bosom of Jesus.

PAUL LAURENCE DUNBAR (1872–1906)

We Wear the Mask

We wear the mask that grins and lies,
It hides our cheeks and shades our eyes,—
This debt we pay to human guile;
With torn and bleeding hearts we smile,
And mouth with myriad subleties.

Why should the world be over-wise,
In counting all our tears and sighs?
Nay, let them only see us, while
    We wear the mask.

We smile, but, O great Christ, our cries
To thee from tortured souls arise.
We sing, but oh the clay is vile
Beneath our feet, and long the mile;
But let the world dream otherwise,
    We wear the mask.

Sympathy

I know what the caged bird feels, alas!
When the sun is bright on the upland slopes;
When the wind stirs soft through the springing grass
And the river flows like a stream of glass;
When the first bird sings and the first bud opes,
And the faint perfume from its chalice steals—
I know what the caged bird feels!

I know why the caged bird beats his wing
Till its blood is red on the cruel bars;
For he must fly back to his perch and cling
When he fain would be on the bough a-swing;
And a pain still throbs in the old, old scars
And they pulse again with a keener sting—
I know why he beats his wing!

I know why the caged bird sings, ah me,
When his wing is bruised and his bosom sore,—
When he beats his bars and would be free;
It is not a carol of joy or glee,
But a prayer that he sends from his heart's deep core,
But a plea, that upward to Heaven he flings—
I know why the caged bird sings!

Frederick Douglass

A hush is over all the teeming lists,
    And there is pause, a breath-space in the strife;
A spirit brave has passed beyond the mists
    And vapors that obscure the sun of life.
And Ethiopia, with bosom torn,
Laments the passing of her noblest born.

She weeps for him a mother's burning tears—
    She loved him with a mother's deepest love.
He was her champion thro' direful years,
    And held her weal all other ends above.
When Bondage held her bleeding in the dust,
He raised her up and whispered, "Hope and Trust."

For her his voice, a fearless clarion, rung
    That broke in warning on the ears of men;
For her the strong bow of his power he strung,
    And sent his arrows to the very den
Where grim Oppression held his bloody place
And gloated o'er the mis'ries of a race.

And he was no soft-tongued apologist;
    He spoke straightforward, fearlessly uncowed;
The sunlight of his truth dispelled the mist,
    And set in bold relief each dark-hued cloud;
To sin and crime he gave their proper hue,
And hurled at evil what was evil's due.

Through good and ill report he cleaved his way
    Right onward, with his face set toward the heights,
Nor feared to face the foeman's dread array,—
    The lash of scorn, the sting of petty spites.
He dared the lightning in the lightning's track,
And answered thunder with his thunder back.

When Malindy Sings

G'way an' quit dat noise, Miss Lucy—
　Put dat music book away;
What's de use to keep on tryin'?
　Ef you practise twell you're gray,
You cain't sta't no notes a-flyin'
　Lak de ones dat rants and rings
From the kitchen to de big woods
　When Malindy sings.

You ain't got de nachel o'gans
　Fu' to make de soun' come right,
You ain't got de tu'ns an' twistin's
　Fu' to make it sweet an' light.
Tell you one thing now, Miss Lucy,
　An' I'm tellin' you fu' true,
When hit comes to raal right singin',
　Tain't no easy thing to do.

Easy 'nough fu' folks to hollah,
　Lookin' at de lines an' dots,
When dey ain't no one kin sence it,
　An' de chune comes in, in spots;
But fu' real melojous music,
　Dat jes' strikes yo' hea't and clings,
Jes' you stan' an listen wif me
　When Malindy sings.

Ain't you nevah hyeahd Malindy?
　Blessed soul, tek up de cross!
Look hyeah, ain't you jokin', honey?
　Well, you don't know whut you los'.
Y'ought to hyeah dat gal a-wa'blin',
　Robins, la'ks, an' all dem things,
Heish dey moufs an' hides dey faces
　When Malindy sings.

Fiddlin' man jes' stop his fiddlin',
　Lay his fiddle on de she'f;
Mockin'-bird quit tryin' to whistle,
　'Cause he jes' so shamed hisse'f.
Folks a-playin' on de banjo
　Draps dey fingahs on de strings—
Bless yo' soul—fu' gits to move 'em,
　When Malindy sings.

She jes' spreads huh mouf and hollahs,
    "Come to Jesus," twell you hyeah
Sinnahs' tremblin' steps and voices,
    Timid-lak a-drawin' neah;
Den she tu'ns to "Rock of Ages,"
    Simply to de cross she clings,
An' you fin' yo' teahs a-drappin'
    When Malindy sings.

Who dat says dat humble praises
    Wif de Master nevah counts?
Heish yo' mouf, I hyeah dat music,
    Ez hit rises up an' mounts—
Floatin' by de hills an' valleys,
    Way above dis buryin' sod,
Ez hit makes its way in glory
    To de very gates of God!

Oh, hit's sweetah dan de music
    Of an edicated band;
An' hit's dearah dan de battle's
    Song o' triumph in de lan'.
It seems holier than evenin'
    When de solemn chu'ch bell rings,
Ez I sit an' ca'mly listen
    While Malindy sings.

Towsah, stop dat ba'kin', hyeah me!
    Mandy, mek dat chile keep still;
Don't you hyeah de echoes callin'
    From de valley to de hill?
Let me listen, I can hyeah it,
    Th'oo de bresh of angel's wings,
Sof' an' sweet, "Swing Low, Sweet Chariot,"
    Ez Malindy sings.

The Paradox

I am the mother of sorrows,
    I am the ender of grief;
I am the bud and the blossom,
    I am the late-falling leaf.

I am thy priest and thy poet,
    I am thy serf and thy king;
I cure the tears of the heartsick,
    When I come near they shall sing.

White are my hands as the snow-drop;
  Swart are my fingers as clay;
Dark is my frown as the midnight,
  Fair is my brow as the day.

Battle and war are my minions,
  Doing my will as divine;
I am the calmer of passions,
  Peace is a nursling of mine.

Speak to me gently or curse me,
  Seek me or fly from my sight;
I am thy fool in the morning,
  Thou art my slave in the night.

Down to the grave will I take thee,
  Out from the noise of the strife;
Then shalt thou see me and know me—
  Death, then, no longer, but life.

Then shalt thou sing at my coming,
  Kiss me with passionate breath,
Clasp me and smile to have thought me
  Aught save the foeman of Death.

Come to me, brother, when weary,
  Come when thy lonely heart swells;
I'll guide thy footsteps and lead thee
  Down where the Dream Woman dwells.

ALICE DUNBAR NELSON (1875–1935)

Sonnet

I had no thought of violets of late,
The wild, shy kind that spring beneath your feet
In wistful April days, when lovers mate
And wander through the fields in raptures sweet.
The thought of violets meant florists' shops,
And bows and pins, and perfumed papers fine;
And garish lights, and mincing little fops
And cabarets and songs, and deadening wine.

So far from sweet real things my thoughts had strayed,
I had forgot wide fields, and clear brown streams;
The perfect loveliness that God has made,—
Wild violets shy and Heaven-mounting dreams.
And now—unwittingly, you've made me dream
Of violets, and my soul's forgotten gleam.

WILLIAM STANLEY BRAITHWAITE
(1878–1962)

To —

Half in the dim light from the hall
I saw your fingers rise and fall
Along the pale, dusk-shadowed keys,
And heard your subtle melodies.

The magic of your mastery leant
Your soul unto the instrument;
Strange-wise, its spell of power seemed
To voice the visions that you dreamed.

The music gave my soul such wings
As bore me through the shadowings
Of mortal bondage; flight on flight
I circled dreams' supremest height.

Above were tender twilight skies,
Where stars were dreams and memories—
The long forgotten raptures of
My youth's dead fires of hope and love.

In a Grave-Yard

In calm fellowship they sleep
Where the graves are dark and deep,
Where nor hate nor fraud nor feud
Mar their perfect brotherhood.

After all was done they went
Into dreamless sleep, content,
That the years would pass them by,
Sightless, soundless, where they lie.

Wines and roses, song and dance,
Have no portion in their trance—
The four seasons are as one,
Dark of night, and light of sun.

Golden Moonrise

When your eyes gaze seaward
Piercing through the dim
Slow descending nightfall,
On the outer rim

Where the deep blue silence
Touches sky and sea,
Hast thou seen the golden
Moon, rise silently?

Seen the great battalions
Of the stars grow pale—
Melting in the magic
Of her silver veil?

I have seen the wonder,
I have felt the balm
Of the golden moonrise
Turn to silver calm.

LESLIE PINCKNEY HILL (1880–1960)

"So Quietly"

News item from the New York Times *on the lynching of a Negro at Smithville, Ga., December 21, 1919:*
   "The train was boarded so quietly . . . members of the train crew did not know that the mob had seized the Negro until informed by the prisoner's guard after the train had left the town. . . . A coroner's inquest held immediately returned the verdict that West came to his death at the hands of unidentified men."

So quietly they stole upon their prey
And dragged him out to death, so without flaw
Their black design, that they to whom the law
Gave him in keeping, in the broad, bright day,

Were not aware when he was snatched away;
And when the people, with a shrinking awe,
The horror of that mangled body saw,
"By unknown hands!" was all that they could say.
So, too, my country, stealeth on apace
The soul-blight of a nation. Not with drums
Or trumpet blare is that corruption sown,
But quietly—now in the open face
Of day, now in the dark—and when it comes,
Stern truth will never write, "By hands unknown."

ANGELINA WELD GRIMKÉ (1880–1958)

The Black Finger

I have just seen a most beautiful thing
    Slim and still,
  Against a gold, gold sky,
  A straight black cypress,
    Sensitive,
    Exquisite,
    A black finger
    Pointing upwards.
Why, beautiful still finger, are you black?
And why are you pointing upwards?

Tenebris

There is a tree, by day,
That, at night,
Has a shadow,
A hand huge and black,
With fingers long and black.
  All through the dark,
Against the white man's house,
  In the little wind,
The black hand plucks and plucks
  At the bricks.
The bricks are the color of blood and very small.
  Is it a black hand,
  Or is it a shadow?

Your Hands

I love your hands:
They are big hands, firm hands, gentle hands;
Hair grows on the back near the wrist . . . .
I have seen the nails broken and stained
From hard work.
And yet, when you touch me,
I grow small . . . . and quiet . . . . . .
 . . . . And happy . . . .
If I might only grow small enough
To curl up into the hollow of your palm,
Your left palm,
Curl up, lie close and cling,
So that I might know myself always there,
 . . . . Even if you forgot.

A Winter Twilight

A silence slipping around like death,
Yet chased by a whisper, a sigh, a breath;
One group of trees, lean, naked and cold,
Inking their crest 'gainst a sky green-gold;
One path that knows where the corn flowers were;
Lonely, apart, unyielding, one fir;
And over it softly leaning down,
One star that I loved ere the fields went brown.

ANNE SPENCER (1882–)

Letter to My Sister

It is dangerous for a woman to defy the gods;
To taunt them with the tongue's thin tip,
Or strut in the weakness of mere humanity,
Or draw a line daring them to cross;

The gods own the searing lightning,
The drowning waters, tormenting fears
And anger of red sins.

Oh, but worse still if you mince timidly—
Dodge this way or that, or kneel or pray,
Be kind, or sweat agony drops
Or lay your quick body over your feeble young;
If you have beauty or none, if celibate
Or vowed—the gods are Juggernaut,
Passing over . . . over . . .

This you may do:
Lock your heart, then, quietly,
And lest they peer within,
Light no lamp when dark comes down
Raise no shade for sun;
Breathless must your breath come through
If you'd die and dare deny
The gods their god-like fun.

Lady, Lady

Lady, Lady, I saw your face,
Dark as night withholding a star . . .
The chisel fell, or it might have been
You had borne so long the yoke of men.

Lady, Lady, I saw your hands,
Twisted, awry, like crumpled roots,
Bleached poor white in a sudsy tub,
Wrinkled and drawn from your rub-a-dub.

Lady, Lady, I saw your heart,
And altared there in its darksome place
Were the tongues of flame the ancients knew,
Where the good God sits to spangle through.

JESSIE REDMOND FAUSET (1882–1961)

Oriflamme

"I can remember when I was a little, young girl, how my old mammy would sit out of doors in the evenings and look up at the stars and groan, and I would say, 'Mammy, what makes you groan so?' And she would say, 'I am groaning to think of my poor children; they do not know where I be and I don't know where they be. I look up at the stars and they look up at the stars!' "—Sojourner Truth.

I think I see her sitting bowed and black,
   Stricken and seared with slavery's mortal scars,
Reft of her children, lonely, anguished, yet
   Still looking at the stars.

Symbolic mother, we thy myriad sons,
   Pounding our stubborn hearts on Freedom's bars,
Clutching our birthright, fight with faces set,
   Still visioning the stars!

RAY GARFIELD DANDRIDGE
(1882–1930)

Time to Die

Black brother, think you life so sweet
That you would live at any price?
Does mere existence balance with
The weight of your great sacrifice?
Or can it be you fear the grave
Enough to live and die a slave?
O Brother! be it better said,
When you are gone and tears are shed,
That your death was the stepping stone
Your children's children cross'd upon.
Men have died that men might live:
Look every foeman in the eye!
If necessary, your life give
For something, ere in vain you die.

Zalka Peetruza

Who Was Christened Lucy Jane

She danced, near nude, to tom-tom beat,
With swaying arms and flying feet,
'Mid swirling spangles, gauze and lace,
Her all was dancing—save her face.

A conscience, dumb to brooding fears,
Companioned hearing deaf to cheers;
A body, marshalled by the will,
Kept dancing while a heart stood still:

And eyes obsessed with vacant stare,
Looked over heads to empty air,
As though they sought to find therein
Redemption for a maiden sin.

'Twas thus, amid force driven grace,
We found the lost look on her face;
And then, to us, did it occur
That, though we saw—we saw not her.

WALTER EVERETTE HAWKINS (1883–)

A Spade Is Just a Spade

As I talk with learned people,
    I have heard a strange remark,
Quite beyond my comprehension,
    And I'm stumbling in the dark.
They advise: Don't be too modest,
    Whatsoever thing is said,
Give to every thing its color,
    Always call a spade a spade.

Now I am not versed in Logic,
    Nor these high-flown classic things,
And am no adept in solving
    Flighty aphoristic flings;

So this proverb seems to baffle
　　All the efforts I have made,—
Now what else is there to call it,
　　When a spade is just a spade?

The Death of Justice

These the dread days which the seers have foretold,
These the fell years which the prophets have dreamed;
Visions they saw in those full days of old,
The fathers have sinned and the children blasphemed,
Hurt is the world, and its heart is unhealed,
Wrong sways the sceptre and Justice must yield.

We have come to the travail of troublous times,
Justice must bow before Moloch and Baal;
Blasphemous prayers for the triumph of crimes,
High sounds the cry of the children who wail.
Hurt is the world, and its heart is unhealed,
Wrong sways the sceptre and Justice must yield.

In the brute strength of the sword men rely,
They count not to Justice in reckoning things;
Whom their lips worship their hearts crucify,
This the oblation the votary brings.
Hurt is the world, and its heart is unhealed,
Wrong sways the sceptre and Justice must yield.

Locked in death-struggle humanity's host,
Seeking revenge with the dagger and sword;
This is the pride which the Pharisees boast,
Man damns his brother in the name of his Lord.
Hurt is the world, and its heart is unhealed,
Wrong sways the sceptre and Justice must yield.

Time dims the glare of the pomp and applause,
Vain-glorious monarchs and proud princes fall;
Until the death of Time revokes his laws,
His awful mandate shall reign over all.
Hurt is the world, and its heart is unhealed,
Wrong sways the sceptre and Justice must yield.

EFFIE LEE NEWSOME (1885–)

Morning Light (The Dew-Drier)

In Africa little black boys, "human brooms," are sent before the explorers into jungle grasses that tower many feet to tread down a path and meet sometimes the lurking leopard or hyena. They are called Dew-driers.

Brother to the firefly—
For as the firefly lights the night,
So lights he the morning—
Bathed in the dank dews as he goes forth
Through heavy menace and mystery
Of half-waking tropic dawn,
Behold a little black boy,
A naked black boy,
Sweeping aside with his slight frame
Night's pregnant tears,
And making a morning path to the light
For the tropic traveler!

Bathed in the blood of battle,
Treading toward a new morning,
May not his race, its body long bared
To the world's disdain, its face schooled to smile
For a light to come,
May not his race, even as the dew-boy leads,
Light onward men's minds toward a time
When tolerance, forbearance
Such as reigned in the heart of One
Whose heart was gold,
Shall shape the earth for that fresh dawning
After the dews of blood?

GEORGIA DOUGLAS JOHNSON (1886–1966)

Old Black Men

They have dreamed as young men dream
Of glory, love and power;
They have hoped as youth will hope
Of life's sun-minted hour.

They have seen as others saw
Their bubbles burst in air,
And they have learned to live it down
As though they did not care.

Common Dust

And who shall separate the dust
Which later we shall be:
Whose keen discerning eye will scan
And solve the mystery?

The high, the low, the rich, the poor,
The black, the white, the red,
And all the chromatique between,
Of whom shall it be said:

Here lies the dust of Africa;
Here are the sons of Rome;
Here lies one unlabelled
The world at large his home!

Can one then separate the dust,
Will mankind lie apart,
When life has settled back again
The same as from the start?

Escape

Shadows, shadows,
Hug me round
So that I shall not be found
By sorrow:
She pursues me
Everywhere,
I can't lose her
Anywhere.

Fold me in your black
Abyss,
She will never look
In this,—
Shadows, shadows,
Hug me round
In your solitude
Profound.

The Suppliant

Long have I beat with timid hands upon life's leaden door,
Praying the patient, futile prayer my fathers prayed before,
Yet I remain without the close, unheeded and unheard,
And never to my listening ear is borne the waited word.

Soft o'er the threshold of the years there comes this counsel cool:
The strong demand, contend, prevail; the beggar is a fool!

Prejudice

These fell miasmic rings of mist, with ghoulish menace bound,
Like noose-horizons tightening my little world around.
They still the soaring will to wing, to dance, to speed away.
And fling the soul insurgent back into its shell of clay.
Beneath incrusted silences, a seething Etna lies,
The fire of whose furnaces may sleep, but never dies!

Credo

I believe in the ultimate justice of Fate;
That the races of men front the sun in their turn;
That each soul holds the title to infinite wealth
In fee to the will as it masters itself;
That the heart of humanity sounds the same tone
In impious jungle, or sky-kneeling fane.
I believe that the key to the life-mystery
Lies deeper than reason and further than death.
I believe that the rhythmical conscience within
Is guidance enough for the conduct of men.

The Riddle

White men's children spread over the earth—
A rainbow suspending the drawn swords of birth,
Uniting and blending the races in one
The world man—cosmopolite—everyman's son!

He channels the stream of the red blood and blue,
Behold him! A Triton—the peer of the two;
Unriddle this riddle of "outside in"
White men's children in black men's skin.

FENTON JOHNSON (1888–1958)

Tired

I am tired of work; I am tired of building up somebody else's civilization.
Let us take a rest, M'Lissy Jane.
I will go down to the Last Chance Saloon, drink a gallon or two of gin, shoot a
game or two of dice and sleep the rest of the night on one of Mike's barrels.
You will let the old shanty go to rot, the white people's clothes turn to dust, and
the Calvary Baptist Church sink to the bottomless pit.
You will spend your days forgetting you married me and your nights hunting the
warm gin Mike serves the ladies in the rear of the Last Chance Saloon.
Throw the children into the river; civilization has given us too many. It is better to
die than to grow up and find that you are colored.
Pluck the stars out of the heavens. The stars mark our destiny. The stars marked my
destiny.
I am tired of civilization.

Aunt Jane Allen

State Street is lonely today. Aunt Jane Allen has driven her chariot to Heaven.
I remember how she hobbled along, a little woman, parched of skin, brown as the
leather of a satchel and with eyes that had scanned eighty years of life.
Have those who bore her dust to the last resting place buried with her the basket of
aprons she went up and down State Street trying to sell?
Have those who bore her dust to the last resting place buried with her the gentle
word *Son* that she gave to each of the seed of Ethiopia?

The Scarlet Woman

Once I was good like the Virgin Mary and the Minister's wife.
My father worked for Mr. Pullman and white people's tips; but he died two days
after his insurance expired.
I had nothing, so I had to go to work.
All the stock I had was a white girl's education and a face that enchanted the men
of both races.
Starvation danced with me.
So when Big Lizzie, who kept a house for white men, came to me with tales of
fortune that I could reap from the sale of my virtue I bowed my head to Vice.
Now I can drink more gin than any man for miles around.
Gin is better than all the water in Lethe.

CLAUDE McKAY (1890–1948)

If We Must Die

If we must die, let it not be like hogs
Hunted and penned in an inglorious spot,
While round us bark the mad and hungry dogs,
Making their mock at our accursèd lot.
If we must die, O let us nobly die,
So that our precious blood may not be shed
In vain; then even the monsters we defy
Shall be constrained to honor us though dead!
O kinsmen! we must meet the common foe!
Though far outnumbered let us show us brave,
And for their thousand blows deal one deathblow!
What though before us lies the open grave?
Like men we'll face the murderous, cowardly pack,
Pressed to the wall, dying, but fighting back!

The Tropics in New York

Bananas ripe and green, and ginger root,
    Cocoa in pods and alligator pears,
And tangerines and mangoes and grape fruit,
    Fit for the highest prize at parish fairs.

Set in the window, bringing memories
    Of fruit-trees laden by low-singing rills,
And dewy dawns, and mystical blue skies
    In benediction over nun-like hills.

My eyes grew dim, and I could no more gaze;
    A wave of longing through my body swept,
And, hungry for the old familiar ways,
    I turned aside and bowed my head and wept.

Outcast

For the dim regions whence my fathers came
My spirit, bondaged by the body, longs.
Words felt, but never heard, my lips would frame;
My soul would sing forgotten jungle songs.

I would go back to darkness and to peace,
But the great western world holds me in fee,
And I may never hope for full release
While to its alien gods I bend my knee.
Something in me is lost, forever lost,
Some vital thing has gone out of my heart,
And I must walk the way of life a ghost
Among the sons of earth, a thing apart.

For I was born, far from my native clime,
Under the white man's menace, out of time.

America

Although she feeds me bread of bitterness,
And sinks into my throat her tiger's tooth,
Stealing my breath of life, I will confess
I love this cultured hell that tests my youth!
Her vigor flows like tides into my blood,
Giving me strength erect against her hate.
Her bigness sweeps my being like a flood.
Yet as a rebel fronts a king in state,
I stand within her walls with not a shred
Of terror, malice, not a word of jeer.
Darkly I gaze into the days ahead,
And see her might and granite wonders there,
Beneath the touch of Time's unerring hand,
Like priceless treasures sinking in the sand.

In Bondage

I would be wandering in distant fields
Where man, and bird, and beast, live leisurely,
And the old earth is kind, and ever yields
Her goodly gifts to all her children free;
Where life is fairer, lighter, less demanding
And boys and girls have time and space for play
Before they come to years of understanding—
Somewhere I would singing, far away.
For life is greater than the thousand wars
Men wage for it in their insatiate lust,
And will remain like the eternal stars,
When all that shines to-day is drift and dust
But I am bound with you in your mean graves,
O black men, simple slaves of ruthless slaves.

The Lynching

His Spirit in smoke ascended to high heaven.
His father, by the cruelest way of pain,
Had bidden him to his bosom once again;
The awful sin remained still unforgiven.
All night a bright and solitary star
(Perchance the one that ever guided him,
Yet gave him up at last to Fate's wild whim)
Hung pitifully o'er the swinging char.
Day dawned, and soon the mixed crowds came to view
The ghastly body swaying in the sun
The women thronged to look, but never a one
Showed sorrow in her eyes of steely blue;
And little lads, lynchers that were to be,
Danced round the dreadful thing in fiendish glee.

To the White Fiends

Think you I am not fiend and savage too?
Think you I could not arm me with a gun
And shoot down ten of you for every one
Of my black brothers murdered, burnt by you?
Be not deceived, for every deed you do
I could match—out-match: am I not Afric's son,
Black of that black land where black deeds are done?
But the Almighty from the darkness drew
My soul and said: Even thou shalt be a light
Awhile to burn on the benighted earth,
Thy dusky face I set among the white
For thee to prove thyself of higher worth;
Before the world is swallowed up in night,
To show thy little lamp: go forth, go forth!

St. Isaac's Church, Petrograd

Bow down my soul in worship very low
And in the holy silences be lost.
Bow down before the marble man of woe,
Bow down before the singing angel host.

What jewelled glory fills my spirit's eye!
What golden grandeur moves the depths of me!

The soaring arches lift me up on high
Taking my breath with their rare symmetry.

Bow down my soul and let the wondrous light
Of Beauty bathe thee from her lofty throne
Bow down before the wonder of man's might.
Bow down in worship, humble and alone;
Bow lowly down before the sacred sight
Of man's divinity alive in stone.

The White House

Your door is shut against my tightened face,
And I am sharp as steel with discontent;
But I possess the courage and the grace
To bear my anger proudly and unbent.
The pavement slabs burn loose beneath my feet,
A chafing savage, down the decent street;
And passion rends my vitals as I pass,
Where boldly shines your shuttered door of glass.
Oh, I must search for wisdom every hour,
Deep in my wrathful bosom sore and raw,
And find in it the superhuman power
To hold me to the letter of your law!
Oh, I must keep my heart inviolate
Against the potent poison of your hate.

After the Winter

Some day, when trees have shed their leaves
    And against the morning's white
The shivering birds beneath the eaves
    Have sheltered for the night,
We'll turn our faces southward, love,
    Toward the summer isle
Where bamboos spire the shafted grove
    And wide-mouthed orchids smile.

And we will seek the quiet hill
    Where towers the cotton tree,
And leaps the laughing crystal rill,
    And works the droning bee.
And we will build a cottage there
    Beside an open glade,
With black-ribbed bluebells blowing near,
    And ferns that never fade.

JEAN TOOMER (1894–1967)

Reapers

Black reapers with the sound of steel on stones
Are sharpening scythes. I see them place the hones
In their hip-pockets as a thing that's done,
And start their silent swinging, one by one.
Black horses drive a mower through the weeds,
And there, a field rat, startled, squealing bleeds,
His belly close to ground. I see the blade,
Blood-stained, continue cutting weeds and shade.

Beehive

Within this black hive to-night
There swarm a million bees;
Bees passing in and out the moon,
Bees escaping out the moon,
Bees returning through the moon,
Silver bees intently buzzing,
Silver honey dripping from the swarm of bees.
Earth is a waxen cell of the world comb,
And I, a drone,
Lying on my back,
Lipping honey,
Getting drunk with silver honey,
Wish that I might fly out past the moon
And curl forever in some far-off farmyard flower.

Georgia Dusk

The sky, lazily disdaining to pursue
    The setting sun, too indolent to hold
    A lengthened tournament for flashing gold,
Passively darkens for night's barbecue,

A feast of moon and men and barking hounds,
    An orgy for some genius of the South
    With blood-hot eyes and cane-lipped scented mouth,
Surprised in making folk-songs from soul sounds.

The sawmill blows its whistle, buzz-saws stop,
    And silence breaks the bud of knoll and hill,
    Soft settling pollen where ploughed lands fulfill
Their early promise of a bumper crop.

Smoke from the pyramidal sawdust pile
    Curls up, blue ghosts of trees, tarrying low
    Where only chips and stumps are left to show
The solid proof of former domicile.

Meanwhile, the men, with vestiges of pomp,
    Race memories of king and caravan,
    High-priests, an ostrich, and a juju-man,
Go singing through the footpaths of the swamp.

Their voices rise . . . the pine trees are guitars,
    Strumming, pine-needles fall like sheets of rain . . .
    Their voices rise . . . the chorus of the cane
Is carolling a vesper to the stars.

O singers, resinous and soft your songs
    Above the sacred whisper of the pines,
    Give virgin lips to cornfield concubines,
Bring dreams of Christ to dusky cane-lipped throngs.

Song of the Son

Pour, O pour that parting soul in song,
O pour it in the saw-dust glow of night,
Into the velvet pine-smoke air to-night,
And let the valley carry it along,
And let the valley carry it along.

O land and soil, red soil and sweet-gum tree,
So scant of grass, so profligate of pines,
Now just before an epoch's sun declines
Thy son, in time, I have returned to thee,
Thy son, I have in time returned to thee.

In time, although the sun is setting on
A song-lit race of slaves, it has not set;
Though late, O soil, it is not too late yet
To catch thy plaintive soul, leaving, soon gone,
Leaving, to catch thy plaintive soul soon gone.

O Negro slaves, dark purple ripened plums,
Squeezed, and bursting in the pine-wood air,
Passing, before they strip the old tree bare
One plum was saved for me, one seed becomes

An everlasting song, a singing tree,
Carolling softly souls of slavery,
What they were, and what they are to me,
Carolling softly souls of slavery.

Brown River, Smile

It is a new America,
To be spiritualized by each new American.

Lift, lift, thou waking forces!
Let us feel the energy of animals,
The energy of rumps and bull-bent heads
Crashing the barrier to man.
It must spiral on!
A million million men, or twelve men,
Must crash the barrier to the next higher form.

    Beyond plants are animals,
    Beyond animals is man,
    Beyond man is the universe.

    The Big Light,
    Let the Big Light in!

O thou, Radiant Incorporeal,
The I of earth and of mankind, hurl
Down these seaboards, across this continent,
The thousand-rayed discus of thy mind,
And above our walking limbs unfurl
Spirit-torsos of exquisite strength!

The Mississippi, sister of the Ganges,
Main artery of earth in the western world,
Is waiting to become
In the spirit of America, a sacred river.
Whoever lifts the Mississippi
Lifts himself and all America;
Whoever lifts himself
Makes that great brown river smile.
The blood of earth and the blood of man
Course swifter and rejoice when we spiritualize.

The old gods, led by an inverted Christ,
A shaved Moses, a blanched Lemur,
And a moulting thunderbird,
Withdrew into the distance and soon died,
Their dust and seed falling down
To fertilize the five regions of America.

We are waiting for a new God.

The old peoples—
The great European races sent wave after wave
That washed the forests, the earth's rich loam,
Grew towns with the seeds of giant cities,
Made roads, laid golden rails,
Sang once of its swift achievement,
And died congested in machinery.
They say that near the end
It was a world of crying men and hard women,
A city of goddam and Jehovah
Baptized in industry
Without benefit of saints,
Of dear defectives
Winnowing their likenesses from weathered rock
Sold by national organizations of undertakers.

Someone said:
        Suffering is impossible
        On cement sidewalks, in skyscrapers,
        In motorcars;
        Steel cannot suffer—
        We die unconsciously
        Because possessed by a nonhuman symbol.

Another cried:
        It is because of thee, O Life,
        That the first prayer ends in the last curse.

Another sang:
        Late minstrels of the restless earth,
        No muteness can be granted thee,
        Lift thy laughing energies
        To that white point which is a star.

The great African races sent a single wave
And singing riplets to sorrow in red fields,
Sing a swan song, to break rocks
And immortalize a hiding water boy.

        I'm leaving the shining ground, brothers,
        I sing because I ache,

I go because I must,
Brothers, I am leaving the shining ground;
Don't ask me where,
I'll meet you there,
I'm leaving the shining ground.

The great red race was here.
In a land of flaming earth and torrent-rains,
Of red sea-plains and majestic mesas,
At sunset from a purple hill
The Gods came down;
They serpentined into pueblo,
And a white-robed priest
Danced with them five days and nights;
But pueblo, priest, and Shalicos
Sank into the sacred earth
To fertilize the five regions of America.

> Hi-ye, hi-yo, hi-yo
> Hi-ye, hi-yo, hi-yo,
> A lone eagle feather,
> An untamed Navaho,
> The ghosts of buffaloes,
> Hi-ye, hi-yo, hi-yo,
> Hi-ye, hi-yo, hi-yo.

We are waiting for a new people.

O thou, Radiant Incorporeal,
The I of earth and of mankind, hurl
Down these seaboards, across this continent,
The thousand-rayed discus of thy mind,
And above our walking limbs unfurl
Spirit-torsos of exquisite strength!

The east coast is masculine,
The west coast is feminine,
The middle region is the child—
Forces of reconciling
And generator of symbols.

> Thou, great fields, waving thy growths across the world,
> Couldest thou find the seed which started thee?
> Can you remember the first great hand to sow?
> Have you memory of His intention?
> Great plains, and thou, mountains,
> And thou, stately trees, and thou,
> America, sleeping and producing with the seasons,
> No clever dealer can divide,
> No machine can undermine thee.

The prairie's sweep is flat infinity,
The city's rise is perpendicular to farthest star,
I stand where the two directions intersect,
At Michigan Avenue and Walton Place,
Parallel to my countrymen,
Right-angled to the universe.

It is a new America,
To be spiritualized by each new American.

The Lost Dancer

Spatial depths of being survive
The birth to death recurrences
Of feet dancing on earth of sand;
Vibrations of the dance survive
The sand; the sand, elect, survives
The dancer. He can find no source
Of magic adequate to bind
The sand upon his feet, his feet
Upon his dance, his dance upon
The diamond body of his being.

Five Vignettes

1

The red-tiled ships you see reflected,
Are nervous,
And afraid of clouds.

2

There, on the clothes-line
Still as she pinned them,
Pieces now the wind may wear.

3

The old man, at ninety,
Eating peaches,
Is he not afraid of worms?

4

Wear my thimble of agony
And when you sew,
No needle points will prick you.

5

In Y. Don's laundry
A Chinese baby fell
And cried as any other.

JOSEPH SEAMAN COTTER, JR.
(1895–1919)

And What Shall You Say?

Brother, come!
And let us go unto our God.
And when we stand before Him
I shall say—
"Lord, I do not hate,
I am hated.
I scourge no one,
I am scourged.
I covet no lands,
My lands are coveted.
I mock no peoples,
My people are mocked."
And, brother, what shall you say?

Sonnet to Negro Soldiers

They shall go down unto Life's Borderland,
    Walk unafraid within that Living Hell,
    Nor heed the driving rain of shot and shell
That round them falls; but with uplifted hand
Be one with mighty hosts, an armed band
    Against man's wrong to man—for such full well
    They know. And from their trembling lips shall swell
A song of hope the world can understand.

All this to them shall be a glorious sign,
A glimmer of that resurrection morn
When age-long faith, crowned with a grace benign,
Shall rise and from their brows cast down the thorn
Of prejudice. E'en though through blood it be,
There breaks this day their dawn of liberty.

MELVIN B. TOLSON (1898–1966)

PSI

Black Boy,
let me get up from the white man's Table of Fifty Sounds
in the kitchen; let me gather the crumbs and cracklings
of this autobio-fragment,
before the curtain with the skull and bones descends.

Many a *t* in the ms.
I've left without a cross,
many an *i* without a dot.
A dusky Lot
with a third degree and a second wind and a seventh turn
of pitch-and-toss,
my psyche escaped the Sodom of Gylt
and the Big White Boss.

Black Boy,
you stand before your heritage,
naked and agape;
cheated like a mockingbird
pecking at a Zeuxian grape,
pressed like an awl to do
duty as a screw-
driver, you
ask the American Dilemma in you:
"If the trying plane
of Demos fail,
what will the trowel
of Uncle Tom avail?"

Black Boy,
in this race, at this time, in this place,
to be a Negro artist is to be
a flower of the gods, whose growth
is dwarfed at an early stage—

a Brazilian owl moth,
a giant among his own in an acreage
dark with the darkman's designs,
where the milieu moves back downward like the sloth.

Black Boy,
true—you
have not
dined and wined
(*ignoti nulla cupido*)
in the El Dorado of aeried Art,
for unreasoned reasons;
and your artists, not so lucky as the Buteo,
find themselves without a
skyscape sanctuary
in the
season of seasons:
in contempt of the contemptible,
refuse the herb of grace, the rue
of Job's comforter;
take no
lie-tea in lieu
of Broken Orange Pekoe.
Doctor Nkomo said: "*What* is he who smacks
his lips when dewrot eats away the golden grain
of self-respect exposed like flax
to the rigors of sun and rain?"

Black Boy,
every culture,
every caste,
every people,
every class,
facing the barbarians
with lips hubris-curled,
believes its death rattle omens
the *Dies Irae* of the world.

Black Boy,
summon Boas and Dephino,
Blumenbach and Koelreuter,
from their posts
around the gravestone of Bilbo,
who, with cancer in his mouth,
orated until he quaked the magnolias of the South,
while the pocketbooks of his weeping black serfs
shriveled in the drouth;
summon the ghosts
of scholars with rams' horns from Jericho
and facies in letters from Jerusalem,

so
we may ask them:
"What is a Negro?"

Black Boy,
what's in a people's name that wries the brain
like the neck of a barley bird?
Can sounding brass create
an ecotype with a word?

Black Boy,
beware of the thin-bladed mercy
stroke, for one drop of Negro blood
(V. *The Black Act of the F. F. V.*)
opens the flood-
gates of the rising tide of color
and jettisons
the D. A. R. in the Heraclitean flux
with Uncle Tom and
Crispus Attucks.
The Black Belt White,
painstaking as a bedbug in
a tenant farmer's truckle bed,
rabbit-punched old Darrow
because
he quoted Darwin's sacred laws
(instead of the Lord God Almighty's)
and gabbled that the Catarrhine ape
(the C from a Canada goose nobody knows)
appears,
after X's of years,
in the vestigial shape
of the Nordic's thin lips, his aquiline nose,
his straight hair,
orangutanish on legs and chest and head.
Doctor Nkomo, a votary of touch-and-go,
who can stand the gaff
of Negrophobes and, like Aramis,
parry a thrust with a laugh,
said:

"In spite of the pig in the python's coils,
in spite of Blake's lamb in the jaws of the tiger,
Nature is kind, even in the raw: she toils
. . . aeons and aeons and aeons . . .
gives the African a fleecy canopy
to protect the seven faculties of the brain
from the burning convex lens of the sun;

she foils
whiteness
(without disdain)
to bless the African
(as Herodotus marvels)
with the birthright of a burnt skin for work or fun;
she roils
the Aryan
(as his eye and ear repose)
to give the African an accommodation nose
that cools the drying-up air;
she entangles the epidermis in broils
that keep the African's body free from lice-infested hair.
As man to man,
the Logos is
Nature is on the square
with the African.
If a black man circles the rim
of the Great White World, he will find
(even if Adamness has made him half blind)
the bitter waters of Marah *and*
the fresh fountains of Elim."

Although his transition
was a far cry
from Shakespeare to Sardou,
the old Africanist's byplay gave
no soothing feverfew
to the Dogs in the Zulu Club;
said he:
"A Hardyesque artistry
of circumstance
divides the Whites and Blacks in life,
like the bodies of the dead
eaten by vultures
in a Tower of Silence.
Let, then, the man with a maggot in his head
lean . . . lean . . . lean
on race or caste or class,
for the wingless worms of blowflies shall grub,
dry and clean,
the stinking skeletons of these,
when the face of the macabre weathercock turns to the torrid wind of misanthropy;
and later their bones shall be swept together
(like the Parsees')
in the Sepulchre of Anonymity."
A Zulu Wit cleared away his unsunned
mood with dark laughter;
but I sensed the thoughts of Doctor Nkomo

pacing nervously to and fro
like Asscher's, after
he'd cleaved the giant Cullinan Diamond.

Black Boy,
the vineyard is the fittest place
in which to booze (with Omar) and study
soil and time and integrity—
the telltale triad of grape and race.

Palates that can read the italics
of *salt* and *sugar* know
a grapevine
transplanted from Bordeaux
to Pleasant Valley
cannot give grapes that make a Bordeaux wine.

Like the sons of the lone mother of dead empires,
who boasted their ancestors,
page after page—
wines are peacocky
in their vintage and their age,
disdaining the dark ways of those engaging
in the profits
of chemical aging.
When the bluebirds sing
their perennial anthem
a capriccio, in the Spring,
the sap begins to move up the stem
of the vine, and the wine in the bed of the deep
cask stirs in its winter sleep.
Its bouquet
comes with the years, dry or wet;
so the connoisseurs say:
"The history of the wine
is repeated by the vine."

Black Boy,
beware of wine labels,
for the Republic does not guarantee
what the phrase "Château Bottled" means—
the estate, the proprietor, the quality.
This ignominy will baffle you, Black Boy,
because the white man's law
has raked your butt many a time
with fang and claw.
Beware of the waiter who wraps
a napkin around your Clos Saint Thierry,
if Chance takes you into high-hat places
open to all creeds and races

born to be or not to be.
Beware of the pop
of a champagne cork:
like the flatted fifth and octave jump in Bebop,
it is theatrical
in Vicksburg or New York.
Beware of the champagne cork
that does not swell up like your ma when she had you—*that*
comes out flat,
because the bottle of wine
is dead . . . dead
like Uncle Tom and the Jim Crow Sign.
Beware . . . yet
your dreams in the Great White World
shall be unthrottled
by pigmented and unpigmented lionhearts,
for we know *without no*
every people, by and by, produces its "Château Bottled."

White Boy,
as regards the ethnic origin
of Black Boy and me,
the *What* in Socrates' *"Tò tí?"*
is for the musk-ox habitat of anthropologists;
but there is another question,
dangerous as a moutaba tick,
secreted in the house
of every Anglo-Saxon sophist and hick:

Who is a Negro?
(I am a White in deah ole Norfolk.)
Who is a White?
(I am a Negro in little old New York.)
Since my mongrelization is invisible
and my Negroness a state of mind conjured up
by Stereotypus, I am a chameleon
on *that* side of the Mason-Dixon
that a white man's conscience
is not on.
My skin is as white
as a Roman's toga when he sought an office on the sly;
my hair is as blond
as xanthein;
my eyes are as blue
as the hawk's-eye.
At the Olympian powwow of curators,
when I revealed my Negroness,
my peers became shocked like virgins in a house
where satyrs tattooed on female thighs heralds of success.

White Boy,
counterfeit scholars have used
the newest brush-on Satinlac,
to make our ethnic identity
crystal clear for the lowest IQ
in every mansion and in every shack.
Therefore,
according to the myth that Negrophobes bequeath
to the Lost Gray Cause, since Black Boy is the color
of betel-stained teeth,
he and I
(from ocular proof
that cannot goof)
belong to races
whose dust-of-the-earth progenitors
the Lord God Almighty created
of different bloods,
in antipodal places.
However,
even the F. F. V. pate
is aware that laws defining a Negro
blackjack each other with*in* and with*out* a state.
The Great White World, White Boy, leaves you in a sweat
like a pitcher with three runners on the bases;
and, like Kant, you seldom get
your grammar straight—yet,
you are the wick that absorbs the oil in my lamp,
in all kinds of weather;
and we are teeth in the pitch wheel
that work together.

White Boy,
when I hear the word *Negro* defined,
why does it bring to mind
the chef, the gourmand, the belly-god,
the disease of kings, the culinary art
in alien lands, Black Mammy in a Dixie big house,
and the dietitian's chart?
Now, look at Black Boy scratch his head!
It's a stereotypic gesture of Uncle Tom,
a learned Gentleman of Color said
in his monumental tome,
The *Etiquette of the New Negro,*
which,
the publishers say,
by the way,
should be in every black man's home.

The Negro is a dish in the white man's kitchen—
a potpourri,

an ola-podrida,
a mixie-maxie,
a hotchpotch of lineal ingredients;
with UN guests at his table,
the host finds himself a Hamlet on the spot,
for, in spite of his catholic pose,
the Negro dish is a dish nobody knows:
to some . . . tasty,
like an exotic condiment—
to others . . . unsavory
and inelegant.

White Boy,
the Negro dish is a mix
like . . . and *un*like
pimiento bisque, chop suey,
eggs à la Goldenrod, and eggaroni;
tongue-and-corn casserole, mulligan stew,
baked fillets of halibut, and cheese fondue;
macaroni milanaise, egg-milk shake,
mulligatawny soup, and sour-milk cake.

Just as the Chinese lack
an ideogram for "to be,"
our lexicon has no definition
for an ethnic amalgam like Black Boy and me.

Behold a Gordian knot without
the *beau geste* of an Alexander's sword!
Water, O Modern Mariner, water, everywhere,
unfit for *vitro di trina* glass
or the old-oaken-bucket's gourd!

For dark hymens on the auction block,
the lord of the mansion knew the macabre score:
not a dog moved his tongue,
not a lamb lost a drop of blood to protect a door.
O
Xenos of Xanthos,
what midnight-to-dawn lecheries,
in cabin and big house,
produced these brown hybrids and yellow motleys?

White Boy,
Buchenwald is a melismatic song
whose single syllable is sung to blues notes
to dark wayfarers who listen for the gong
at the crack of doom along
. . . that Lonesome Road . . .
before they travel on.

A Pelagian with the *raison d'être* of a Negro,
 I cannot say I have outwitted dread,
 for I am conscious of the noiseless tread
of the Yazoo tiger's ball-like pads behind me
   in the dark
  as I trudge ahead,
up and up . . . that Lonesome Road . . . up and up.

   In a Vision in a Dream,
 from the frigid seaport of the proud Xanthochroid,
   the good ship *Défineznegro*
 sailed fine, under an unabridged moon,
  to reach the archipelago
   Nigeridentité.
  In the Strait of Octoroon,
   off black Scylla,
after the typhoon Phobos, out of the Stereotypus Sea,
 had rived her hull and sail to a **T**,
  the *Défineznegro* sank the rock
  and disappeared in the abyss
   (*Vanitas vanitatum!*)
   of white Charybdis.

The Sea-Turtle and the Shark

  Strange but true is the story
 of the sea-turtle and the shark—
the instinctive drive of the weak to survive
   in the oceanic dark.
    Driven,
     riven
    by hunger
   from abyss to shoal,
  sometimes the shark swallows
   the sea-turtle whole.
  The sly reptilian marine
   withdraws,
    into the shell
  of his undersea craft,
his leathery head and the rapacious claws
   that can rip
  a rhinoceros' hide
   or strip
a crocodile to fare-thee-well;

now,
inside the shark,
the sea-turtle begins the churning seesaws
of his descent into pelagic hell;
then . . . *then*
with ravenous jaws
that can cut sheet steel scrap,
the sea-turtle gnaws
. . . and gnaws . . . and gnaws . . .
his way in a way that appalls—
his way to freedom,
beyond the vomiting dark,
beyond the stomach walls
of the shark.

African China

I

A connoisseur of pearl
necklace phrases,
Wu Shang disdains
his laundry, lazes
among his bric-a-brac
metaphysical;
and yet dark customers,
on Harlem's rack
quizzical,
sweat and pack
the forked caldera of
his Stygian shop:
some worship God,
and some Be-Bop.

Wu Shang discovers
the diademed word to be,
on the sly,
a masterkey
to Harlem pocketbooks,
outjockeyed by
policy
and brimstone
theology
alone!

II

As bust and hips
her corset burst,
An Amazonian fantasy,
A Witness of Jehovah
by job and husband curst,
lumbers in.
A yellow mummy in a mummery
a tip-toe,
Wu Shang unsheathes a grin,
and then, his fingers sleeved,
gulps an ugh and eats his crow,
disarmed by ugliness disbelieved!

At last he takes his wits
from balls of moth,
salaams. "Dear Lady, I, for you,
wear goats' sackcloth
to mark this hour and place;
cursed be the shadow of delay
that for a trice conceals a trace
of beauty in thy face!"

Her jug of anger emptied, now he sighs:
"Her kind cannot play euchre.
The master trick belongs to him
who holds the joker."
His mind's eye sees a black hand drop
a red white poker.

III

The gingered gigolo,
vexed by the harrow of a date
and vanity torn,
goddamns the yellow sage,
four million yellow born,
and yellow fate!

The gigolo
a wayward bronco
seen but unheard,
Wu Shang applies the curb-bit word:
"Wise lovers know
that in their lottery success
belongs to him who plays a woman
with titbits of a guess."

The sweet man's sportive whack
Paralyzes Wu Shang's back.
"Say, Yellah Boy, I call yo' stuff
the hottest dope in town!
That red hot mama'll never know
she got her daddy down."

IV

Sometimes the living dead
stalk in and sue for grace,
the tragic uncommon
in the comic commonplace,
the evil that the good
begets in love's embrace,
a Harlem melodrama
like that in Big John's face

as Wu Shang peers at him
and cudgels a theorem.
The sage says in a voice ilang-ilang,
"Do you direct the weathercock?"
And then his lash, a rackarock,
descends with a bang,
"Show me the man who has not thrown
a boomerang!"

. . . words, no longer pearls,
but drops of Gilead's balm.
Later, later, Wu Shang remarks,
"Siroccos mar the toughest palm."
The bigger thing, as always, goes unsaid:
the look behind the door of Big John's eyes,
awareness of the steps of *Is,*
the freedom of the wise.

V

When Dixie Dixon breaks a leg
on arctic Lenox Avenue
and Wu Shang homes her, pays her fees,
old kismet knots the two
unraveled destinies.
The unperfumed
wag foot, forefinger, head;
and belly laughter waifs ghost rats
foxed by the smell of meat and bread;
and black walls blab, "Good Gawd,
China and Africa gits wed!"

VI

Wu Shang, whom nothing sears,
says Dixie is a dusky passion flower
unsoiled by envious years.
And Dixie says
her Wu Shang is a Mandarin
with seven times seven ways of love,
her very own oasis in
the desert
of Harlem men.

In dignity, Wu Shang and Dixie walk
the gauntlet, Lenox Avenue;
their son has Wu Shang's cast
and Dixie's hue.

The dusky children roll
their oyster eyes
at Wu Shang, Junior, flash
a premature surmise,
as if afraid:
in accents Carolina
on the streets they never made,
the dusky children tease,
"African China!"

FRANK HORNE (1899–)

Notes Found Near a Suicide

TO ALL OF YOU

My little stone
Sinks quickly
Into the bosom of this deep, dark pool
Of oblivion . . .
I have troubled its breast but little
Yet those far shores
That knew me not
Will feel the fleeting, furtive kiss
Of my tiny concentric ripples . . .

TO MOTHER

I came
In the blinding sweep
Of ecstatic pain,
I go
In the throbbing pulse
Of aching space—
In the eons between
I piled upon you
Pain on pain
Ache on ache
And yet as I go
I shall know
That you will grieve
And want me back . . .

TO CATALINA

Love thy piano, Oh girl,
It will give you back
Note for note
The harmonies of your soul.
It will sing back to you
The high songs of your heart.
It will give
As well as take . . .

TO TELIE

You have made my voice
A rippling laugh
But my heart
A crying thing . . .
'Tis better thus:
A fleeting kiss
And then,
The dark . . .

TO "CHICK"

Oh Achilles of the moleskins
And the gridiron
Do not wonder
Nor doubt that this is I
That lies so calmly here—
This is the same exultant beast
That so joyously
Ran the ball with you
In those far-flung days of abandon.

You remember how recklessly
We revelled in the heat and the dust
And the swirl of conflict?
You remember they called us
The Terrible Two?
And you remember
After we had battered our heads
And our bodies
Against the stonewall of their defense,—
You remember the signal I would call
And how you would look at me
In faith and admiration
And say "Let's go," . . .
How the lines would clash
And strain,
And how I would slip through
Fighting and squirming
Over the line
To victory.
You remember, Chick? . . .
When you gaze at me here
Let that same light
Of faith and admiration
Shine in your eyes
For I have battered the stark stonewall
Before me . . .
I have kept faith with you
And now
I have called my signal,
Found my opening
And slipped through
Fighting and squirming
Over the line
To victory. . . .

TO WANDA

To you, so far away
So cold and aloof,
To you, who knew me so well,
This is my last Grand Gesture
This is my last Great Effect
And as I go winging
Through the black doors of eternity
Is that thin sound I hear
Your applause? . . .

TO JAMES

Do you remember
How you won
That last race . . . ?
How you flung your body
At the start . . .
How your spikes
Ripped the cinders
In the stretch . . .
How you catapulted
Through the tape . . .
Do you remember . . . ?
Don't you think
I lurched with you
Out of those starting holes . . . ?
Don't you think
My sinews tightened
At those first
Few strides . . .
And when you flew into the stretch
Was not all my thrill
Of a thousand races
In your blood . . . ?
At your final drive
Through the finish line
Did not my shout
Tell of the
Triumphant ecstasy
Of victory . . . ?
Live
As I have taught you
To run, Boy—
It's a short dash
Dig your starting holes
Deep and firm
Lurch out of them
Into the straightaway
With all the power
That is in you
Look straight ahead
To the finish line
Think only of the goal
Run straight
Run high
Run hard
Save nothing
And finish
With an ecstatic burst

That carries you
Hurtling
Through the tape
To victory . . .

TO THE POETS

Why do poets
Like to die
And sing raptures to the grave?

They seem to think
That bitter dirt
Turns sweet between the teeth.

I have lived
And yelled hosannas
At the climbing stars

I have lived
And drunk deep
The deceptive wine of life . . .

And now, tipsy and reeling
From its dregs
I die . . .

Oh, let the poets sing
Raptures to the grave.

TO HENRY

I do not know
How I shall look
When I lie down here
But I really should be smiling
Mischievously . . .
You and I have studied
Together
The knowledge of the ages
And lived the life of Science
Matching discovery for discovery—
And yet
In a trice
With a small explosion
Of this little machine
In my hand
I shall know

All
That Aristotle, Newton, Lavoisier, and Galileo
Could not determine
In their entire
Lifetimes . . .
And the joke of it is,
Henry,
That I have
Beat you to it . . .

TO ONE WHO CALLED ME "NIGGER"

You are Power
And send steel ships hurtling
From shore to shore . . .

You are Vision
And cast your sight through eons of space
From world to world . . .

You are Brain
And throw your voice endlessly
From ear to ear . . .

You are Soul
And falter at the yawning chasm
From White to Black . . .

TO CAROLINE

Your piano
Is the better instrument . . .
Yesterday
Your fingers
So precisely
Touched the cold keys—
A nice string
Of orderly sounds
A proper melody . . .
Tonight
Your hands
So wantonly
Caressed my tingling skin—
A mad whirl
Of cacophony,
A wild chanting . . .
Your piano
Is the better instrument.

TO ALFRED

I have grown tired of you
And your wife
Sitting there
With your children,
Little bits of you
Running about your feet
And you two so calm
And cold together . . .
It is really better
To lie here
Insensate
Than to see new life
Creep upon you
Calm and cold
Sitting there . . .

TO YOU

All my life
They have told me
That You
Would save my Soul
That only
By kneeling in Your House
And eating of Your Body
And drinking of Your Blood
Could I be born again . . .
And yet
One night
In the tall black shadow
Of a windy pine
I offered up
The Sacrifice of Body
Upon the altar
Of her breast . . .
You
Who were conceived
Without ecstasy
Or pain
Can you understand
That I knelt last night
In Your House
And ate of Your Body
And drank of Your Blood.
. . . and thought only of her?

On Seeing Two Brown Boys
in a Catholic Church

It is fitting that you be here,
Little brown boys
With Christ-like eyes
And curling hair.

Look you on yonder crucifix
Where He hangs nailed and pierced
With head hung low
And eyes all blind with blood that drips
From a thorny crown . . .
Look you well,
You shall know this thing.

Judas' kiss shall burn your cheek
And you will be denied
By your Peter—

And Gethsemane . . .
You shall know full well. . . .
Gethsemane . . .

You, too, will suffer under Pontius Pilate
And feel the rugged cut of rough-hewn cross
Upon your surging shoulder—
They will spit in your face
And laugh . . .
They will nail you up twixt thieves
And gamble for your garments.

And in this you will exceed God
For on this earth
You shall know Hell—

O little brown boys
With Christ-like eyes
And curling hair,
It is fitting that you be here.

Kid Stuff

December, 1942

The wise guys
tell me
that Christmas
is Kid Stuff . . .
Maybe they've got
something there—
Two thousand years ago
three wise guys
chased a star
across a continent
to bring
frankincense and myrrh
to a Kid
born in a manger
with an idea in his head . . .

And as the bombs
crash
all over the world
today
the real wise guys
know
that we've all
got to go chasing stars
again
in the hope
that we can get back
some of that
Kid Stuff
born two thousand years ago.

Resurrection

Some of us
these days
will kneel before altars
resplendent with cloth and gold
redolent with incense
exalted by homage
to a Jew
crucified, dead and buried

—Forgive them, Father, they know not what they do—
who rose from the tomb
with nail holes in His hands and feet
and spear in His side
to teach us
that love conquers all . . .

And others of us
will sit around the family table
lift high the cup of wine
and answer four questions
in homage to Jehovah
and Moses
for delivering us in the exodus
out of bondage in Egypt
into the promised land
to live in freedom and light
under the laws of the prophets . . .

And then
there are some of us
—sons and daughters of Ham
—they say
who still toil under the yoke
of bondage and oppression
in a dark and weary land . . .
sometimes we wonder
in anguish—
where is He
that brings love and freedom?
—why hast Thou forsaken me—
where is Moses
to strike off our chains
and lead us into the promised land?

But that still small voice
is thundering louder and louder:
Love ye all men
—yeah even Ross Barnett
    and Faubus and Bull Connor
Love ye all men . . .
and you yourself
press against the yoke
with ballots
and dignity
—and holes in hands and feet
and compassion
even for him
who wields the lash—
—they know not what they do—

and you may save his soul
and theirs that break unleavened bread
—for you were strangers in the land of Egypt
and theirs that eat of His Body and Blood
—love thy neighbor as thyself
and your own
as you impel the world to recall
the triumph of Golgotha
and the glory of love
and the laws of the prophets.

LEWIS ALEXANDER (1900–1945)

Negro Woman

The sky hangs heavy tonight
Like the hair of a Negro woman.
The scars of the moon are curved
Like the wrinkles on the brow of a Negro woman.

The stars twinkle tonight
Like the glaze in a Negro woman's eyes,
Drinking the tears set flowing by an aging hurt
Gnawing at her heart.

The earth trembles tonight
Like the quiver of a Negro woman's eye-lids cupping tears.

Enchantment

Part I

Night

The moonlight:
Juice flowing from an over-ripe pomegranate
bursting

The cossack-crested palm trees:
motionless

The leopard spotted shade:
inciting fear

silence seeds sown . . .

Part II

Medicine Dance

A body smiling with black beauty
Leaping into the air
Around a grotesque hyena-faced monster:
The Sorcerer—
A black body—dancing with beauty
Clothed in African moonlight,
Smiling more beauty into its body.
The hyena-faced monster yelps!
Echo!
Silence—
The dance
Leaps—
Twirls—
The twirling body comes to a fall
At the feet of the monster.
Yelps—
Wild—
Terror-filled—
Echo—

The hyena-faced monster jumps
starts,
runs,
chases his own yelps back to the wilderness.
The black body clothed in moonlight
Raises up its head,
Holding a face dancing with delight.

Terror reigns like a new crowned king.

Dream Song

Walk with the sun,
Dance at high noon;
And dream when night falls black;
But when the stars
Vie with the moon,
Then call the lost dream back.

Nocturne Varial

I came as a shadow,
I stand now a light;
The depth of my darkness
Transfigures your night.

My soul is a nocturne
Each note is a star;
The light will not blind you
So look where you are.

The radiance is soothing.
There's warmth in the light.
I came as a shadow,
To dazzle your night!

STERLING A. BROWN (1901–)

Strong Men

> The strong men keep coming on.—*Sandburg*

They dragged you from the homeland,
They chained you in coffles,
They huddled you spoon-fashion in filthy hatches,
They sold you to give a few gentlemen ease.

They broke you in like oxen,
They scourged you,
They branded you,
They made your women breeders,
They swelled your numbers with bastards . . . . .
They taught you the religion they disgraced.
You sang:
      Keep a-inchin' along
      Lak a po' inch worm . . .
You sang:
      By and bye
      I'm gonna lay down this heaby load . . .
You sang:
      Walk togedder, chillen,
      Dontcha git weary . . .
            The strong men keep a-comin' on
            The strong men get stronger.

They point with pride to the roads you built for them,
They ride in comfort over the rails you laid for them.
They put hammers in your hands
And said—Drive so much before sundown.
You sang:
>   Ain't no hammah
>   In dis lan'
>   Strikes lak mine, bebby,
>   Strikes lak mine.

They cooped you in their kitchens,
They penned you in their factories,
They gave you the jobs that they were too good for,
They tried to guarantee happiness to themselves
By shunting dirt and misery to you.
You sang:
>   Me an' muh baby gonna shine, shine
>   Me an' muh baby gonna shine.
>   The strong men keep a-comin' on
>   The strong men git stronger . . .

They bought off some of your leaders
You stumbled, as blind men will . . .
They coaxed you, unwontedly soft-voiced . . .
You followed a way.
Then laughed as usual.
They heard the laugh and wondered;
Uncomfortable;
Unadmitting a deeper terror . . .
>   The strong men keep a-comin' on
>   Gittin' stronger . . .

What, from the slums
Where they have hemmed you,
What, from the tiny huts
They could not keep from you—
What reaches them
Making them ill at ease, fearful?
Today they shout prohibition at you
"Thou shalt not this"
"Thou shalt not that"
"Reserved for whites only"
You laugh.

One thing they cannot prohibit—

>   The strong men . . . coming on
>   The strong men gittin' stronger.
>   Strong men . . .
>   Stronger . . .

Strange Legacies

One thing you left with us, Jack Johnson.
One thing before they got you.

You used to stand there like a man,
Taking punishment
With a golden, spacious grin;
Confident.
Inviting big Jim Jeffries, who was boring in:
"Heah ah is, big boy; yuh sees whah Ise at.
Come on in. . . ."

Thanks, Jack, for that.

John Henry, with your hammer;
John Henry, with your steel driver's pride,
You taught us that a man could go down like a man,
Sticking to your hammer till you died.
Sticking to your hammer till you died.

Brother,
When, beneath the burning sun
The sweat poured down and the breath came thick,
And the loaded hammer swung like a ton
And the heart grew sick;
You had what we need now, John Henry.
Help us get it.

So if we go down
Have to go down
We go like you, brother,
'Nachal' men. . . .

Old nameless couple in Red River Bottom,
Who have seen floods gutting out your best loam,
And the boll weevil chase you
Out of your hard-earned home,
Have seen the drought parch your green fields,
And the cholera stretch your porkers out dead;
Have seen year after year
The commissary always a little in the lead;
Even you said
That which we need
Now in our time of fear,—

Routed your own deep misery and dread,
Muttering, beneath an unfriendly sky,
"Guess we'll give it one mo' try.
Guess we'll give it one mo' try."

Remembering Nat Turner

For R. C. L.

We saw a bloody sunset over Courtland, once Jerusalem,
As we followed the trail that old Nat took
When he came out of Cross Keys down upon Jerusalem,
In his angry stab for freedom a hundred years ago.
The land was quiet, and the mist was rising,
Out of the woods and the Nottaway swamp,
Over Southampton the still night fell,
As we rode down to Cross Keys where the march began.

When we got to Cross Keys, they could tell us little of him,
The Negroes had only the faintest recollections:
    "I ain't been here so long, I come from up roun' Newsome;
    Yassah, a town a few miles up de road,
    The old folks who coulda told you is all dead an' gone.
    I heard something, sometime; I doan jis remember what.
    'Pears lak I heard that name somewheres or other.
    So he fought to be free. Well. You doan say."

An old white woman recalled exactly
How Nat crept down the steps, axe in his hand,
After murdering a woman and child in bed,
"Right in this here house at the head of these stairs"
(In a house built long after Nat was dead).
She pointed to a brick store where Nat was captured,
(Nat was taken in the swamp, three miles away)
With his men around him, shooting from the windows
(She was thinking of Harper's Ferry and old John Brown).
She cackled as she told how they riddled Nat with bullets
(Nat was tried and hanged at Courtland, ten miles away).

She wanted to know why folks would comes miles
Just to ask about an old nigger fool.
    "Ain't no slavery no more, things is going all right,
    Pervided thar's a good goober market this year.
    We had a sign post here with printing on it,
    But it rotted in the hole, and thar it lays,
    And the nigger tenants split the marker for kindling.
    Things is all right, naow, ain't no trouble with the niggers.
    Why they make this big to-do over Nat?"

As we drove from Cross Keys back to Courtland,
Along the way that Nat came down upon Jerusalem,
A watery moon was high in the cloud-filled heavens,
The same moon he dreaded a hundred years ago.
The tree they hanged Nat on is long gone to ashes,
The trees he dodged behind have rotted in the swamps.

The bus for Miami and the trucks boomed by,
And touring cars, their heavy tires snarling on the pavement.
Frogs piped in the marshes, and a hound bayed long,
And yellow lights glowed from the cabin windows.

As we came back the way that Nat led his army,
Down from Cross Keys, down to Jerusalem,
We wondered if his troubled spirit still roamed the Nottaway,
Or if it fled with the cock-crow at daylight,
Or lay at peace with the bones in Jerusalem,
Its restlessness stifled by Southampton clay.

We remembered the poster rotted through and falling,
The marker split for kindling a kitchen fire.

Foreclosure

Father Missouri takes his own.
These are the fields he loaned them,
Out of hearts' fullness; gratuitously;
Here are the banks he built up for his children—
Here are the fields; rich, fertile silt.

Father Missouri, in his dotage
Whimsical and drunkenly turbulent,
Cuts away the banks; steals away the loam;
Washes the ground from under wire fences,
Leaves fenceposts grotesquely dangling in the air;
And with doddering steps approaches the shanties.

Father Missouri; far too old to be so evil.

Uncle Dan, seeing his garden lopped away,
Seeing his manured earth topple slowly in the stream,
Seeing his cows knee-deep in yellow water,
His pig-sties flooded, his flower beds drowned,
Seeing his white leghorns swept down the stream—

Curses Father Missouri, impotently shakes
His fist at the forecloser, the treacherous skinflint;
Who takes what was loaned so very long ago,
And leaves puddles in his parlor, and useless lakes
In his fine pasture land.

Sees years of work turned to nothing—
Curses, and shouts in his hoarse old voice,
"Ain't got no right to act dat way at all"
And the old river rolls on, slowly to the gulf.

After Winter

He snuggles his fingers
In the blacker loam
The lean months are done with,
The fat to come.

    His eyes are set
    On a brushwood-fire
    But his heart is soaring
    Higher and higher.

Though he stands ragged
An old scarecrow,
This is the way
His swift thoughts go,

    "Butter beans fo' Clara
    Sugar corn fo' Grace
    An' fo' de little feller
    Runnin' space.

"Radishes and lettuce
Eggplants and beets
Turnips fo' de winter
An' candied sweets.

    "Homespun tobacco
    Apples in de bin
    Fo' smokin' an' fo' cider
    When de folks draps in."

He thinks with the winter
His troubles are gone;
Ten acres unplanted
To raise dreams on.

The lean months are done with,
The fat to come.
His hopes, winter wanderers,
Hasten home.

"Butterbeans fo' Clara
Sugar corn fo' Grace
An' fo' de little feller
Runnin' space. . . ."

Sister Lou

Honey
When de man
Calls out de las' train
You're gonna ride,
Tell him howdy.

Gather up yo' basket
An' yo' knittin' an' yo' things,
An' go on up an' visit
Wid frien' Jesus fo' a spell.

Show Marfa
How to make yo' greengrape jellies,
An' give po' Lazarus
A passel of them Golden Biscuits.

Scald some meal
Fo' some rightdown good spoonbread
Fo' li'l box-plunkin' David.

An' sit aroun'
An' tell them Hebrew Chillen
All yo' stories. . . .

Honey
Don't be feared of them pearly gates,
Don't go 'round to de back,
No mo' dataway
Not evah no mo'.

Let Michael tote yo' burden
An' yo' pocketbook an' evah thing
'Cept yo' Bible,
While Gabriel blows somp'n
Solemn but loudsome
On dat horn of his'n.

Honey
Go Straight on to de Big House,
An' speak to yo' God
Widout no fear an' tremblin'.

Then sit down
An' pass de time of day awhile.

Give a good talkin' to
To yo' favorite 'postle Peter,
An' rub the po' head
Of mixed-up Judas,
An' joke awhile wid Jonah.

Then, when you gits de chance,
Always rememberin' yo' raisin',
Let 'em know youse tired
Jest a mite tired.

Jesus will find yo' bed fo' you
Won't no servant evah bother wid yo' room.
Jesus will lead you
To a room wid windows
Openin' on cherry trees an' plum trees
Bloomin' everlastin'.

An' dat will be yours
Fo' keeps.

Den take yo' time. . . .
Honey, take yo' blessed time.

Southern Road

Swing dat hammer—hunh—
Steady, bo';
Swing dat hammer—hunh—
Steady, bo';
Ain't no rush, bebby,
Long ways to go.

Burner tore his—hunh—
Black heart away;
Burner tore his—hunh—
Black heart away;
Got me life, bebby,
An' a day.

Gal's on Fifth Street—hunh—
Son done gone;
Gal's on Fifth Street—hunh—
Son done gone;
Wife's in de ward, bebby,
Babe's not bo'n.

My ole man died—hunh—
Cussin' me;
My ole man died—hunh—
Cussin' me;
Ole lady rocks, bebby,
Huh misery.

Doubleshackled—hunh—
Guard behin';
Doubleshackled—hunh—
Guard behin';
Ball an' chain, bebby,
On my min'.

White man tells me—hunh—
Damn yo' soul;
White man tells me—hunh—
Damn yo' soul;
Got no need, bebby,
To be tole.

Chain gang nevah—hunh—
Let me go;
Chain gang nevah—hunh—
Let me go;
Po' los' boy, bebby,
Evahmo'. . . .

An Old Woman Remembers

Her eyes were gentle; her voice was for soft singing
In the stiff-backed pew, or on the porch when evening
Comes slowly over Atlanta. But she remembered.

She said: "After they cleaned out the saloons and the dives
The drunks and the loafers, they thought that they had better
Clean out the rest of us. And it was awful.
They snatched men off of street-cars, beat up women.
Some of our men fought back, and killed too. Still
It wasn't their habit. And then the orders came

For the milishy, and the mob went home,
And dressed up in their soldiers' uniforms,
And rushed back shooting just as wild as ever.
Some leaders told us to keep faith in the law,
In the governor; some did not keep that faith,
Some never had it: he was white too, and the time
Was near election, and the rebs were mad.
He wasn't stopping hornets with his head bare.
The white folks at the big houses, some of them
Kept all their servants home under protection
But that was all the trouble they could stand.
And some were put out when their cooks and yard-boys
Were thrown from cars and beaten, and came late or not at all.
And the police they helped the mob, and the milishy
They helped the police. And it got worse and worse.

"They broke into groceries, drug-stores, barber shops,
It made no difference whether white or black.
They beat a lame bootblack until he died,
They cut an old man open with jack-knives
The newspapers named us black brutes and mad dogs,
So they used a gun butt on the president
Of our seminary where a lot of folks
Had sat up praying prayers the whole night through.

"And then," she said, "our folks got sick and tired
Of being chased and beaten and shot down.
All of a sudden, one day, they all got sick and tired.
The servants they put down their mops and pans,
And brooms and hoes and rakes and coachman whips,
Bad niggers stopped their drinking Dago red,
Good Negroes figured they had prayed enough,
All came back home—they'd been too long away—
A lot of visitors had been looking for them.

"They sat on their front stoops and in their yards,
Not talking much, but ready; their welcome ready:
Their shotguns oiled and loaded on their knees.

"And then
There wasn't any riot any more."

Old Lem

I talked to old Lem
and old Lem said:
      "They weigh the cotton
      They store the corn

We only good enough
To work the rows;
They run the commissary
They keep the books
    We gotta be grateful
    For being cheated;
Whippersnapper clerks
Call us out of our name
    We got to say mister
    To spindling boys
They make our figgers
Turn somersets
We buck in the middle
    Say, 'Thankyuh, sah.'
        They don't come by ones
        They don't come by twos
        But they come by tens.

"They got the judges
They got the lawyers
They got the jury-rolls
They got the law
        They don't come by ones
They got the sheriffs
They got the deputies
        They don't come by twos
They got the shotguns
They got the rope
    We git the justice
    In the end
        And they come by tens.

"Their fists stay closed
Their eyes look straight
    Our hands stay open
    Our eyes must fall
        They don't come by ones
They got the manhood
They got the courage
        They don't come by twos
    We got to slink around
    Hangtailed hounds.
They burn us when we dogs
They burn us when we men
        They come by tens . . .

"I had a buddy
Six foot of man
Muscled up perfect
Game to the heart

They don't come by ones
Outworked and outfought
Any man or two men
    They don't come by twos
He spoke out of turn
At the commissary
They gave him a day
To git out the county.
He didn't take it.
He said 'Come and get me.'
They came and got him
    And they came by tens.
He stayed in the county—
He lays there dead.

    They don't come by ones
    They don't come by twos
    But they come by tens."

CLARISSA SCOTT DELANY (1901–1927)

Solace

My window opens out into the trees
And in that small space
Of branches and of sky
I see the seasons pass
Behold the tender green
Give way to darker heavier leaves.
The glory of the autumn comes
When steeped in mellow sunlight
The fragile, golden leaves
Against a clear blue sky
Linger in the magic of the afternoon
And then reluctantly break off
And filter down to pave
A street with gold.
Then bare, gray branches
Lift themselves against the
Cold December sky
Sometimes weaving a web
Across the rose and dusk of late sunset
Sometimes against a frail new moon
And one bright star riding
A sky of that dark, living blue
Which comes before the heaviness

Of night descends, or the stars
Have powdered the heavens.
Winds beat against these trees;
The cold, but gentle rain of spring
Touches them lightly
The summer torrents strive
To lash them into a fury
And seek to break them—
But they stand.
My life is fevered
And a restlessness at times
An agony—again a vague
And baffling discontent
Possesses me.
I am thankful for my bit of sky
And trees, and for the shifting
Pageant of the seasons.
Such beauty lays upon the heart
A quiet.
Such eternal change and permanence
Take meaning from all turmoil
And leave serenity
Which knows no pain.

LANGSTON HUGHES (1902–1967)

The Negro Speaks of Rivers

To W. E. B. Du Bois

I've known rivers:
I've known rivers ancient as the world and older than
   the flow of human blood in human veins.

My soul has grown deep like the rivers.

I bathed in the Euphrates when dawns were young.
I built my hut near the Congo and it lulled me to sleep.
I looked upon the Nile and raised the pyramids above it.
I heard the singing of the Mississippi when Abe
   Lincoln went down to New Orleans, and I've seen
   its muddy bosom turn all golden in the sunset.

I've known rivers:
Ancient, dusky rivers.

My soul has grown deep like the rivers.

Christ in Alabama

Christ is a nigger,
Beaten and black:
Oh, bare your back!

Mary is His mother:
Mammy of the South,
Silence your mouth.

God is His father:
White Master above
Grant Him your love.

Most holy bastard
Of the bleeding mouth,
    Nigger Christ
    On the cross
    Of the South.

Cross

My old man's a white old man
And my old mother's black.
If ever I cursed my white old man
I take my curses back.

If ever I cursed my black old mother
And wished she were in hell,
I'm sorry for that evil wish
And now I wish her well.

My old man died in a fine big house.
My ma died in a shack.
I wonder where I'm gonna die,
Being neither white nor black?

Song for a Dark Girl

Way Down South in Dixie
   (Break the heart of me)
They hung my dark young lover
   To a cross roads tree.

Way Down South in Dixie
　　(Bruised body high in air)
I asked the white Lord Jesus
　　What was the use of prayer.

Way Down South in Dixie
　　(Break the heart of me)
Love is a naked shadow
　　On a gnarled and naked tree.

Dream Variation

To fling my arms wide
In some place of the sun,
To whirl and to dance
Till the white day is done.
Then rest at cool evening
Beneath a tall tree
While night comes on gently,
　　Dark like me—
That is my dream!

To fling my arms wide
In the face of the sun,
Dance! Whirl! Whirl!
Till the quick day is done.
Rest at pale evening . . .
A tall, slim tree . . .
Night coming tenderly
　　Black like me.

Juke Box Love Song

I could take the Harlem night
and wrap around you,
Take the neon lights and make a crown,
Take the Lenox Avenue buses,
Taxis, subways,
And for your love song tone their rumble down.
Take Harlem's heartbeat,
Make a drumbeat,
Put it on a record, let it whirl,
And while we listen to it play,
Dance with you till day—
Dance with you, my sweet brown Harlem girl.

I, Too, Sing America

I, too, sing America.

I am the darker brother.
They send me to eat in the kitchen
When company comes,
But I laugh,
And eat well,
And grow strong.

Tomorrow,
I'll be at the table
When company comes.
Nobody'll dare
Say to me,
"Eat in the kitchen,"
Then.

Besides,
They'll see how beautiful I am
And be ashamed—

I, too, am America.

Motto

I play it cool
And dig all jive—
That's the reason
I stay alive.

My motto,
As I live and learn
        Is
Dig and be dug
In return.

Dream Deferred

What happens to a dream deferred?

Does it dry up
like a raisin in the sun?
Or fester like a sore—
And then run?
Does it stink like rotten meat?
Or crust and sugar over—
like a syrupy sweet?

Maybe it just sags
like a heavy load.

Or does it explode?

Prime

Uptown on Lenox Avenue
Where a nickel costs a dime,
In these lush and thieving days
When million-dollar thieves
Glorify their million-dollar ways
In the press and on the radio and TV—
But won't let me
Skim even a dime—
I, black, come to my prime
In the section of the niggers
Where a nickel costs a dime.

Cultural Exchange

In the Quarter of the Negroes
Where the doors are doors of paper
Dust of dingy atoms
Blows a scratchy sound.
Amorphous jack-o'-lanterns caper
and the wind won't wait for midnight
For fun to blow doors down.

By the river and the railroad
With fluid far-off going

Boundaries bind unbinding
A whirl of whistles blowing.
No trains or steamboats going—
Yet Leontyne's unpacking.

In the Quarter of the Negroes
Where the doorknob lets in Lieder
More than German ever bore,
Her yesterday past grandpa—
Not of her own doing—
In a pot of collard greens
Is gently stewing.

Pushcarts fold and unfold
In a supermarket sea.
And we better find out, mama,
Where is the colored laundromat
Since we moved up to Mount Vernon.

In the pot behind the paper doors
On the old iron stove what's cooking?
What's smelling, Leontyne?
Lieder, lovely Lieder
And a leaf of collard green.
Lovely Lieder, Leontyne.

You know, right at Christmas
They asked me if my blackness,
Would it rub off?
I said, *Ask your mama.*

Dreams and nightmares!
Nightmares, dreams, oh!
Dreaming that the Negroes
Of the South have taken over—
Voted all the Dixiecrats
Right out of power—
Comes the COLORED HOUR:
Martin Luther King is Governor of Georgia,
Dr. Rufus Clement his Chief Adviser,
A. Philip Randolph the High Grand Worthy.
In white pillared mansions
Sitting on their wide verandas,
Wealthy Negroes have white servants,
White sharecroppers work the black plantations,
And colored children have white mammies:
            Mammy Faubus
            Mammy Eastland
            Mammy Wallace
Dear, dear darling old white mammies—

Sometimes even buried with our family.
   Dear old
   Mammy Faubus!
Culture, they say, *is a two-way street:*
Hand me my mint julep, mammy.
    Hurry up!
    Make haste!

Freedom

Freedom will not come
Today, this year
  Nor ever
Through compromise and fear.

I have as much right
As the other fellow has
  To stand
On my two feet
And own the land.

I tire so of hearing people say,
Let things take their course.
Tomorrow is another day.
I do not need my freedom when I'm dead.
I cannot live on tomorrow's bread.
   Freedom
   Is a strong seed
   Planted
   In a great need.
   I live here, too.
   I want freedom
   Just as you.

October 16: The Raid

Perhaps
You will remember
John Brown.

John Brown
Who took his gun,
Took twenty-one companions
White and black,
Went to shoot your way to freedom
Where two rivers meet

And the hills of the
South
Look slow at one another—
And died
For your sake.

Now that you are
Many years free,
And the echo of the Civil War
Has passed away,
And Brown himself
Has long been tried at law,
Hanged by the neck,
And buried in the ground—
Since Harpers Ferry
Is alive with ghosts today,
Immortal raiders
Come again to town—

Perhaps
You will recall
John Brown.

Death in Yorkville

James Powell, Summer, 1964

How many bullets does it take
To kill a fifteen-year-old kid?
How many bullets does it take
To kill me?

How many centuries does it take
To bind my mind—chain my feet—
Rope my neck—lynch me—
Unfree?

From the slave chain to the lynch rope
To the bullets of Yorkville,
Jamestown, 1619 to 1963:
Emancipation Centennial—
100 years NOT free.

Civil War Centennial: 1965.
How many Centennials does it take
To kill me,

Still alive?
When the long hot summers come
Death ain't
No jive.

Militant

Let all who will
Eat quietly the bread of shame.
I cannot,
Without complaining loud and long,
Tasting its bitterness in my throat,
And feeling to my very soul
It's wrong.
For honest work
You proffer me poor pay,
For honest dreams
Your spit is in my face,
And so my fist is clenched
Today—
To strike your face.

Special Bulletin

Lower the flags
For the dead become alive,
Play hillbilly dirges
That hooded serpents may dance,
Write obituaries
For white-robed warriors
Emerging to the fanfare
Of death rattles.
Muffled drums in Swanee River tempo.
Hand-high salutes—*heil!*
Present arms
With ax handles
Made in Atlanta,
     Sieg
     Heil!
Oh, run, all who have not
Changed your names.
As for you others—
The skin on your black face,
Peel off the skin,
     Peel peel
     Peel off
     The skin.

GWENDOLYN B. BENNETT (1902–)

Heritage

I want to see the slim palm-trees,
Pulling at the clouds
With little pointed fingers. . . .

I want to see lithe Negro girls,
Etched dark against the sky
While sunset lingers.

I want to hear the silent sands,
Singing to the moon
Before the Sphinx-still face. . . .

I want to hear the chanting
Around a heathen fire
Of a strange black race.

I want to breathe the Lotus flow'r,
Sighing to the stars
With tendrils drinking at the Nile. . . .

I want to feel the surging
Of my sad people's soul
Hidden by a minstrel-smile.

To a Dark Girl

I love you for your brownness
And the rounded darkness of your breast.
I love you for the breaking sadness in your voice
And shadows where your wayward eye-lids rest.

Something of old forgotten queens
Lurks in the lithe abandon of your walk
And something of the shackled slave
Sobs in the rhythm of your talk.

Oh, little brown girl, born for sorrow's mate,
Keep all you have of queenliness,
Forgetting that you once were slave,
And let your full lips laugh at Fate!

Sonnet I

He came in silvern armor, trimmed with black—
A lover come from legends long ago—
With silver spurs and silken plumes a-blow,
And flashing sword caught fast and buckled back
In a carven sheath of Tamarack.
He came with footsteps beautifully slow,
And spoke in voice meticulously low.
He came and Romance followed in his track. . . .

I did not ask his name—I thought him Love;
I did not care to see his hidden face.
All life seemed born in my intaken breath;
All thought seemed flown like some forgotten dove.
He bent to kiss and raised his visor's lace . . .
All eager-lipped I kissed the mouth of Death.

Sonnet II

Some things are very dear to me—
Such things as flowers bathed by rain
Or patterns traced upon the sea
Or crocuses where snow has lain . . .
The iridescence of a gem,
The moon's cool opalescent light,
Azaleas and the scent of them,
And honeysuckles in the night.
And many sounds are also dear—
Like winds that sing among the trees
Or crickets calling from the weir
Or Negroes humming melodies.
But dearer far than all surmise
Are sudden tear-drops in your eyes.

Hatred

I shall hate you
Like a dart of singing steel
Shot through still air
At even-tide.

Or solemnly
As pines are sober
When they stand etched
Against the sky.
Hating you shall be a game
Played with cool hands
And slim fingers.
Your heart will yearn
For the lonely splendor
Of the pine tree;
While rekindled fires
In my eyes
Shall wound you like swift arrows.
Memory will lay its hands
Upon your breast
And you will understand
My hatred.

ARNA BONTEMPS (1902–)

Southern Mansion

Poplars are standing there still as death
and ghosts of dead men
meet their ladies walking
two by two beneath the shade
and standing on the marble steps.

There is a sound of music echoing
through the open door
and in the field there is
another sound tinkling in the cotton:
chains of bondmen dragging on the ground.

The years go back with an iron clank,
a hand is on the gate,
a dry leaf trembles on the wall.
Ghosts are walking.
They have broken roses down
and poplars stand there still as death.

The Day-breakers

We are not come to wage a strife
with swords upon this hill:
it is not wise to waste the life
against a stubborn will.

Yet would we die as some have done:
beating a way for the rising sun.

The Return

I

Once more, listening to the wind and rain,
Once more, you and I, and above the hurting sound
Of these comes back the throbbing of remembered rain,
Treasured rain falling on dark ground.
Once more, huddling birds upon the leaves
And summer trembling on a withered vine.
And once more, returning out of pain,
The friendly ghost that was your love and mine.

II

Darkness brings the jungle to our room:
The throb of rain is the throb of muffled drums.
Darkness hangs our room with pendulums
Of vine and in the gathering gloom
Our walls recede into a denseness of
Surrounding trees. This is a night of love
Retained from those lost nights our fathers slept
In huts; this is a night that must not die.
Let us keep the dance of rain our fathers kept
And tread our dreams beneath the jungle sky.

III

And now the downpour ceases.
Let us go back once more upon the glimmering leaves
And as the throbbing of the drums increases
Shake the grass and dripping boughs of trees.
A dry wind stirs the palm; the old tree grieves.

Time has charged the years: the old days have returned.

Let us dance by metal waters burned
With gold of moon, let us dance
With naked feet beneath the young spice trees.
What was that light, that radiance
On your face?—something I saw when first
You passed beneath the jungle tapestries?

A moment we pause to quench our thirst
Kneeling at the water's edge, the gleam
Upon your face is plain: you have wanted this.
Let us go back and search the tangled dream
And as the muffled drum-beats throb and miss
Remember again how early darkness comes
To dreams and silence to the drums.

IV

Let us go back into the dusk again,
Slow and sad-like following the track
Of blowing leaves and cool white rain
Into the old gray dream, let us go back.
Our walls close about us we lie and listen
To the noise of the street, the storm and the driven birds.
A question shapes your lips, your eyes glisten
Retaining tears, but there are no more words.

A Black Man Talks of Reaping

I have sown beside all waters in my day.
I planted deep, within my heart the fear
That wind or fowl would take the grain away.
I planted safe against this stark, lean year.

I scattered seed enough to plant the land
In rows from Canada to Mexico
But for my reaping only what the hand
Can hold at once is all that I can show.

Yet what I sowed and what the orchard yields
My brother's sons are gathering stalk and root,
Small wonder then my children glean in fields
They have not sown, and feed on bitter fruit.

Close Your Eyes!

Go through the gates with closed eyes.
Stand erect and let your black face front the west.
Drop the axe and leave the timber where it lies;
A woodman on the hill must have his rest.

Go where leaves are lying brown and wet.
Forget her warm arms and her breast who mothered you,
And every face you ever loved forget.
Close your eyes; walk bravely through.

COUNTEE CULLEN (1903–1946)

In Memory of Colonel Charles Young

Along the shore the tall, thin grass
That fringes that dark river,
While sinuously soft feet pass,
Begins to bleed and quiver.

The great dark voice breaks with a sob
Across the womb of night;
Above your grave the tom-toms throb,
And the hills are weird with light.

The great dark heart is like a well
Drained bitter by the sky,
And all the honeyed lies they tell
Come there to thirst and die.

No lie is strong enough to kill
The roots that work below;
From your rich dust and slaughtered will
A tree with tongues will grow.

Saturday's Child

Some are teethed on a silver spoon,
  With the stars strung for a rattle;
I cut my teeth as the black raccoon—
  For implements of battle.

Some are swaddled in silk and down,
    And heralded by a star;
They swathed my limbs in a sackcloth gown
    On a night that was black as tar.

For some, godfather and goddame
    The opulent fairies be;
Dame Poverty gave me my name,
    And Pain godfathered me.

For I was born on Saturday—
    "Bad time for planting a seed,"
Was all my father had to say,
    And, "One mouth more to feed."

Death cut the strings that gave me life,
    And handed me to Sorrow,
The only kind of middle wife
    My folks could beg or borrow.

From the Dark Tower

To Charles S. Johnson

We shall not always plant while others reap
The golden increment of bursting fruit,
Not always countenance, abject and mute,
That lesser men should hold their brothers cheap;
Not everlastingly while others sleep
Shall we beguile their limbs with mellow flute,
Not always bend to some more subtle brute;
We were not made eternally to weep.

The night whose sable breast relieves the stark,
White stars is no less lovely being dark,
And there are buds that cannot bloom at all
In light, but crumple, piteous, and fall;
So in the dark we hide the heart that bleeds,
And wait, and tend our agonizing seeds.

Yet Do I Marvel

I doubt not God is good, well-meaning, kind,
And did He stoop to quibble could tell why
The little buried mole continues blind,
Why flesh that mirrors Him must some day die,

Make plain the reason tortured Tantalus
Is baited by the fickle fruit, declare
If merely brute caprice dooms Sisyphus
To struggle up a never-ending stair.
Inscrutable His ways are, and immune
To catechism by a mind too strewn
With petty cares to slightly understand
What awful brain compels His awful hand.
Yet do I marvel at this curious thing:
To make a poet black, and bid him sing!

Heritage

For Harold Jackman

What is Africa to me:
Copper sun or scarlet sea,
Jungle star or jungle track,
Strong bronzed men, or regal black
Women from whose loins I sprang
When the birds of Eden sang?
One three centuries removed
From the scenes his fathers loved,
Spicy grove, cinnamon tree,
What is Africa to me?

So I lie, who all day long
Want no sound except the song
Sung by wild barbaric birds
Goading massive jungle herds,
Juggernauts of flesh that pass
Trampling tall defiant grass
Where young forest lovers lie,
Plighting troth beneath the sky.
So I lie, who always hear,
Though I cram against my ear
Both my thumbs, and keep them there,
Great drums throbbing through the air.
So I lie, whose fount of pride,
Dear distress, and joy allied,
Is my somber flesh and skin,
With the dark blood dammed within
Like great pulsing tides of wine
That, I fear, must burst the fine
Channels of the chafing net
Where they surge and foam and fret.

Africa? A book one thumbs
Listlessly, till slumber comes.
Unremembered are her bats
Circling through the night, her cats
Crouching in the river reeds,
Stalking gentle flesh that feeds
By the river brink; no more
Does the bugle-throated roar
Cry that monarch claws have leapt
From the scabbards where they slept.
Silver snakes that once a year
Doff the lovely coats you wear,
Seek no covert in your fear
Lest a mortal eye should see;
What's your nakedness to me?
Here no leprous flowers rear
Fierce corollas in the air;
Here no bodies sleek and wet,
Dripping mingled rain and sweat,
Tread the savage measures of
Jungle boys and girls in love.
What is last year's snow to me,
Last year's anything? The tree
Budding yearly must forget
How its past arose or set—
Bough and blossom, flower, fruit,
Even what shy bird with mute
Wonder at her travail there,
Meekly labored in its hair.
One three centuries removed
From the scenes his fathers loved,
Spicy grove, cinnamon tree,
What is Africa to me?

So I lie, who find no peace
Night or day, no slight release
From the unremittent beat
Made by cruel padded feet
Walking through my body's street.
Up and down they go, and back,
Treading out a jungle track.
So I lie, who never quite
Safely sleep from rain at night—
I can never rest at all
When the rain begins to fall;
Like a soul gone mad with pain
I must match its weird refrain;
Ever must I twist and squirm,
Writhing like a baited worm,

While its primal measures drip
Through my body, crying, "Strip!
Doff this new exuberance.
Come and dance the Lover's Dance!"
In an old remembered way
Rain works on me night and day.

Quaint, outlandish heathen gods
Black men fashion out of rods,
Clay, and brittle bits of stone,
In a likeness like their own,
My conversion came high-priced;
I belong to Jesus Christ,
Preacher of humility;
Heathen gods are naught to me.

Father, Son, and Holy Ghost,
So I make an idle boast;
Jesus of the twice-turned cheek,
Lamb of God, although I speak
With my mouth thus, in my heart
Do I play a double part.

Ever at Thy glowing altar
Must my heart grow sick and falter,
Wishing He I served were black,
Thinking then it would not lack
Precedent of pain to guide it,
Let who would or might deride it;
Surely then this flesh would know
Yours had borne a kindred woe.
Lord, I fashion dark gods, too,
Daring even to give You
Dark despairing features where,
Crowned with dark rebellious hair,
Patience wavers just so much as
Mortal grief compels, while touches
Quick and hot, of anger, rise
To smitten cheek and weary eyes.
Lord, forgive me if my need
Sometimes shapes a human creed.

All day long and all night through,
One thing only must I do:
Quench my pride and cool my blood,
Lest I perish in the flood.
Lest a hidden ember set
Timber that I thought was wet
Burning like the dryest flax,

Melting like the merest wax,
Lest the grave restore its dead.
Not yet has my heart or head
In the least way realized
They and I are civilized.

Four Epitaphs

For My Grandmother

This lovely flower fell to seed;
Work gently sun and rain;
She held it as her dying creed
That she would grow again.

For John Keats, Apostle of Beauty

Not writ in water nor in mist,
Sweet lyric throat, thy name.
Thy singing lips that cold death kissed
Have seared his own with flame.

For Paul Laurence Dunbar

Born of the sorrowful of heart
Mirth was a crown upon his head;
Pride kept his twisted lips apart
In jest, to hide a heart that bled.

For a Lady I Know

She even thinks that up in heaven
    Her class lies late and snores,
While poor black cherubs rise at seven
    To do celestial chores.

Incident

For Eric Walrond

Once riding in old Baltimore,
    Heart-filled, head-filled with glee,
I saw a Baltimorean
    Keep looking straight at me.

Now I was eight and very small,
   And he was no whit bigger,
And so I smiled, but he poked out
   His tongue, and called me, "Nigger."

I saw the whole of Baltimore
   From May until December;
Of all the things that happened there
   That's all that I remember.

Black Majesty

   After reading John W. Vandercook's chronicle of sable glory

These men were kings, albeit they were black,
Christophe and Dessalines and L'Ouverture;
Their majesty has made me turn my back
Upon a plaint I once shaped to endure.
These men were black, I say, but they were crowned
And purple-clad, however brief their time.
Stifle your agony; let grief be drowned;
We know joy had a day once and a clime.

Dark gutter-snipe, black sprawler-in-the-mud,
A thing men did a man may do again.
What answers filter through your sluggish blood
To these dark ghosts who knew so bright a reign?
"Lo, I am dark, but comely," Sheba sings.
"And we were black," three shades reply, "but kings."

For a Mouthy Woman

God and the devil still are wrangling
   Which should have her, which repel;
God wants no discord in his heaven;
   Satan has enough in hell.

Tableau

Locked arm in arm they cross the way,
The black boy and the white,
The golden splendor of the day
The sable pride of night.

From lowered blinds the dark folk stare
And here the fair folk talk,
Indignant that these two should dare
In unison to walk.

Oblivious to look and word
They pass, and see no wonder
That lightning brilliant as a sword
Should blaze the path of thunder.

Brown Boy to Brown Girl

Remembrance on a hill

For Yolande

"As surely as I hold your hand in mine,
As surely as your crinkled hair belies
The enamoured sun pretending that he dies
While still he loiters in its glossy shine,
As surely as I break the slender line
That spider linked us with, in no least wise
Am I uncertain that these alien skies
Do not our whole life measure and confine.
No less, once in a land of scarlet suns
And brooding winds, before the hurricane
Bore down upon us, long before this pain,
We found a place where quiet water runs;
I held your hand this way upon a hill,
And felt my heart forbear, my pulse grow still."

Scottsboro, Too, Is Worth Its Song

A poem to American poets

I said:
Now will the poets sing,—
Their cries go thundering
Like blood and tears
Into the nation's ears,
Like lightning dart
Into the nation's heart.

Against disease and death and all things fell,
And war,
Their strophes rise and swell
To jar
The foe smug in his citadel.

Remembering their sharp and pretty
Tunes for Sacco and Vanzetti,
I said:
Here too's a cause divinely spun
For those whose eyes are on the sun,
Here in epitome
Is all disgrace
And epic wrong,
Like wine to brace
The minstrel heart, and blare it into song.

Surely, I said,
Now will the poets sing.
    But they have raised no cry.
    I wonder why.

DONALD JEFFREY HAYES (1904–)

Appoggiatura

It was water I was trying to think of all the time
Seeing the way you moved about the house. . . .
It was water, still and grey—or dusty blue
Where late at night the wind and a half-grown moon
Could make a crazy quilt of silver ripples
And it little mattered what you were about;
Whether painting in your rainbow-soiled smock
Or sitting by the window with the sunlight in your hair
That boiled like a golden cloud about your head
Or whether you sat in the shadows
Absorbed in the serious business
Of making strange white patterns with your fingers—
Whether it was any of these things
The emotion was always the same with me
And all the time it was water I was trying to recall,
Water, silent, breathless, restless,
Slowly rising, slowly falling, imperceptibly. . . .
It was the memory of water and the scent of air
Blown from the sea
That bothered me!

When you laughed, and that was so rare a festival,
I wanted to think of gulls dipping—
Grey wings, white-faced, into a rising wind
Dipping . . .
Do you remember the day
You held a pale white flower to the sun
That I might see how the yellow rays
Played through the petals?
As I remember now
The flower was beautiful—
And the sunrays playing through—
And your slim fingers
And your tilting chin
But then:
There was only the indistinguishable sound of water silence;
The inaudible swish of one wave breaking. . . .

And now that you have moved on into the past;
You and your slim fingers
And your boiling hair,
Now that you have moved on into the past,
And I have time to stroll back through the corridors of memory,
It is like meeting an old friend at dawn
To find carved here deep in my mellowing mind
These words:
    "Sea-Woman—slim-fingered-water-thing . . ."

FRANK MARSHALL DAVIS (1905–)

Flowers of Darkness

Slowly the night blooms, unfurling
Flowers of darkness, covering
The trellised sky, becoming
A bouquet of blackness
Unending
Touched with sprigs
Of pale and budding stars

Soft the night smell
Among April trees
Soft and richly rare
Yet commonplace
Perfume on a cosmic scale

I turn to you Mandy Lou
I see the flowering night
Cameo condensed
Into the lone black rose
Of your face

The young woman-smell
Of your poppy body
Rises to my brain as opium
Yet silently motionless
I sit with twitching fingers
Yea, even reverently
Sit I
With you and the blossoming night
For what flower, plucked,
Lingers long?

Giles Johnson, Ph.D.

Giles Johnson
had four college degrees
knew the whyfore of this
the wherefore of that
could orate in Latin
or cuss in Greek
and, having learned such things
he died of starvation
because he wouldn't teach
and he couldn't porter.

Robert Whitmore

Having attained success in business
possessing three cars
one wife and two mistresses
a home and furniture
talked of by the town
and thrice ruler of the local Elks
Robert Whitmore
died of apoplexy
when a stranger from Georgia
mistook him
for a former Macon waiter.

Four Glimpses of Night

I

Eagerly
Like a woman hurrying to her lover
Night comes to the room of the world
And lies, yielding and content
Against the cool round face
Of the moon.

II

Night is a curious child, wandering
Between earth and sky, creeping
In windows and doors, daubing
The entire neighborhood
With purple paint.
Day
Is an apologetic mother
Cloth in hand
Following after.

III

Peddling
From door to door
Night sells
Black bags of peppermint stars
Heaping cones of vanilla moon
Until
His wares are gone
Then shuffles homeward
Jingling the gray coins
Of daybreak.

IV

Night's brittle song, sliver-thin
Shatters into a billion fragments
Of quiet shadows
At the blaring jazz
Of a morning sun.

I Sing No New Songs

Once I cried for new songs to sing . . . a black rose . . . a brown sky . . . the moon for my buttonhole . . . pink dreams for the table

Later I learned life is a servant girl . . . dusting the same pieces yesterday, today, tomorrow . . . a never ending one two three one two three one two three

The dreams of Milton were the dreams of Lindsay . . . drinking corn liquor, wearing a derby, dancing a foxtrot . . . a saxophone for a harp

Ideas rise with new mornings but never die . . . only names, places, people change . . . you are born, love, fight, tire and stop being . . . Caesar died with a knife in his guts . . . Jim Colosimo from revolver bullets

So I shall take aged things . . . bearded dreams . . . a silver dollar moon worn thin from the spending . . . model a new dress for this one . . . get that one a new hat . . . teach the other to forget the minuet . . . then I shall send them into the street

And if passersby stop and say "Who is that? I never saw this pretty girl before" or if they say . . . "Is that old woman still alive? I thought she died years ago" . . . if they speak these words, I shall neither smile nor swear . . . those who walked before me, those who come after me, may make better clothes, teach a more graceful step . . . but the dreams of Homer neither grow nor wilt. . . .

Snapshots of the Cotton South

Listen, you drawing men
I want a picture of a starving black
I want a picture of a starving white
Show them bitterly fighting down on the dark soil
Let their faces be lit by hate
Above there will stand
The rich plantation owner, holder of the land
A whip in his red fist
Show his pockets bulging with dollars spilled
From the ragged trousers of the fighting men
And I shall call it
"Portrait of the Cotton South."

Co'n pone, collard greens, side meat
Sluggish sorghum and fat yams
Don't care who eats them.
The popping bolls of cotton
Whiter than the snobbish face
Of the plantation owner's wife
Never shrink in horror
At the touch of black croppers' hands.
And when the weevils march
They send no advance guard
Spying at doors, windows
Reporting back
"This is a privileged place
We shall pass it by
We want only nigger cotton."
Death
Speeding in a streamlined racing car
Or hobbling on ancient crutches
Sniffs at the color line;
Starvation, privation, disease, disaster
Likewise embarrass Social Tradition
By indiscriminately picking victims
Instead of arranging
Black folk later—
But otherwise
Life officially flows
In separate channels.

Chisel your own statue of God.
Have him blonde as a Viking king
A celestial czar of race separation
Roping off a jim crow section
On the low lying outskirts of heaven
Hard by the platinum railroad tracks
Where there will dwell for eternity
Good darkies inferiority-conscious
Of their brothers and sisters
In the Methodist Episcopal Church, South
Or
Have him a dealer of vengeance
Punishing in hell's hot fires
Lynchers, quick trigger sheriffs,
Conniving land owners, slave driving overseers
While today's black Christians
Look down at their endless torture
Then travel the golden streets of paradise
To the biggest mansions
In the best districts
And there feast themselves

On milk and honey
As say the preachers
In the little colored churches.
Of course
There is no intermingling socially
Between the races
Such is absolutely unthinkable
Oh my yes
Still
At regular intervals
The wife of Mobtown's mayor
Sees an Atlanta specialist
For syphilis contracted from her husband
Who got it from their young mulatto cook
Who was infected by the chief of police
Who received it from his washerwoman
Who was made diseased by the shiftless son
Of the section's richest planter
One night before
He led the pack that hanged
The black bastard who broke into
A farm woman's bedroom—
But
As was mentioned before
There is no intermingling socially . . . .

Neither Socialist nor Communist lingers here.
The Southern Tenant Farmers Union
Is officially a Grave Menace
Here we have Democracy at its best
Amid "native American"
"Bedrock of the nation"
Untouched by "The Foreign Element"
They have "Rugged Individualism"
"Any man may be President"
"Equality of Opportunity"
Which, translated, means
The rich men grow richer
Big planters get bigger
Controlling the land and the towns
Ruling their puppet officials
Feeding white croppers and tenant farmers
Banquets of race hate for the soul
Sparse crumbs for their thin bodies
Realizing
The feast of animosity
Will dull their minds
To their own plight

So the starving po' whites
Contemptuous of neighboring blacks
Filled with their pale superiority
Live in rotting cabins
Dirt floored and dirty
Happy hunting ground of hookworm and vermin
Overrun with scrawny children
Poverty sleeping on the front stoop
Enslaved on islands of rundown clay
And to the planter-owned commissaries;
Dying, then dumped into the grinning graves
Their worm-picked bones resting silently
In a white burial ground
Separated even in death
As were their fathers before them.

No matter what the cost in taxes
Sacrificed by penniless croppers
Unmissed by money-grabbing land owners
There must be separate accommodations
And public institutions
For each race.
Impoverished white schools
Loosing tidewaters
Of anti-Negro propaganda
While the fallen-in buildings
For black children
Have courses in Manual Arts,
Writing, and a little figuring
In between cotton picking and sowing
And of course
Care must be taken
By public officials
Not to make jails too strong
And thus inconvenience
The hungry lynchers.
Now
There are some who say
Voteless blacks never get
A proportionate return of taxes paid
But since so many
Land in the hoosegow
On copyrighted charges
And the county pays their keep
In stockade, on chain gang,
They really use their share
Of public funds—
The arithmetic and logic
Are indisputable.

At sunrise
Into the broad fields they go—
Cropper, tenant, day laborer
Black and white—
Leaving behind
Shacks of logs and rough planks.
Arching their crooked backs
Slowly, like long mistreated cats,
They throttle the living cotton,
Hustle it, dead and grayish white,
Into the gaping sacks
Portable tombs
For the soft body
Of the South's Greatest Industry—
While, nearby
Overseers stand
Throttling the living souls
Of the broken workers
Choking their spirit
Until
Worn out and useless
They are crammed into
The waiting earth—
Another industry
Of the Cotton South.

Well, you remakers of America
You apostles of Social Change
Here is pregnant soil
Here are grass roots of a nation.
But the crop they grow is Hate and Poverty.
By themselves they will make no change
Black men lack the guts
Po' whites have not the brains
And the big land owners want Things As They Are.
You disciples of Progress
Of the Advancing Onward
Communist, Socialist, Democrat, Republican
See today's picture—
It is not beautiful to look upon.
Meanwhile paint pots drip over
There is fresh canvas for the asking.
Will you say,
"But that is not my affair"
Or will you mold this section
So its portrait will fit
In the sunlit hall
Of Ideal America?

HELENE JOHNSON (1907–)

Magalu

Summer comes.
The ziczac hovers
'Round the greedy-mouthed crocodile.
A vulture bears away a foolish jackal.
The flamingo is a dash of pink
Against dark green mangroves,
Her slender legs rivalling her slim neck.
The laughing lake gurgles delicious music in its throat
And lulls to sleep the lazy lizard,
A nebulous being on a sun-scorched rock.
In such a place,
In this pulsing, riotous gasp of color,
I met Magalu, dark as a tree at night,
Eager-lipped, listening to a man with a white collar
And a small black book with a cross on it.
Oh Magalu, come! Take my hand and I will read you poetry,
Chromatic words,
Seraphic symphonies,
Fill up your throat with laughter and your heart with song.
Do not let him lure you from your laughing waters,
Lulling lakes, lissome winds.
Would you sell the colors of your sunset and the fragrance
Of your flowers, and the passionate wonder of your forest
For a creed that will not let you dance?

Poem

Little brown boy,
Slim, dark, big-eyed,
Crooning love songs to your banjo
Down at the Lafayette—
Gee, boy, I love the way you hold your head,
High sort of and a bit to one side,
Like a prince, a jazz prince. And I love
Your eyes flashing, and your hands,
And your patent-leathered feet,
And your shoulders jerking the jig-wa.
And I love your teeth flashing,
And the way your hair shines in the spotlight
Like it was the real stuff.

Gee, brown boy, I loves you all over.
I'm glad I'm a jig. I'm glad I can
Understand your dancin' and your
Singin', and feel all the happiness
And joy and don't-care in you.
Gee, boy, when you sing, I can close my ears
And hear tom-toms just as plain.
Listen to me, will you, what do I know
About tom-toms? But I like the word, sort of,
Don't you? It belongs to us.
Gee, boy, I love the way you hold your head,
And the way you sing and dance,
And everything.
Say, I think you're wonderful. You're
All right with me,
You are.

Bottled: New York

Upstairs on the third floor
Of the 135th Street library
In Harlem, I saw a little
Bottle of sand, brown sand
Just like the kids make pies
Out of down at the beach.
But the label said: "This
Sand was taken from the Sahara desert."
Imagine that! The Sahara desert!
Some bozo's been all the way to Africa to get some sand.

And yesterday on Seventh Avenue
I saw a Negro dressed fit to kill
In yellow gloves and swallow-tail coat
And twirling a cane. And everyone
Was laughing at him. Me too,
At first, till I saw his face
When he stopped to hear a
Organ grinder grind out some jazz.
Boy! You should a seen that fellow's face!
It just shone. Gee, he was happy!
And he began to dance. No
Charleston or Black Bottom for him.
No sir. He danced just as dignified
And slow. No, not slow either.
Dignified and *proud!* You couldn't
Call it slow, not with all the
Cuttin' up he did. You would a died to see him.

The crowd kept yellin' but he didn't hear,
Just kept on dancin' and twirlin' that cane
And yellin' out loud every once in a while.
I know the crowd thought he was coo-coo.
But say, I was where I could see his face,
And somehow, I could see him dancin' in a jungle,
A real honest-to-goodness jungle, and he wouldn't have on them
Trick clothes—those yellow shoes and yellow gloves
And swallow-tail coat. He wouldn't have on nothing.
And he wouldn't be carrying no cane.
He'd be carrying a spear with a sharp fine point
Like the bayonets we had "over there."
And the end would be dipped in some kind of
Hoodoo poison. And he'd be dancin' black and naked and gleaming.
And he'd have rings in his ears and on his nose
And bracelets and necklaces of elephants' teeth.
Gee, I bet he'd be beautiful then all right.

No one would laugh at him then, I bet.
Say! That man that took that sand from the Sahara desert
And put it in a little bottle on a shelf in the library,
That's what they done to this dancer, ain't it? Bottled him.
Trick shoes, trick coat, trick cane, trick everything—all glass—
But inside—
Gee, that poor guy!

RICHARD WRIGHT (1908–1960)

I Have Seen Black Hands

I

I am black and I have seen black hands, millions and millions of them—
Out of millions of bundles of wool and flannel tiny black fingers have reached
   restlessly and hungrily for life.
Reached out for the black nipples at the black breasts of black mothers,
And they've held red, green, blue, yellow, orange, white, and purple toys in the
   childish grips of possession,
And chocolate drops, peppermint sticks, lollypops, wineballs, ice cream cones, and
   sugared cookies in fingers sticky and gummy,
And they've held balls and bats and gloves and marbles and jack-knives and sling-
   shots and spinning tops in the thrill of sport and play,

And pennies and nickels and dimes and quarters and sometimes on New Year's,
　　Easter, Lincoln's Birthday, May Day, a brand new green dollar bill,
They've held pens and rulers and maps and tablets and books in palms spotted and
　　smeared with ink,
And they've held dice and cards and half-pint flasks and cue sticks and cigars and
　　cigarettes in the pride of new maturity . . .

II

I am black and I have seen black hands, millions and millions of them—
They were tired and awkward and calloused and grimy and covered with hangnails,
And they were caught in the fast-moving belts of machines and snagged and
　　smashed and crushed,
And they jerked up and down at the throbbing machines massing taller and taller
　　the heaps of gold in the banks of bosses,
And they piled higher and higher the steel, iron, the lumber, wheat, rye, the oats,
　　corn, the cotton, the wool, the oil, the coal, the meat, the fruit, the glass, and
　　the stone until there was too much to be used,
And they grabbed guns and slung them on their shoulders and marched and groped
　　in trenches and fought and killed and conquered nations who were customers
　　for the goods black hands had made.
And again black hands stacked goods higher and higher until there was too much
　　to be used,
And then the black hands held trembling at the factory gates the dreaded lay-off slip,
And the black hands hung idle and swung empty and grew soft and got weak and
　　bony from unemployment and starvation,
And they grew nervous and sweaty, and opened and shut in anguish and doubt and
　　hesitation and irresolution . . .

III

I am black and I have seen black hands, millions and millions of them—
Reaching hesitantly out of days of slow death for the goods they had made, but the
　　bosses warned that the goods were private and did not belong to them,
And the black hands struck desperately out in defence of life and there was blood,
　　but the enraged bosses decreed that this too was wrong,
And the black hands felt the cold steel bars of the prison they had made, in despair
　　tested their strength and found that they could neither bend nor break them,
And the black hands fought and scratched and held back but a thousand white hands
　　took them and tied them,
And the black hands lifted palms in mute and futile supplication to the sodden
　　faces of mobs wild in the revelries of sadism,
And the black hands strained and clawed and struggled in vain at the noose that
　　tightened about the black throat,
And the black hands waved and beat fearfully at the tall flames that cooked and
　　charred the black flesh . . .

IV

I am black and I have seen black hands
Raised in fists of revolt, side by side with the white fists of white workers,
And some day—and it is only this which sustains me—
Some day there shall be millions and millions of them,
On some red day in a burst of fists on a new horizon!

Between the World and Me

And one morning while in the woods I stumbled suddenly upon the thing,
Stumbled upon it in a grassy clearing guarded by scaly oaks and elms.
And the sooty details of the scene rose, thrusting themselves between the world
and me. . . .

There was a design of white bones slumbering forgottenly upon a cushion of ashes.
There was a charred stump of a sapling pointing a blunt finger accusingly at the sky.
There were torn tree limbs, tiny veins of burnt leaves, and a scorched coil of greasy
hemp;
A vacant shoe, an empty tie, a ripped shirt, a lonely hat, and a pair of trousers stiff
with black blood.
And upon the trampled grass were buttons, dead matches, butt-ends of cigars and
cigarettes, peanut shells, a drained gin-flask, and a whore's lipstick;
Scattered traces of tar, restless arrays of feathers, and the lingering smell of gasoline.
And through the morning air the sun poured yellow surprise into the eye sockets of
a stony skull. . . .
And while I stood my mind was frozen with a cold pity for the life that was gone.
The ground gripped my feet and my heart was circled by icy walls of fear—
The sun died in the sky; a night wind muttered in the grass and fumbled the leaves
in the trees; the woods poured forth the hungry yelping of hounds; the darkness
screamed with thirsty voices; and the witnesses rose and lived:
The dry bones stirred, rattled, lifted, melting themselves into my bones.
The grey ashes formed flesh firm and black, entering into my flesh.
The gin-flask passed from mouth to mouth; cigars and cigarettes glowed, the whore
smeared the lipstick red upon her lips,
And a thousand faces swirled around me, clamoring that my life be burned. . . .

And then they had me, stripped me, battering my teeth into my throat till I
swallowed my own blood.
My voice was drowned in the roar of their voices, and my black wet body slipped
and rolled in their hands as they bound me to the sapling.
And my skin clung to the bubbling hot tar, falling from me in limp patches.
And the down and quills of the white feathers sank into my raw flesh, and I
moaned in my agony.
Then my blood was cooled mercifully, cooled by a baptism of gasoline.
And in a blaze of red I leaped to the sky as pain rose like water, boiling my limbs.
Panting, begging I clutched childlike, clutched to the hot sides of death.
Now I am dry bones and my face a stony skull staring in yellow surprise at the
sun. . . .

Hokku Poems

I am nobody
A red sinking autumn sun
Took my name away

Make up your mind snail!
You are half inside your house
And halfway out!

In the falling snow
A laughing boy holds out his palms
Until they are white

Keep straight down this block
Then turn right where you will find
A peach tree blooming

With a twitching nose
A dog reads a telegram
On a wet tree trunk

The spring lingers on
In the scent of a damp log
Rotting in the sun

Whose town did you leave
O wild and drowning spring rain
And where do you go?

The crow flew so fast
That he left his lonely caw
Behind in the fields

PAULI MURRAY (1910–)

Without Name

Call it neither love nor spring madness,
Nor chance encounter nor quest ended.
Observe it casually as pussy willows
Or pushcart pansies on a city street.

Let this seed growing in us
Granite-strong with persistent root
Be without name, or call it the first
Warm wind that caressed your cheek
And traded unshared kisses between us.
Call it the elemental earth
Bursting the clasp of too-long winter
And trembling for the plough-blade.

Let our blood chant it
And our flesh sing anthems to its arrival,
But our lips shall be silent, uncommitted.

Mr. Roosevelt Regrets

Detroit Riot, 1943

Upon reading PM newspaper's account of Mr. Roosevelt's statement on the recent race clashes: "I share your feeling that the recent outbreaks of violence in widely spread parts of the country endanger our national unity and comfort our enemies. I am sure that every true American regrets this."

What'd you get, black boy,
When they knocked you down in the gutter,
And they kicked your teeth out,
And they broke your skull with clubs
And they bashed your stomach in?
What'd you get when the police shot you in the back,
And they chained you to the beds
While they wiped the blood off?
What'd you get when you cried out to the Top Man?
When you called on the man next to God, so you thought,
And you asked him to speak out to save you?
What'd the Top Man say, black boy?
"Mr. Roosevelt regrets . . . ."

Harlem Riot, 1943

Not by hammering the furious word,
Nor bread stamped in the streets,
Nor milk emptied in gutter,
Shall we gain the gates of the city.

But I am a prophet without eyes to see;
I do not know how we shall gain the gates of the city.

August 1943

Death of a Friend

There was one among us who rose
And leaving by an outer door
Closed it silently.
Why have I felt a chill upon the earth
And songs of dead poets haunted me all day?

Berkeley, April 1945

For Mack C. Parker

Victim of lynching in Mississippi, 1959

> In the hour of death,
> In the day of judgment,
>   *Good Lord, deliver us!*
>   —*The Book of Common Prayer*

The cornered and trapped,
The bludgeoned and crushed,
The hideously slain,
Freed from the dreaded waiting,
The tortured body's pain,
On death's far shore cast mangled shrouds
To clothe the damned whose fear
Decreed a poisoned harvest,
Garnered a bitter grain.
For these who wear the cloak of shame
Must eat the bread of gall,
Each vainly rubbing the 'cursed spot
Which brands him Cain.

April 1959

ROBERT HAYDEN (1913–)

Middle Passage

I

Jesús, Estrella, Esperanza, Mercy:

Sails flashing to the wind like weapons,
sharks following the moans the fever and the dying;
horror the corposant and compass rose.

Middle Passage:
>   voyage through death
>>   to life upon these shores.

"10 April 1800—
Blacks rebellious. Crew uneasy. Our linguist says
their moaning is a prayer for death,
ours and their own. Some try to starve themselves.
Lost three this morning leaped with crazy laughter
to the waiting sharks, sang as they went under."

Desire, Adventure, Tartar, Ann:

Standing to America, bringing home
black gold, black ivory, black seed.

>   *Deep in the festering hold thy father lies,*
>   *of his bones New England pews are made,*
>   *those are altar lights that were his eyes.*

Jesus Saviour Pilot Me
Over Life's Tempestuous Sea

We pray that Thou wilt grant, O Lord,
safe passage to our vessels bringing
heathen souls unto Thy chastening.

Jesus Saviour

"8 bells. I cannot sleep, for I am sick
with fear, but writing eases fear a little
since still my eyes can see these words take shape
upon the page & so I write, as one
would turn to exorcism. 4 days scudding,
but now the sea is calm again. Misfortune
follows in our wake like sharks (our grinning
tutelary gods). Which one of us
has killed an albatross? A plague among
our blacks—Ophthalmia: blindness—& we
have jettisoned the blind to no avail.
It spreads, the terrifying sickness spreads.
Its claws have scratched sight from the Capt.'s eyes
& there is blindness in the fo'c'sle
& we must sail 3 weeks before we come
to port."

>   *What port awaits us, Davy Jones'*
>   *or home? I've heard of slavers drifting, drifting,*
>   *playthings of wind and storm and chance, their crews*

gone blind, the jungle hatred
crawling up on deck.

Thou Who Walked On Galilee

"Deponent further sayeth *The Bella J*
left the Guinea Coast
with cargo of five hundred blacks and odd
for the barracoons of Florida:

"That there was hardly room 'tween-decks for half
the sweltering cattle stowed spoon-fashion there;
that some went mad of thirst and tore their flesh
and sucked the blood:

"That Crew and Captain lusted with the comeliest
of the savage girls kept naked in the cabins;
that there was one they called The Guinea Rose
and they cast lots and fought to lie with her:

"That when the Bo's'n piped all hands, the flames
spreading from starboard already were beyond
control, the negroes howling and their chains
entangled with the flames:

"That the burning blacks could not be reached,
that the Crew abandoned ship,
leaving their shrieking negresses behind,
that the Captain perished drunken with the wenches:

"Further Deponent sayeth not."

Pilot Oh Pilot Me

II

Aye, lad, and I have seen those factories,
Gambia, Rio Pongo, Calabar;
have watched the artful mongos baiting traps
of war wherein the victor and the vanquished

Were caught as prizes for our barracoons.
Have seen the nigger kings whose vanity
and greed turned wild black hides of Fellatah,
Mandingo, Ibo, Kru to gold for us.

And there was one—King Anthracite we named him—
fetish face beneath French parasols
of brass and orange velvet, impudent mouth
whose cups were carven skulls of enemies:

He'd honor us with drum and feast and conjo
and palm-oil-glistening wenches deft in love,
and for tin crowns that shone with paste,
red calico and German-silver trinkets

Would have the drums talk war and send
his warriors to burn the sleeping villages
and kill the sick and old and lead the young
in coffles to our factories.

Twenty years a trader, twenty years,
for there was wealth aplenty to be harvested
from those black fields, and I'd be trading still
but for the fevers melting down my bones.

III

Shuttles in the rocking loom of history,
the dark ships move, the dark ships move,
their bright ironical names
like jests of kindness on a murderer's mouth;
plough through thrashing glister toward
fata morgana's lucent melting shore,
weave toward New World littorals that are
mirage and myth and actual shore.

Voyage through death,
                              voyage whose chartings are unlove.

A charnel stench, effluvium of living death
spreads outward from the hold,
where the living and the dead, the horribly dying,
lie interlocked, lie foul with blood and excrement.

Deep in the festering hold thy father lies,
the corpse of mercy rots with him,
rats eat love's rotten gelid eyes.

But, oh, the living look at you
with human eyes whose suffering accuses you,
whose hatred reaches through the swill of dark
to strike you like a leper's claw.

You cannot stare that hatred down
or chain the fear that stalks the watches
and breathes on you its fetid scorching breath;
cannot kill the deep immortal human wish,
the timeless will.

"But for the storm that flung up barriers
of wind and wave, *The Amistad,* señores,
would have reached the port of Príncipe in two,
three days at most; but for the storm we should
have been prepared for what befell.
Swift as the puma's leap it came. There was
that interval of moonless calm filled only
with the water's and the rigging's usual sounds,
then sudden movement, blows and snarling cries
and they had fallen on us with machete
and marlinspike. It was as though the very
air, the night itself were striking us.
Exhausted by the rigors of the storm,
we were no match for them. Our men went down
before the murderous Africans. Our loyal
Celestino ran from below with gun
and lantern and I saw, before the cane-
knife's wounding flash, Cinquez,
that surly brute who calls himself a prince,
directing, urging on the ghastly work.
He hacked the poor mulatto down, and then
he turned on me. The decks were slippery
when daylight finally came. It sickens me
to think of what I saw, of how these apes
threw overboard the butchered bodies of
our men, true Christians all, like so much jetsam
Enough, enough. The rest is quickly told:
Cinquez was forced to spare the two of us
you see to steer the ship to Africa,
and we like phantoms doomed to rove the sea
voyaged east by day and west by night,
deceiving them, hoping for rescue,
prisoners on our own vessel, till
at length we drifted to the shores of this
your land, America, where we were freed
from our unspeakable misery. Now we
demand, good sirs, the extradition of
Cinquez and his accomplices to La
Havana. And it distresses us to know
there are so many here who seem inclined
to justify the mutiny of these blacks.
We find it paradoxical indeed
that you whose wealth, whose tree of liberty
are rooted in the labor of your slaves
should suffer the august John Quincy Adams
to speak with so much passion of the right
of chattel slaves to kill their lawful masters
and with his Roman rhetoric weave a hero's
garland for Cinquez. I tell you that
we are determined to return to Cuba

with our slaves and there see justice done. Cinquez—
or let us say 'the Prince'—Cinquez shall die."

The deep immortal human wish,
the timeless will:

Cinquez its deathless primaveral image,
life that transfigures many lives.

Voyage through death
                to life upon these shores.

A Ballad of Remembrance

Quadroon mermaids, Afro angels, black saints
balanced upon the switchblades of that air
and sang. Tight streets unfolding to the eye
like fans of corrosion and elegiac lace
crackled with their singing: Shadow of time. Shadow of blood.

Shadow, echoed the Zulu king, dangling
from a cluster of balloons. Blood,
whined the gun-metal priestess, floating
over the courtyard where dead men diced.

What will you have? she inquired, the sallow vendeuse
of prepared tarnishes and jokes of nacre and ormolu,
what but those gleamings, oldrose graces,
manners like scented gloves? Contrived ghosts
rapped to metronome clack of lavalieres.

Contrived illuminations riding a threat
of river, masked Negroes wearing chameleon
satins gaudy now as a fortuneteller's
dream of disaster, lighted the crazy flopping
dance of love and hate among joys, rejections.

Accommodate, muttered the Zulu king,
toad on a throne of glaucous poison jewels.
Love, chimed the saints and the angels and the mermaids.
Hate, shrieked the gun-metal priestess
from her spiked bellcollar curved like a fleur-de-lis:

As well have a talon as a finger, a muzzle as a mouth,
as well have a hollow as a heart. And she pinwheeled
away in coruscations of laughter, scattering
those others before her like foil stars.

But the dance continued—now among metaphorical
doors, coffee cups floating poised
hysterias, decors of illusion; now among
mazurka dolls offering death's-heads
of cocaine roses and real violets.

Then you arrived, meditative, ironic,
richly human; and your presence was shore where I rested
released from the hoodoo of that dance, where I spoke
with my true voice again.

And therefore this is not only a ballad of remembrance
for the down-South arcane city with death
in its jaws like gold teeth and archaic cusswords;
not only a token for the troubled generous friends
held in the fists of that schizoid city like flowers,
but also, Mark Van Doren,
a poem of remembrance, a gift, a souvenir for you.

O Daedalus, Fly Away Home

Drifting night in the Georgia pines,
coonskin drum and jubilee banjo.
    Pretty Malinda, dance with me.

Night is juba, night is conjo.
    Pretty Malinda, dance with me.

Night is an African juju man
weaving a wish and a weariness together
    to make two wings.

    O fly away home fly away

Do you remember Africa?

    O cleave the air fly away home

My gran, he flew back to Africa,
just spread his arms and
    flew away home.

Drifting night in the windy pines;
night is a laughing, night is a longing.
    Pretty Malinda, come to me.

Night is a mourning juju man
weaving a wish and a weariness together
    to make two wings.

O fly away home fly away

Homage to the Empress of the Blues

Because there was a man somewhere in a candystripe silk shirt,
gracile and dangerous as a jaguar and because a woman moaned
for him in sixty-watt gloom and mourned him Faithless Love
Twotiming Love Oh Love Oh Careless Aggravating Love,

> She came out on the stage in yards of pearls, emerging like
> a favorite scenic view, flashed her golden smile and sang.

Because grey laths began somewhere to show from underneath
torn hurdygurdy lithographs of dollfaced heaven;
and because there were those who feared alarming fists of snow
on the door and those who feared the riot-squad of statistics,

> She came out on the stage in ostrich feathers, beaded satin,
> and shone that smile on us and sang.

Mourning Poem for the Queen of Sunday

> Lord's lost Him His mockingbird,
> His fancy warbler;
> Satan sweet-talked her,
> four bullets hushed her.
> Who would have thought
> she'd end that way?

Four bullets hushed her. And the world a-clang with evil.
Who's going to make old hardened sinner men tremble now
and the righteous rock?
Oh who and oh who will sing Jesus down
to help with struggling and doing without and being colored
all through blue Monday?
Till way next Sunday?

> All those angels
> in their cretonne clouds and finery
> the true believer saw
> when she rared back her head and sang,
> all those angels are surely weeping.

Who would have thought
she'd end that way?

Four holes in her heart. The gold works wrecked.
But she looks so natural in her big bronze coffin
among the Broken Hearts and Gates-Ajar,
it's as if any moment she'd lift her head
from its pillow of chill gardenias
and turn this quiet into shouting Sunday
and make folks forget what she did on Monday.

Oh, Satan sweet-talked her,
and four bullets hushed her.
Lord's lost Him His diva,
His fancy warbler's gone.
Who would have thought,
who would have thought she'd end that way?

"Summertime and the Living . . ."

Nobody planted roses, he recalls,
but sunflowers gangled there sometimes,
tough-stalked and bold
and like the vivid children there unplanned.
There circus-poster horses curveted
in trees of heaven
above the quarrels and shattered glass,
and he was bareback rider of them all.

No roses there in summer—
oh, never roses except when people died—
and no vacations for his elders,
so harshened after each unrelenting day
that they were shouting-angry.
But summer was, they said, the poor folks' time
of year. And he remembers
how they would sit on broken steps amid

The fevered tossings of the dusk, the dark,
wafting hearsay with funeral-parlor fans
or making evening solemn by
their quietness. Feels their Mosaic eyes
upon him, though the florist roses
that only sorrow could afford
long since have bidden them Godspeed.

Oh, summer summer summertime—

Then grim street preachers shook
their tambourines and Bibles in the face
of tolerant wickedness;
then Elks parades and big splendiferous
Jack Johnson in his diamond limousine
set the ghetto burgeoning
with fantasies
of Ethiopia spreading her gorgeous wings.

The Whipping

The old woman across the way
   is whipping the boy again
and shouting to the neighborhood
   her goodness and his wrongs.

Wildly he crashes through elephant ears,
   pleads in dusty zinnias,
while she in spite of crippling fat
   pursues and corners him.

She strikes and strikes the shrilly circling
   boy till the stick breaks
in her hand. His tears are rainy weather
   to woundlike memories:

My head gripped in bony vise
   of knees, the writhing struggle
to wrench free, the blows, the fear
   worse than blows that hateful

Words could bring, the face that I
   no longer knew or loved . . .
Well, it is over now, it is over,
   and the boy sobs in his room,

And the woman leans muttering against
   a tree, exhausted, purged—
avenged in part for lifelong hidings
   she has had to bear.

Those Winter Sundays

Sundays too my father got up early
and put his clothes on in the blueblack cold,
then with cracked hands that ached
from labor in the weekday weather made
banked fires blaze. No one ever thanked him.

I'd wake and hear the cold splintering, breaking.
When the rooms were warm, he'd call,
and slowly I would rise and dress,
fearing the chronic angers of that house,

Speaking indifferently to him,
who had driven out the cold
and polished my good shoes as well.
What did I know, what did I know
of love's austere and lonely offices?

Frederick Douglass

When it is finally ours, this freedom, this liberty, this beautiful
and terrible thing, needful to man as air,
usable as earth; when it belongs at last to all,
when it is truly instinct, brain matter, diastole, systole,
reflex action; when it is finally won; when it is more
than the gaudy mumbo jumbo of politicians:
this man, this Douglass, this former slave, this Negro
beaten to his knees, exiled, visioning a world
where none is lonely, none hunted, alien,
this man, superb in love and logic, this man
shall be remembered. Oh, not with statues' rhetoric,
not with legends and poems and wreaths of bronze alone,
but with the lives grown out of his life, the lives
fleshing his dream of the beautiful, needful thing.

Runagate Runagate

I

Runs falls rises stumbles on from darkness into darkness
and the darkness thicketed with shapes of terror
and the hunters pursuing and the hounds pursuing
and the night cold and the night long and the river
to cross and the jack-muh-lanterns beckoning beckoning
and blackness ahead and when shall I reach that somewhere
morning and keep on going and never turn back and keep on going

    Runagate
        Runagate
            Runagate

Many thousands rise and go
many thousands crossing over

> O mythic North
> O star-shaped yonder Bible city

Some go weeping and some rejoicing
some in coffins and some in carriages
some in silks and some in shackles

> Rise and go or fare you well

No more auction block for me
no more driver's lash for me

> If you see my Pompey, 30 yrs of age,
> new breeches, plain stockings, negro shoes;
> if you see my Anna, likely young mulatto
> branded E on the right cheek, R on the left,
> catch them if you can and notify subscriber.
> Catch them if you can, but it won't be easy.
> They'll dart underground when you try to catch them,
> plunge into quicksand, whirlpools, mazes,
> turn into scorpions when you try to catch them.

And before I'll be a slave
I'll be buried in my grave

> North star and bonanza gold
> I'm bound for the freedom, freedom-bound
> and oh Susyanna don't you cry for me

> Runagate

> Runagate

II

Rises from their anguish and their power,

> Harriet Tubman,

> woman of earth, whipscarred,
> a summoning, a shining

> Mean to be free

And this was the way of it, brethren brethren,
way we journeyed from Can't to Can.

Moon so bright and no place to hide,
the cry up and the patterollers riding,
hound dogs belling in bladed air.
And fear starts a-murbling, Never make it,
we'll never make it. *Hush that now,*
and she's turned upon us, levelled pistol
glinting in the moonlight:
Dead folks can't jaybird-talk, she says;
you keep on going now or die, she says.

Wanted   Harriet Tubman   alias The General
alias Moses   Stealer of Slaves

In league with Garrison   Alcott   Emerson
Garrett   Douglass   Thoreau   John Brown

Armed and known to be Dangerous

Wanted   Reward   Dead or Alive

Tell me, Ezekiel, oh tell me do you see
mailed Jehovah coming to deliver me?

Hoot-owl calling in the ghosted air,
five times calling to the hants in the air.
Shadow of a face in the scary leaves,
shadow of a voice in the talking leaves:

Come ride-a my train

Oh that train, ghost-story train
through swamp and savanna movering movering,
over trestles of dew, through caves of the wish,
Midnight Special on a sabre track movering movering,
first stop Mercy and the last Hallelujah.

Come ride-a my train

Mean mean mean to be free.

Bahá'u'lláh in the Garden of Ridwan

Agonies confirm His hour,
    and swords like compass-needles turn
        toward His heart.

The midnight air is forested
   with presences that shelter Him
      and sheltering praise

The auroral darkness which is God
   and sing the word made flesh again
      in Him,

Eternal exile whose return
   epiphanies repeatedly
      foretell.

He watches in a borrowed garden,
   prays. And sleepers toss upon
      their armored beds,

Half-roused by golden knocking at
   the doors of consciousness. Energies
      like angels dance

Glorias of recognition.
   Within the rock the undiscovered suns
      release their light.

El-Hajj Malik El-Shabazz

Malcolm X

O masks and metamorphoses of Ahab, Native Son

I

The icy evil that struck his father down
and ravished his mother into madness
trapped him in violence of a punished self
struggling to break free.

As Home Boy, as Dee-troit Red,
he fled his name, became the quarry of
his own obsessed pursuit.

He conked his hair and Lindy-hopped,
zoot-suited jiver, swinging those chicks
in the hot rose and reefer glow.

His injured childhood bullied him.
He skirmished in the Upas trees
and cannibal flowers of the American Dream—

but could not hurt the enemy
powered against him there.

II

Sometimes the dark that gave his life
its cold satanic sheen would shift
a little, and he saw himself
floodlit and eloquent;

yet how could he, "Satan" in The Hole,
guess what the waking dream foretold?

Then false dawn of vision came;
he fell upon his face before
a racist Allah pledged to wrest him from
the hellward-thrusting hands of Calvin's Christ—

to free him and his kind
from Yakub's white-faced treachery.
He rose redeemed from all but prideful anger,

though adulterate attars could not cleanse
him of the odors of the pit.

III

Asalam alaikum!

He X'd his name, became his people's anger,
exhorted them to vengeance for their past;
rebuked, admonished them,

their scourger who
would shame them, drive them from
the lush ice gardens of their servitude.

Asalam alaikum!

Rejecting Ahab, he was of Ahab's tribe.
"Strike through the mask!"

IV

Time. "The martyr's time," he said.
Time and the karate killer,
knifer, gunman. Time that brought
ironic trophies as his faith

twined sparking round the bole,
the fruit of neo-Islam.
"The martyr's time."

But first, the ebb time pilgrimage
toward revelation, hejira to
his final metamorphosis;

Labbayk! Labbayk!

He fell upon his face before
Allah the raceless in whose blazing Oneness all
were one. He rose renewed renamed, became
much more than there was time for him to be.

Aunt Jemima of the Ocean Waves

I

Enacting someone's notion of themselves
(and me), The One And Only Aunt Jemima
and Kokimo The Dixie Dancing Fool
do a bally for the freak show.

I watch a moment, then move on,
pondering the logic that makes of them
(and me) confederates
of The Spider Girl, The Snake-skinned Man. . .

Poor devils have to live somehow.

I cross the boardwalk to the beach,
lie in the sand and gaze beyond
the clutter at the sea.

II

Trouble you for a light?
I turn as Aunt Jemima settles down
beside me, her blue-rinsed hair
without the red bandanna now.

I hold the lighter to her cigarette.
Much obliged. Unmindful (perhaps)
of my embarrassment, she looks
at me and smiles: You sure

do favor a friend I used to have.
Guess that's why I bothered you
for a light. So much like him that I—
She pauses, watching white horses rush

to the shore. Way them big old waves
come slamming whopping in,
sometimes it's like they mean to smash
this no-good world to hell.

　　Well, it could happen. A book I read—
Crossed that very ocean years ago.
London, Paris, Rome,
Constantinople too—I've seen them all.

Back when they billed me everywhere
as the Sepia High Stepper.
Crowned heads applauded me.
Years before your time. Years and years.

I wore me plenty diamonds then,
and counts or dukes or whatever they were
would fill my dressing room
with the costliest flowers. But of course

there was this one you resemble so.
Get me? The sweetest gentleman.
Dead before his time. Killed in the war
to save the world for another war.

High-stepping days for me
were over after that. Still I'm not one
to let grief idle me for long.
I went out with a mental act—

mind-reading—Mysteria From
The Mystic East—veils and beads
and telling suckers how to get
stolen rings and sweethearts back.

One night he was standing by my bed,
seen him plain as I see you,
and warned me without a single word:
Baby, quit playing with spiritual stuff.

So here I am, so here I am,
fake mammy to God's mistakes.
And that's the beauty part,
I mean, ain't that the beauty part.

She laughs, but I do not, knowing what
her laughter shields. And mocks.
I light another cigarette for her.
She smokes, not saying any more.

Scream of children in the surf,
adagios of sun and flashing foam,
the sexual glitter, oppressive fun. . . .
An antique etching comes to mind:

"The Sable Venus" naked on
a baroque Cellini shell—voluptuous
imago floating in the wake
of slave-ships on fantastic seas.

Jemima sighs, Reckon I'd best
be getting back. I help her up.
Don't you take no wooden nickels, hear?
Tin dimes neither. So long, pal.

OWEN DODSON (1914–)

Mary Passed This Morning

Letters from Joseph to Martha

i

Martha
Mary passed this morning
funeral this evening   stop
Near six o'clock
tell the others   stop
Raising bus fare for you
stop
        signed Joseph

ii

Dear Martha,
I'm sorry you missed the bus
for the funeral and what not.
I had raised the fare.

Mary didn't look dead
as we took her out to go . . .
Peter began to sing:
'Leaving for home,
leaving for home,
Mary's going home . . .'
I felt like crying,
but I wept. Oh Martha.
Peter kept singing:
'Leaving for home,
going to home,
Mary's almost there . . .'

It was dark twilight
and the sun came out
to go back in again
and hide us all
'leaving for home . . .'

Then John joined Peter:
'Going to home,
Mary's almost there'.
Oh Martha.
                    signed Joseph

iii

Dear Martha,
we laid her flat in the earth
where lilies of the valley
and poppies grew with grass;
then there was the laying on
of hands: Peter touched Mary's
face, then the disciples kissed
his hand in equal turn like prayer:
then in equal turn they bowed to me
(Judas was not there)
all the disciples bowed to me.
Mary seemed to smile.
A hallelujah crossed the air.
Some bird began to cry.
I picked some poppies and some lilies:
it was all I could do,
to sprinkle over her.
The bird wept on like a child.
We left her lying there.
Oh oh Martha.
                    signed Joseph

iv

Dear Martha,
Mary just finished
baking sesame biscuits
for the poor
before she passed.
Can't find my way clear
to take them out of the oven,
they smell so fresh and good.
Ah Martha . . .
                    signed Joseph

v

Dear Martha,
after Mary passed
I carried out her orders:
I dialled her friend
(that I never saw):
his secretary said
he was not in . . .
out somewhere looking
at Sunday for a while.
I thought he should be present
to view the remains and make
remarks. When I called again
she said he was still out there
looking at lilies and the birds.
He should have been in when I called!
    signed Joseph

vi

Dear Martha,
I don't know Lazarus' address
so I am sending these to you.
Mary said Jesus wanted him
to have these garments:
here they are. Tell him
to keep warm and what not.
    signed Joseph

vii

Dear Martha,
you asked how it happened—
from the beginning. Well, when Mary
was sixteen, I noticed her,
then I had to move away

to carve some Roman crosses
for a time. When I came back
some years ahead, I courted her;
we were married before Jesus came.
  signed Joseph

viii

Dear Martha,
I thought Judas had killed himself.
I strolled in the cool gardens
last night to get cool,
to take a stroll.
The darkness was thick
as a wailing wall.
When the moon appeared:
sitting on the wall
under a tree,
smelling a flower,
I saw a man the spit
and image of Judas.
He began to cry at me,
then ran up the hill.
I thought Judas had killed himself!
Burn this letter.
                signed Joseph

ix

Dear Martha,
I'm glad you have the copy of
the Beatitudes which Jesus wrote
in his own hand. I'm happy Paul
was in your neighborhood.
He tells me you have
rheumatism and arthritis
at the same time . . . (smile)
Walk in the sun
to bake them out.
The weathers here are chancey.
  signed Joseph

x

Dear Martha,
I don't write so much now these days:
my hands are getting shaky.
I must be getting old.
I sat at her grave tonight
just to linger there with her.

I wanted to talk with her:
about our life together
and the son. She answered me
in tongues when I whispered
to the grave. I only spoke
the words I knew: 'Mene, mene
teckle uppharsin'.
When I got them out,
she ceased to speak.
What do these words mean?
Oh Martha, answer me. You're wise.
What do these words mean?
What do these words mean?
What did I say?

I'm weary now. I'm tired out.
So I sign my friend to thee,
so I sign my life to her,
so I sign my love to her,
so I sign my love to her.
I must be getting old.
Goodnight, goodnight.
    signed Joseph

from: Poems for My Brother Kenneth

VII

Sleep late with your dream.
The morning has a scar
To mark on the horizon
With the death of the morning star.

The color of blood will appear
And wash the morning sky,
Aluminum birds flying with fear
Will scream to your waking,
Will send you to die;

Sleep late with your dream.
Pretend that the morning is far,
Deep in the horizon country,
Unconcerned with the morning star.

Sorrow Is the Only Faithful One

Sorrow is the only faithful one:
The lone companion clinging like a season
To its original skin no matter what the variations.

If all the mountains paraded
Eating the valleys as they went
And the sun were a coiffure on the highest peak,

Sorrow would be there between
The sparkling and the giant laughter
Of the enemy when the clouds come down to swim.

But I am less, unmagic, black,
Sorrow clings to me more than to doomsday mountains
Or erosion scars on a palisade.

Sorrow has a song like a leech
Crying because the sand's blood is dry
And the stars reflected in the lake

Are water for all their twinkling
And bloodless for all their charm.
I have blood, and song.

Sorrow is the only faithful one.

Yardbird's Skull

For Charlie Parker

The bird is lost,
Dead, with all the music:
Whole sunsets heard the brain's music
Faded to last horizon notes.
I do not know why I hold
This skull, smaller than a walnut's,
Against my ear,
Expecting to hear
The smashed fear
Of childhood from . . . bone;

Expecting to see
Wind nosing red and purple,
Strange gold and magic
On bubbled windowpanes
Of childhood. Shall I hear?
I should hear: this skull
Has been with violets
Not Yorick, or the gravedigger,
Yapping his yelling story,
This skull has been in air,
Sensed his brother, the swallow,
(Its talent for snow and crumbs).
Flown to lost Atlantis islands,
Places of dreaming, swimming, lemmings.
O I shall hear skull skull,
Hear your lame music,
Believe music rejects undertaking,
Limps back.
Remember tiny lasting, we get lonely:
Come sing, come sing, come sing sing
And sing.

I Break the Sky

Only the deep well
With its reflecting echo
Knows the long dismay
I call this afternoon.

Because my voice is downward
Leaning over shale and torture rock
Surrounding the narrow of this well,
Nothing hears as I cry your name.

There are trees,
The birds they nest are deaf;
All the animals have rejected
The emotion my echo mourns.

Far, far down, the end is prepared
In the sky that breaks as I fall.
I see my face coming, foreshorted descent,
The whiz, the slime—and the sky is whole.

MARGARET DANNER

Far From Africa: Four Poems

"are you beautiful still?"

1. GARNISHING THE AVIARY

Our moulting days are in their twilight stage.
These lengthy dreaded suns of draggling plumes.
These days of moods that swiftly alternate between
The former preen (ludicrous now) and a downcast rage
Or crestfallen lag, are fading out. The initial bloom;
Exotic, dazzling in its indigo, tangerine

Splendor; this rare, conflicting coat had to be shed.
Our drooping feathers turn all shades. We spew
This unamicable aviary, gag upon the worm, and fling

Our loosening quills. We make a riotous spread
Upon the dust and mire that beds us. We do not shoo
So quickly; but the shades of the pinfeathers resulting

From this chaotic push, though still exotic,
Blend in more easily with those on the wings
Of the birds surrounding them; garnishing
The aviary, burnishing this zoo.

2. DANCE OF THE ABAKWETA

Imagine what Mrs. Haessler would say
If she could see the Watusi youth dance
Their well-versed initiation. At first glance
As they bend to an invisible barre
You would know that she had designed their costumes.

For though they were made of pale beige bamboo straw
Their lines were the classic tutu. Nothing varied.
Each was cut short at the thigh and carried
High to a degree of right angles. Nor was there a flaw
In their leotards. Made of leopard skin or the hide

Of a goat, or the Gauguin-colored Okapi's striped coat
They were cut in her reverenced "tradition."
She would have approved their costumes and positions.

And since neither Iceland nor Africa is too remote
For her vision she would have wanted to form

A "traditional" ballet. Swan Lake, Scheherazade or
(After seeing their incredible leaps)
Les Orientales. Imagine the exotic sweep
Of such a ballet, and from the way the music pours
Over these dancers (this tinkling of bells, talking
Of drums, and twanging of tan, sandalwood harps)
From this incomparable music, Mrs. Haessler of Vassar can
Glimpse strains of Tchaikovsky, Chopin
To accompany her undeviatingly sharp
"Traditional" ballet. I am certain that if she could
Tutor these potential protégés, as
Quick as Aladdin rubbing his lamp, she would.

3. THE VISIT OF THE PROFESSOR OF AESTHETICS

To see you standing in the sagging bookstore door
So filled me with chagrin that suddenly you seemed as
Pink and white to me as a newborn, hairless mouse. For

I had hoped to delight you at home. Be a furl
Of faint perfume and Vienna's cordlike lace.
To shine my piano till a shimmer of mother-of-pearl

Embraced it. To pleasantly surprise you with the grace
That transcends my imitation and much worn
"Louis XV" couch. To display my Cathedrals and ballets.

To plunge you into Africa through my nude
Zulu Prince, my carvings from Benin, forlorn
Treasures garnered by much sacrifice of food.

I had hoped to delight you, for more
Rare than the seven-year bloom of my
Chinese spiderweb fern is a mind like yours

That concedes my fetish for this substance
Of your trade. And I had planned to prove
Your views of me correct at even every chance

Encounter. But you surprised me. And the store which
Had shown promise until you came, arose
Like a child gone wild when company comes or a witch

At Hallowe'en. The floor, just swept and mopped,
Was persuaded by the northlight to deny it.
The muddy rag floor rugs hunched and flopped

Away from the tears in the linoleum that I wanted
Them to hide. The drapes that I had pleated
In clear orchid and peach feverishly flaunted

Their greasiest folds like a banner.
The books who had been my friends, retreated—
Became as shy as the proverbial poet in manner

And hid their better selves. All glow had been deleted
By the dirt. And I felt that you whose god is grace
Could find no semblance of it here. And unaware

That you were scrubbing, you scrubbed your hands.
Wrung and scrubbed your long white fingers. Scrubbed
Them as you smiled and I lowered my eyes from despair.

4. ETTA MOTEN'S ATTIC
(*Filled with mementos of African journeys*)

It was as if Gauguin
had upset a huge paint pot
of his incomparable tangerine,

splashing wherever my startled eyes ran
here and there, and at my very hand on
masques and paintings and carvings not seen

here before, spilling straight as a stripe
spun geometrically in a Nbeble rug
flung over an ebony chair,

or dripping round as a band on a type
of bun the Watusi warriors
make of their pompadoured hair,

splashing high as a sunbird or fly moving
over a frieze of mahogany trees,
or splotching out from low underneath as a root,

shimmering bright as a ladybug grooving
a green bed of moss, sparkling as a beetle,
a bee, shockingly dotting the snoot

of an ape or the nape of its neck or as clue
to its navel, stamping a Zulu's
intriguing masque, tipping

the lips of a chief of Ashantis who
was carved to his stool so he'd sit
there forever and never fear a slipping

of rule or command, dyeing the skirt
(all askew) that wouldn't stay put on the
Pygmy in spite of his real leather belt,

quickening and charming till we felt the bloom
of veldt and jungle flow through the room.

The Elevator Man Adheres to Form

I am reminded, by the tan man who wings
the elevator, of Rococo art. His ways
are undulating waves that shepherd and swing
us cupid-like from floor to floor.

He sweethearts us
with polished pleasantries; gallantly
flourishing us up and up. No casual "Hi's" from him.

His greetings, Godspeedings, display his Ph.D.
aplomb, and I should feel like a cherubim,
be fleur-de-lis and pastel-shell-like, but

instead, I vision other tan and deeper much than tan
early-Baroque-like men, who (seeing themselves still strutlessly
groping, winding down subterranean

grottoes of injustice, down dark spirals) feel
with such tortuous, smoked-stone greyed intensity
that they exhale a hurricane of gargoyles, then reel

into it. I see these others boggling in their misery
and wish this elevator artisan would fill his flourishing form
with warmth for them and turn his lettered zeal
toward lifting them above their crippling storm.

Best Loved of Africa

Dedicated to the first Gorilla at Lincoln Park Zoo in Chicago.

It is New Year's Day.
The blasé people rise.
They face a sleek-like ray of light
The low slung skys send shadows down . . .
It's dark.

The earth is treacherous to the tread
And deep in the bedroom
Of his terraced suite in Lincoln Park
Lies Bushman, Best Loved of Africa,
Huge and beautifully black as he ever was . . .
But dead.

Sadie's Playhouse

Over the warts on the bumpy
half-plastered wall
just recently slapped with peach-
colored calcimine,
Carter the artist curved tan
mahogany chalk African women, tall
and arched with a swaying grace.

He then conjured nine
green palm trees and three Egyptian
perfume urns,
so that those whom some might call
flotsam, pimps, jadies,
after tippling their cheap, heady
drinks, could discern
the palms, waving cool, green, shady,
over the (dancing now) African ladies.

DUDLEY RANDALL (1914–)

Legacy: My South

What desperate nightmare rapts me to this land
Lit by a bloody moon, red on the hills,
Red in the valleys? Why am I compelled
To tread again where buried feet have trod,
To shed my tears where blood and tears have flowed?
Compulsion of the blood and of the moon
Transports me. I was molded from this clay
My blood must ransom all the blood shed here,
My tears redeem the tears. Cripples and monsters
Are here. My flesh must make them whole and hale.
I am the sacrifice.

See where the halt
Attempt again and again to cross a line
Their minds have drawn, but fear snatches them back
Though health and joy wait on the other side.
And there another locks himself in a room
And throws away the key. A ragged scarecrow
Cackles an antique lay, and cries himself
Lord of the world. A naked plowman falls
Famished upon the plow, and overhead
A lean bird circles.

The Southern Road

There the black river, boundary to hell.
And here the iron bridge, the ancient car,
And grim conductor, who with surly yell
Forbids white soldiers where the black ones are.
And I re-live the enforced avatar
Of desperate journey to a dark abode
Made by my sires before another war;
And I set forth upon the southern road.

To a land where shadowed songs like flowers swell
And where the earth is scarlet as a scar
Friezed by the bleeding lash that fell (O fell)
Upon my fathers' flesh. O far, far, far
And deep my blood has drenched it. None can bar
My birthright to the loveliness bestowed
Upon this country haughty as a star.
And I set forth upon the southern road.

This darkness and these mountains loom a spell
Of peak-roofed town where yearning steeples soar
And the holy holy chanting of a bell
Shakes human incense on the throbbing air
Where bonfires blaze and quivering bodies char.
Whose is the hair that crisped, and fiercely glowed?
I know it; and my entrails melt like tar
And I set forth upon the southern road.

O fertile hillsides where my fathers are,
From which my griefs like troubled streams have flowed,
I have to love you, though they sweep me far.
And I set forth upon the southern road.

Memorial Wreath

For the more than 200,000 Negroes who served
in the Union Army during the Civil War

In this green month when resurrected flowers,
Like laughing children ignorant of death,
Brighten the couch of those who wake no more,
Love and remembrance blossom in our hearts
For you who bore the extreme sharp pang for us,
And bought our freedom with your lives.

                                                  And now,
Honoring your memory, with love we bring
These fiery roses, white-hot cotton flowers
And violets bluer than cool northern skies
You dreamed of in the burning prison fields
When liberty was only a faint north star,
Not a bright flower planted by your hands
Reaching up hardy nourished with your blood.

Fit gravefellows you are for Lincoln, Brown
And Douglass and Toussaint . . . all whose rapt eyes
Fashioned a new world in this wilderness.

American earth is richer for your bones;
Our hearts beat prouder for the blood we inherit.

Black Magic

Black girl black girl
lips as curved as cherries
full as grape bunches
sweet as blackberries

Black girl black girl
when you walk you are
magic as a rising bird
or a falling star

Black girl black girl
what's your spell to make
the heart in my breast
jump   stop   shake

The Profile on the Pillow

After our fierce loving
in the brief time we found to be together,
you lay in the half light
exhausted, rich,
with your face turned sideways on the pillow,
and I traced the exquisite
line of your profile, dark against the white,
delicate and lovely as a child's.

Perhaps
you may cease to love me,
or we may be consumed in the holocaust,
but I keep, against the ice and the fire,
the memory of your profile on the pillow.

On Getting a Natural

For Gwendolyn Brooks

She didn't know she was beautiful
though her smiles were dawn,
her voice was bells,
and her skin deep velvet Night.
She didn't know she was beautiful,
although her deeds,
kind, generous, unobtrusive,
gave hope to some,
and help to others,
and inspiration to us all. And
beauty is as beauty does,
they say.
Then one day there blossomed
a crown upon her head,
bushy, bouffant, real Afro-down,
Queen Nefertiti again.
And now her regal woolly crown
declares,
I know
I'm black
AND
beautiful.

The Intellectuals

The intellectuals talked.
They had to decide on principles.
Nothing should be done, nothing legislated
Till a rationale had been established.

The intellectuals talked.

Meanwhile the others,
Who believed in action,
And that they should be up and all others down,
Stormed the hall, shot the leaders and arrested the remainder,
Whom they later hanged.

There was no more talking.

Roses and Revolutions

Musing on roses and revolutions,
I saw night close down on the earth like a great dark wing,
and the lighted cities were like tapers in the night,
and I heard the lamentations of a million hearts
regretting life and crying for the grave,
and I saw the Negro lying in the swamp with his face blown off,
and in northern cities with his manhood maligned and felt the writhing
of his viscera like that of the hare hunted down or the bear at bay,
and I saw men working and taking no joy in their work
and embracing the hard-eyed whore with joyless excitement
and lying with wives and virgins in impotence.

And as I groped in darkness
and felt the pain of millions,
gradually, like day driving night across the continent,
I saw dawn upon them like the sun a vision
of a time when all men walk proudly through the earth
and the bombs and missiles lie at the bottom of the ocean
like the bones of dinosaurs buried under the shale of eras,
and men strive with each other not for power or the accumulation of paper
but in joy create for others the house, the poem, the game of athletic beauty.

Then washed in the brightness of this vision,
I saw how in its radiance would grow and be nourished and suddenly
burst into terrible and splendid bloom
the blood-red flower of revolution.

JOHN HENRIK CLARKE (1915–)

Sing Me A New Song

Sing me a new song, young black singer,
Sing me a song with some thunder in it,
And a challenge that will
Drive fear into the hearts of those people
Who think that God has given them
The right to call you their slave.

Sing me a song of strong men growing stronger
And bold youth facing the sun and marching.
Sing me a song of an angry sharecropper,
Who is not satisfied with his meager share
Of the products that he squeezed from the earth
While watering the earth with his sweat and tears.

Sing me a song of two hundred million Africans
Revising the spirit of Chaka, Moshesh and Menelik,
And shouting to the world:
"This is my land and I shall be free upon it!"
Put some reason in my song and some madness too.

Let the reason be the kind of reason
Frederick Douglass had,
When he was fighting against slavery in America.
Let the madness be the kind of madness
Henri Christophe had when
He was driving Napoleon's army from Haitian soil.

Sing me a song with some hunger in it, and a challenge too
Let the hunger be the kind of hunger
Nat Turner and Denmark Vesey had
When they rose from bondage and inspired
Ten thousand black hands to reach for freedom.

Let the challenge be the kind of challenge
Crispus Attucks had
While dying for American Independence.

Don't put "I ain't gonna study war no more" in my song.
Sing me a song of a people hungry for freedom,
Who will study war until they are free!

Determination

My feet have felt the sands
Of many nations,
I have drunk the water
Of many springs,
I am old,
Older than the Pyramids,
I am older than the race
That oppresses me,
I will live on . . .
I will outlive oppression,
I will outlive oppressors.

MARGARET WALKER (1915–)

For My People

For my people everywhere singing their slave songs repeatedly: their dirges and
their ditties and their blues and jubilees, praying their prayers nightly to an
unknown god, bending their knees humbly to an unseen power;

For my people lending their strength to the years, to the gone years and the now
years and the maybe years, washing ironing cooking scrubbing sewing mending
hoeing plowing digging planting pruning patching dragging along never gain-
ing never reaping never knowing and never understanding;

For my playmates in the clay and dust and sand of Alabama backyards playing
baptizing and preaching and doctor and jail and soldier and school and mama
and cooking and playhouse and concert and store and hair and Miss Choomby
and company;

For the cramped bewildered years we went to school to learn to know the reasons
why and the answers to and the people who and the places where and the days
when, in memory of the bitter hours when we discovered we were black and
poor and small and different and nobody cared and nobody wondered and
nobody understood;

For the boys and girls who grew in spite of these things to be man and woman, to
laugh and dance and sing and play and drink their wine and religion and
success, to marry their playmates and bear children and then die of consump-
tion and anemia and lynching;

For my people thronging 47th Street in Chicago and Lenox Avenue in New York and Rampart Street in New Orleans, lost disinherited dispossessed and happy people filling the cabarets and taverns and other people's pockets needing bread and shoes and milk and land and money and something—something all our own;

For my people walking blindly spreading joy, losing time being lazy, sleeping when hungry, shouting when burdened, drinking when hopeless, tied and shackled and tangled among ourselves by the unseen creatures who tower over us omnisciently and laugh;

For my people blundering and groping and floundering in the dark of churches and schools and clubs and societies, associations and councils and committees and conventions, distressed and disturbed and deceived and devoured by money-hungry glory-craving leeches, preyed on by facile force of state and fad and novelty, by false prophet and holy believer;

For my people standing staring trying to fashion a better way from confusion, from hypocrisy and misunderstanding, trying to fashion a world that will hold all the people, all the faces, all the adams and eves and their countless generations;

Let a new earth rise. Let another world be born. Let a bloody peace be written in the sky. Let a second generation full of courage issue forth; let a people loving freedom come to growth. Let a beauty full of healing and a strength of final clenching be the pulsing in our spirits and our blood. Let the martial songs be written, let the dirges disappear. Let a race of men now rise and take control.

We Have Been Believers

We have been believers believing in the black gods of an old land, believing in the secrets of the seeress and the magic of the charmers and the power of the devil's evil ones.

And in the white gods of a new land we have been believers believing in the mercy of our masters and the beauty of our brothers, believing in the conjure of the humble and the faithful and the pure.

Neither the slavers' whip nor the lynchers' rope nor the bayonet could kill our black belief. In our hunger we beheld the welcome table and in our nakedness the glory of a long white robe. We have been believers in the new Jerusalem.

We have been believers feeding greedy grinning gods, like a Moloch demanding our sons and our daughters, our strength and our wills and our spirits of pain. We have been believers, silent and stolid and stubborn and strong.

We have been believers yielding substance for the world. With our hands have we fed a people and out of our strength have they wrung the necessities of a nation. Our song has filled the twilight and our hope has heralded the dawn.

Now we stand ready for the touch of one fiery iron, for the cleansing breath of many
molten truths, that the eyes of the blind may see and the ears of the deaf may
hear and the tongues of the people be filled with living fire.

Where are our gods that they leave us asleep? Surely the priests and the preachers
and the powers will hear. Surely now that our hands are empty and our hearts
too full to pray they will understand. Surely the sires of the people will send
us a sign.

We have been believers believing in our burdens and our demigods too long. Now
the needy no longer weep and pray; the long-suffering arise, and our fists
bleed against the bars with a strange insistency.

October Journey

Traveler take heed for journeys undertaken in the dark of the year.
Go in the bright blaze of Autumn's equinox.
Carry protection against ravages of a sun-robber, a vandal, and a thief.
Cross no bright expanse of water in the full of the moon.
Choose no dangerous summer nights;
no heady tempting hours of spring;
October journeys are safest, brightest, and best.

I want to tell you what hills are like in October
when colors gush down mountainsides
and little streams are freighted with a caravan of leaves.
I want to tell you how they blush and turn in fiery shame and joy,
how their love burns with flames consuming and terrible
until we wake one morning and woods are like a smoldering plain—
a glowing caldron full of jeweled fire:
the emerald earth a dragon's eye
the poplars drenched with yellow light
and dogwoods blazing bloody red.

Traveling southward earth changes from gray rock to green velvet.
Earth changes to red clay
with green grass growing brightly
with saffron skies of evening setting dully
with muddy rivers moving sluggishly.

In the early spring when the peach tree blooms
wearing a veil like a lavender haze
and the pear and plum in their bridal hair
gently snow their petals on earth's grassy bosom below
then the soughing breeze is soothing
and the world seems bathed in tenderness,

but in October
blossoms have long since fallen.
A few red apples hang on leafless boughs;
wind whips bushes briskly.
And where a blue stream sings cautiously
a barren land feeds hungrily.

An evil moon bleeds drops of death.
The earth burns brown.
Grass shrivels and dries to a yellowish mass.
Earth wears a dun-colored dress
like an old woman wooing the sun to be her lover,
be her sweetheart and her husband bound in one.
Farmers heap hay in stacks and bind corn in shocks
against the biting breath of frost.

The train wheels hum, "I am going home, I am going home,
I am moving toward the South."
Soon cypress swamps and muskrat marshes
and black fields touched with cotton will appear.

I dream again of my childhood land
of a neighbor's yard with a redbud tree
the smell of pine for turpentine
an Easter dress, a Christmas eve
and winding roads from the top of a hill.
A music sings within my flesh
I feel the pulse within my throat
my heart fills up with hungry fear
while hills and flatlands stark and staring
before my dark eyes sad and haunting
appear and disappear.

Then when I touch this land again
the promise of a sun-lit hour dies.
The greenness of an apple seems
to dry and rot before my eyes.
The sullen winter rains
are tears of grief I cannot shed.
The windless days are static lives.
The clock runs down
timeless and still.
The days and nights turn hours to years
and water in a gutter marks the circle of another world
hating, resentful, and afraid
stagnant, and green, and full of slimy things.

+

Childhood

When I was a child I knew red miners
dressed raggedly and wearing carbide lamps.
I saw them come down red hills to their camps
dyed with red dust from old Ishkooda mines.
Night after night I met them on the roads,
or on the streets in town I caught their glance;
the swing of dinner buckets in their hands,
and grumbling undermining all their words.

I also lived in low cotton country
where moonlight hovered over ripe haystacks,
or stumps of trees, and croppers' rotting shacks
with famine, terror, flood, and plague near by;
where sentiment and hatred still held sway
and only bitter land was washed away.

Lineage

My grandmothers were strong.
They followed plows and bent to toil.
They moved through fields sowing seed.
They touched earth and grain grew.
They were full of sturdiness and singing.
My grandmothers were strong.

My grandmothers are full of memories
Smelling of soap and onions and wet clay
With veins rolling roughly over quick hands
They have many clean words to say.
My grandmothers were strong.
Why am I not as they?

Girl Held Without Bail

"In an unjust state the only place for a just man is in jail."

I like it here just fine
And I don't want no bail
My sister's here
My mother's here
And all my girl friends too.

I want my rights
I'm fighting for my rights
I want to be treated
Just like *anybody* else
I want to be treated
Just like *everybody* else

I like it fine in Jail
And I don't want no Bail.

Birmingham

1.

With the last whippoorwill call of evening
Settling over mountains
Dusk dropping down shoulders of red hills
And red dust of mines
Sifting across somber sky
Setting the sun to rest in a blue blaze of coal fire
And shivering memories of Spring
With raw wind out of woods
And brown straw of last year's needle-shedding-pines
Cushions of quiet underfoot
Violets pushing through early new spring ground
And my winging heart flying across the world
With one bright bird—
Cardinal flashing through thickets—
Memories of my fancy-ridden life
Come home again.

2.

I died today.
In a new and cruel way.
I came to breakfast in my night-dying clothes
Ate and talked and nobody knew
They had buried me yesterday.
I slept outside city limits
Under a little hill of butterscotch brown
With a dusting of white sugar
Where a whistling ghost kept making a threnody
Out of a naked wind.

3.

Call me home again to my coffin bed of soft warm clay.
I cannot bear to rest in frozen wastes

Of a bitter cold and sleeting northern womb.
My life dies best on a southern cross
Carved out of rock with shooting stars to fire
The forge of bitter hate.

For Malcolm X

All you violated ones with gentle hearts;
You violent dreamers whose cries shout heartbreak;
Whose voices echo clamors of our cool capers,
And whose black faces have hollowed pits for eyes.
All you gambling sons and hooked children and bowery bums
Hating white devils and black bourgeoisie,
Thumbing your noses at your burning red suns,
Gather round this coffin and mourn your dying swan.

Snow-white moslem head-dress around a dead black face!
Beautiful were your sand-papering words against our skins!
Our blood and water pour from your flowing wounds.
You have cut open our breasts and dug scalpels in our brains.
When and where will another come to take your holy place?
Old man mumbling in his dotage, or crying child, unborn?

RAY DUREM (1915–1963)

Friends

Some of my best friends are white boys.
When I meet 'em
I treat 'em
Just the same as if
They was people.

Vet's Rehabilitation

Doctor, doctor, it fits real fine
But the leg you gave me worries my mind!

Doctor, doctor, hear me beg.
Get me a black artificial leg.

I'm going home to a Georgia town.
This leg would make the white folks frown.

Doctor, doctor, hear me beg:
I want a *black* artificial leg.

I Know I'm Not Sufficiently Obscure

I know I'm not sufficiently obscure
to please the critics—nor devious enough.
Imagery escapes me.
I cannot find those mild and gracious words
to clothe the carnage.
Blood is blood and murder's murder.
What's a lavender word for lynch?
Come, you pale poets, wan, refined and dreamy:
here is a black woman working out her guts
in a white man's kitchen
for little money and no glory.
How should I tell that story?
There is a black boy, blacker still from death,
face down in the cold Korean mud.
Come on with your effervescent jive
explain to him why he ain't alive.
Reword our specific discontent
into some plaintive melody,
a little whine, a little whimper,
not too much—and no rebellion!
God, no! Rebellion's much too corny.
You deal with finer feelings,
very subtle—an autumn leaf
hanging from a tree—I see a body!

Problem in Social Geometry—The Inverted Square!

For Ferlinghetti

I have seen the smallest minds of my generation
assume the world ends at Ellis Island,
that its capital is North Beach,
and Fillmore is a nighttown Street
for weary intellectuals.

Man, there were no hypes at Stalingrad,
and Malcolm X is real!
Spare us the cavils of the nihilistic beats

who criticize the cavities and contours of their nest,
but never leave it.
Warm in its filth,
maggots in a rotten apple
with their little pens or paintbrush
They deride the filth they feed on,
they flutter but they never fly.

Little beat bearded Bohemian brother
There are capitals in this universe
beyond your bagel shops and book stores,
Bandung was no chimera, nor Cairo
you think we are so different from Egyptians?
or those in Tres Marias with Zapata?
Bird sang sweet, but sweeter is the song of La Habana
and its echo deep in Monroe County
swings, man, and you are not with it

Man, like,

When you tire of pot
Try thought.

Award

A Gold Watch to the FBI Man who has followed me for 25 **Years.**

Well, old spy
looks like I
led you down some pretty blind alleys,
took you on several trips to Mexico,
fishing in the high Sierras,
jazz at the Philharmonic.
You've watched me all your life,
I've clothed your wife,
put your two sons through college.
What good has it done?
Sun keeps rising every morning.
Ever see me buy an Assistant President?
or close a school?
or lend money to Somoza?
I bought some after-hours whiskey in L.A.
but the Chief got his pay.
I ain't killed no Koreans,
or fourteen-year-old boys in Mississippi
neither did I bomb Guatemala,
or lend guns to shoot Algerians.
I admit I took a Negro child

to a white rest room in Texas,
but she was my daughter, only three,
and she had to pee,
and I just didn't know what to do,
would you?
See, I'm so light, it don't seem right
to go to the colored rest room;
my daughter's brown, and folks frown on that in Texas,
I just don't know how to go to the bathroom in the free world!

Now, old FBI man,
you've done the best you can,
you lost me a few jobs,
scared a couple landlords,
you got me struggling for that bread,
but I ain't dead.
And before it's all through,
I may be following you!

GWENDOLYN BROOKS (1917–)

A Song in the Front Yard

I've stayed in the front yard all my life.
I want a peek at the back
Where it's rough and untended and hungry weed grows.
A girl gets sick of a rose.

I want to go in the back yard now
And maybe down the alley,
To where the charity children play.
I want a good time today.

They do some wonderful things.
They have some wonderful fun.
My mother sneers, but I say it's fine
How they don't have to go in at a quarter to nine.
My mother she tells me that Johnnie Mae
Will grow up to be a bad woman.
That George'll be taken to jail soon or late.
(On account of last winter he sold our back gate.)

But I say it's fine. Honest I do.
And I'd like to be a bad woman too,
And wear the brave stockings of night-black lace.
And strut down the streets with paint on my face.

The Egg Boiler

Being you, you cut your poetry from wood.
The boiling of an egg is heavy art.
You come upon it as an artist should,
With rich-eyed passion, and with straining heart.
We fools, we cut our poems out of air,
Night color, wind soprano, and such stuff.
And sometimes weightlessness is much to bear.
You mock it, though, you name it Not Enough.
The egg, spooned gently to the avid pan,
And left the strict three minutes, or the four,
Is your Enough and art for any man.
We fools give courteous ear—then cut some more,
Shaping a gorgeous Nothingness from cloud.
You watch us, eat your egg, and laugh aloud.

The Bean Eaters

They eat beans mostly, this old yellow pair.
Dinner is a casual affair.
Plain chipware on a plain and creaking wood,
Tin flatware.

Two who are Mostly Good.
Two who have lived their day,
But keep on putting on their clothes
And putting things away.

And remembering . . .
Remembering, with twinklings and twinges,
As they lean over the beans in their rented back room that
        is full of beads and receipts and dolls and cloths,
        tobacco crumbs, vases and fringes.

The Old-Marrieds

But in the crowding darkness not a word did they say.
Though the pretty-coated birds had piped so lightly all the day.
And he had seen the lovers in the little side streets.
And she had heard the morning stories clogged with sweets.
It was quite a time for loving. It was midnight. It was May.
But in the crowding darkness not a word did they say.

The Last Quatrain of the Ballad of Emmett Till

after the murder,
after the burial

Emmett's mother is a pretty-faced thing;
      the tint of pulled taffy.
She sits in a red room,
      drinking black coffee.
She kisses her killed boy.
      And she is sorry.
Chaos in windy grays
      through a red prairie.

The Chicago "Defender" Sends a Man to Little Rock

Fall, 1957

In Little Rock the people bear
Babes, and comb and part their hair
And watch the want ads, put repair
To roof and latch. While wheat toast burns
A women waters multiferns.

Time upholds or overturns
The many, tight, and small concerns.

In Little Rock the people sing
Sunday hymns like anything,
Through Sunday pomp and polishing.

And after testament and tunes,
Some soften Sunday afternoons
With lemon tea and Lorna Doones.

I forecast
And I believe
Come Christmas Little Rock will cleave
To Christmas tree and trifle, weave,
From laugh and tinsel, texture fast.

In Little Rock is baseball; Barcarolle.
That hotness in July . . . the uniformed figures raw and implacable
And not intellectual,
Batting the hotness or clawing the suffering dust.
The Open Air Concert, on the special twilight green . . .
When Beethoven is brutal or whispers to lady-like air.
Blanket-sitters are solemn, as Johann troubles to lean
To tell them what to mean . . .

There is love, too, in Little Rock. Soft women softly
Opening themselves in kindness,
Or, pitying one's blindness,
Awaiting one's pleasure
In azure
Glory with anguished rose at the root . . .
To wash away old semi-discomfitures.
They re-teach purple and unsullen blue.
The wispy soils go. And uncertain
Half-havings have they clarified to sures.

In Little Rock they know
Not answering the telephone is a way of rejecting life,
That it is our business to be bothered, is our business
To cherish bores or boredom, be polite
To lies and love and many-faceted fuzziness.

I scratch my head, massage the hate-I-had.
I blink across my prim and pencilled pad.
The saga I was sent for is not down.
Because there is a puzzle in this town.
The biggest News I do not dare
Telegraph to the Editor's chair:
'They are like people everywhere.'

The angry Editor would reply
In hundred harryings of why.

And true, they are hurling spittle, rock
Garbage and fruit in Little Rock.
And I saw coiling storm a-writhe
On bright madonnas. And a scythe
Of men harassing brownish girls.
(The bows and barrettes in the curls
And braids declined away from joy.)

I saw a bleeding brownish boy . . .

The lariat lynch-wish I deplored.

The loveliest lynchee was our Lord.

We Real Cool

THE POOL PLAYERS.
SEVEN AT THE GOLDEN SHOVEL.

We real cool. We
Left school. We

Lurk late. We
Strike straight. We

Sing sin. We
Thin gin. We

Jazz June. We
Die soon.

Bronzeville Man with a Belt in the Back

In such an armor he may rise and raid
The dark cave after midnight, unafraid,
And slice the shadows with his able sword
Of good broad nonchalance, hashing them down.

And come out and accept the gasping crowd,
Shake off the praises with an airiness.
And, searching, see love shining in an eye,
But never smile.

In such an armor he cannot be slain.

Strong Men, Riding Horses

Lester after the Western

Strong Men, riding horses. In the West
On a range five hundred miles. A Thousand. Reaching
From dawn to sunset. Rested blue to orange.
From hope to crying. Except that Strong Men are
Desert-eyed. Except that Strong Men are
Pasted to stars already. Have their cars
Beneath them. Rentless, too. Too broad of chest
To shrink when the Rough Man hails. Too flailing
To redirect the Challenger, when the challenge
Nicks; slams; buttonholes. Too saddled.

I am not like that. I pay rent, am addled
By illegible landlords, run, if robbers call.

What mannerisms I present, employ,
Are camouflage, and what my mouths remark
To word-wall off that broadness of the dark
Is pitiful.
I am not brave at all.

Medgar Evers

For Charles Evers

The man whose height his fear improved he
arranged to fear no further. The raw
intoxicated time was time for better birth or a final death.

Old styles, old tempos, all the engagement of
the day—the sedate, the regulated fray—
the antique light, the Moral rose, old gusts,
tight whistlings from the past, the mothballs
in the Love at last our man forswore.

Medgar Evers annoyed confetti and assorted
brands of businessmen's eyes.

The shows came down: to maxims and surprise.
And palsy.

Roaring no rapt arise-ye to the dead, he
leaned across tomorrow. People said that
he was holding clean globes in his hands.

Malcolm X

For Dudley Randall

Original.
Ragged-round.
Rich-robust.

He had the hawk-man's eyes.
We gasped. We saw the maleness.
The maleness raking out and making guttural the air
and pushing us to walls.

And in a soft and fundamental hour
a sorcery devout and vertical
beguiled the world.

He opened us—
who was a key,

who was a man.

Martin Luther King Jr.

A man went forth with gifts.

He was a prose poem.
He was a tragic grace.
He was a warm music.

He tried to heal the vivid volcanoes.
His ashes are
    reading the world.

His Dream still wishes to anoint
    the barricades of faith and of control.

His word still burns the center of the sun,
    above the thousands and the
    hundred thousands.

The word was Justice. It was spoken.

So it shall be spoken.
So it shall be done.

The Blackstone Rangers

I

AS SEEN BY DISCIPLINES

There they are.
Thirty at the corner.
Black, raw, ready.
Sores in the city
that do not want to heal.

II

THE LEADERS

Jeff. Gene. Geronimo. And Bop.
They cancel, cure and curry.
Hardly the dupes of the downtown thing
the cold bonbon,
the rhinestone thing. And hardly
in a hurry.
Hardly Belafonte, King,
Black Jesus, Stokely, Malcolm X or Rap.
Bungled trophies.
Their country is a Nation on no map.

Jeff, Gene, Geronimo and Bop
in the passionate noon,
in bewitching night
are the detailed men, the copious men.
They curry, cure,
they cancel, cancelled images whose Concerts
are not divine, vivacious; the different tins
are intense last entries; pagan argument;
translations of the night.

The Blackstone bitter bureaus
(bureaucracy is footloose) edit, fuse
unfashionable damnations and descent;
and exulting, monstrous hand on monstrous hand,
construct, strangely, a monstrous pearl or grace.

III

GANG GIRLS

A Rangerette

Gang Girls are sweet exotics.
Mary Ann
uses the nutrients of her orient,
but sometimes sighs for Cities of blue and jewel
beyond her Ranger rim of Cottage Grove.
(Bowery Boys, Disciples, Whip-Birds will
dissolve no margins, stop no savory sanctities.)

Mary is
a rose in a whiskey glass.

Mary's
Februaries shudder and are gone. Aprils
fret frankly, lilac hurries on.
Summer is a hard irregular ridge.
October looks away.
And that's the Year!
                    Save for her bugle-love.
Save for the bleat of not-obese devotion.

Save for Somebody Terribly Dying, under
the philanthropy of robins. Save for her Ranger
bringing
an amount of rainbow in a string-drawn bag.
"Where did you get the diamond?" Do not ask:
but swallow, straight, the spirals of his flask
and assist him at your zipper; pet his lips
and help him clutch you.

Love's another departure.
Will there be any arrivals, confirmations?
Will there be gleaning?

Mary, the Shakedancer's child
from the rooming-flat, pants carefully, peers at
her laboring lover. . . .
                    Mary! Mary Ann!
Settle for sandwiches! settle for stocking caps!
for sudden blood, aborted carnival,
the props and niceties of non-loneliness—
the rhymes of Leaning.

from: Two Dedications

II

THE WALL

August 27, 1967

For Edward Christmas

"The side wall of a typical slum building on the corner of 43rd and
Langley became a mural communicating black dignity. . . ."
—*Ebony*

A drumdrumdrum.
Humbly we come.
South of success and east of gloss and glass are
sandals;

flowercloth;
grave hoops of wood or gold, pendant
from black ears, brown ears, reddish-brown
and ivory ears;

black boy-men.
Black
boy-men on roofs fist out "Black Power!" Val,
a little black stampede
in African
images of brass and flowerswirl,
fists out "Black Power!"—tightens pretty eyes,
leans back on mothercountry and is tract,
is treatise through her perfect and tight teeth.

Women in wool hair chant their poetry.
Phil Cohran gives us messages and music
made of developed bone and polished and honed cult.
It is the Hour of tribe and of vibration,
the day-long Hour. It is the Hour
of ringing, rouse, of ferment-festival.

On Forty-third and Langley
black furnaces resent ancient
legislatures
of ploy and scruple and practical gelatin.
They keep the fever in,
fondle the fever.

All
worship the Wall.

I mount the rattling wood. Walter
says, "She is good." Says, "She
our Sister is." In front of me
hundreds of faces, red-brown, brown, black, ivory,
yield me hot trust, their yea and their Announcement
that they are ready to rile the high-flung ground.
Behind me, Paint.
Heroes.
No child has defiled
the Heroes of this Wall this serious Appointment
this still Wing
this Scald this Flute this heavy Light this Hinge.

An emphasis is paroled.
The old decapitations are revised,
the dispossessions beakless.

And we sing.

The Sermon on the Warpland

"The fact that we are black is our ultimate reality."—*Ron Karenga*

And several strengths from drowsiness campaigned
but spoke in Single Sermon on the warpland.

And went about the warpland saying No.
"My people, black and black, revile the River.
Say that the River turns, and turn the River.

Say that our Something in doublepod contains
seeds for the coming hell and health together.
Prepare to meet
(sisters, brothers) the brash and terrible weather;
the pains;
the bruising; the collapse of bestials, idols.
But then oh then!—the stuffing of the hulls!
the seasoning of the perilously sweet!
the health! the heralding of the clear obscure!

Build now your Church, my brothers, sisters. Build
never with brick nor Corten nor with granite.
Build with lithe love. With love like lion-eyes.
With love like morningrise.
With love like black, our black—
luminously indiscreet;
complete; continuous."

The Second Sermon on the Warpland

For Walter Bradford

1.

This is the urgency: Live!
and have your blooming in the noise of the whirlwind.

2.

Salve salvage in the spin.
Endorse the splendor splashes;
stylize the flawed utility;
prop a malign or failing light—
but know the whirlwind is our commonwealth.
Not the easy man, who rides above them all,

not the jumbo brigand,
not the pet bird of poets, that sweetest sonnet,
shall straddle the whirlwind.
Nevertheless, live.

3.

All about are the cold places,
all about are the pushmen and jeopardy, theft—
all about are the stormers and scramblers but
what must our Season be, which starts from Fear?
Live and go out.
Define and
medicate the whirlwind.

4.

The time
cracks into furious flower. Lifts its face
all unashamed. And sways in wicked grace.
Whose half-black hands assemble oranges
is tom-tom hearted
(goes in bearing oranges and boom).
And there are bells for orphans—
and red and shriek and sheen.
A garbageman is dignified
as any diplomat
Big Bessie's feet hurt like nobody's business,
but she stands—bigly—under the unruly scrutiny, stands in the wild weed.

In the wild weed
she is a citizen,
and is a moment of highest quality; admirable.

It is lonesome, yes. For we are the last of the loud.
Nevertheless, live.

Conduct your blooming in the noise and whip of the whirlwind.

Riot

A riot is the language of the unheard.—*Martin Luther King*

John Cabot, out of Wilma, once a Wycliffe,
all whitebluerose below his golden hair,
wrapped richly in right linen and right wool,
almost forgot his Jaguar and Lake Bluff;
almost forgot Grandtully (which is The
Best Thing That Ever Happened To Scotch); almost

forgot the sculpture at the Richard Gray
and Distelheim; the kidney pie at Maxim's,
the Grenadine de Boeuf at Maison Henri.

Because the Negroes were coming down the street.

Because the Poor were sweaty and unpretty
(not like Two Dainty Negroes in Winnetka)
and they were coming toward him in rough ranks.
In seas. In windsweep. They were black and loud.
And not detainable. And not discreet.

Gross. Gross. *"Que tu es grossier!"* John Cabot
itched instantly beneath the nourished white
that told his story of glory to the World.
"Don't let It touch me! the blackness! Lord!" he whispered
to any handy angel in the sky.

But, in a thrilling announcement, on It drove
and breathed on him: and touched him. In that breath
the fume of pig foot, chitterling and cheap chili,
malign, mocked John. And, in terrific touch, old
averted doubt jerked forward decently,
cried "Cabot! John! You are a desperate man,
and the desperate die expensively today."

John Cabot went down in the smoke and fire
and broken glass and blood, and he cried "Lord!
Forgive these nigguhs that know not what they do."

Paul Robeson

That time
we all heard it,
cool and clear,
cutting across the hot grit of the day.
The major Voice.
The adult Voice
forgoing Rolling River,
forgoing tearful tale of bale and barge
and other symptoms of an old despond.
Warning, in music-words
devout and large,
that we are each other's
harvest:
we are each other's
business:
we are each other's
magnitude and bond.

SAMUEL ALLEN (PAUL VESEY) (1917–)

A Moment Please

When I gaze at the sun
   I walked to the subway booth
   for change for a dime.
and know that this great earth
   Two adolescent girls stood there
   alive with eagerness to know
is but a fragment from it thrown
   all in their new found world
   there was for them to know
in heat and flame a billion years ago,
   they looked at me and brightly asked
   "Are you Arabian?"
that then this world was lifeless
   I smiled and cautiously
   —for one grows cautious—
   shook my head.
as, a billion hence,
   "Egyptian?"
it shall again be,
   Again I smiled and shook my head
   and walked away.
what moment is it that I am betrayed,
   I've gone but seven paces now
oppressed, cast down,
   and from behind comes swift the sneer
or warm with love or triumph?
   "Or Nigger?"

   A moment, please
What is it that to fury I am roused?
   for still it takes a moment
What meaning for me
   and now
in this homeless clan
   I'll turn
the dupe of space
   and smile
the toy of time?
   and nod my head.

Dylan, Who Is Dead

He is wasted now
Time which bled has thrown him back
    on the height of his insolent ways
The fevered brow, the trembling hand that bore,
    that lifted, now are still.
He is forever gone out from us
The belfry rung
The last furious anthem sprung
    beyond the steeples of his infancy
In rock his word wound round in flame
    the wreath of his going
Struck to his measure there is none
Nor seed in womb to bring forth the glory that is fallen
Bitter is the wind that whirls up out of the shorn isle
And voiceless the void of his farewell
Hail oracle, shine
               in that dark night!

To Satch

Sometimes I feel like I will never stop
Just go forever
Till one fine morning
I'll reach up and grab me a handful of stars
And swing out my long lean leg
And whip three hot strikes burning down the heavens
And look over at God and say
How about that!

The Staircase

The stairs mount to his eternity
the rotted floor, the dripping faucet
all now abide within him,
the cracked ceiling, the rusted bed in his dark squalid chamber
abide with him now
    in the hour that is upon him.

The balance is tenuous
as his twin comes running after
the infant he let unprotected go
—the hail of steel, stopped for a moment, lurks in the shadows.

The staircase turns and panting turns
the completely vile woman assails him
throwing livid screams from her den
far up the dark filthy hallway
until she hears the twin come running after
and falls sobbing and senseless to her knees.

A massive form stood out against the sky.
Come down, Death, come!
Take me away.

The hail of steel begins
the twin goes exalted to his worms
hail cried 'hail'.

If the Stars Should Fall

Again the day
The low bleak day of the stricken years
And now the years.

The huge slow grief drives on
And I wonder why
And I grow cold
And care less
And less and less I care.

If the stars should fall,
I grant them privilege;
Or if the stars should rise to a brighter flame
The mighty dog, the buckled Orion
To excellent purposes appear to gain—
I should renew their privilege
To fall down.

It is all to me the same
The same to me
I say the great Gods, all of them,
All—cold, pitiless—
Let them fall down
Let them buckle and drop.

NANINA ALBA (1917–1968)

Be Daedalus

Be Daedalus: make wings,
Make feathered wings;
Bind them with wax.
   Avoid the parching sun that brings
   Death as its tax.
   Suns can be brutal things.

Be Daedalus; make wings,
If Icarus be unwise
And swing up toward the flame,
   Forget his prejudice and prize,
   The price, the name.

Be Daedalus; make wings,
Make even feathered wings . . .

For Malcolm X

". . . indomitable that obelisk of a beard admonishes
the heavens."—*Malcolm Cowley.*

From my personal album
Two photos—from the news—
Hand raised by handsome chin
   toward head;
Words pouring out to resurrect the dead
Who walk among us, as Baldwin has said.

Then prostrate on a stretcher,
Eyes opened toward a sightless sky
And every passerby;
The shock as close It neared;
One remembers Sunday-school cards,
History's stoning of Stephens.
One sees— ". . . indomitable that
   obelisk of a beard admonishes the heavens."

MYRON O'HIGGINS (1918–)

Young Poet

Somebody,
Cut his hair
And send him out to play.

Someone,
While there is time,
Call him down from his high place.

Tell him,
Before terror marks his face,
He will belong to the hunted.

Say
He will be betrayed,
Or high on some fruited hill
Die naked with thieves.

Go to him
While fire is in his flesh:
Take him whole
And kiss his young mouth into wisdom
And healing.

Two Lean Cats . . .

I remember Wednesday was the day
the rain came down in ragged jets
and made a grave along my street . . .

And Friday was the day that brought
impatient winds to swell the
blood-stained garments on my line

But that day in between
comes back with two lean cats
who run in checkered terror
through a poolroom door
and bolting from a scream
a keen knife marks with sudden red
the gaming green
. . . a purple billiard ball
explodes the color scheme.

Vaticide

For Mohandas Gandhi

. . . he is murdered upright in the day
his flesh is opened and displayed. . . .

Into that stricken hour the hunted had gathered.
You spoke . . . some syllable of terror. *Ram!*
They saw it slip from your teeth and dangle, ablaze
Like a diamond on your mouth.
In that perilous place you fell—extinguished.
The instrument, guilt. The act was love.

Now they have taken your death to their rooms
And here in this far city a false Spring
Founders in the ruins of your quiet flesh
And deep in your marvelous wounds
The sun burns down
And the seas return to their imagined homes.

BRUCE McM. WRIGHT (1918–)

The African Affair

Black is what the prisons are,
The stagnant vortex of the hours
Swept into totality,
Creeping in the perjured heart,
Bitter in the vulgar rhyme,
Bitter on the walls;

Black is where the devils dance
With time within
The creviced wall. Time pirouettes
A crippled orbit in a trance,
And crawls below, beneath the flesh
Where darkness flows;

Black is where the deserts burn,
The Niger and Sasandra flow,
From where the Middle Passage went
Within the Continent of Night
From Cameroons to Carisbrooke
And places conscience cannot go;

Black is where thatched temples burn
Incense to carved ebon-wood;
Where traders shaped my father's pain,
His person and his place,
Among dead statues in a frieze,
In the spectrum of his race.

ALFRED A. DUCKETT (1918–)

Sonnet

Where are we to go when this is done?
Will we slip into old, accustomed ways,
finding remembered notches, one by one?
Thrashing a hapless way through quickening haze?

Who is to know us when the end has come?
Old friends and families, but could we be
strange to the sight and stricken dumb
at visions of some pulsing memory?

Who will love us for what we used to be
who now are what we are, bitter or cold?
Who is to nurse us with swift subtlety
back to the warm and feeling human fold?

Where are we to go when this is through?
We are the war-born. What are we to do?

LANCE JEFFERS (1919–)

How High the Moon

(first the melody, clean and hard,
and the flat slurs are faint;
the down-knotted mouth, tugged in deprecation,
is not there. But near the end of the first chorus
the slurs have come, and the street is there,
street of the quiet pogrom,
the beat of the street—talk flares strong,
the rhythm of the street talk pounds hard,
and the gestures and the laughter cut the air.)

'BLOW!' 'BLOW!' the side-men shout,

and the thin black young man with an old man's face lungs up;
   the   high tissue of a trumpet from his deep-cancered corners
racks out a high and searing curse!
   Full   from the sullen grace of his street it sprouts:
         NEVER YOUR CAPTIVE

On Listening to the Spirituals

When the master lived a king and I a starving hutted slave beneath the lash, and

when my five-year-old son was driven at dawn to cottonfield to pick until he could
   no longer see the sun, and

when master called my wife to the big house when mistress was gone, took her
   against her will and gave her a dollar to be still, and when she turned upon her
   pride and cleavered it, cursed her dignity and stamped on it, came back to me
   with his evil on her thighs, hung her head when I condemned her with my eyes,

what broken mettle of my soul wept steel, cracked teeth in self-contempt upon my
   flesh, crept underground to seek new roots and secret breathing place?

When all the hatred of my bones was buried in a forgotten county of my soul,
then from beauty muscled from the degradation of my oaken bread,
I stroked on slavery soil the mighty colors of my song, a passionate heaven rose no
   God in heaven could create!

Grief Streams Down My Chest

Grief streams down my chest
like spittle from the baby's mouth,
and in the corridors behind my eyes,
   Vietnamese mothers dry-eyed walk and hand me stone
   tablets and motion me to inscribe my name thereon that
   I have seen and dimly understood their suffering.
My black grief's a pygmy pyramid beside the grassy mountain of their thorn as high as the Asian continent is long.

My Blackness Is the Beauty of This Land

My blackness is the beauty of this land,
my blackness,
tender and strong, wounded and wise,
my blackness:
I, drawling black grandmother, smile muscular and sweet,

unstraightened white hair soon to grow in earth,
work-thickened hand thoughtful and gentle on grandson's head,
my heart is bloody-razored by a million memories' thrall:

> remembering the crook-necked cracker who spat
>   on my naked body,
> remembering the splintering of my son's spirit
>   because he remembered to be proud
> remembering the tragic eyes in my daughter's
>   dark face when she learned her color's meaning,

and my own dark rage a rusty knife with teeth to gnaw
   my bowels,
my agony ripped loose by anguished shouts in Sunday's
   humble church,
my agony rainbowed to ecstasy when my feet oversoared
   Montgomery's slime,

ah, this hurt, this hate, this ecstasy before I die,
and all my love a strong cathedral!
My blackness is the beauty of this land!

Lay this against my whiteness, this land!
Lay me, young Brutus stamping hard on the cat's tail,
gutting the Indian, gouging the nigger,
booting Little Rock's Minniejean Brown in the buttocks and boast,
   my sharp white teeth derision-bared as I the conqueror crush!
Skyscraper-I, white hands burying God's human clouds beneath
   the dust!
Skyscraper-I, slim blond young Empire
   thrusting up my loveless bayonet to rape the sky,
then shrink all my long body with filth and in the gutter lie
as lie I will to perfume this armpit garbage,
While I here standing black beside
wrench tears from which the lies would suck the salt
to make me more American than America . . .
But yet my love and yet my hate shall civilize this land,
this land's salvation.

M. CARL HOLMAN (1919–)

Notes for a Movie Script

Fade in the sound of summer music,
Picture a hand plunging through her hair,
Next his socked feet and her scuffed dance slippers
Close, as they kiss on the rug-stripped stair.

Catch now the taxi from the station,
Capture her shoulders' sudden sag;
Switch to him silent in the barracks
While the room roars at the corporal's gag.

Let the drums dwindle in the distance,
Pile the green sea above the land;
While she prepares a single breakfast,
Reading the v-mail in her hand.

Ride a cold moonbeam to the pillbox,
Sidle the camera to his feet
Sprawled just outside in the gummy grasses,
Swollen like nightmare and not neat.

Now doorbell nudges the lazy morning:
She stills the sweeper for a while,
Twitches her dress, swings the screendoor open,
Cut—with no music—on her smile.

And on This Shore

I

Alarm and time clock still intrude too early,
Sun on the lawns at morning is the same,
Across the cups we yawn at private murders,
Accustomed causes leave us gay or glum.

(I feel the streaming wind in my eyes,
the highway swimming under the floor,
music flung comically over the hills,
Remember your profile, your pilot's body at ease,
the absolute absence of boredom, the absence of fear)

The swingshift workers are snoring at noon,
The armywife's offspring dumb in his crib,
The private, patron of blackmarket still,
Sleeps long past reveille stark on his slab.

(The chimes were musing far beyond soft hills,
I brushed an ant from your arm,
The leaves lifted, shifted like breathing to pour
Light on your lids, seemed then no end of time)

The streets re-wind to spools of home,
Dials usher in the bland newscaster,

From the mail box's narrow room
Lunges the cobra of disaster.

(Kissed and were happy at the door,
showered, pretending this would last,
Stones down dead wells, the calendar
counts summers that are lost, are lost)

II

Is it yourself he loves
Or the way you arranged your hair?
The book which taught you to listen while he talked?
The cute dance steps and that night on the Navy pier?
Did he see yours or another's face when he waked?
On what does this shadow feed
And shall it not fade?

Is it yourself she loves
Or the easy-come money you breezily spend?
The 4-F, convertible, "A" coupons, dark market Scotch?
Would she stick if she found she could interest your friend:
When the man on her dresser returns will you prove his match?
On what does this shadow feed
And shall it not fade?

Is it yourself they love
Or the victories panted with vibrant voice?
(Mellow for brave boys sleeping their last long sleep)
Will sponsor and fan abide when bulletins burst in your face,
Raw stumps and barricades explode through the map?
On what does this shadow feed,
And shall it not fade?

Is it yourself they love,
You brief-cased and lens-familiar,
Invoking spring from the smoke of our heaviest winter?
Their mouths adore—but fangs may lurk for anger;
Watching night wither do you not sometimes wonder
On what does this shadow feed
And shall it not fade?

Picnic: The Liberated

En route to the picnic they drive through their history,
Telling jokes and watching the road, but averting their eyes
From the rows of sun-flayed faces barely darker than theirs
Through which they pass like foreigners or spies.

The children play word games, count cows, inspect
Their armament of softballs, glasses, rods and hooks,
Survey the molten prairies overhead for signs of rain,
Retreat like crayfish to their comic books.

Grown-up laughter dwindles; they enter the wool-hat town
Like a gangster funeral, under the chastening eye
Of Confederate cannon, depot, First Baptist Church,
The white frame hospital that would let them die.

But out of sight is as safe as out of mind:
Dust lifts a protective screen half a mile down a winding road
Opening into a grove of pines, the green lake beyond
And the smoky pungence of barbecue as the cars unload.

So the long day blossoms in the sumptuous shade
Where the velvet-limbed girls parade their peacock beauty
In slacks and shorts, ignoring, excited by the clashing glances
Of waspish wives who lose track of matronly duty

And the men rotating their drinks in dixie cups,
Absently talking of civil rights, money and goods
But stirred by audacious dreams of rendezvous,
Boar-ramping conquests deep in the secret woods.

The tadpole hunters soak their shoes at the scummy edge
Of the lake where a boat capsizes but nobody drowns,
The badminton birds veer off course toward the tables
Where the gold-toothed winner grins, the loser frowns.

The sky contracts, the country dark creeps in,
Flicking a chilly tongue across the grass.
Uneasily the motors cough, headlights blink on,
Goodbys go flat, and tempers turn to glass.

Their tags are passports as they straggle home
To sprinklered lawns on Circles, Lanes and Drives,
Claiming once more the preferential signs
With which the Southern city stamps their lives.

Deep in the night the wind walks past the lake,
Leaps the pinewoods, lays an impartial hand
On cannon, croppers' shacks, touches at last
The handsome mortgaged houses where they sleep—
Mounting their private myths of freedom and command,
Privileged prisoners in a haunted land.

JAMES A. EMANUEL (1921–)

The Treehouse

To every man
His treehouse,
A green splice in the humping years,
Spartan with narrow cot
And prickly door.

To every man
His twilight flash
Of luminous recall
    of tiptoe years
    in leaf-stung flight;
    of days of squirm and bite
    that waved antennas through the grass;
    of nights
    when every moving thing
    was girlshaped,
    expectantly turning.

To every man
His house below
And his house above—
With perilous stairs
Between.

Church Burning: Mississippi

In fragrant Dixie's arms
Christ came down in flames,
A smoke-smile on His lips
And black of face
Before the furtive, nail-pierced can
And upthrust beam
Broke charcoal thorns
Across His brow.

The gloried ashes rose
And crossed the heart of Him
Evicted from the land,

Unfisted King whose love was fire enough
To forge the ages,
Martyred Lord, his circling men now weaponed
Only in their eyes.

Some muttered aging prophecies,
Denim pockets bulging knuckles.
Wonder, vague as smoke, if Christ had bled before
He really died
Took some, like coughing, by the throat.
Some rooted young ones broke from Dixie's arms
And dropped like firebrands on the fragrant hearth.

Emmett Till

I hear a whistling
Through the water.
Little Emmett
Won't be still.
He keeps floating
Round the darkness,
Edging through
The silent chill.

Tell me, please,
That bedtime story
Of the fairy
River Boy
Who swims forever,
Deep in treasures,
Necklaced in
A coral toy.

Get Up, Blues

Blues
Never climb a hill
Or sit on a roof
In starlight.

Blues
Just bend low
And moan in the street
And shake a borrowed cup.

Blues
Just sit around
Sipping,
Hatching yesterdays.

Get up, Blues.
Fly.
Learn what it means
To be up high.

Old Black Men Say

They say "Son"
(always start with son)
"watch out, cause them folks
is MEAN
when you rile em"—
as if I cant be mean
(grandaddy walked like
old Black men,
bent over where they hit im
ridin drinkin cussin laughin
throwed their bottle on his street
the sheriff didnt do a thing),

yeah they say "Listen. I KNOW"
(daddy didnt listen
didnt know, mamma never
told how he died)
and they squint and chew on how I feel
hearin that old jive
bout what they KNOW
(they know they took that crap
they died
they dead right now
xcep for me
not listenin).

"Boy you aint listenin"
(but somethin in they voice
say go head
say if you strong enough
go be a fool,
somethin turns me loose
stays at the door
like fist on that old walkin cane
they didnt need,
took just to poke they minds
around the ground).

When I leave
them old men's noses
suck in like they painin smart,
spittin sideways
lookin me up and down
like a crop they raised.

Im gonna rile them folks
like I been riled,
gonna be a fool
maybe,
whatever they raised—
them old Black men.

ADAM DAVID MILLER (1922–)

The Hungry Black Child

lord
forgive me
if i twist the sunset
but when evening twist my belly
i see red
walking the field the woods
the houses on my street
white
burning burning

Crack in the Wall Holds Flowers

After each Quake
New cracks appear in the wall;
These fissures forced by cataclysm
Hold flowers.

This vast natural damage
Presaged always by rumblings
Deep in things maternal breeds lilacs
That hang in a nook near the edge of the sun.

My uneasiness
Reminded by a niche now brown,
Is not soothed by the prospect of flowers.

NAOMI LONG MADGETT (1923–)

Mortality

This is the surest death
Of all the deaths I know.
The one that halts the breath,
The one that falls with snow
Are nothing but a peace
Before the second zone,
For Aprils never cease
To resurrect their own,
And in my very veins
Flows blood as old as Eve.
The smallest cell contains
Its privileged reprieve.
But vultures recognize
This single mortal thing
And watch with hungry eyes
When hope starts staggering.

Simple

For Langston Hughes

He sits at the bar in the Alhambra
looking down Seventh Avenue
through the open door.
He wants to talk, but the stool beside him
is empty
and no one he knows is coming down the street.

> Hey man, I got problems—ya know?
> Could ya let me have another fin
> jes till nex' Friday, huh?
> I gotta get in to change my clothes
> but my lan'lady's bolted the door again.
> If Joyce don't get to go to that show
> again tonight, man,
> my name really be mud!

The landlady's bolted the door for good
this time
and he will never go home.

Joyce will tap her toe impatiently awhile
and then go out alone.
Through a long, long night
he will stare at his empty beer glass
and the vacant stool
and soon he will wonder what it was
he wanted to say.

Her Story

They gave me the wrong name, in the first place.
They named me Grace and waited for a light and agile dancer.
But some trick of the genes mixed me up
And instead I turned out big and black and burly.

In the second place, I fashioned the wrong dreams.
I wanted to dress like Juliet and act
Before applauding audiences on Broadway.
I learned more about Shakespeare than he knew about himself.
But of course, all that was impossible.
"Talent, yes," they would tell me,
"But an actress has to look the part."
So I ended up waiting on tables in Harlem
And hearing uncouth men yell at me:
"Hey, momma, you can cancel that hamburger
And come on up to 102."

In the third place, I tried the wrong solution.
The stuff I drank made me deathly sick
And someone called a doctor.
Next time I'll try a gun.

Black Woman

My hair is springy like the forest grasses
That cushion the feet of squirrels—
Crinkled and blown in a south breeze
Like the small leaves of native bushes.

My black eyes are coals burning
Like a low, full, jungle moon
Through the darkness of being.

In a clear pool I see my face,
Know my knowing.

My hands move pianissimo
Over the music of the night:
Gentle birds fluttering through leaves and grasses
They have not always loved,
Nesting, finding home.

Where are my lovers?
Where are my tall, my lovely princes
Dancing in slow grace
Toward knowledge of my beauty?
Where
Are my beautiful
Black men?

GLORIA C. ODEN (1923–)

Review from Staten Island

The skyline of New York does not excite me
(ferrying towards it) as mountains do in snow-steeped
                              hostility to sun.
There is something in the view—spewed up from water
                    to pure abandonment in air—
                    that snakes my spine with cold
and mouse-tracks over my heart.

Strewn across the meet of wave and wind, it seems
the incompleted play of some helter-skeltering child whose
                              hegira (as all
our circles go) has not yet led him back, but will, ripe
                    with that ferocious glee which
                    can boot these building-blocks
to earth, then heel under.

One gets used to dying living. Growth is an
end to many things—even the rose disposes of summer—
                    but still I
wince at being there when the relentless foot kicks down;
                    and the tides come roaring over
                    to pool within
the unlearned depths of me.

The Carousel

"I turned from side to side, from image to image
to put you down."—*Louise Bogan*

An empty carousel in a deserted park
rides me round and round,
forth and back,
from end to beginning,
like the tail that drives the dog.

I cannot see:
sight focusses shadow where once
pleased scenery,
and in this whirl of space
only the indefinite is constant.

This is the way of grief:
spinning in the rhythm of memories
that will not let you up
or down,
but keeps you grinding through
a granite air.

The Riven Quarry

In my dry cell
of love's heat
here, in May,
in lover's weather,
I hunch over these words,
shaping them to the image of
my hunger, clothing them
in the many-colored robes
woven upon the loom of
your absence.

Scarlet and summer-yellow
with jungle excess, vivid
appetites of love hob
the green grounds of my
anxiety; and I observe
myself the riven quarry
of lust, the red demon.

I would not have it other.
Let me not run to
beauty on timid feet;
but in whatever error
my journeying may prove to be,
arrive forwardly as
sea exposing itself to
the high-ribbed attractions of
shore.   Love that cannot
shoulder its own torment
forfeits the name. Or so
I voice to myself
voyaging these Saharas
between our contract,
wolves sharp-eyed at the
heels of spirit.

Man White, Brown Girl and All That Jazz

Upon the Occasion of his Marriage

It is essential I remember
ours was a fair exchange.
We were a happy consequence
to paths of darkness
in a world
no less terrible or strange
for all our years of toiling
through it.

I valued you for what I took.
That burning in you bright
illumined our collision;
your phosphorescence still
must be reckoned with
when night
heretic with your memory
trespasses.

God knows we were; though such love
did not a kingdom come to us,
each the other's
wood of destiny
has lit.
You found your clearing;
I fathom mine.
We have had the best of it.

MARI EVANS

. . . And the Old Women Gathered

The Gospel Singers

and the old women gathered
and sang His praises
standing
resolutely together
like supply sergeants who
have seen
everything
and are still
Regular Army: It
was fierce and
not melodic and
although we ran
the sound of it
stayed in our ears . . .

The Rebel

When I
die
I'm sure
I will have a
Big Funeral

Curiosity
seekers

coming to see
if I
am really
Dead

or just
trying to make
Trouble

Black jam for dr. negro

Pullin me in off the corner to wash my face an
cut my fro off turn
my collar
down
when that aint my
thang I
walk heels first
nose round an tilted
up
my ancient
eyes
see your thang
baby
an it aint
shit
your thang
puts my eyes out baby
turns my seeking fingers
   into splintering fists
messes up my head
an I scream you out
your thang
is what's   wrong
   an' you keep
   pilin it on rubbin it
   in
   smoothly
   doin it
   to death

what you sweatin
baby
        your guts
puked an rotten
waitin'

to be defended

Vive Noir!

i
am going to rise
en masse
from Inner City

               sick
             of newyork ghettos
             chicago tenements
        l   a's slums
weary
      of exhausted lands
      sagging privies
      saying yessuh yessah
      yesSIR
      in an assortment
      of geographical dialects i
have seen my last
broken down plantation
even from a
distance
        i
will load all my goods
in '50 Chevy pickups '53
Fords fly United and '66
caddys i
      have packed in
      the old man and the old lady and
      wiped the children's noses
              I'm tired
             of hand me downs
           shut me ups
            pin me ins
                keep me outs
                  messing me over have
              just had it
            baby
          from
        you . . .
i'm
gonna spread out
over America
          intrude
my proud blackness
all
      over the place
             i have wrested wheat fields
             from the forests
             turned rivers
             from their courses
             leveled mountains
             at a word
             festooned the land with
             bridges
                     gemlike
                   on filaments of steel

                        moved
        glistening towersofBabel in place
                like blocks
        sweated a whole
        civilization

            now
                    i'm
        gonna breathe fire
        through flaming nostrils BURN
                a place for

                    me

        in the skyscrapers and the
        schoolrooms on the green
        lawns and the white
        beaches
                    i'm
        gonna wear the robes and
        sit on the benches
        make the rules and make
        the arrests say
        who can and who
        can't
                    baby you don't stand
                    a
                    chance
i'm
        gonna put black angels
        in all the books and a black
        Christchild in Mary s arms i'm
        gonna make black bunnies black
        fairies black santas black
        nursery rhymes and
                        black
        ice cream
                    i'm
gonna make it a
    crime
            to be anything BUT   black

gonna make white
a twentyfourhour
lifetime
J.O.B.

into blackness softly

the hesitant door chain
back forth back
forth
      the
stealthy
   soft
      final
          sssshuuu t
jubilantly
    stepping down
       stepping down
            step
ping lightly across the lower
     hall
the shocking airfingers
   the
      receiving
          blackness
   sigh

To Mother and Steve

All I wanted
was your
love

when I roiled down
Brewster blew
soft pot clouds on
subs when
I lay in nameless rooms
cold-sweating
horse in nameless arms
crawled
thru white hell owning
no one no one no one save
one purple-bruised soul
pawned
in exchange for
oblivion
   all I wanted
was
your love

not twice but
constantly
I tried
to free you

it was all
such cold shit
then
the last day
of the
last year
of my raw-edged anguish
I was able wearily
at last—
to roll.

(all I wanted
was
your love)
I bought this final
battered gift

(do not refuse—for it
was all
I had)

with my back supported
by the tolerant
arms
of a picket fence and my
legs crumpled crazily in front
and love fell
soft and cold and
covered me in
blanket
like

the one you
tucked around me
centuries
ago and like that
later
gently pulled
across my face
and in this season
of peace and
goodwill and the smell
of cedar
remembered

thru warm yellow
windows—
   all I wanted
and it was more than
I could stand and
more than a thousand passions and
I could not
mainline it
away

     was your
     love

OLIVER PITCHER (1924–)

Salute

   Murderers
of Emmett Till
I salute you
and the men
who set the
   murderers
free I salute
you. Twice.

   I salute
the brothers
of charity
who let Bessie
Smith bleed to
death. She
had the wrong
blood type.
It wasn't white.

   I salute
all self-anointed
   men
who dole out freedoms to other
   men.

I could go on. But won't. I
salute everything, all things
that infect me with this knot
twisted in my subconscious; knot
of automatic distrust, unravelled.

I salute everything, all things
worthy of my confusion, my awe,
my fury, my cursing, which never
looks good in print . . . worthy of
my tears . . . ALL HONORABLE MEN!
I salute you.

You could go on . . . But won't.

The Pale Blue Casket

Why don't we rock the casket here in the moonlight?

A man begins in the cradle and ends in the casket.
That's if he's a two time winner. In between? The
echo of a long lament. A mosaic of sleep. A marble
laugh. A few grapes. A short wail from the other
shore. The scattered moldly crumbs of best intentions
and the insecure peace of distance. The moon and
the sun go on playing an eternal game Show-me-your!
and I'll-show-you-mine but words fail us. We say,
here lies a man in a telephone booth, already cold
and without direct communication to the moon to
warm himself. And rock so soon!

Rock, rock, rock the casket here in the moonlight.

ZACK GILBERT (1925–)

My Own Hallelujahs

I do not want to stand
Beside you at the feast;
You eat of rot. Or walk
Beside you; your pace is
Not my pace. To follow
You or be with you I lose.
I'll turn back to my roots
Making my own way through
Fields you'll never know
Singing my own songs
To a different tune,
Shouting my own
Hallelujahs.

When I Heard Dat White Man Say

When I heard dat
   White man say on radio
Duh uder day,
"Gwen Brooks don broke
Wid der establishment. Don
Got in der black militant camp.
I said, "You faggot fool,
Where you think she been all der' time?
'Cause she use what you call
Good Englis don mean she aint
     Black.
There's uh lotta them like that
Going 'round fooling you, baby.
      An' you better believe it."

For Stephen Dixon

News Item: 18 year old black southside youth fatally shot by white policemen.

This is my last cry
My last memorial
To the fallen slain
My last black eulogy
To the dying young.

To whale spout angry
Words is close to folly
Now in this our time of
Blood and bombs and bullets.
Ears are turned to
Stone and do not hear.
We goose step to our tomb;
The unheard tune is death.

My pen is broken
My ink is drained and dried
My only message now
Is knife and gun.
How eloquent is that
Future flow of blood
How lovely the head
Made gourd.

For Angela

1.

When you were
A baby in diapers
Or even before you made
Your first yelp into life
Our own black Richard had
Penned "The God that failed."
Even if you didn't
Listen to his voice
Or those of others
Yours was the right to move
To the drumming of
Your own beating heart.

2.

Yes, some stroked
Their paths in fire,
Others in blood—
In Watts, in Howe,
In Detroit
And in Newark.
Remember the "Algiers" dead?
Some knew
The whip of Bill Conners,
The dogs and the hose.
In Birmingham we still
Remember the children.
Huey Newton and Cleaver
Fred Hampton and Clark
Martin and Malcolm
Evers and the
Mississippi three.
The line is long
And painful.
The line is endless.
Must we go on
To sanctify a point?

3.

So we evolve.
Each step, each
Link to link.
We evolve.

Some move to
Individual tunes,
Others to a whole
Orchestra playing.
Whatever your music, Angela
We embrace. We condone
And we evolve.

RUSSELL ATKINS (1926–)

It's Here In The

Here in the newspaper—the wreck of the East Bound.
A photograph bound to bring on cardiac asthenia.
There is a blur that mists the page!
On one side is a gloom of dreadful harsh.
Then breaks flash lights up sheer.
There is much huge about. I suppose then
      those no's are people
  between that suffering of—
   (what more have we? for Christ's sake, no!)
Something of a full stop of it
crash of blood and the still shock   .
  of stark sticks and an immense swift gloss,
And two dead no's lie aghast still.
One casts a crazed eye and the other's
Closed dull.
    the heap up twists
     such
as to harden the unhard and unhard
the hardened.

On the Fine Arts Garden, Cleveland

  The Park's beautiful
               really
something so serious about it
serene and gloomy
              mildly gloomy
mildly touching, all things
                 softly
and pouring with
mellows the silver fountain

                         silent figures
move reposefully into the living shadows
and then the golden lamps
the while

        slowly filtering—

Night and a Distant Church

Forward abrupt
                    up
then mmm
            mmm
wind mmm   m
    mmm
            m

upon
the mm
            mm
wind mmm   m
    mmm
into the mm wind
rain now and again
the mm
            wind
    ells
b
        ells
    b

Narrative

I sat with John Brown. That night moonlight framed
    the blown of his beard like a portent's undivulged.
He came and said 'It's Harpers, men!'

Now Harpers was a place in which death thousand'd
    for us!
Already our faces, even as he told of how,
    sweated. And then suddenly, he,
with fierced spark'd eye—incredible heavens!

Horses dreadful appearance had of exhumed:
    our boots strode the ready. We dared off.

As generally seeming of the trail
   smooth—and so whist!
   i.e., save sounded thunder
   of us in a rush
   passed swift fierce "ft
   'ierce shsh!!
   'ss'd in a w'isk!
   'ierced passed "ft!
Harpers a!p!p!e!a!r!e!d!
   —into it we went in a dust!

"ft passed 'ierced
   "if's, in, ss'd
   shsh "erced
   "ft
   "isk

BETTE DARCIE LATIMER (1927–)

For William Edward Burghardt Du Bois on His Eightieth Birthday

He does not lounge with the old men
on their thrones in the sun. . . .

I have awakened from the unknowing to the knowing
hoping to see the fathomless. . . .

But I saw the old men
on their thrones in the sun,
with aged eyes
and dust in their beards.

    Mixed with the shadows,
    veiled and unthroned,
    the brown one smiles.

I meet them at the turnpike,
but they point signward,
waving the crutches of empty years.

    The brown one, smiling, led me on
    with wisdom as a sturdy cane.
    "The masterpiece is there," he said—
    and the dread beauty of living
    crushed us into reverence.

HOYT W. FULLER (1928–)

Seravezza

There are no nightmares now. Only when memory settles,
a gentle, vaporous presence, over some rare silence as today
do I scramble again down the shell-ripped mountain,
over cobblestones worn glassy by the boots of centuries
and strewn now with the debris of shattered walls and limbs

It was familiar then: the stink of death, the cries beseeching God
hanging like dry mist in the breathless night

In darkness we marched in single-file down the surreal street
past the vile-smelling latrine and into the swift canal
The mountain loomed like some monster of pre-history,
a hulking beast great beyond belief napping in the receding dawn
The column of men, a toy brigade, wound through the valley,
Lilliputians stalking a vast unwary prey
It was when the column's tail swished across the broad canal
that the sly beast roused, turned its terrible venom on the valley
and spat down a rain of doom

The senses rebel at massacre: it is unreal: it must be denied

This was the dream that came and came again
in those first years of peace,
firing the flesh until it singed the touch,
racing the pulse until it soared near pain

And meaning besieged the mind: desperate was the need to know

Now, memory recaptures stricken voices babbling final prayer,
startled bodies crashing dully in the stream
and cold rushing water running rose with blood
This I recall with merely a stab of visceral heat
That soft pang, plus one small gratitude among
these thankless things:
Beside me, a boy named Henry Edwards gasps in profound surprise,
turns his afflicted face and stares with imploring eyes,
opens trembling lips but finds no voice to speak
I could not have endured it had he called my name

Lost Moment

Some thoughts on the occasion of a tribute to Gwen

When it is all over
when we have stomped our feet
and shook our fists
and moaned in wordless bitterness
like choruses of cadavers robed in gloom
when we have drained ourselves of rage
and stand silent and impotent
alone
will we know at last
will we understand
that passion builds no bridges
that rhetoric is no music
that pain is not panacea nor power
    though it teaches spirit
    and defines the god in man
will we see, will we know
that evil is a solid thing
real like iron
that it bends and breaks
only when the strength of fire
the weight of worlds
conspire to confront it?

When it is ended—
this bombast and this bluff—
will we move quietly then
into the shadows
out in the storm
into the sea
will we finally seek the wisdom
and like wise children
hold hands against the dark?

This crime we would commit
against our beauty
this crime of eloquence and fear
against our children
will doom us
to walk the empty plains of hell
forever and ever
more.

December 31, 1969

LERONE BENNETT, JR. (1928–)

Blues and Bitterness

For Billie Holiday

Ice tinkled in glasses,
froze and rolled away
from hearts
in tombs where she slept.
Smoke noosed,
coiled and dangled from ceilings
in caves where she wept.

I woke up this morning
Just befo' the break of day.
I was bitter, blue and black, Lawd.
There ain't nothing else to say.

In saloons
festooned with trumpets
she prayed—sang
love songs to dead men
waiting with hammers
at the bottom of syringes.
She sang it in a song
before Sartre put it into a book.
She was Bigger
before Wright wrote,
was with Nekeela
in a slave coffle,
was stripped, branded
and eaten by the sharks
and rose again
on the third day in Georgia.

I wondered why God made me.
I wondered why He made me black.
I wondered why Mama begat me—
And I started to give God His ticket back.

And Was Not Improved

Let them keep it
whatever it is
for white only hides.
And smiles.
I was in the pale inn
after the writs
after the whores
after the hilariously lonely
convention men
and was not improved
and wondered why
anyone bothered.
I was in the mausoleum
with the corpses
and counted the bones
and was sad.
I went up high
and came down
and hurried home
to you
and hugged the broken-glass ghetto
and was glad
and wondered again
why anyone bothered.

SARAH WEBSTER FABIO (1928–)

Black Man's Feast

His desires, growing
from timid heights
on homecomings, birthdays,
holiday celebrations,
looming tall on his
taste buds and leaden;
then, in the exuberance
of his black mood, he'd
call for greens, pot likker,
cole slaw, cracklin' bread,

and chitterlings; hog head
and maw, pig feet and ears
and black-eyed peas—
these gourmet dishes of his
impoverished past.

Confronted with this repast,
he'd conjure up the memory
of his ugly-money days when
it maddened him to spend his
torn-muscle treasures for
the trivial idiocies of
a second-hand civilization.
Dressed to kill in hard-pressed,
outmoded garments, he'd survey
his store of pinched-penny
purchases and mourn the passing
of his thin, rainy-day dimes
dribbled away on pews and prayers,
grave plots, and poll tax
irrelevancies.

He'd remember when he,
African bushman, (or his
father or father's father)
had stalked big game, absorbing
the animal strength of his prize
in the ritual of eating viscera:
later, it was he,
American slave, (or his
mother, or mother's mother)
whose reward for soulless toil
was special rations of
these same intestines,
burnt-out bacon ends, bone-
and-gristle inedibles
to turn with will and magic
into succulent sustenance.

Now, basking in the warmth
of his gladder money days,
he swallows hungrily
his easy-purchased pleasure food—
yet still feasts on the gall
of his gastronomical past.

Evil Is No Black Thing

1.

Ahab's gaily clad fisherfriends,
questing under the blue skies after
the albino prize find the green sea
cold and dark at its deep center,
but calm—unperturbed by the fates
of men and whales.

Rowing shoreward, with wet and empty
hands, their sun-rich smiles fuzz
with bafflement as the frothing
surf buckles underneath and their
sea-scarred craft is dashed to pieces
near the shore: glancing backward,
the spiralling waves are white-capped.

2.

Evil is no black thing: black
the rain clouds attending a storm
but the fury of it neither begins
nor ends there. Weeping tear-clear
rain, trying to contain the hoarse
blue-throated thunder and the fierce
quick-silver tongue of lightning, bands
of clouds wring their hands.

Once I saw dark clouds in Texas
stand by idly while a Northeaster
screamed its icy puffs, ringtailing
rainddrops, rolling them into baseballs
of hail, then descending upon the
tin-roofed houses, unrelentingly
battering them down.

3.

And the night is blackest where
gay throated cuckoos sing among the
dense firs of the Black Forest, where
terrible flurries of snow are blinding
bright: somewhere, concealed here deeply,
lies a high-walled town, whitewashed.

Seen at sunset, only the gaping ditch
and overhanging, crooked tree are painted
pitch to match the night: but I've seen
a dying beam of light reach through
the barred windows of a shower chamber,
illuminating its blood-scratched walls.

4.

Evil is no black thing: black
may be the undertaker's hearse
and so many of the civil trappings
of death, but not its essence:
the riderless horse, the armbands
and veils of mourning, the grave shine
darkly; but these are the rituals
of the living.

One day I found its meaning as I
rushed breathless through a wind-parched
field, stumbling unaware: suddenly there
it was, laying at my feet, hidden
beneath towering golden rods,
a criss-crossed pile of
sun-bleached bones.

TED JOANS (1928–)

Its Curtains

All god's SPADES wear dark shades
        and some of god's SPADES
(you'll never be able to figger what nigger)
    carry l   o   n   g   sharp
            protective blades
                            so I repeat, though
he may be raggedy or neat
        All god's SPADES got SHADES

Scenery

the flowers are dead
the vase is broken
water leaked out   drowned a family
of roaches

they are gone   the table is bare   toilet dont flush
fleas/rats/mice/ and dead roaches
legions of bandit bed bugs   called chinches   patrol
the rock'n'roll squeaky sex bed
everywhere   flowers   are dead
vases are broke   like maiden head   on a roof
slumlord's   throat   slashed   as expected   like a
                              punchline of a black joke

The Protective Grigri

the protective grigri
that I wear
that I never take off
is the spiritual grigri
that I hear
that I adhere and believe
As natural as a leopard's
night cough

SUN RA

Nothing Is

At first nothing is;
Then nothing transforms itself to be air
Sometimes the air transforms itself to be water;
And the water becomes rain and falls to earth;
Then again, the air through friction becomes fire.
So the nothing and the air and the water
And the fire are really the same—
Upon different degrees.

The Plane: Earth

Every planet is a small plane
In the universe
Planet means
Small plane
When considered
According to a certain standard.

Every plane is a plane T
Planet three is Plane T three
T, then, is a symbol for the plane earth.

Primary Lesson: The Second Class Citizens

The second class is the second grade
And the second grade is the second dimension
of learning: Another phase of wisdom.

The second grade is the root of the
secondary education . . . . .
The secondary education is the
Higher form of wisdom,
The magnificent and advanced precept.
It is given as the Secondary Word
From the Secondary God
To the secondary citizens of the

Second Class.
To "on" the advance is to "own" the advance.
The Advance Prophet transcends the
Law concerning "A prophet."

RAYMOND R. PATTERSON (1929–)

When I Awoke

When I awoke, she said:
Lie still, do not move.
They are all dead,
She said.

Who?
I said.

The world,
She said.

I had better go,
I said.

Why?
She said,

What good
Will it do?

I have to see,
I said.

I've Got a Home in That Rock

I had an uncle once who kept a rock in his pocket—
Always did, up to the day he died.
And as far as I know, that rock is still with him,
Holding down some dust of his thighbone.

From Mississippi he'd got that rock, he'd say—
Or, sometimes, from Tennessee: a different place each time
He told it, how he'd picked it up when he first left home—
Running, he'd say—to remind him when times got hard
Enough to make him homesick, what home was really like.

You Are the Brave

You are the brave who do not break
In the grip of the mob when the blow comes straight
To the shattered bone; when the sockets shriek;
When your arms lie twisted under your back.

Good men holding their courage slack
In their frightened pockets see how weak
The work that is done; and feel the weight
Of your blood on the ground for their spirits' sake;

And build their anger, stone on stone;
Each silently, but not alone.

Birmingham 1963

Sunday morning and her mother's hands
Weaving the two thick braids of her springing hair,
Pulling her sharply by one bell-rope when she would
Not sit still, setting her ringing,
While the radio church choir prophesied the hour
With theme and commercials, while the whole house tingled;
And she could not stand still in that awkward air;
Her dark face shining, her mother now moving the tiny buttons,

Blue against blue, the dress which took all night making,
That refused to stay fastened;
There was some pull which hurried her out to Sunday School
Toward the lesson and the parable's good news,
The quiet escape from the warring country of her feelings,
The confused landscape of grave issues and people.

But now we see
Now we see through the glass of her mother's wide screaming
Eyes into the room where the homemade bomb
Blew the room down where her daughter had gone:
Under the leaves of hymnals, the plaster and stone,
The blue dress, all undone—
The day undone to the bone—
Her still, dull face, her quiet hair;
Alone amid the rubble, amid the people
Who perish, being innocent.

At That Moment

When they shot Malcolm Little down
On the stage of the Audubon Ballroom,
When his life ran out through bullet holes
(Like the people running out when the murder began)
His blood soaked the floor
One drop found a crack through the stark
Pounding thunder—slipped under the stage and began
Its journey: burrowed through concrete into the cellar,
Dropped down darkness, exploding like quicksilver
Pellets of light, panicking rats, paralyzing cockroaches—
Tunneled through rubble and wrecks of foundations,
The rocks that buttress the bowels of the city, flowed
Into pipes and powerlines, the mains and cables of the city:
A thousand fiery seeds.
At that moment,
Those who drank water where he entered . . .
Those who cooked food where he passed . . .
Those who burned light while he listened . . .
Those who were talking as he went, knew he was water
Running out of faucets, gas running out of jets, power
Running out of sockets, meaning running along taut wires—
To the hungers of their living. It is said
Whole slums of clotted Harlem plumbing groaned
And sundered free that day, and disconnected gas and light
Went on and on and on. . . .
They rushed his riddled body on a stretcher
To the hospital. But the police were too late.
It had already happened.

Letter in Winter

Under my window
The soot bangs as it falls down the shaft.
The cold smoke scrapes
Against the frozen walls.
From somewhere a child screams through its skin.
Behind the plaster the pipes kick.
The dark corners boil. The toilet strangles in the hall.
Only the angry smells are silent.

In the dark
Through the flaking walls, I hear
My neighbor, the old man and his rotting leg.
Hiss and thump in his heatless rage.

We are all locked in.
No one bothers
To clean the blood from the stairs.
I have no money
And there is nothing between my soul
And the iron weather
But one ruined candle
And your tears.

Night-Piece

I do not sleep at night.
Rain does not lull me, and the withered wind
Is always out of tune, when there is wind
Or moon enough for light.

The sounds, up from the street,
Fall back again, unclaimed: The dispossessed
Call out with longing to the dispossessed.
The sounds repeat, repeat . . .

But never call my name;
Though I have heard the footsteps mount the stair,
The steady tread that echoes down the stair—
And trembled just the same . . .

As if someone had come
But could not find me, passing by my room,
And did not know I waited in my room,
Lonely, sleepless and dumb.

Black All Day

This morning, when he looked at me,
I saw how black I was
though there was nothing I could see
to give him any cause.

But I was black all day, and mean;
and leaving none to doubt,
I showed all day what I had seen
this morning stepping out.

He looked me into rage and shame;
no less, the day was grim.
Tomorrow, by another name,
I'll do as much for him.

SARAH E. WRIGHT

To Some Millions Who Survive Joseph E. Mander, Senior*

I.

Sunday strollers along a sewage-choked Schuylkill
May soon forget where he died;
And many will point with second-hand authority
To the place in the liquid darkness,
Showing only
where death
gave birth
to a hero.

But they might glory in any
Novel bit of newsprint knowledge
Quite as pridefully:
  Great men often become great curiosities—
  Too often become conversation pieces
  And nothing more.

But something should be said
About Joseph E. Mander, Senior,
Lest the lesson he died to teach
  follow him to death:

---

* See page 538 (Sarah E. Wright) for historical note.

Joseph E. Mander, Senior, hero today,
And contemporary choice for parlor pledges,
Is more than a name to you now.

Yesterday you didn't know him—
Didn't care to meet him—
     To some of you (and I speak to that some of you)
He was any black man
Walking the streets of a segregated housing project,
"keeping in his proper place,"
Staying close to his particular breed
Of dark-skinned humanity,
Fenced in by stronger walls than stone and steel,
Forced in by will—your will, your fears, your hate.
Squeezed by your financial and legislative strength
Into a specified, had to be enough, little plot of ground
To raise his three born and one more on the way
     safely away from yours.

And after that yesterday,
When you didn't know him, in that short hour—
Before he became your favorite obligation,
Joseph E. Mander died;
        Died proving what so many have tried
        To obliterate with blood.
            Remember Warsaw—
            Remember Gettysburg—
            Remember blood?
        You have poured out years of it!
        Red human-life substance
        Spilling all over your consciences
        Trying to wash away brotherhood—
        And yet
        It lives!
Mander knew it, proved it,
Died because of it and you
With the memories of blood.
        Yes, one of your infant kind,
        Whose fear of the lone big silence
        Forced out one anguished, strangled plea for help,
        Cared not at all that it was a black
        Fully-clothed Mander
        Whose love-directed body
        Plunged into the river's filth,
        Reaching out with his black hands—
        His life—
        To grasp a small white hand—
        To give back life—
        Even if it meant his own . . .
        And it did.

And it should be said,
That greater fatherhood has no man than he
Who would leave those he has begat
To return to life one
Whose so-called "superiority"
Might one day deny his flesh—
His infant images—
Full and equal right to life.

II.

Now I have seen monuments:
Great geometric heaps of stone,
Lifeless towers raised to keep alive the dead;
And I have seen you, the people,
Anxious to write off your obligation to Mander
And his survivors (there are 16 million of them)
With a hurried check,
A few high-sounding speeches;
And if nothing spectacular happens
To claim the moments you've allowed for bigness,
You will remember the black man long enough
To raise a great grey stone thing—
A feelingless symbol,
In final-ended payment.

But I ask,

Cannot a monument that breathes be built?
A grateful people are bigger than all the tall piled stones
In our wide and waiting world;
A grateful people are wise
When their living grows into a growing monument.

And I ask,

Will not a monument breathe for Mander?
Spring out of the hearts of people who
Have grown wise in the ways of brotherhood
As taught by brave dead Mander?

And I ask,

When you walk through the spring that won't come this year for
Joseph E. Mander, Senior,

Will you turn those fingers that point to say,
"That's where a hero died"
back to yourselves—
point to your hearts
saying,
"But this is where he lives!"

Until They Have Stopped

Dedicated to Paul Robeson, Sr.

Until they have stopped glutting me with slop from
    the kitchen's garbage to make fat profit of me like a hog,
Until they have stopped slitting my throat like the defenseless animal's
    in the near-Christmas time killing for the Christmas feast,
Until they stop the knife which in my tenderest years
    I had learned to anticipate,
Until they stop the bloodletting, the blood purging, and the
    Joyful shouts over the slaughter for the feast—
Exultantly saying in many ways: She has borne enough pigs
    that will grow up to be hogs for the next year's feast,
Until they have stopped, my Mother of Christ,
I will not desist from saying, "No!"

Until they have stopped standard-branding me
    on the television and radio
With the junk of how a real he-man is one who prefers the blondest,
    less-gray-hair type of woman,
One who sails a speedboat going umpteen too-many fast
    miles an hour,
While smoking a famous name brand cancer-producing cigarette;
And a real she-woman is one who adores the sexual sell—loves nothing
    better than running a home with brainless effortlessness
While indulging herself in a profusion of useless commodities
    And purring like a little tiger kitten,
Until they have stopped, my earth, my people,
I will not desist from saying, "No!"

Until they have stopped filling my lungs with tear gas in
    Alabama, U.S.A.
And vomiting gas in Vietnam—knowing that to rob a person
    of will is to rob them of life,
Until they have stopped disgracing the languages of the
    peoples of this globe
By calling these murderous attacks "humane"—and out-and-out
    war "deterrent activity,"
Until they have stopped this assault to my natural intelligence,
I will not desist from saying, "No!"

"No!" to the would-be destroyers of my mother's milk,
Full of earth and determination and broken fingernails—
Hurting to the quick from digging and groveling and
Making this and that do when she know by the standards of her Christ

Nothing else would do except
A more equitable distribution of the wealth of this earth.
Until they stop the necessity of millions of mothers
All over this earth from having to feed children on
Fairy tales as a substitute for food,
Until they stop! I will not desist from saying, "No!"
For no fairy tale will do when the belly bleeds
    from the claws of hunger.
No fancy hair sprays will do when the body is aging
Or frightened from economic illnesses unattended.
Nothing will do but another borning of humanity,
A clean new day free of degrading wars,
Against the working people of this earth—
A tomorrow lit by the suns of peace
And the stars of constructive human achievement.
Nothing will do except the coming of a time for love
For the spirit of Paul Robeson—for the hallowed spirit
Of the great man Robeson—nothing but a time for love.

CARL GARDNER (1931–)

The Dead Man Dragged from the Sea

The dead man dragged from the sea
Lay on the beach on his heels, buttocks, shoulders.
Like the figure "X",
His arms and legs stretched outward, so the crowd,
Lunching on fingernails, had melted
Backward, there
Was nothing more that they could do.
On the quiet sea
A motorboat made disturbances.
This was the end of the sea . . .
What had he learned there?
Patience from the jellyfish?
    Had he learned the fruits of
Sensitive waiting, the turning
In wet seasons?—so the drift—
His mouth gaped wide, but someone had closed his eyes,
Denying all instruction
of the crystal mackerel.
"I live because I'm caught,
I fear and find no end to fear.
I never wanted to die,
Because I never thought of living."

And he came with a message from the anemones,
But though his tongue stared out
It never blinked—so then
The message of the squid
Was lost, and the revelations of the eels
Were lost,
And the warnings of the turtles—
For none could read
The darkening lips, the lids of salt.
They were never sad enough
In burying the dead man dragged from the sea.

Reflections

I saw myself leaving
And welcomed myself back
In the mirrors, I ran by too fast,
And had to retrace, to see.
I have watched myself too much
In the polished hubcaps,
Found myself smiling
Too widely in the window glass.
I stood on the corner, a statue.
Phidias would have been proud.
Too far was I leaning
Over the puddle in its peace.
I have been too witty,
Heard too much applause,
Become too wise, too full of knowing.
My chest has caught fire with the medals
For the good that I have done.
I have ordered too many executions.

GERALD W. BARRAX (1933–)

Efficiency Apartment

My sons.
sometimes I can / not name you
until this magic room is sleeping
and the stretched out ends our lives make
curl around
and stitch you thru the interstices
behind my eyes.

*

(And ceremonies changed us
And equaled what we became
And ceremonial words preceded us
Into flesh and spirit and aborted us
Into the ends our lives made
With marvelous cadences to tell us what we were
And would be.)

*

One, Two, and Three
when the room is awake and shrugs the shadows off its walls
I see the papered magic I've added
    scraps left over from the ends the world made.
Roger is jolly on the wall and says hi
Hippity Hop skips under the breast of a dragon's shadow
   that burns yellow leaves in green flame

    the moonmen's marbled earth
    (that I gave your names to remember me)
floats in space above the telephone

and what you drew and gave me once on a visit
   One, your seraped boy with the cactus grin
   Two, your Sopwith Camel firing four lines
    of wavery pencil rounds into the dragon's mouth
      (I arranged it that way to conserve the forest)
   and Three's cycloptic snaggletoothed house

I call children's art when visitors ask

*

(Dear, lost, penultimate love
Poorer for, richer for rituals
Of birth and mortgage
We made formality of ceremony
And two or three and ten years
Was too long to live the deaths
That did us part.)

*

Your schoolday weather.

   (Did she know the probability of rain?)

Winter mornings close the room.
She wakes you before leaving
  and unthreads you from my sleep.

(Did she hear the forecast at all?)

Twelve and ½ miles and one river
is close enough to dress you in three warm apologies

                              for being here.

In bells and voices at noon
in the center of a cross
                         of church, funeral home and two schools
it opens   and   I am imprisoned
by the shouting sons of other fathers

  playing (

                         *

Did I play with you?

            (We gave us One for our youth
            Two for love
            Three the image of me.)

Is a father with no sons
a nursery with no rimes
songs, music
now
roses no rings
but ashes   ashes
down the hill we fell
rolling One   sliding Two   tumbling Three

out of the ends of our lives

now

I am black sheep
three boys empty

I will go hi
            (Spy in her eye)
round my base is

round my base
   hidingO seekand
daddy's
(*find me!*)
(lost)
  it

＊

(I wed thee
I ring this with what we were
In seeming real
One   in
Two   seemly
Three   black
        sons.)

＊

Books all over the place

my little people   big people
slim and fat   —boys

daddy does well in school—

they hunch in bookcase caves
and a box under the table
and squat on top of the closet
in my efficient kitchen

they are a comfort these days
chatting away in my unsleeping
exorcising the square deific

After opening the doors out of your lives
   boys
        I followed the little people leading the piper

and here I am
12½ miles and one river

   wondering:what if I kill them

will they drown or burn

                    and then?

But no I guess
I have already given my only begotten sons
to save them
                and
every week
it seems
I buy at least one
more

＊

Hello.   Hello.   Hello.

and to make him laugh I play my old game

       Is that you, Sam?

I have no son by that name.

It was funnier when
they'd come home from
school and I'd keep
them waiting outside the
back door asking who
they were *Is that
you Sam Harry Joe?*
and they'd fall all
over each other shrieking

no daddy
it's *us!*

Hello,Hello.   hello.
what were you doing
how is school
are there grapes on the vine yet
I'll see you soon   I dont know
goodnite goodnite goodnite
no   tell her goodnite for me

               *

      (Even now
      The cadence of our changes remains in phase.
      I had only to become what I am
      And you what you will not.
      Hotter than a pepper sprout.
      I am learning to play the guitar you gave me
      Trying not to smoke
      So much.
      Peace. Your hold forever
      And now speak.)

            *

Here we go round
here we go round
the Supremes hover above my feet
   the 3 girls I'll never have
the telephone is sorry
the room is raining, efficiently
the room rains and rings
the ends are stitched together

One, Two and Three
                    will be fine

the fit will survive

I have made us all typical
now
true to myself
the nigger daddy for social statistics

(is it asleep?   yes
sleeping and raining and ringing)

goodnite   goodnite   goodnite
Dennis   Jerry   Josh

To a Woman Who Wants Darkness and Time

where light is
where your body is blacker
where light is

where love lights love
out of sight
of all other reason

we will take the guts out of night
and lay its old breezes and moons
on the altars of afternoons

where light is
where your body is blacker
in a room in the sun

if this is treason
compound it in a room with wrens and sparrows
streaming dust in stiletto beams

like flecks of sun
we will be striped and bound
and listen to nightingales dying

But first we must sit in intellectual talk
and smile across a room
and walk around the edges of your years

And I will tell you about time
lover please
listen

New grass springs from reluctant
as well as eager lovers
ultimately a mass

of melting flesh brings
spring   yes   spring
and hell

while waiting to glisten in dewdrops
on grass from melting
flesh

woman   lover   mine
melts   now   now
hush   ah hush   then

when it stops
may my prodding of you
answer me with spring
If you would live in my untrodden ways
where the judgment of the body
is valid as the mind's

and lovers are garroted by twisting eyebeams
and the moon strangles in its own congealed blood
and an hour forgets nothing years remember

but tell me that love must wear yellow leaves
and I will build pyramids for you of robins' eggs
and mountains of aspen leaves

It will come
when we are covered with the yellow leaves of God's head
shedding

it will
and I will remember the carnage
where light is the black taste of your body
between my savage teeth

Black Narcissus

You want to integrate me into your anonymity
because it is my right
you think
to be like you.

I want your right to be like yourself.
Integrate me for this reason:
    because I will die with you.

But remember
each day I will look into a mirror
and if you have not taken more than you have given
I will laugh when I see that I am still black.

For Malcolm: After Mecca

My whole life has been a chronology of—*changes*.

You lie now in many coffins
in parlors where your name
is dropped more heavily even than Death
sent you crashing to the stage
on which you had exorcised our shame.

In little rooms they gather now
bringing their own memories of your pilgrimage
they come and go
speaking of revolution
without knowing as you learned
how static hate is
without recognizing the man you were
lay in our shame
and your growth into martyrdom.

Your Eyes Have Their Silence

Your eyes have their silence in giving words
back more beautifully than trees can rain
and give back in swaying the rain
that makes silence mutable and startles nesting birds.

And so it rains. And so I speak or not
as your eyes go from silence suddenly
at love to wonder (as those quiet birds suddenly
at rain) letting, finally, myself be taught

silence before your eyes conceding everything
spoken as experience, as love, as reason
enough not to speak of them and my reason
crawls into the silence of your eyes. Spring

always promises something, sometimes only more
beauty: and so it rains. And so I take
whatever promise there is in silence as you take
words as rain and give them back in silence before

there are ways to say that more beauty is nothing
for you before my hands can memorize
the beauty of your slender movements and nothing
is beautiful as words nesting in your eyes.

Fourth Dance Poem

In legend, the appearance of White Ladies usually forbodes death. In Normandy they lurk on bridges and other narrow places and ask the traveller to dance. If he refuses the Lady he is thrown into a ditch.

The White Lady has asked me to dance.
She had been lurking under the bridge I had to cross
   to go anywhere.
I've considered my answer
and since I've stopped denying it
                she knows I have natural rhythm
so will she believe I dont know this dance?

"Why dance we not? Why stand we still?"

She has seen the white feather
I wear in my cap like a plume
and doubts my honesty
but I say to her anyway
ah White Lady
but I dont know this dance.

She hasnt believed me.

"They flee from me that sometime did me seek."

Oh White Lady
now you've said it

for me it was a long walk from Alabama

and I was on my way anywhere

HERBERT MARTIN (1933–)

Antigone I

For Shoko

Perhaps
This is the way
The world looks from the moon
If it has sight at all
To see me in my dreams
Loving your tiny sinews.

Moon tighten sea.
River run through grass.
There is a pool of dust
On the desert tonight.

Whatever light there is, comes from the false sight of the moon.
But consider as I do the past winter love, leaf to my finger.
There are winds that revolve around the stars.
There is a certain clarity to their sight,
Should they, too, chance to see. You must know that.
This year the losses are great: several Negroes, a number of whites,
One Siamese, silverpoint, beautiful, all, in a forest of grass.
Truly there was a love among us. So, the increment of vanity.
There is, however, a certain clarity to understanding possessions lost.
You, who lost a lover, that loss I know, remembering
There was a year when twice I lost a love
And have not touched that music again.

Antigone VI

All day walking with a yellow rose

For Rachel, a girl in Central Park

I choose not to walk among ghosts
(The wind this summer moves softly over the voices of children)
or with the young girl in the purple gown,
with mascara eyes, distributing yellow roses
as if they were answers.

She is as blatant as the sun.
Velvet is the metaphor of her rose.
The stem has thorns, on which flesh will bleed
(even when the children's voices are gone)
and murder its odor.

Lines

For my students 1967–1970

The age
requires this task;
create
a different image;
re-animate
the mask.—*Dudley Randall*

Singularly and in pairs the decade has been ripped by bullets.
The wind has reft the flame from the tabernacle.
Somewhere in the night reason staggers;
We peep guilt through our fingers.
Sniffle regret in our handkerchiefs;
Bathe the brain in tears to forget,
And slowly the age loses its face.
> The summer desert offers no water.
> The snake makes no love.
> The tree branches give no shade.
> The land is fire.
> The wind is a ghost of no relief.
> Lay down the roses, love is for the night.
> Lay gentle the lilies down, grief stalks the day.
> Time feasts at the center of everything.
The cradle that seeds the flesh demands the fire.
The heart must beat as the times require.

A Negro Soldier's Viet Nam Diary

The day he discovered a mother and child in the river, he wrote

They had been there a month; the water had begun to tear them apart.
The mother had not relaxed, even in death she held to her child.
I lowered my gun slowly into the water, walked away.
My stomach screamed empty, there was nothing there.

What little warm water I had would not Pilot away the mud or stench.
It was like a dead body we could not discover.
Death hangs on the rice.
The ground is watered with blood.
The land bears no fruit.
Grass is an amenity.
It is a luxury forever to notice so much as a flower,
Or clear water in a stream.
Bullets, here, kill with the same deliberate speed that they do at home.
Fear destroys the thing it is unacquainted with.
I never want to kill again.
Do not celebrate me when and if I come home.
I step around the smallest creatures these days.
I am cautious to pray.
I am cautious to believe the day will come when we can
Take up our sharing again with deliberate speed.
Have you prayed, lately, for that?

ETHERIDGE KNIGHT (1933–)

Cell Song

Night   Music   Slanted
Light strike the cave
of sleep.   I alone
tread the red circle
and twist the space
with speech.

Come   now,   etheridge,   don't
be a savior; take
your words and scrape
the sky, shake rain

on the desert, sprinkle
salt on the tail
of a girl,

can there anything
good come out of
prison

The Sun Came

And if sun comes
How shall we greet him?—*Gwendolyn Brooks*

The Sun came, Miss Brooks,—
After all the night years.
He came spitting fire from his lips.
And we flipped—We goofed the whole thing.
It looks like our ears were not equipped
For the fierce hammering.

And now the Sun has gone, has bled red,
Weeping behind the hills.
Again the night year shadows form.
But beneath the placid faces a storm rages.
The rays of Red have pierced the deep, have struck
The core.   We cannot sleep.
The shadows sing: Malcolm, Malcolm, Malcolm.
The darkness ain't like before.

The Sun came, Miss Brooks.
And we goofed the whole thing.
I think.
(Though ain't no vision visited my cell).

The Idea of Ancestry

I

Taped to the wall of my cell are 47 pictures: 47 black
faces: my father, mother, grandmothers (1 dead), grand
fathers (both dead), brothers, sisters, uncles, aunts,
cousins (1st & 2nd), nieces, and nephews. They stare
across the space at me sprawling on my bunk. I know
their dark eyes, they know mine. I know their style,
they know mine. I am all of them, they are all of me;
they are farmers, I am a thief, I am me, they are thee.

I have at one time or another been in love with my mother,
1 grandmother, 2 sisters, 2 aunts (1 went to the asylum),
and 5 cousins. I am now in love with a 7 year old niece
(she sends me letters written in large block print, and
her picture is the only one that smiles at me).

I have the same name as 1 grandfather, 3 cousins, 3 nephews,
and 1 uncle. The uncle disappeared when he was 15, just took
off and caught a freight (they say). He's discussed each year
when the family has a reunion, he causes uneasiness in
the clan, he is an empty space. My father's mother, who is 93
and who keeps the Family Bible with everybody's birth dates
(and death dates) in it, always mentions him. There is no
place in her Bible for "whereabouts unknown."

2

Each Fall the graves of my grandfathers call me, the brown
hills and red gullies of mississippi send out their electric
messages, galvanizing my genes. Last yr/like a salmon quitting
the cold ocean—leaping and bucking up his birthstream/I
hitchhiked my way from L.A. with 16 caps in my pocket and a
monkey on my back.   and I almost kicked it with the kinfolks.
I walked barefooted in my grandmother's backyard/I smelled the old
land and the woods/I sipped cornwhiskey from fruit jars with the men/
I flirted with the women/I had a ball till the caps ran out
and my habit came down. That night I looked at my grandmother
and split/my guts were screaming for junk/but I was almost
contented/I had almost caught up with me.
(The next day in Memphis I cracked a croaker's crib for a fix.)

This yr there is a gray stone wall damming my stream, and when
the falling leaves stir my genes, I pace my cell or flop on my bunk
and stare at 47 black faces across the space. I am all of them,
they are all of me, I am me, they are thee, and I have no sons
to float in the space between.

To Dinah Washington

I have heard your voice floating, royal and real,
Across the dusky neighborhoods,
And the eyes of old men grow bright, remembering;
Children stop their play to listen,
Remembering—though they have never heard you before,
You are familiar to them:
Queen of the Blues, singing an eternal song.

In the scarred booths of Forty-Third street,
"Long Johns" suck in their bellies,
On the brass studded leather of Elite-town,
Silk-suited Bucks raise their chins . . .

Wherever a man is without a warm woman,
Or a woman without her muscled man,
The eternal song is sung.

Some say you're sleeping,
But I say you're singing.

Unforgettable Queen.

He Sees Through Stone

He sees through stone
he has the secret
eyes this old black one
who under prison skies
sits pressed by the sun
against the western wall
his pipe between purple gums

the years fall
like overripe plums
bursting red flesh
on the dark earth

his time is not my time
but I have known him
in a time gone

he led me trembling cold
into the dark forest
taught me the secret rites
to take a woman
to be true to my brothers
to make my spear drink
the blood
of my enemies

now black cats circle him
flash white teeth
snarl at the air
mashing green grass beneath
shining muscles
ears peeling his words
he smiles
he knows
the hunt   the enemy
he has the secret eyes
he sees through stone

It Was a Funky Deal

It was a funky deal.
The only thing real was red,
Red blood around his red, red beard.

It was a funky deal.

In the beginning was the word,

And in the end the deed.
Judas did it to Jesus
For the same Herd.   Same reason.
You made them mad, Malcolm. Same reason.

It was a funky deal.

You rocked too many boats, man.
Pulled too many coats, man.
Saw through the jive.
You reached the wild guys
Like me   You and Bird. (And that
Lil LeRoi cat.)

It was a funky deal.

Portrait of Malcolm X

For Charles Baker

He has the sign
of the time shining
in his eyes   the high sign

His throat moans
Moses on Sinai and cracks
stones

His lips lay full and flowered
by the breast of Mother Africa

His forehead is red
and sacrosanct and
smooth as time and
love for you

For Black Poets Who Think of Suicide

Black Poets should live—not leap
From steel bridges, like the white boys do.
Black Poets should *live*—not lay
Their necks on railroad tracks, (like the white boys do.
Black Poets should seek, but not search
Too much in sweet dark caves
Or hunt for snipes down psychic trails—
(Like the white boys do;

For Black Poets belong to Black People.
Are the flutes of Black Lovers—Are
The organs of Black Sorrows—Are
The trumpets of Black Warriors.
Let all Black Poets die as trumpets,
And be buried in the dust of marching feet.

CONRAD KENT RIVERS (1933–1968)

Prelude

Night and the hood,
soft plain and rape that tears apart.
One man, one child, two human hearts,
    destroyed.

Vengeful black hands,
a white body slain. A pause for breath.
One land, one man—then kill again,
a land apart, to dust, to clay.

Watts

Must I shoot the
white man dead
to free the nigger
in his head?

To Richard Wright

You said that your people
Never knew the full spirit of
Western Civilization.
To be born unnoticed
Is to be born black,
And left out of the grand adventure.

Miseducation, denial,
Are lost in the cruelty of oppression.
And the faint cool kiss of sensuality
Lingers on our cheeks.

The quiet terror brings on silent night.
They are driving us crazy. And our father's
Religion warps his life.

To live day by day
    Is not to live at all.

Four Sheets to the Wind

And a One Way Ticket to France

As a child
I bought a red scarf and women told me how beautiful it looked,
wandering through the sous-sols as France wandered through me.

In the evenings
I would watch the funny people make love the way Maupassant said,
my youth allowed me the opportunity to hear all those strange
verbs conjugated in erotic affirmations. I knew love at twelve.

When Selassie went before his peers and Dillinger goofed
I read in two languages, not really caring which one belonged to me.

My mother lit a candle for King George, my father went broke, we died.
When I felt blue the Champs understood, and when it was crowded
the alley behind Harry's New York Bar soothed my restless spirit.

I liked to watch the nonconformists gaze at the paintings
along Gauguin's bewildered paradise.

Braque once passed me in front of the Café Musique.
I used to watch those sneaky professors examine the populace.
Americans never quite fitted in but they tried, so we smiled.

I guess the money was too much for my folks.
Hitler was such a prig and a scare. We caught the long boat.
I stayed.

Main Street was never the same. I read Gide and tried to
translate Proust. Now nothing is real except French wine.
For absurdity is reality, my loneliness unreal, my mind tired.

And I shall die an old Parisian.

On the Death of William Edward Burghardt Du Bois by African Moonlight and Forgotten Shores

"Work out your own salvation."—*Buddha*

True to your might winds on dusky shores
      the kingdom bowed down at last,
there you were, the chosen scholar home.

True you were among the earth's unborn
      a sheik of justice and almighty intellect,
killer of liberals, brother to a distant
      universe, not easily explained to bands
of hungry black men experiencing a real truth
      spelled-out, propagated, in slums born
more vigorous each day and year of triumph,
      unemployment, wine and sweet vermouth
            squeezed against death's cool
                  cocoa brown hands.

True to your souls of black folks, all hell sweeps
      our land; this moment fulfills your truths
which the State department burned, Crisis censored,
      Marx allowed, and I see you now an old man
opening a door marked entrance, making your mark
      for the bravest party you discovered, knowing
full well that none dare give what the NAACP demands;
      but, somehow hoping your shadow fell over all
those trusting black brothers, who depend and follow
      the whites of this or any diseased land
instead of their hearts and brains and fountain pens;

men who are ashamed to curse one another, to wail
against tyranny, power structures, famous names,
  men against the greatness of themselves.

Sage, can there be no more hope for everyman?
  Do we walk so close to devils, lose sight of Sun,
struggle against autumnal air, quench thirst of life?
      I stand dumb and chilled to understand
      W.E.B., your search, your loneliness,
and my own debt for the etchings from those lonely hills
    which now and forever hold communion over you.

If Blood Is Black Then Spirit Neglects My Unborn Son

For Malcolm X in Substance

You must remember structures beyond cotton plains
  filled
      by joes voting for godot,
        stealing the white man's thunder,
          avarice,

        Songs of silence parade your dead body
        Distracted by housemaids' bending backs
        Gold dusted, not sinned in the angry silence
        Surrounding fetid breaths and heavy sighs
        As your actor friend tells of tall trees
        Addressing that tenth talented mind
        Bowing for recognition under the sun shining
        Cameras shaping your body

You must remember that and this second whirl of
  care
      while black brothers grieve
        your unbroken Upanishads passing the white
          man's understanding of your new peace
      without hate.
        Your new love with sweet words
      articulating complete manhood,
          directly questioning the whole and famous
      words you said.
          Let my women mourn for days
      in flight.

The Train Runs Late to Harlem

Each known mile comes late.
Faces that leave with me earlier,
Return, sit and wait.
We made eight gruesome hours today.
And lunch; lunch we barely ate,
Watching today tick away.

One bravado is going to crash
One of those pine paneled suites
Where the boss sits, laying before
Him mankind's pleas. Old Boss
In his wild sophisticated way,
He'll quote from Socrates or Plato,
Then confess to be one of us.

I'll take Sunday's long way home,
Ride those waves;
Book passage around the world.
New house: boarding school for my
Kids, free rides at Riverside, buy
Out Sherman's barbecue,
Lift my people from poverty,
Until my train pops 133rd square
In her tiger's mouth
Returning me, returning me.

The Still Voice of Harlem

Come to me broken dreams and all,
bring me the glory of your wayward souls;
I shall find a place for them in my garden.

Weep not for the golden sun of California,
think not of the fertile soil of Alabama,
nor of your father's eyes, your mother's
body twisted by the washing board.

    I am the hope
    and tomorrow
    of your unborn.

Truly, when there is no more of me
there shall be no more of you . . .

CALVIN C. HERNTON (1934–)

The Patient: Rockland County Sanitarium

For Portia

I

Here is a place that is no place
And here is no place that is a place
A place somewhere beyond time
And beyond the reaches of those who in time
Bring flowers and fruit to this place,
Yet here is a definite place
And a definite time, fixed
In a timelessness of precise vantage
From which to view flowers and view fruit
And view those who come bearing them.

Those who come by Sunday's habit are weary
And kiss us half-foreign but sympathetic;
Spread, eat noisily to crack the unbearable
Silence of this place—
They do not know that something must always come
From something and that nothing must come always
From nothing, and that nothing is always a thing

To drive us mad.

II

A little at a time. Time is little,
Obsolescent and eternal.
Those who come Sundayly kiss us
And place flowers in our windows
While their minds grow smaller than the Eyes
Of the serpent who is at the gate:
Christ was not a man but a woman who wept for man.

Time is absolute, fluid, and infinite,
Origin and destiny, beginning and end,
Wedded and unwedded in the endless beginningless—

Faces that are distorted and terrified, faces
That are marble and mellow, all laugh the same
And weep the same both here and there.
Society is the hero.
Society is the villian.

Here, however, in Rockland Sanitarium, one can see them
Existentially;
Know, at last, that neither exist!

III

But if I were to speak mouth fully
Eat it and grow fat like you, oh so
Fat—and lielays, of course with discretion,
Laylies, and vagina centric like you,
I could not, with the help of God, distinguish
Trash from trash: the fragments of shattered lives
Hang in broken windows—
Throw them out!

I choose rather to speak confusedly with the
World that swirls around within and without the gate;
Trapped now here and trapped there everywhere
And nowhere in wellsfargoland, ambushed at the hour
Of birth and before and after, set upon by rats and roaches
Between definitional montanas, between left and left
And right and right and nothing and everything between
No place and some place without and within:
The whole world is our patient, dear ones.

IV

So it is best to keep silent
Ask no questions, give no answers, make no
Responses.
At least, this way, we know them that know us not;
The world knows us not, Portia;
For we are nolonger dwellers in the world,
But, having once been a part of it and learned
Its awful truth, have passed beyond that terrible place,

Passed beyond struggle, beyond the motives that lead
To madness
Now to sit here resigned, dumb as dead soldiers are
And stare out upon the great hecatomb of life with cold,
Immobile, terrified eyes.

Jitterbugging in the Streets

To Ishmael Reed

There will be no Holyman crying out this year
No seer, no trumpeter, no George Fox walking barefoot
    up and down the hot land
The only Messiah we shall see this year
Staggers
To and fro
On the LowerEastSide
Being laughed at by housewives in Edsel automobiles
    who teach their daughters the fun of deriding a terror
    belched up from the scatological asphalt of America
Talking to himself

An unshaven idiot
A senile derelict
A black nigger
Laughter and scorn on the lips of Edsel automobiles
    instructing the populace to love God, be kind to puppies
    and the Chase Manhattan National Bank
Because of this there will be no Fourth of July this year
No shouting, no popping of firecrackers, no celebrating,
    no parade
But the rage of a hopeless people
Jitterbugging
    in the streets.

Jacksonville, Florida
Birmingham, Atlanta, Rochester, Bedford-Stuyvesant
Jackson, Mississippi, Harlem, New York
Jitterbugging
    in
    the streets
To ten thousand rounds of ammunition
To waterhoses, electric prods, phallic sticks
    hound dogs, black boots stepping in soft places
    of the body—
Venom in the mouths of Christian housewives, smart young
    Italians, old Scandinavians in Yorkville, suntanned
    suburban organization men, clerks and construction
    workers, poor white trash and gunhappy cops every-
    where:
"Why don't we kill all niggers
Not one or two
But every damn black of them. Niggers will do anything.
I better never catch a nigger messing with my wife, and

most of all never with my daughter! Aughter grab 'em up
and ship every black clean out of the country . . .
aughter just line 'em up and mow 'em down
MachineGunFire!"
All American—housewives, businessmen, civil service
Employees, loving their families, going to church, regularly
    depositing money in their neighborhood bank
All Fourth of July celebrators belched up from the guilt-
    ridden, cockroach, sick-sex terror of America
Talking to themselves
In bars
On street corners
Fantasizing hatred
At bridge clubs
Lodge meeting, on park benches
In fashionable mid-town restaurants.

No Holyman shall cry out upon the black ghetto this year
No trombonist
The only Messiah we will know this year is a bullet
In the belly
    of a Harlem youth shot down by a coward crouched
    behind an outlaw's badge—

Mississippi
Georgia
Tennessee, Alabama
Your mother your father your brothers, sisters, wives
    and daughters
Up and down the hot land
There is a specter haunting America
Spitfire of clubs, pistols, shotguns, and the missing
Murdered
Mutilated
Bodies of relatives and loved ones
Be the only Santa Claus niggers will remember this year
Be the only Jesus Christ born this year
    curled out dead on the pavement, torso floating
    the bottom of a lake
Being laughed at by housewives in Edsel automobiles.

You say there are four gates to the ghetto
Make your own bed hard that is where you have got
To lay
You say there is violence in Harlem, niggers run amuck
    perpetrating crimes against property, looting stores,
    breaking windows, flinging beer bottles at officers
    of the law
You say a certain virgin gave birth to a baby
Through some mysterious process, some divine conjure,

A messenger turned his walking cane into a serpent
  and the serpent stood up and walked like a natural man
You say . . .
America, why are you afraid of the phallus!

I say there is no "violence" in Harlem.
There is TERROR in Harlem!
Terror that shakes the foundation of the very assholes
  of the people
And fear! And corruption! And murder!

Harlem is the asphalt plantation of America
Rat-infested tenements totter like shanty houses
  stacked upon one another

Circular plague of the welfare check brings vicious wine
  every semi-month, wretched babies twice a year, death
  and hopelessness every time the sun goes down
Big-bellied agents of downtown landlords with trousers
  that fit slack in the crotch
Forcing black girls to get down and do the dog before they
  learn to spell their names
If you make your own bed hard

He said he was fifteen years old, and he walked beside us
  there in the littered fields of the ghetto
He spoke with a dignity of the language that shocked us
  and he said he had a *theory* about what *perpetrated* the
Horror that was upon us as we walked among flying bullets,
  broken glass, curses and the inorganic phalluses of
  cops whirling about our heads
He said he was a business major at George Washington High
And he picked up a bottle and hurled it above the undulating
  crowd
Straight into the chalk face of a black helmet!

Thirty-seven properties ransacked, steel gates ripped from
  their hinges, front panes shattered; pawn shops, dry
  cleaners, liquor stores
Ripped apart and looted—

"Niggers will do anything. Aughter grab 'em up . . . If they
  ever try to eat my children I'll personally get a
  shotgun and mow down everyone I set eyes on."

And if your church don't support the present police action,
In dingy fish-n-chip and bar-b-que joints
Niggers will be doing business as usual—
From river to river,
Signboard to signboard

Scattering Schaefuer sex-packs all over the ghetto,
Like a bat out of hell,
Marques Haynes is a dribbling fool.

TERROR is in Harlem.
A Fear so constant

Black men crawl the pavement as if they were snakes,
    and snakes turn to bully sticks that beat the heads
    of those who try to stand up—
A Genocide so blatant
Every third child will do the junky-nod in the whore-scented
    night before semen leaps from his loins—
And Fourth of July comes with the blasting bullet in the belly
    of a teenager
Against which no Holyman, no Christian housewife
In Edsel automobile
Will cry out this year

Jitterbugging
    in the streets.

Fall Down

In memory of Eric Dolphy

All men are locked in their cells.
Though we quake
In the fist of the body
Keys rattle, set us free.

I remember and wonder why?
In fall, in summer; times we had
Will be no more. Journeys have
Their end.
I remember and wonder why?

In the sacred suffering of lung
Spine and groin,
You cease, fly away

To what? To autumn, to
Winter, to brown leaves, to
Wind where no lark sings; yet
Through dominion of air, jaw and fire

I remember!

Eric Dolphy, you swung
A beautiful axe. You lived a clean
Life. You were young
Then
You
Died.

D Blues

D blues
What you woke up wit
Dhis mourning
What you toss and turn
All night in your bed wit
Nothing,   no
One in your arms
Nobody.

Dats
What D blues
Is.

AUDRE LORDE (1934–)

Coal

I
is the total black, being spoken
from the earth's inside.
There are many kinds of open.
How a diamond comes into a knot of flame
how sound comes into a word, coloured
by who pays what for speaking.

Some words are open
like a diamond on glass windows
singing out within the crash of passing sun
Then there are words like stapled wagers
in a perforated book—buy and sign and tear apart—
and come whatever wills all chances
the stub remains
an ill-pulled tooth with a ragged edge.
Some words live in my throat
breeding like adders. Others know sun

seeking like gypsies over my tongue
to explode through my lips
like young sparrows bursting from shell.
Some words
bedevil me.

Love is a word another kind of open—
as a diamond comes into a knot of flame
I am black because I come from the earth's inside
Take my word for jewel in the open light.

Summer Oracle

Without expectation
there is no end
to the shocks of morning
or even a small summer.

Now the image is fire
blackening the vague lines
into defiance across the city.
The image is fire
sun warming us in a cold country
barren of symbols for love.

Now I have forsaken order
and imagine you into fire
untouchable in a magician's coat
covered with signs of destruction and birth
sewn with griffins and arrows and hammers
and gold sixes stitched into your hem
your fingers draw fire
but still the old warlocks shun you
for no gourds ring in your sack
no spells bring forth peace
and I am still fruitless and hungry
this summer
the peaches are flinty and juiceless
and cry sour worms.

The image is fire
flaming over you burning off excess
like the blaze planters start
to burn off bagasse from the canefields
after a harvest.

The image is fire
the high sign that rules our summer

I smell it in the charred breeze blowing over
your body
close
hard
essential
under its cloak of lies.

Father, the Year Is Fallen

Father, the year is fallen.
Leaves bedeck my careful flesh like stone.
One shard of brilliant summer pierced me
And remains.
By this only,—unregenerate bone
I am not dead, but waiting.
When the last warmth is gone
I shall bear in the snow.

Now That I Am Forever with Child

How the days went
while you were blooming within me
I remember, each upon each
The swelling changed planes of my body
and how you first fluttered, then jumped
and I thought it was my heart.

How the days wound down
and the turning of winter
I recall, with you growing heavy
against the wind. I thought
now her hands are formed, and her hair
has started to curl
now her teeth are done
now she sneezes.
Then the seed opened.
I bore you one morning just before spring
My head rang like a fiery piston
my legs were towers between which
A new world was passing.

From then
I can only distinguish
one thread within running hours
You . . . flowing through selves
toward you.

And What About the Children

Now we've made a child.
And the dire predictions
have changed into
wild
grim
speculations.
Still the negatives
are waiting
watching
and the relatives
Keep Right On
Touching . . .
    and how much curl
    is right for a girl?

But if it's said
at some future date
that my son's head
is on straight
he won't care
about his
hair
nor give a damn
whose wife
I am.

What My Child Learns of the Sea

What my child learns of the sea
of the summer thunder
of the bewildering riddles that hide within spring
she will learn in my twilights
and childlike
revise every autumn.

What my child learns
as her winters fall out of time
ripened in my own body
to enter her eyes with first light.

This is why
more than blood
or the milk I have given her

one day a strange girl will step
to the back of a mirror
cutting my ropes
of sea and thunder and sun.
Of the way she will taste her autumns—
toast-brittle, or warmer than sleep—
and the words she will use for winter,
I stand already condemned.

Father Son and Holy Ghost

I have not ever seen my father's grave.
Not that his judgment eyes have been forgotten
Nor his great hands print
On our evening doorknobs
One half turn each night and he would come
Misty from the world's business
Massive and silent as the whole day's wish, ready
To re-define each of our shapes—
But that now the evening doorknobs
Wait, and do not recognize us as we pass.

Each week a different woman
Regular as his one quick glass each evening—
Pulls up the grass his stillness grows
Calling it weed. Each week
A different woman has my mother's face
And he, who time has
Changeless
Must be amazed, who knew and loved but one.

My father died in silence, loving creation
And well-defined response.
He lived still judgments on familiar things
And died, knowing a January fifteenth that year me.

Lest I go into dust
I have not ever seen my father's grave.

Suffer the Children

Pity for him who suffers from his waste.
Water that flows from the earth
For lack of roots to hold it
And children who are murdered
Before their lives begin.

Who pays his crops to the sun
When the fields are parched by drought
Will mourn the lost water while waiting another rain.
But who shall dis-inter these girls
To love the women they were to become
Or read the legends written beneath their skin?

Those who loved them remember their child's laughter.
But he whose hate has robbed him of their good
Has yet to weep at night above their graves.

Years roll out and rain shall come again.
But however many girls be brought to sun
Someday
A man will thirst for sleep in his southern night
Seeking his peace where no peace is
And come to mourn these children
Given to the dust.

Rites of Passage

   To MLK jr.

Now rock the boat to a fare-thee-well.
Once we suffered dreaming
into the place where the children are playing
their child's games
where the children are hoping
knowledge survives
if unknowing
they follow the game
without winning.

Their fathers are dying
back to the freedom of wise children playing
at knowing
their fathers are dying
whose deaths will not free them
of growing from knowledge
of knowing
when the game becomes foolish
a dangerous pleading
for time out of power.

Quick
children kiss us
we are growing through dream.

IMAMU AMIRI BARAKA (LEROI JONES)

(1934–)

Each Morning

Section 4 from "Hymn for Lanie Poo"

Each morning
I go down
to Gansevoort St.
and stand on the docks.
I stare out
at the horizon
until it gets up
and comes to embrace
me. I
make believe
it is my father.
This is known
as genealogy.

Preface to a Twenty Volume Suicide Note

For Kellie Jones, born 16 May 1959

Lately, I've become accustomed to the way
The ground opens up and envelopes me
Each time I go out to walk the dog.
Or the broad edged silly music the wind
Makes when I run for a bus . . .

Things have come to that.

And now, each night I count the stars,
And each night I get the same number.
And when they will not come to be counted,
I count the holes they leave.

Nobody sings anymore.

And then last night, I tiptoed up
To my daughter's room and heard her
Talking to someone, and when I opened
The door, there was no one there . . .
Only she on her knees, peeking into

Her own clasped hands.

The Invention of Comics

I am a soul in the world: in
the world of my soul the whirled
light from the day
the sacked land
of my father.

In the world, the sad
nature of
myself. In myself
nature is sad. Small
prints of the day. Its
small dull fires. Its
sun, like a greyness
smeared on the dark.

The day of my soul, is
the nature of that
place. It is a landscape. Seen
from the top of a hill. A
grey expanse; dull fires
throbbing on its seas.

The man's soul, the complexion
of his life. The menace
of its greyness. The
fire, throbs, the sea
moves. Birds shoot
from the dark. The edge
of the waters lit
darkly for the moon.

And the moon, from the soul. Is
the world, of the man. The man
and his sea, and its moon, and
the soft fire throbbing. Kind
death. O
my dark and sultry
love.

Way Out West

For Gary Snyder

As simple an act
as opening the eyes. Merely
coming into things by degrees.

Morning: some tear is broken
on the wooden stairs
of my lady's eyes. Profusions
of green. The leaves. Their
constant prehensions. Like old
junkies on Sheridan Square, eyes
cold and round. There is a song
Nat Cole sings . . . This city
& the intricate disorder
of the seasons.

Unable to mention
something as abstract as time.

Even so, (bowing low in thick
smoke from cheap incense; all
kinds questions filling the mouth,
till you suffocate & fall dead
to opulent carpet.) Even so,

shadows will creep over your flesh
& hide your disorder, your lies.

There are unattractive wild ferns
outside the window
where the cats hide. They yowl
from there at nights. In heat
& bleeding on my tulips.

Steel bells, like the evil
unwashed Sphinx, towing in the twilight.
Childless old murderers, for centuries
with musty eyes.

I am distressed. Thinking
of the seasons, how they pass,
how I pass, my very youth, the
ripe sweet of my life; drained off . . .

Like giant rhesus monkeys;
picking their skulls,
with ingenious cruelty
sucking out the brains.

No use for beauty
collapsed, with moldy breath
done in. Insidious weight
of cankered dreams. Tiresias'
weathered cock.

Walking into the sea, shells
caught in the hair. Coarse
waves tearing the tongue.

Closing the eyes. As
simple an act. You float

Legacy

For Blues People

In the south, sleeping against
the drugstore, growling under
the trucks and stoves, stumbling
through and over the cluttered eyes
of early mysterious night. Frowning
drunk waving moving a hand or lash.
Dancing kneeling reaching out, letting
a hand rest in shadows. Squatting
to drink or pee. Stretching to climb
pulling themselves onto horses near
where there was sea (the old songs
lead you to believe). Riding out
from this town, to another, where
it is also black. Down a road
where people are asleep. Towards
the moon or the shadows of houses.
Towards the songs' pretended sea.

Letter to E. Franklin Frazier

Those days when it was all right
to be a criminal, or die, a postman's son,
full of hallways and garbage, behind the hotdog store
or in the parking lots of the beautiful beer factory.

Those days I rose through the smoke of chilling Saturdays
hiding my eyes from the shine boys, my mouth and my flesh
from their sisters. I walked quickly and always alone
watching the cheap city like I thought it would swell
and explode, and only my crooked breath could put it together
again.

By the projects and small banks of my time. Counting my steps
on tar or new pavement, following the sun like a park. I imagined
a life, that was realer than speech, or the city's anonymous
fish markets. Shuddering at dusk, with a mile or so up the hill

to get home. Who did you love
then, Mussolini? What were you thinking,
Lady Day? A literal riddle of image
was me, and my smell was a continent
of familiar poetry. Walking the long way,
always the long way, and up the steep hill.

Those days like one drawn-out song, monotonously
promising. The quick step, the watchful march march,
All were leading here, to this room, where memory
stifles the present. And the future, my man, is long
time gone.

W.W.

Back home the black women are all beautiful,
and the white ones fall back, cutoff from 1000
years stacked booty, and Charles of The Rits
where jooshladies turn into billy burke in
        blueglass
kicks. With wings, and jingly bew-teeful things.
The black women in Newark are fine. Even with
all that grease in their heads. I mean even
the ones where the wigs a
slide around, and they coming at you 75 degrees
        off course.
I could talk to them. Bring them around.
To something.
Some kind of quick course, on the sidewalk,
    like Hey baby,
why don't you take that thing off yo' haid.
You look like
Miss Muffett in a runaway ugly machine.
I mean, like that.

A Poem for Black Hearts

For Malcolm's eyes, when they broke
the face of some dumb white man. For
Malcolm's hands raised to bless us
all black and strong in his image
of ourselves, for Malcolm's words
fire darts, the victor's tireless
thrusts, words hung above the world
change as it may, he said it, and
for this he was killed, for saying,
and feeling, and being/ change, all
collected hot in his heart, For Malcolm's
heart, raising us above our filthy cities,
for his stride, and his beat, and his address
to the grey monsters of the world, For Malcolm's
pleas for your dignity, black men, for your life,
black men, for the filling of your minds
with righteousness, For all of him dead and
gone and vanished from us, and all of him which
clings to our speech black god of our time.
For all of him, and all of yourself, look up,
black man, quit stuttering and shuffling, look up,
black man, quit whining and stooping, for all of him,
For Great Malcolm a prince of the earth,
    let nothing in us rest
until we avenge ourselves for his death, stupid animals
that killed him, let us never breathe a pure breath if
we fail, and white men call us faggots till the end of
the earth.

leroy

I wanted to know my mother when she sat
looking sad across the campus in the late 20's
into the future of the soul, there were black angels
straining above her head, carrying life from our ancestors,
and knowledge, and the strong nigger feeling. She sat
(in that photo in the yearbook I showed Vashti) getting into
new blues, from the old ones, the trips and passions
showered on her by her own. Hypnotizing me, from so far
ago, from that vantage of knowledge passed on to her passed on
to me and all the other black people of our time.

When I die, the consciousness I carry I will to
black people. May they pick me apart and take the
useful parts, the sweet meat of my feelings. And leave
the bitter bullshit rotten white parts
alone.

Bumi

I forgotten who
I is
I wanted to be some body
and lost it
I lost my self
I *lost love*
I left a girl
   dying
I see her
   all the time
I dont know
   what
   to do
    I
   wish my mind
   wd stay here

Dust ocean a city
faces like napkins
fire hydrants catch
them I cd walk
if I want to
I used to run
I can sing a little
bit but that still
don't say I can heal
or bring back
the dead

A Guerrilla Handbook

In the palm
the seed
is burned up
in the wind.
      In their rightness
the tree trunks are socialists

leaves murder the silence and are brown
and old when they blow to the sea.
                              Convinced
of the lyric. Convinced
of the man's image (since
he will not look at substance
other than his ego. Flowers, grapes
the shadows of weeds, as the weather
is colder, and women walk
with their heads down.
                      Silent political rain
against the speech
of friends. (We love them
trapped in life, knowing no way out
except description. Or black soil
floating in the arm.
                      We must convince the living
                      that the dead
                      cannot sing.

We Own the Night

We are unfair
And unfair
We are black magicians
Black arts we make
in black labs of the heart

The fair are fair
And deathly white

The day will not save them
And we own the night

SOS

Calling black people
Calling all black people, man woman child
Wherever you are, calling you, urgent, come in
Black People, come in, wherever you are, urgent, calling
you, calling all black people
calling all black people, come in, black people, come
on in.

Study Peace

Out of the shadow, I am come in to you whole a black holy man
whole of heaven in my hand in my head look out two yeas to ice
what does not belong in the universe of humanity and love. I am
the black magician you have heard of, you knew was on you in you now
my whole self, which is the star beneath the knower's arc, when the star it
self rose and its light illuminated the first prophet, the five pointed being
of love.
I have come through my senses
The five the six the fourteen
of them. And I am a fourteen point star
of the cosmic stage, spinning in my appointed orbit
giving orders to my dreams, ordering my imagination
that the world it gives birth to is the beautiful quranic vision

We are phantoms and visions, ourselves
Some star's projection, some sun's growth beneath that holy star
And all the other worlds there are exist alive beneath their own beautiful fires
real and alive, just as we are
beings of the star's mind
images cast against the eternally shifting
heavens.

QUANDRA PRETTYMAN

Photograph

For L. McL.

i

What cannot be committed to memory, this can save.
We can look saying, "thus it was."
The sun has not been really caught,
The clouds, less solid then, kept moving.
Pull from our pockets loved ones we have not kept,
"This is he," we point.
He no longer has the beard
And his hair now is cut,
But this was one moment he,
Now held forever

And here that moment the eye so swiftly loses
When gravity put down, the dancer rises,
Flies.

ii

Nor can this capture what the eye sees
                              or mind desires.
Walking is to put one leg before the other
                              again and again.
A smile is a light rising and falling in the eye,
A child is a growing thing,
A trumpet is to sound,
An open mouth is to cover.

iii

The picture is not real.
Still, neither is the word.
But the eye makes pictures,
The mouth words,
Pressing order
Where none is.

We hear some song and look for birds,
We see a hand and we call it love.

Still Life: Lady With Birds

She, in dowdy dress and dumpy,
clutching her black purse and brown paper bag,
comes bounty bearing and love bestows.

She, with birds for epaulets,
thrusts such crusts as she has, such crumbs.
They cluster and grab and grabbing sometimes claw.

She, alone in this agony,
feeds them swiftly, firmly brushes them away,
speaking wild rantings to no one I see.

Sometimes one comes late,
finds no where to rest at her shoulders,
finds no crumb to eat at her feet.

To that one, she
holds out her arm.
Him, she brings in.

When Mahalia Sings

We used to gather at the high window
of the holiness church and, on tip-toe,
look in and laugh at the dresses, too small
on the ladies, and how wretched they all
looked—an old garage for a church, for pews,
old wooden chairs. It seemed a lame excuse
for a church. Not solemn or grand,
with no real robed choir, but a loose jazz band,
or so it sounded to our mocking ears.
So we responded to their hymns with jeers.

Sometimes those holiness people would dance,
and this we knew sprang from deep ignorance
of how to rightly worship God, who after
all was pleased not by such foolish laughter
but by the stiffly still hands in our church
where we saw no one jump or shout or lurch
or weep. We laughed to hear those holiness
rhythms making a church a song fest:
we heard this music as the road to sin,
down which they traveled toward that end.

I, since then, have heard the gospel singing
of one who says I worship with clapping
hands and my whole body, God, whom we must
thank for all this richness raised from dust.
Seeing her high-thrown head reminded
me of those holiness high-spirited,
who like angels, like saints, worshiped as whole
men with rhythm, with dance, with singing soul.
Since then, I've learned of my familiar God—
He finds no worship alien or odd.

The Mood

All that I ran from,
I held
in my hands.
When I did jump,
I landed where
I leapt from.
The stairs up
only descended.

When I looked
the other way,
time's face
confronted me
with all I
had turned from.
I fell down,
but my knees
would not bend.
I could not
be saved.

JOSEPH WHITE

Black Is a Soul

Down
Down into the fathomless depths
Down into the abyss beneath the stone
Down still farther, to the very bottom
    of the infinite
Where black-eyed peas & greens are stored
Where de lawd sits among melon rinds.
A dark blue sound (funky & barefooted)
    entered & sang a tear for the People
Of black women (buxom & beautiful)
With nappy heads & cocoa filled breasts
    nippled with molasses,
      & their legs sensual & long beneath
    short bright dresses
& of black men greasy from the sun-soaked
    fields sitting in the shade,
    their guitars, the willow & the
    squatting sun weeping authentic blues

These quantums of pure soul
Who pick cotton under the rant rays of the sun
Who eat hot greasy fish, chitlins, corn pone,
    pig feet, fat back & drink wine
    on Sat. nights
Who get happy & swing tambourines & sing
    them there spirituals
Who are blessed by the power of poverty

Who bathe their feet in streamlets of
    simplicity
Who are torn by the insolence & depression
    of bigot blonde America,
Are the essence of beauty
The very earth
The good earth
The black earth

In these moments when my man preaches
    about a no good nigger woman who did
    him wrong
My fingers begin to pop
My feet jump alive
The blue sound clutches me to its bosom
    until I become that sound
In these moments when the sun is blue
When the rivers flow with wine
When the neck bone tree is in blossom
I raise my down bent kinky head to charlie
    & shout
I'm black. I'm black
& I'm from Look Back

BOB KAUFMAN (1935–)

Mingus

String-chewing bass players,
Plucking rolled balls of sound
From the jazz-scented night.

Feeding hungry beat seekers
Finger-shaped heartbeats,
Driving ivory nails
Into their greedy eyes.

Smoke crystals, from the nostrils
Of released jazz demons,
Crash from foggy yesterday
To the light
Of imaginary night.

Blues Note

For Ray Charles's birthday
N.Y.C./1961

Ray Charles is the black wind of Kilimanjaro,
Screaming up-and-down blues,
Moaning happy on all the elevators of my time.

Smiling into the camera, with an African symphony
Hidden in his throat, and (*I Got a Woman*) wails, too.

He burst from Bessie's crushed black skull
One cold night outside of Nashville, shouting,
And grows bluer from memory, glowing bluer, still.

At certain times you can see the moon
Balanced on his head.

From his mouth he hurls chunks of raw soul.
He separated the sea of polluted sounds
And led the blues into the Promised Land.

Ray Charles is a dangerous man ('way cross town),
And I love him.

African Dream

In black core of night, it explodes
Silver thunder, rolling back my brain,
Bursting copper screens, memory worlds
Deep in star-fed beds of time,
Seducing my soul to diamond fires of night.
Faint outline, a ship—momentary fright
Lifted on waves of color,
Sunk in pits of light,
Drummed back through time,
Hummed back through mind,
Drumming, cracking the night.
Strange forest songs, skin sounds
Crashing through—no longer strange.
Incestuous yellow flowers tearing
Magic from the earth.

Moon-dipped rituals, led
By a scarlet god,
Caressed by ebony maidens
With daylight eyes,
Purple garments,
Noses that twitch,
Singing young girl songs
Of an ancient love
In dark, sunless places
Where memories are sealed,
Burned in eyes of tigers.

Suddenly wise, I fight the dream:
Green screams enfold my night.

Patriotic Ode on the Fourteenth Anniversary of the Persecution of Charlie Chaplin

Come on out of there with your hands up, Chaplin,
In your Sitting Bull suit, with your amazing new Presto Lighter.
We caught you. We found your fingerprints on the World's Fair.
Give us back the money and start over as a cowboy.
Come on, Chaplin, we mean business.

I Have Folded My Sorrows

I have folded my sorrows into the mantle of summer night,
Assigning each brief storm its allotted space in time,
Quietly pursuing catastrophic histories buried in my eyes.
And yes, the world is not some unplayed Cosmic Game,
And the sun is still ninety-three million miles from me,
And in the imaginary forest, the shingled hippo becomes the gay unicorn.
No, my traffic is not with addled keepers of yesterday's disasters,
Seekers of manifest disembowelment on shafts of yesterday's pains.
Blues come dressed like introspective echoes of a journey.
And yes, I have searched the rooms of the moon on cold summer nights.
And yes, I have refought those unfinished encounters.
     Still, they remain unfinished.
And yes, I have at times wished myself something different.

The tragedies are sung nightly at the funerals of the poet;
The revisited soul is wrapped in the aura of familiarity.

Walking Parker Home

Sweet beats of jazz impaled on slivers of wind
Kansas Black Morning/ First Horn Eyes/
Historical sound pictures on New Bird wings
People shouts/boy alto dreams/Tomorrow's
Gold belled pipe of stops and future Blues Times
Lurking Hawkins/ shadows of Lester/ realization
Bronze fingers—brain extensions seeking trapped sounds
Ghetto thoughts/ bandstand courage/ solo flight
Nerve-wracked suspicions of newer songs and doubts
New York altar city/ black tears/ secret disciples
Hammer horn pounding soul marks on unswinging gates
Culture gods/ mob sounds/ visions of spikes
Panic excursions to tribal Jazz wombs and transfusions
Heroin nights of birth/ and soaring/ over boppy new ground.
Smothered rage covering pyramids of notes spontaneously exploding
Cool revelations/shrill hopes/beauty speared into greedy ears
Birdland nights on bop mountains, windy saxophone revolutions
Dayrooms of junk/ and melting walls and circling vultures/
Money cancer/ remembered pain/ terror flights/
Death and indestructible existence

In that Jazz corner of life
Wrapped in a mist of sound
His legacy, our Jazz-tinted dawn
Wailing his triumphs of oddly begotten dreams
Inviting the nerveless to feel once more
That fierce dying of humans consumed
In raging fires of Love.

To My Son Parker, Asleep in the Next Room

On ochre walls in ice-formed caves shaggy Neanderthals
     marked their place in time.
On germinal trees in equatorial stands embryonic giants
     carved beginnings.
On Tasmanian flatlands mud-clothed first men hacked rock,
     still soft.
On Melanesian mountain peaks barked heads were reared
     in pride and beauty.
On steamy Java's cooling lava stooped humans raised stones
     to altar height.
On newborn China's plain mythless sons of Han acquired
     peaked gods with teak faces.

On holy India's sacred soil future gods carved worshipped
    reflections.
On Coptic Ethiopia's pimple rock pyramid builders tore
    volcanoes from earth.
On death-loving Egypt's godly sands living sacrifices carved
    naked power.
On Sumeria's cliffs speechless artists gouged messages
    to men yet uncreated.
On glorious Assyria's earthen dens art priests chipped
    figures of awe and hidden dimensions.
On splendored Peru's gold-stained body filigreed temples
    were torn from severed hands.
On perfect Greece's bloody sites marble stirred
    under hands of men.
On degenerate Rome's trembling sod imitators sculpted lies
    into beauty.
On slave Europe's prostrate form chained souls shaped free
    men.
On wild America's green torso original men painted
    glacial languages.
On cold Arctica's snowy surface leathery men raised totems
    in frozen air.
On this shore, you are all men, before, forever, eternally
    free in all things.
On this shore, we shall raise our monuments of stones,
      of wood, of mud, of color, of labor, of belief, of being,
      of life, of love, of self, of man expressed
      in self-determined compliance, or willful revolt,
      secure in this avowed truth, that no man is our master,
      nor can any ever be, at any time in time to come.

Falling

Cool shadows blanked dead cities, falling,
Electric anthills, where love was murdered.
Daily crucifixions, on stainless steel crosses,
In the gardens of pillbox subdivisions, falling.
Poets, like free reeds, drift over fetid landscapes,
Bearded Phoenix, burning themselves, falling.
Death patterns capture the eyes, falling.
A saving madness, cast by leafless trees, falling,
Cushions the songs, filtered through smoking ruins,
From the nostrils of unburied dead gods.
Cool shadows, fall over drawn eyelids, falling,
Cutting off the edge of time, falling, endlessly.

HENRY DUMAS (1935–1968)

Black Trumpeter

we must kill our gods before they kill us
not because we will to kill but because
our gods think themselves gods
they are only actors who have lost their script
cannot remember the lines, and fake visions
of themselves without mirrors
phantoms screaming without voices

we must kill our gods before they kill us
this then is the law and the testament
with malice toward none we give you warning
when the statue falls the pedestal remains
black birds do not light upon the roots of trees
the wing praises the root by taking to the limbs
we are Americans looking in the mirror of Africa

Buffalo

I caught the American bull
and brought him down.
Dust, like drops of blood,
spurted into the air,
and all the time I was
thinking, that if I ever
caught the American bull
   I would die.

America

If an eagle be imprisoned
on the back of a coin,
and the coin be tossed
into the sky,
the coin will spin,
the coin will flutter,
but the eagle will never fly.

knock on wood

i go out to totem street
   we play
   neon monster
     and watusi feet

killer sharks chasin behind
   we play hide
   siren!
     and out-run cops
they catch
   willie
   and me
     splittin over fence
they knock
   in willie's head
   hole
they kick me watusi
   down
     for dead
like yesterday
   runnin feet in my brain
   won't stop willie lookin blood
     beggin me
cut off blackjack pain

so whenever you see me comin
   crazy watusi
     you call me watusi
i keep a wooden willie
   blade and bone outa that fence
a high willie da conqueror
   listen! up there he talkin
wooden willie got all the sense

i go out to siren street
   don't play no more
me and willie beat a certain beat
   aimin wood carvin shadows

sometimes i knock on wood
   with fist
me and willie play *togetherin*
   and we don't miss

Black Star Line

My black mothers I hear them singing.

   Sons, my sons,
dip into this river with your ebony cups.
A vessel of knowledge sails under power.
Study stars as well as currents.
Dip into this river with your ebony cups.

My black fathers I hear them chanting.

   My sons, my sons,
let ebony strike the blow that launches the ship!
Send cargoes and warriors back to sea.
Remember the pirates and their chains of nails.
Let ebony strike the blow that launches this ship!
Make your heads not idle sails, blown about
by any icy wind like a torn page from a book.

   Bones of my bones,
all you golden-black children of the sun,
lift up! and read the sky
written in the tongue of your ancestors.
It is yours, claim it.
Make no idle sails, my sons.
Make heavy-boned ships
to bring back sagas from Melle, Songhay, Kongo,
deeds and words of Malik, Marcus, Toussaint,
and statues of Mahdi.
Make no idle ships of pleasure.
Remember the pirates.
For it is the sea who owns the pirates,
not the pirates the sea.

My black mothers I hear them singing.

   Children of my flesh,
dip into this river with your ebony cups.
A ship of knowledge sails unto wisdom.
Study what mars and what lifts up.
Dip into this river with your ebony cups.

JAMES W. THOMPSON (1935–)

You Are Alms

For: Cecil Taylor, Black composer/pianist & musicologist

You are alms—love
  —all lilting legs
      lending light
    in shadowed streets;
        strolling beneficent
beneath star's steel, morning's mauve,
      noon's amalgamate frenzy:
rain wind and the rage of raucous Rotarians
reeling to unwind from the stupor of acquisition
    in an alcohol-acquired feel
        of ready red-bloodedness
and rage; rage for your alms, your acquisition
          being the essential (yourself)
        not bi-leveled rooms
              attached
          entombed.

You are alms—love
  —the lyricism of the living.
          unfettered even in your needs
            strolling beneficent
              lending light
      to pallid thugs hunched on corners
            hopping in a frantic step:
the brown posture—clutching, anguished,
      at their acquisition of manhood
          (not being men but postures to penises attendant);
in envy without knowledge of need which makes being
      vital, and acquisition—an attendant factor
              of living—
          not itself a life;
without knowledge of why the language of African
    or Red Indian—wedded in a mellow mouth
          raised an idiom
            and an esthetic felt,
              formulated through the ritual
of maintaining life in the outrageous streets of the settlers.

You are alms—love
　　—raised in an idiom and an esthetic
　　　　felt and formulated
　　　　　　before the brain could record the feeling
　　　　　　　　in the introspective isolation of intellect
　　　　to art—attending:
　　　　　　yours is the art and record of itself
and though time visits the vital with remonstrances
　　　　art is the living—not the dead.

The Yellow Bird

Mandarin
in a silent film
he wings
into the night
past
painted women
chalked in doorways
gesturing
with fragile
lacquered hands.

Large yellow bird
he alights
in a foreign land
his buttocks fan
the perch
of a stool
fluttering
his eyes
rise
swallow the eddy
of human forms
swabbed in denim
shod in boots.

His stemmed drink
stands clear
among tumblers
of foaming beer
and he sips—
with an ease
of Eliot
attending
an effusive reading—
as the music grinds
in 4/4 time . . .

The stranger
steals
from the Victorian bed
combs
a hard hand
through his
blond head
gazing
in sandalwood
scented gloom
at the soft
yellow bird
asleep in the room.

JAY WRIGHT (1935–)

Wednesday Night Prayer Meeting

On Wednesday night,
the church still opens at seven,
and the boys and girls have to come in
from their flirting games of tag,
with the prayers they've memorized,
the hymns they have to start.
Some will even go down front,
with funky bibles,
to read verses from Luke,
where Jesus triumphs, or Revelations,
where we all come to no good end.
Outside, the pagan kids
scramble in the darkness,
kissing each other with a sly humility,
or urinating boldly against the trees.
The older people linger
in the freshly lit night,
not in a hurry to enter,
having been in the battle of voices
far too long, knowing that the night
will stretch and end only
when some new voice rises
in ecstasy, or deceit, only
when some arrogant youth
comes cringing down front,
screaming about sin, begging
the indifferent faced women

for a hand, for a touch,
for a kiss, for help,
for forgiveness, for being young
and untouched by the grace
of pain, innocent of the insoluble
mysteries of being black
and sinned against, black
and sinning in the compliant cities.
What do the young know
about some corpulent theologian,
sitting under his lamp,
his clammy face wet,
his stomach trying to give up
the taste of a moderate wine,
kissing God away with a labored
toss of his pen?
How would these small black singers
know which Jesus is riding
there over the pulpit,
in the folds of the banner
left over from Sunday,
where the winners were the ones
who came, who dropped their nickels
into the felted platters with a flourish?
And how can they be expected
to remember the cadences
that will come again,
the same heart-rending release
of the same pain, as the clock turns
toward the certainty
of melancholic afternoons,
roast and left-over prayers,
the dampened hours that last through the night?
But Christ will come,
feeling injured, having gone
where beds were busy without him,
having seen pimps cane their number running boys,
the televisions flicker over heaped up bodies,
having heard some disheveled man
shout down an empty street, where women
slither in plastic boots, toward light,
their eyes dilated and empty;
will come like a tired workman
and sit on a creaky bench,
in hope, in fear, wanting to be pleased again,
so anxious that his hands move,
his head tilts for any lost accent
He seems to be home,
where he's always been.
His intense smile is fixed

to the rhythm of hands,
to the unhurried intensity
of this improvised singing.
He seems not to know
the danger of being here,
among these lonely singers,
in the middle of a war
of spirits who will not wait for him,
who cannot take his intense glare
to heart anymore, who cannot justify
the Wednesday nights given up
in these stuffy, tilted rooms,
while the work piles up for Thursday,
and the dogs mope around empty garbage pails,
and the swingers swing into the night
with a different ecstasy.
Caught in this unlovely music,
he spills to the floor.
The sisters circle him,
and their hands leap from bone to bone,
as if their touch would change him,
would make him see
the crooked lights like stars.
The bible-reading boy tags him with verses,
and he writhes like a boy
giving up stolen kisses,
the free play of his hand on his own body,
the unholy clarity of his worldly speech.
He writhes as if he would be black,
on Wednesday, under the uncompromising
need of old black men and women,
who know that pain is what
you carry in the mind,
in the solemn memory of small triumphs,
that you get, here,
as the master of your pain.
He stands up to sing,
but a young girl,
getting up from the mourner's bench,
tosses her head in a wail.
The women rise,
the men collect the banners
and the boys drop their eyes,
listening to the unearthly wind
whisper to the peeping-tom trees.
This is the end of the night,
and he has not come there yet,
has not made it into the stillness
of himself, or the flagrant uncertainty
of all these other singers.

They have taken his strangeness,
and given it back, the way a lover
will return the rings and letters
of a lover that hurts him.
They have closed their night
with what certainty they could,
unwilling to change their freedom for a god.

An Invitation to Madison County

I ride through Queens,
out to International Airport,
on my way to Jackson, Tougaloo, Mississippi.
I take out a notebook,
write "my southern journal," and the date.
I write something,
but can't get down the apprehension,
the strangeness, the uncertainty
of zipping in over the Sunday streets,
with the bank clock flashing the weather
and time, as if it were a lighthouse
and the crab-like cars mistook it
for their own destination.
The air terminal looks
like a city walled in, waiting for war.
The arrivals go down to the basement,
recruits waking at five AM to check out their gear,
to be introduced to the business end of the camp.
Fifteen minutes in the city,
and nothing has happened.
No one has asked me to move over
for a small parade of pale women,
or called me nigger, or asked me where I'm from.
Sure only of my destination, I wait.

Now, we move out through the quiet city,
past clean brick supermarkets,
past clean brick houses with nameplates
and bushy lawns, past the sleepy-eyed
travelers, locked tightly in their cars.
No one speaks. The accent I've been
waiting to hear is still far off,
still only part of that apprehension
I had on the highway, in Queens.

The small campus springs up
out of the brown environment,
half-green, half-brown, covered over

with scaly white wooden houses.
It seems to be fighting this atmosphere,
fighting to bring some beauty
out of the dirt roads, the tense isolation of this place.

Out to Mama's T's, where farmers, young instructors
and students scream for hamburgers and beer,
rub each other in the light of the jukebox,
and talk, and talk. I am still
not in Jackson, not in Mississippi,
still not off that highway in Queens,
nor totally out of Harlem, still
have not made it into this place,
where the tables creak, and the crickets
close up Sunday, just at evening,
and people are saying goodnight early.
Afraid now, I wonder how I'll get into it,
how I can make my hosts forget
these impatient gestures, the matching socks and tie
I wonder how long I'll have to listen
to make them feel I listen, wonder
what I can say that will say,
"It's all right. I don't understand
a thing. Let me meet you here, in your home.
Teach me what you know,
for I think I'm coming home."

Then I meet a teen-aged girl,
who knows that I can read.
I ride with her to Madison County,
up backroads that stretch
with half-fulfilled crops,
half-filled houses, half-satisfied
cows, and horses, and dogs.
She does all the talking,
challenging me to name the trees,
the plants, the cities in Mississippi, her dog.
We reach her house,
a shack dominated by an old stove,
with its smoky outline going up the wall
into the Mississippi air, mattresses tossed
around the table, where a small piece of cornbread
and a steaming plate of greens wait for her.
Her mother comes out, hands folded before her
like a madonna. She speaks to me,
moving step by step back into the house,
asking me to come again,
as if I were dismissed,
as if there were nothing more
that I could want from her, from Madison County,

no secret that I could ask her to repeat,
not even ask about the baby resting there on her belly,
nor if she ever knew anyone with my name
in Madison County, in Mississippi.

Since I can't, and will not, move,
she stays, with her head coming up,
finally, in a defiant smile.
She watches me sniff the greens,
look around at the bare trees
heaving up out of the bare ground.
She watches my surprise
as I look at her manly nine-year-old
drive a tractor through the fields.
I think of how she is preparing him
for death, how one day he'll pack
whatever clothes remain from the generations,
and go off down the road,
her champion, her soldier, her lovable boy,
her grief, into Jackson, and away,
past that lighthouse clock,
past the sleepy streets,
and come up screaming,
perhaps on the highway in Queens,
thinking that he'll find me,
the poet with matching socks and tie,
who will tell him all about the city,
who will drink with him in a bar
where lives are crackling, with the smell
of muddy-rooted bare trees, half-sick cows
and simmering greens still in his nose.

But I'm still not here,
still can't ask any easy question,
or comment on the boy, the bright girl,
the open fields, the smell of the greens;
can't even say, yes, I remember this,
or heard of it, or want to know it;
can't apologize for my clean pages,
or assert that I must change, after being here;
can't say that I'm after spirits in Mississippi,
that I've given up my apprehension
about pale and neatly dressed couples
speeding past the lighthouse clock,
silently going home to their own apprehensions;
can't say, yes, you're what I really came for,
you, your scaly hands, your proud, surreptitious
smile, your commanding glance at your son,
that's what I do not search, but discover.

I stand in Madison County,
where you buy your clothes, your bread,
your very life, from hardline politicians,
where the inessential cotton still comes up
as if it were king, and belonged to you,
where the only escape is down that road,
with your slim baggage, into war,
into some other town that smells the same,
into a relative's crowded house
in some uncertain city, into the arms
of poets, who would be burned,
who would wake in the Mississippi rain,
listening for your apprehension,
standing at the window in different shadows,
finally able to say, "I don't understand.
But I would be taught your strength."

The father comes down the road,
among his harness bells and dust,
straight and even, slowly, as if each step
on that hard ground were precious.
He passes with a nod,
and stands at the door of his house,
making a final, brief inventory
all around and in it.
His wife goes in, comes out with a spoon,
hands it to you with a gracious little nod,
and says, "Such as . . ."

"Such as . . .," as I heard
when my mother invited the preacher in,
or some old bum, who had fallen off
a box-car into our small town
and come looking for bread-crumbs,
a soup bowl of dish water beans,
a glass of tap water, served up
in a murky glass.
"Such as . . .," as I heard
when I would walk across the tracks
in Bisbee, or Tucson, or El Paso, or Santa Fe,
bleeding behind the eyes,
cursing the slim-butted waitresses
who could be so polite.
"Such as . . .," as I heard
when I was invited behind leaky doors,
into leaky rooms, for my loneliness,
for my hunger, for my blackness.
"Such as . . .," as I hear
when people, who have only themselves to give,
offer you their meal.

The Homecoming Singer

The plane tilts in to Nashville,
coming over the green lights
like a toy train skipping past
the signals on a track.
The city is livid with lights,
as if the weight of all the people
shooting down her arteries
had inflamed them.
It's Friday night,
and people are home for the homecomings.
As I come into the terminal,
a young black man, in a vested gray suit,
paces in the florid Tennessee air,
breaks into a run like a halfback
in open field, going past the delirious faces,
past the shiny poster of Molly Bee,
in her shiny chaps, her hips tilted forward
where the guns would be, her legs set,
as if she would run, as if she were
a cheerleader who doffs her guns
on Saturday afternoon and careens
down the sidelines after some broken field runner,
who carries it in, for now,
for all the state of Tennessee
with its nut-smelling trees,
its stolid little stone walls
set out under thick blankets of leaves,
its crisp lights dangling on the porches
of homes that top the graveled driveways,
where people who cannot yodel or yell
putter in the grave October afternoons,
waiting for Saturday night and the lights
that spatter on Molly Bee's silver chaps.
I don't want to think of them,
or even of the broken field runner in the terminal,
still looking for his girl, his pocket
full of dates and parties, as I come
into this Friday night of homecomings
and hobble over the highway in a taxi
that has its radio tuned to country music.
I come up to the campus,
with a large wreath jutting up
under the elegant dormitories,
where one girl sits looking down at the shrieking cars,
as the lights go out, one by one, around her

and the laughter drifts off, rising, rising,
as if it would take flight away
from the livid arteries of Nashville.
Now, in sleep, I leave my brass-headed bed,
and see her enter with tall singers,
they in African shirts, she in a robe.
She sits, among them, as a golden lance
catches her, suddenly chubby, with soft lips
and unhurried eyes, quite still in the movement
around her, waiting, as the other voices fade,
as the movement stops, and starts to sing,
her voice moving up from its tart entrance
until it swings as freely
as an ecstatic dancer's foot,
rises and plays among the windows
as it would with angels and falls,
almost visible, to return to her,
and leave her shaking with the tears
I'm ashamed to release, and leave her
twisting there on that stool with my shame
for the livid arteries, the flat Saturdays,
the inhuman homecomings of Nashville.
I kneel before her. She strokes my hair,
as softly as she would a cat's head
and goes on singing, her voice shifting
and bringing up the Carolina calls,
the waterboy, the railroad cutter, the jailed,
the condemned, all that had been forgotten
on this night of homecomings, all
that had been misplaced in those livid arteries.
She finishes, and leaves,
her shy head tilted and wrinkled,
in the green-tinged lights of the still campus.
I close my eyes and listen,
as she goes out to sing this city home.

Death As History

i

They are all dying,
all the ones who make
living worth the price,
and there is hardly time
to lament the passing
of their historical necessity.
Young poets sit in their rooms
like perverted Penelopes,

unraveling everything,
kicking the threads
into the wind,
and I stop,
woolly-eyed,
trying to record
this peculiar American game.
But they are dying,
the living ones,
and I am sapped of all resolve,
fleeced, finally, of the skill
to live among these others.

To be charged with so much living
is such an improbability,
to be improbable about living
is such a charge to hold
against oneself,
against those who are dying.

ii

Dropping his history books,
a young man, lined against the horizon
like an exclamation point with nothing to assert,
stumbles into the dance.
The dancers go round and round
like drones on an unhappy flight.
They look to him for another possibility.
They hum.
They plead.
They circle him with outstretched hands.
They offer him their own salvation.
And he moves forward with a rose.
All that long search
to bring back death.
Who wants that old mystery?

iii

But still there is the probable.
And even in Madrid
the golden ages settle
in their sturdy coffins.
Oh, you can say that there
where the olive trees burst up
through the asphalt cells,
where well-endowed bulls butt
the tail-end of tame Sundays,
and the coquettish river flings

its hips at the cattle-mouthed mountains,
everything there is an imitation.
The girls always advance on the square,
repeating the vital moments,
needing no bookish priests
to redeem that dance.
And it is always the credible dance.

iv

It is always like the beginning.
It is always having the egg
and seven circles,
always casting about in the wind
on that particular spot;
it is that African myth
we use to challenge death.
What we learn is that
death is not complete in itself,
only the final going from self to self.

v

And death is the reason
to begin again, without letting go.
And who can lament
such historical necessity?
If they are all dying,
the living ones,
they charge us with the improbable.

A. B. SPELLMAN (1935–)

zapata & the landlord

For allen dulles

the thief in me is running a
round in circles. what will he
do? how will he
                    fight an army?
hide somewhere, a shade
                              among shadows?
o the embarrassment, the tedium of coming
so far & failing.

eg., the mexicans, emiliano
& anthony, touched
        by the thief, run off to the
mountains by the thief, returned with their 3000
brothers
    & brought back the mountain.
                well, i
have only one
      brother, roland, 18,
& he has never fought
        a thief.

john coltrane

an impartial review

may he have new life like the fall
fallen tree, wet moist rotten enough
to see shoots stalks branches & green
leaves (& may the roots) grow into his side.

around the back of the mind, in its closet
is a string, i think, a coil around things.
listen to *summertime,* think of spring, negroes
cats in the closet, anything that makes a rock

of your eye. imagine you steal. you are frightened
you want help. you are sorry you are born with ears.

For My Unborn & Wretched Children

if i bring back
life to a home of want
let it be me.

let me be, if i come
back, new, hands in first,
the mouth in.

if hands & mouth are in,
the belly, filled, clothes
the body. *then* want.

if want & hurt are clothed, bring
back life to home. if
want decides, let it be me.

when black people are

when black people are
with each other
we sometimes fear ourselves
whisper over our shoulders
about unmentionable acts
& sometimes we fight & lie.
these are somethings we sometimes do.

& when alone i sometimes walk
from wall to wall fighting visions
of white men fighting me
& black men fighting white men
& fighting me & i lose my
self between walls &
ricocheting shots & can't say
for certain who i have killed
or been killed by.

it is the fear of winter passing
& summer coming & the killing
i have called for coming
to my door saying
hit it a.b., you're in it too.

& the white army moves like thieves
in the night mass producing beautiful
black corpses & then stealing them away
while my frequent death watches me
from orangeburg on cronkite &
i'm oiling my gun & cooking my food
& saying "when the time comes"
to myself, over & over, hopefully.

but i remember driving from atlanta
to the city with stone & featherstone
& cleve & on the way feather talked
about ambushing a pair of klansmen
& cleve told how they hunted
chaney's body in the white night
of the haunted house in the mississippi
swamp while a runaway survivor
from orangeburg slept between wars
on the back seat.

times like this
are times when black people
are with each other & the strength flows
back & forth between us like
borrowed breath.

in orangeburg my brothers did

in orangeburg my brothers did
the african twist around a bonfire they'd built
at the gate to keep the hunkies out. the day
before they'd caught one shooting up
the campus like the white hunter
he was. but a bonfire? only conjures
up the devil. up popped the devil from behind a bush
the brothers danced the fire
danced the bullets cut their flesh
like bullets. black death
black death black death black
brothers black sisters black me with no white blood on my hands
we are so beautiful
we study our history backwards
& that must be the beast's most fatal message
that we die to learn it well.

tomorrow the heroes

tomorrow the heroes
will be named willie. their
hair will the bushes that grow
everywhere the beast walks. america

is white. america is not. white
is not the slow kerneling of seed
in earth like the willies, the grass
the roots that grapple the beast

in the swamps. the williecong are earth
walking. ile-ife succor the williecong.
there is no other hope.

SONIA SANCHEZ (1935–)

homecoming

i have been a
way so long
once after college
i returned tourist
style to watch all
the niggers killing
themselves with
3 for oners
with
needles
that
cd
not support
their
stutters.
       now woman
i have returned
leaving behind me
all those hide and
seek faces peeling
with freudian dreams.
this is for real.
            black
     niggers
          my beauty.
baby.
i have learned it
ain't like they say
in the newspapers.

poem at thirty

it is midnight
no magical bewitching
hour for me
i know only that
i am here waiting
remembering that
once as a child
i walked two
miles in my sleep.

did i know
then where i
was going?
traveling. i'm
always traveling.
i want to tell
you about me
about nights on a
brown couch when
i wrapped my
bones in lint and
refused to move.
no one touches
me anymore.
father do not
send me out
among strangers.
you you black man
stretching scraping
the mold from your body.
here is my hand.
i am not afraid
of the night.

right on: white america

this country might have
been a pio
            neer land
once.
    but.   there ain't
no mo
        indians   blowing
custer's mind
            with a different
image of america.
                    this country
might have
            needed shoot/
outs/ daily/
        once.
                but. there ain't
no mo real/ white/   allamerican
                          bad/guys.
just.
    u & me.
            blk/ and un/armed.

this country might have
been a pion
                eer land.   once.
                                and it still is.
check out
            the falling
gun/shells   on our blk/tomorrows.

poem

for dc's 8th graders—1966–67

look at me 8th
grade
        i am black
beautiful. i have a
man who looks at
my face and smiles.
on my face
are black warriors
riding in ships
of slavery;
            on my face
                        is malcolm
                            spitting his metal seeds
on a country of sheep;
on my face
            are young eyes
breathing in black crusts.
                        look at us
8th grade
            we are black
beautiful and our black
ness sings out
            while america wanders
dumb with her wet bowels.

definition for blk / children

a policeman
            is a pig
and he shd be in
        a zoo
with all the other piggy
                animals.   and

until he stops
     killing blk/people
cracking open their heads
remember.
       the policeman
  is a pig.
      (oink/
        oink.)

hospital / poem

    for etheridge. 9/26/69

they have sed
u will die in
this nite room
of tubes/
      red/death/screams.
                   how do
they ima
    gine death?
          becuz yo/body
stops its earth
       movements
           does not
mean it dies.
     blk/
        mass can
not die maaan.
       it regroups
          to move
in to   another
       space.   a
             nother time.
it is mor/ning
      maaaan.   still u do not
move
   and yo/hrs
       slide into days
     and i watch u
        as i
begin the talk
      of HYenaaaAAS.

to all sisters

hurt.
        u worried abt a
    little hurting.
                    man
hurt ain't the bag u
    shd be in.
                loving is
the bag. man.
                there ain't
no MAN like a
                    black man.
he puts it where it is
and makes u
                turn in/side out.

now poem.   for us.

don't let them die out
all these old / blk / people
don't let them cop out
with their memories
of slavery / survival.
                        it is our
heritage.
            u know. part / african.
part / negro.
                part / slave
sit down with em brothas & sistuhs.
                        talk to em. listen to their
tales of victories / woes / sorrows.
                            listen to their blk /
myths.
        record them talken their ago talk
for our tomorrows.
                    ask them bout the songs of
births.   the herbs
            that cured
                their aches.   the crazy /
                            niggers blowen
                            some cracker's cool.
the laughter
comen out of tears.
let them tell us of their juju years
        so ours will be that much stronger.

JOHARI AMINI (1935–)

to a poet i knew

on the ridiculous occasion of his death

u bet u wer
left ther to die. die
just like u wasted yrself. out.
ok ure gon & that/this aint
no tribute now not now
cause tributes r meaning/less than
seeing a soul beyond th body & yrs was.
ther. to be seen which i dug(& still
is(but just th parts u
stopped to leave befor u went takin
all yr yetpoems with u befor
u split to becom
one of th wasted ones

positives

positives.positives.ain u sumthin
.u. i see u ther .yea i see u
ure a lyric physical blk
when u wait ther watchin
watchin me n th velvet
of yr flesh .yeah i see u.
yea. watchin me watchin
me & makin nite/noises
2 me .yea. nite/noises
2 me 2 touch th fingertips
of my mine. yea ure a
velvet worship lyric 4 me
th same 4 me th same watchin
watchin watchin me move
movin warm/waitin movin 2 u 2
u 2 u takin a fertile step & nu
breath 2 u 2 u velvet sumthin blkman

signals

(1)

is yo eye so empty
in the moonlight of yo smoke
u cant see me waitin
for u to sway my way
sway fine & black & o so cool
a swift swayin tree
swayin bendin down
& catchin me up into yo movement
pleasin u?
is yo eye so empty
in the moonlight of yo smoke
u cant see me waitin

(2)

o my man
our beginning will be
as beginnings be
total through all the sweet secretions
from your prime cause

and i will be a womanfire
orbiting your night

and you will protect my burning softness
because you wont be
out
of
it
when i need you

SAM CORNISH (1935–)

The River

we move from one
land
to another

my sister died
in the river

the cradle
on your sister's
back
is empty

& the water
rises

mother

why do we go
on

if we are
dying

my father carried
a fish over his back
its tail touched the ground

grandmother
used to chain herself
to the postoffice
for woman rights

Montgomery

For Rosa Parks

white woman have you heard
she is too tired to sit in the back
her feet are two hundred years old

move to the back or walk
around to the side door how
long can a woman be a cow

your feet will not move
and you never listen
but even if it rains empty

seats will ride through town
i walk for my children
my feet two hundred years old

One Eyed Black Man in Nebraska

The skin quickens to noises.
The ground beneath a black man opens.

His wife in her nightgown
hears horses and men in her husband's
deathbed.

White horses move through the fields
lifting men out of darkness.

In the pillows, she keeps
a rifle and twenty two,
for hunting rabbits and keeping alive.

Still he dies,
one eye closed on the ground.

Frederick Douglass

my mother twice in her life on worn feet
walked an afternoon against the southern
heat to bring me a ginger cake
her face lined with scars in wrinkled
skin was only twenty three

my mother carried me in the fields and slept
on black ground as i turned within our skin
and as a child white fingers walked into her
mouth to count the teeth and raise the price

i was born somewhere between the shacks
and evenings when shadows were tired across
the fields and dresses grey with dust

To a Single Shadow Without Pity

you are all these people
and will die soon they wade
in the filth of my mind
with tender feet extend
through my fingers with a quiet

uncertain voice each face
reflecting the greys
of small compromise
i live somewhere in the lines
in their faces and cannot convince
them of my intentions there is some
meaning on the hesitation
of a lip the quick
of the eye learning
the description of a different
street when it sees you
on a sudden corner where my
eyes will not let them alone
from all the minutes i am pushed from
where i hear music they do not understand
i wish there could be a silence of them
behind their faces i wish we could never
think of speaking behind these faces
without this music learning itself
within me
not knowing how to die
without music can be pain
unless you are someone who
understands all you want
is only sleep
and the music
touching the blankness
in the spaces where
the body hurts

not knowing how to die
i find myself in music
because the fingers
extend only the lies
of your own mind
my obscure words
too much like yours
where there is walking
in this city drinks a
dull mind

not knowing how to listen
because so many stone
structures are dead
with exhaustion
not wanting to die
because the fingers
want to extend themselves
i constantly feel
rhythm

we are drifting westward
where no landmarks are visible

the earth turns
on the edge
of the plow

red house
near the bridge
a corpse came home
& went to sleep

crows
on distant fences
near the river
cannot mourn

eyes have turned
to stone
white
except the trees
the sky almost
reaches the red
house
almost touches
his hands

                under the trees
                the stone and you
                shall go no further

                under the trees
                the flowers sleep
                with memory

                you will feel
                no more winter
                branches will spread

                and you
                feel no more

Death of Dr. King

#1

we sit outside
the bars   the dime stores
everything is closed today

we are mourning
our hands filled with bricks
a brother is dead

my eyes are white and cold
water is in my hands

this is grief

#2

after the water
the broken bread
we return
to our separate
places

in our heads
bodies collapse
and grow again

the city boils
black men
jump out of trees

Panther

Bobby Hutton, murdered by the Oakland police

three black boys
listen to the sounds
around them

in the trees policemen
are growing sticks

there are 20 holes
in bobby
his life runs through
them

A Black Man

a black man
in the water
stands
in sand and cold
stones
push on his feet
like any other man

did I expect something
different
because
we are another kind
of man

the first
and last
the one who the convoy
comes for
the new man in the ovens

CLARENCE MAJOR (1936–)

Vietnam #4

a cat said
on the corner

the other day
dig man

how come so many
of us
niggers

are dying over there
in that white
man's war

they say more of us
are dying

than them peckerwoods
& it just
      don't make sense

unless it's true
that the honkeys

are trying to kill us out
with the same stone

they killing them other cats
with

you know, he said
two birds with one stone

Vietnam

he was just back
from the war

said man they got
whites

over there now
fighting
us

and blacks over there
too

fighting us

and we can't tell
our whites
from the others

nor our blacks
from the others

& everybody
is just killing

& killing
like crazy

Blind Old Woman

spots on black skin.
                    she is dry.
how time, how she waits here
in her dingy wool, shabby
                    the fingers on her cup.
so frail, a woven face, so oval
such empty charity. how she remains
so quiet, quiet please.
                    how the cup shakes. and
it is not straight. nothing
is.
She does not sell candy nor rubber
bands. like the blind man
at the other end. of the silence. the sounds
                    of one or two pennies
in the bent up tin. up her canvas stool
at the end of the shadows.
                    how they return before her,
through these 1960 Indiana streets.
as she shuffles into street sounds.

The Design

          the music and its harmony
measures in the space of my boredom,
remains stale the air, the music.

The house. The things around
          the little things around my terms with you.
You never come to terms with
my brain. My music is difficult, you never

          empty the ashtrays. I am tired of the
apartment is dull a place but it comes
to this each

item you left, a few belongings: the african woman
with a shrunken leg, one with
a jug, a king dancing. The harmony
does not change the paradox of my birth.

They talk about Mao Tse-tung these days, small
talk, you know. This is simply
a letter of what I might say.

In our cold rooms a mocking laugh
rattles inside the walls. Inside the planks
          of our mind, we think alike.

Well, let me tell you
of my new lady. But she says she belongs to
nobody, or the world. A coddle for a poor fool's
          pride. And pleasure. Contemporary moments.

Exist, these melodies, difficult phrases, the
          stray bits of speech, exist thru her presence.
SHE HAS COME DOWN
                    front, baby. In the spaces, the music.

You say, they say, everybody says, even I say
          the important thing is her virtue: her sins
the building she lives in she lives in
chaos, in roots. In her cracked mirror in her mission
she lives in us, in everybody
          she lives in you.

We live anywhere, by the water, perhaps.
The blade of the water
          does not wake her, cutting her.
When it runs low, the fire sweeps her face but
          does not burn into her sleep. I know
she is peaceful, I

sometimes sleep like a fifteen year old dog
          beside her fire. Warm, losing my touch
I face rough walls in terrible moments, a finger
          might knock the edge, tilt the concerto

but I stop to think. It would be like picking up
a little man, a huge black beard
          weighing down his face, his legs
are goat legs. He sings, like a bird.
And it does not puzzle, nor amaze
          any of us. Not even under the effect
of her capsules; she, in her aspects makes no excuses
for such rhythm out of context.

          I say it is because of motherhood and she
remains abstract, not giving anything away. Sometime, like this time
          she leaves me feeling as commercial, plastic
as a sunrise on that post card
          you sent us from your vacation.

I say to her, Come
        into this home, this blue house of black
music. She knows the score
already, she was not as snowed as you, dear.

Now, things are working, we think alike.
No matter what I might say
        she is not bored.

Swallow the Lake

Gave me things I
could not use. Then. Now.
Rain night bursting upon & into. I
shine updown into Lake Michigan

like the glow from the cold lights of the Loop.
Walks. Deaths. Births.
Streets. Things I could not give back. Nor
use. Or night or day or night or

loneliness. Other ways   feelings I could not
put into words   into themselves into people.
Blank monkeys of the hierarchy. More deaths—
stupidity & death turning them on

into the beat of my droopy heart   my middle
passage blues my corroding hate my release
while I come to become neon iron eyes stainless lungs
blood zincgripped steel I
come up abstract

not able to take their bricks. Tar. Nor their flesh.
I ran: stung. Loop fumes hung
                        in my smoky lungs.

ideas I could not break nor form. Gave me
things I
see break & run down the crawling down the
game.

Illusion illusion, and you
would swear before screaming somehow
choked voices in me.

The crawling thing in the blood, the
huge immune loneliness. One becomes immune

to the bricks the feelings. One becomes
death.
One becomes each one and every person I
become. I could not
I COULD NOT
I could not whistle and walk in storms
along Lake Michigan's shore. Concrete walks.
I could not swallow the lake

JUNE JORDAN (1936–)

All the World Moved

All the world moved next to me strange
I grew on my knees
in hats and taffeta trusting
the holy water to run
like grief from a brownstone
cradling.

Blessing a fear of the anywhere
face too pale to be family
my eyes wore ribbons
for Christ on the subway
as weekly as holiness
in Harlem.

God knew no East no West no South
no Skin nothing I learned like
traditions of sin but later
life began and strangely
I survived His innocence
without my own.

The New Pietà: For the Mothers and Children of Detroit

They wait like darkness not becoming stars
long and early in a wrong one room
he moves no more

Weeping thins the mouth a poor escape from fire
lights to claim to torch the body
burial by war

She and her knees lock slowly closed (a burning door)
not to continue as they bled before
he moves no more

Uncle Bull-boy

His brother   after dinner
once a year would play the piano
short and tough in white shirt
plaid suspenders   green tie and
checked trousers.
Two teeth were gold.   His eyes
were pink with alcohol.   His fingers
thumped for Auld Lang Syne.
He played St. Louis Woman
Boogie, Blues, the light
pedestrian.

        But one night   after dinner
after chitterlings and pigs' feet
after bourbon rum and rye
after turnip greens and mustard greens
and sweet potato pie
Bullboy looking everywhere
realized his brother was not there.

Who would emphasize the luxury
of ice cream by the gallon who would
repeat effusively the glamour not the gall
of five degrees outstanding on the wall?
Which head would nod and then recall
the crimes   the apples stolen from the stalls
the soft coal stolen by the pile?
Who would admire
the eighteenth pair of forty
dollar shoes?
Who could extol their mother with good
brandy as his muse?

        His brother   dead from drinking
Bullboy drank to clear his thinking
saw the roach inside the riddle.
Soon the bubbles from his glass
were the only bits of charm
which overcame his folded arms.

In Memoriam: Martin Luther King, Jr.

I

honey people murder mercy U.S.A.
the milkland turn to monsters teach
to kill to violate pull down destroy
the weakly freedom growing fruit
from being born

America

tomorrow yesterday rip rape
exacerbate despoil disfigure
crazy running threat the
deadly thrall
appall belief dispel
the wildlife burn the breast
the onward tongue
the outward hand
deform the normal rainy
riot sunshine shelter wreck
of darkness derogate
delimit blank
explode deprive
assassinate and batten up
like bullets fatten up
the raving greed
reactivate a springtime
terrorizing

by death by men by more
than you or I can

STOP

II

They sleep who know a regulated place
or pulse or tide or changing sky
according to some universal
stage direction obvious
like shorewashed shells

we share an afternoon of mourning
in between no next predictable
except for wild reversal hearse rehearsal

bleach the blacklong lunging
ritual of fright insanity and more
deplorable abortion
more and
more

LUCILLE CLIFTON (1936–)

Good Times

My Daddy has paid the rent
and the insurance man is gone
and the lights is back on
and my uncle Brud has hit
for one dollar straight
and they is good times
good times
good times

My Mama has made bread
and Grampaw has come
and everybody is drunk
and dancing in the kitchen
and singing in the kitchen
oh these is good times
good times
good times

oh children think about the
good times

For deLawd

people say they have a hard time
understanding how I
go on about my business
playing my Ray Charles
hollering at the kids—
seem like my Afro
cut off in some old image
would show I got a long memory
and I come from a line
of black and going on women
who got used to making it through murdered sons

and who grief kept on pushing
who fried chicken
ironed
swept off the back steps
who grief kept
for their still alive sons
for their sons coming
for their sons gone
just pushing

Miss Rosie

When I watch you
wrapped up like garbage
sitting, surrounded by the smell
of too old potato peels
or
when I watch you
in your old man's shoes
with the little toe cut out
sitting, waiting for your mind
like next week's grocery
I say
when I watch you
you wet brown bag of a woman
who used to be the best looking gal in Georgia
used to be called the Georgia Rose
I stand up
through your destruction
I stand up

Those Boys That Ran Together

those boys that ran together
at Tillman's
and the poolroom
everybody see them now
think it's a shame

everybody see them now
remember they was fine boys

we have some fine black boys

don't it make you want to cry?

My Mama Moved Among the Days

My Mama moved among the days
like a dreamwalker in a field;
seemed like what she touched was hers
seemed like what touched her couldn't hold,
she got us almost through the high grass
then seemed like she turned around and ran
right back in
right back on in

listen children

listen children
keep this in the place
you have for keeping
always
keep it all ways

we have never hated black

listen
we have been ashamed
hopeless   tired   mad
but always
all ways
we loved us

we have always loved each other
children   all ways

pass it on

to Bobby Seale

feel free.
like my daddy
always said
jail wasn't made
for dogs,
was made for
men

LEBERT BETHUNE (1937–)

A Juju of My Own

To make a Juju of my own
For I was tired of strange ghosts
Whose cool bones
Lived on the green furnace of my blood
Was always my destiny
So she warned me—my grandmother,
And now and now
When I kindle again her small eyes with their quick
lights
Darting ancient love into my infancy
And when I break through to her easy voice
That voice like the pliant red clay she baked
She sings the only lullaby she sang me

"Me no care for Bakra whip
Me no care fe fum-fum
Come Juju come"

So I am fashioning this thing
My own Juju
Out of her life and our desire
Out of an old black love
I am baking my destiny to a lullaby—

"Me no care fe Bakra whip
Me no care fe fum-fum
Come Juju come . . ."

Harlem Freeze Frame

On the corner—116th and Lenox
   all in brown down to his kickers,
   and leaning on a post like some gaudy warrior
   spear planted, patient eyes searching the veldt

This gleaming wrinkled blunthead old sweet-daddy
   smiles a grim smile
   as he hears a voice of Harlem scream
"WE ALL SUPPOSED TO BE DEAD BUT
WE AINT"
And his slow strut moves him on again.

Bwagamoyo

Safari to Bwagamoyo
Safari to Bwagamoyo
For a lost son of Africa
Black sun, blue dust
On the way to Bwagamoyo
May eyes catch meanings in tears . . .

Bwagamoyo—beginning and end.

Myself, coming in love
The path to my destination
A jumble of holes
Red clay black
Slim hipped bridges
Swaying above dry gullies
The way to this place
Brings back old terrors . . .

Bwagamoyo—crush your heart for all is lost now.

What drawn out journey
What endless coffle
What sharp-toothed rivers to cross
What rust-bruised
Blistered flesh and soul
(While dhows like cradles on the tide)
Could flay this meaning there . . .

Bwagamoyo—throw off melancholy the terrible march is
                                                ended.

And now to come
Again to this beginning
Oceans crossed
Quick beaked birds endured
To come anew to meaning
The brown earth
Fat blue winds
Small children roasting fish
Black sun

Bwagamoyo—lay down your heart here on the coast of your
                                            homeland.

Blue Tanganyika

Here its like that . . .
   atmosphere of surprise
   hot sudden rain
   the pulse of things
   swings at different pace . . .
   fruit riper
   putrifying quicker
   (a sharper carcass marks all death in heat . . .)
   you wander at dusk and
   this turn in the path
   meets green eyes
   of a jackal
   disappearing into bush—
Now—sweet singing

EUGENE REDMOND (1937–)

Definition of Nature

In this stoned and
Steely park,
Love is an asphalt
Fact:
        flowers
        birds
        trees
        rushing or creeping brooks
are framed on walls and tv tubes.

But each night when the city shrinks,
      the stars roof us,
And any bush becomes
      our Bantu wonderland.

Gods in Vietnam

Mechanical
Oracles dot the sky,
Casting shadows on the sun.
Instead of manna
Leaflets fall
To resurrect the coals
Dead from the week's bombing.

Below
In the jungle,
Flaming altars
Buckle under prophecies;
And smoke whimpers
In the west wind.
Dry seas hide the
Cringing fold
While fishermen leap from clouds,
Nets blooming
On their lean bodies.

The sun slumps,
Full;
Before it sleeps
Solemn chaplains come,
Their voices choked
In suspicious silence.

MICHAEL S. HARPER (1938–)

Martin's Blues

He came apart in the open,
the slow motion cameras
falling quickly
neither alive nor kicking;
stone blind dead
on the balcony

that old melody
etched his black lips
in a pruned echo:
We shall overcome
some day—
Yes we did!
Yes we did!

Photographs: A Vision of Massacre

We thought the grass
would grow up quickly
to hide the bodies.
A brother sloped across
his brother, the patched
clay road slipping
into our rainy season
of red, our favorite color.

When the pictures came
we spoke of our love
for guns, oiled and glistening
in the rich blood of machines:
bodies, boys and girls, clutching
their private parts, oiled,
now slightly pink,
and never to be used.

Here Where Coltrane Is

Soul and race
are private dominions,
memories and modal
songs, a tenor blossoming,
which would paint suffering
a clear color but is not in
this Victorian house
without oil in zero degree
weather and a forty-mile-an-hour wind;
it is all a well-knit family:
a love supreme.

Oak leaves pile up on walkway
and steps, catholic as apples
in a special mist of clear white
children who love my children.
I play "Alabama"
on a warped record player
skipping the scratches
on your faces over the fibrous
conical hairs of plastic
under the wooden floors.
Dreaming on a train from New York
to Philly, you hand out six
notes which become an anthem
to our memories of you:
oak, birch, maple,
apple, cocoa, rubber.
For this reason Martin is dead;
for this reason Malcolm is dead;
for this reason Coltrane is dead;
in the eyes of my first son are the browns
of these men and their music.

Come Back Blues

For Robert F. Williams

I count black-lipped
children along river-creek,
skimming between bog,
floating garbage
logs, glistening tipped
twilight and night beaks;
the drowned drown again
while their parents
picket the old library and pool
special fish
taken up in poison—
you've come back
to count bodies again
in your own backyard.

Newsletter from My Mother:

8:30 A.M., December 8, '69

"1100 Exposition
 4115 South Central
 and some place on 55th Street
 were all subject to seige
 at 5:30 this morning.
 The police arrived with search warrants.

"At the present time
 1100 Exposition
 and the house on 55th Street
 have fallen.

"4115 South Central
 is still resisting;
 they have sandbagged
 the place and are wearing
 bullet-proof vests,
 tear gas masks;

"the whole area is cordonned off,
 Wadsworth School is closed;
 the police are clearing a hotel
 next door to get a better vantage.

"The police deny this is part
 of a nationwide program to wipe
 out the Panther Party;
 one of the fellows here at work,
 who lives in the area,
 says that they were clearing the streets
 last night, arresting people
 on any pretext,
 and that the jails are full.

"(I have to wait until my boss
 starts her class in the conference
 room so I can turn on the radio
 and get the latest news.)

"10 A.M.:
 The Panthers are surrendering
 1 at a time."

For Katherine Johnson Harper

Barricades

For Ronnie Herndon

Barricades hammered into place,
the beams stake out
in broad daylight
to avert nothing
they've taken; the old second
floor where they write the checks,
synchronize the grades,
or type in correct places
a stream data prognosis
is taken in the night;
the magpies are around, around
the corporate desk.

The blacks are studying
the records kept,
memorizing the numbers,
tallying the secret exits,
remembering the names,
the window pipes, outside,
for the way down.

They've gotten up there
with Frederick Douglass
in a six hour duel
with the overseers,
the first confrontation
to his own man;
DuBois in Atlanta
looking at the fingers
toes of meat market Sam;
and Malcolm in his first
act crumbling his prison
and the bullet proof glass.

Someone is having a familiar
vision of the black-white syndrome
in the academic halls;
in the cigar smoke
one hears the full-bull
rhesis rhetoric
and the black Christmas
in the halls of ivy:
the barricades come down—

Blue Ruth: America

I am telling you this:
the tubes in your nose,
in the esophagus,
in the stomach;
the small balloon
attached to its end
is your bleeding gullet;
yellow in the canned
sunshine of gauze,
stitching, bedsores,
each tactoe cut
sewn back
is America:
I am telling you this:
history is your own heartbeat.

Deathwatch

Twitching in the cactus
hospital gown, a loon
on hairpin wings,
she tells me how
her episiotomy
is perfectly sewn
and doesn't hurt
while she sits in a pile
of blood
which once cleaned
the placenta
my third son should be in.
She tells me how early
he is, and how strong,
like his father,
and long, like a black-
stemmed Easter rose
in a white hand.

Just under five pounds
you lie there, a collapsed
balloon doll, burst in your
fifteenth hour, with the face
of your black father,
his fingers, his toes,

and eight voodoo
adrenalin holes in
your pinwheeled hair-lined
chest; you witness
your parents sign the autopsy
and disposal papers
shrunken to duplicate
in black ink
on white paper
like the country
you were born in,
unreal, asleep,
silent, almost alive.

This is a dedication
to our memory
of three sons—
two dead, one alive—
a reminder of a letter
to DuBois
from a student
at Cornell—on behalf
of his whole history class.
The class is confronted
with a question,
and no one—
not even the professor—
is sure of the answer:
"Will you please tell us
whether or not it is true
that negroes
are not able to cry?"

America needs a killing.
America needs a killing.
Survivors will be human.

Effendi

For McCoy Tyner

The piano hums
again the clear
story of our coming,
enchained, severed,
our tongues gone,
herds the quiet

musings of ten million
years blackening the earth
with blood and our moon women,
children we loved,
the jungle swept up
in our rhapsodic song
giving back
banana leaves and
the incessant beating
of our tom-tom hearts.
We have sung a long time here
with the cross and the cotton field.
Those white faces turned
away from their mythical
beginnings are no art
but that of violence—
the kiss of death.
Somewhere on the inside
of those faces
are the real muscles
of the world;
the ones strengthened
in experience and pain,
the ones wished for in one's lover
or in the mirror
near the eyes
that record this lost, dogged data
and is pure, new, even lovely
and is you.

JULIA FIELDS (1938–)

Alabama

Out of the dark raw earth
Of blood and water
Should spring a song
For whatever beauty there is,
Should spring a prayer
For whoever god is,
Should burst forth a symphony
For all the hearts that are
Upon these barren, rustic hills
These cold and fruitless fields.

The moon hangs eloquent
In the sky
A smoke stack hovers
Blank nearby
Chiffon clouds glide on the air
"There must be eloquence somewhere."

God save the owls
    That perch on trees
    And curse the meals
    Of bread and peas—
    Preacher owls
    Mamma owls
    God owls
    Whore owls
    Hoot owls
    Teacher owls
    Store Keeper owls
    Farmer owls—
    White owls
    Black owls
Grass fed owls—
    For singing
Whatever beauty there is.

Poems: Birmingham 1962–1964

Moths

I have seen them at many hours
There on their corners standing
Almost infested like moths
Eating away the heart of time, slowly
As though they were an interwoven remnant
Of some elegant Eastern city
Where men lay dying like flowers in the street.
"Give them their viols. Let them have music.
Let them labor laborless. Perfume them
In their bathless nights and days.
Let them have their insane music."
Sweet, ironic music exuding the
Timelessness of ancient jungles
And the dance of silent feet as if
They were an interwoven remnant of
Some distant Eastern city
Where men go bathing in balsamic streams.

Their eyes are mad. They burn a
Helpless maddened energy. They have
A new peculiar anger. I have heard
Them curse Jerusalem and tear down
Jacob's ladder from their skies
As if they were apostles of some
Interwoven remnant of some holiness
New and in disguise. As if they think
To sing a music such as the city
Nor the world has ever known
Nor dreamed to know, nor wished to learn thereof.

Birmingham

I play the Masonic Funeral March
Now. Here. Alone. Outside eternity.
Spring has come. My landlady
Pretends within her garden plot.
She is old enough to know
That fairy tales will not
Make Flowers grow.
But she too is part of
The unreality. All spring
She will hoe in her garden
Seeds she forgot to plant
Not knowing that she really
Merely impedes the progress of
The Weeds.

Each twilight time I play
The lonely death defiant dirge
But nothing ever changes—
Except the colors of the seasons,
Half-hearted colors of the seasons.
Spring couldn't care less that
Roses sprout and dance upon
The icy grave of winter,
Or that the sun worn summer
Blasts asunder spring's efforts
To be lush and rich with greens and blues.

Here the worshipping of death
Is elegant with sun-spilled rites.
I play the fitting music
For gardens which will not bloom
And maiden ladies spoon-fed
In their effervescent youth
And for indifferent seasons.

NORMAN JORDAN (1938–)

Black Warrior

At night while
whitey sleeps
the heat of a
thousand African fires
burns across my chest

I hear the beat
of a war drum
dancing from a distant
land
dancing across a mighty
water
telling me to strike

Enchanted by this
wild call
I hurl a brick through
a store front window
and disappear.

Feeding the Lions

They come into
our neighborhood
with the sun
an army of
social workers
carrying briefcases
filled with lies
and stupid grins
Passing out relief
checks
and food stamps
hustling from one
apartment to another
so they can fill
their quota
and get back out
before dark.

July 31,

There are some

secrets

only time can

reveal

for instance:

        All young girls

          are beautiful

and all old men

are hip to it.

August 2,

When the

Sun

moves close

to earth

old men's eyes

become wet,

warriors' hearts

grow bold,

and the inside

of artists' stomachs itch.

KEORAPETSE KGOSITSILE (1938–)

Origins

For Melba

deep in your cheeks
your specific laughter owns
all things south of the ghosts
we once were. straight ahead
the memory beckons from the future
You and I a tribe of colors
this song that dance
godlike rhythms to birth
footsteps of memory
the very soul aspires to. songs
of origins songs of constant beginnings
what is this thing called
love

Ivory Masks in Orbit

For Nina Simone

these new night
babies flying on ivory wings
dig the beginning

do you love me!

son gawdamn
i saw the sun
rise at the midnight hour

300 sounds burn
on the ivory bespeaking
a new kind of air massive
as future memory

this like a finger moves
over 300 mississippis
rock the village
gate with future memory
of this moment's riff

the sun smiles of new
dawn mating with this
burning moment for the memory
can no longer kneel-in

do you love me!

88 times over lovely
ebony lady swims in this
cloud like the crocodile
in the limpopo midnight
hour even here speaking
of love armed with future
memory: desire become memory
i know how you be tonight!

Spirits Unchained

For Brother Max Stanford

Rhythm it is we
walk to against the evil
of monsters that try to kill the Spirit
It is the power of this song
that colors our every act
as we move from the oppressor-made gutter
Gut it is will move us from the gutter
It is the rhythm of guts
blood black, granite hard
and flowing like the river or the mountains
It is the rhythm of unchained Spirit
will put fire in our hands
to blaze our way
to clarity to power
to the rebirth of real men

For Eusi, Ayi Kwei & Gwen Brooks

In us and into us and ours
This movement rises every day
As the day whose fire informs
The rhythm of the sons who must live
After the death of those familiar faces.

We move from origin,
The singular fruit, at times bitter
As the Sophiatown winters we did not create,
To roots, stronger than the grief
Which groans under the weighted
Centuries of systematic rape and ruin.

We move from origin to roots.
Past the rancid face of anger and sorrow
Where I was a stranger to my breath
Rests the color of my eye
Calling my name
In the depths that reclaim
My pulse in the darknesses that alone
Remember the face of the warrior
Whose name knows a multiple doom
Before he is born to follow the eye
To the shapes remembered where the spirit moves
On to the darknesses the eye caresses
In us and into us and ours.

My Name Is Afrika

For Nqabeni Mthimkhulu

All things come to pass
when they do, if they do
All things come to their end
when they do, as they do
so will the day of the stench of oppression
leaving nothing but the lingering
taste of particles of hatred
woven around the tropical sun
while in the belly of the night
drums roll and peal a monumental song . . .
To every birth its blood
All things come to pass
when they do
We are the gods of our day and us
Panthers with claws of fire
And songs of love for the newly born
There will be ruins in Zimbabwe for real
Didn't Rap say,
They used to call it Detroit
And now they call it Destroyed!
To every birth its pain
All else is death or life

ISHMAEL REED (1938–)

Rain Rain on the Splintered Girl

the sun came up
the people yawned and stretched in rat traps whipping mildewed cats,
pomaded and braced in gold bathrooms of baroque toilet boxes,
from chairs with paws, from snuff cases, from the puzzlement of
round square rooms they poured into the streets,
yelling down phantom taxi cabs, jostling old men blowing their noses
    with tired flags
  some came in steel rickshaws
  some in buicks some on weird pack animals talking extinct words
(linguists bought them kool aid) some popped gum some were carried
some grumbled some fondled pistols
others in trench coats jotted down names for the state.   took photos

    babies set up tents and auctioned off errant mothers
jive oatmeal was flung at finger wagging humanists who drew up their
hind legs and split for the cafes covering their faces with *Les Temps
  Moderne*
  with grapefruit and cherries

            a famous editor was hanged on the spot for quoting jeffer-
            son with almost no deliberation his credit cards stamps line
            gauge correspondence and grey pages slid towards the sewer

some sprinted some bopped some leaned on shaky lamp posts
others sat down crossed their legs and marveled as
the old men talked of what was talked of what is talked of what is to
  come
talked crazy talk
toyed with their whiskers
threw difficult finger exercises at each other   white lightning
jumped like birds jumped like lions   yellow thunder
a girl above   on a ledge toes over the edge
knees knocking teeth chattering

    JUMP JUMP JUMP (millions of hands megaphoning razored
      lips)

some danced some sang some vomited
stained themselves pared fingernails
the moon came sick with old testament hang ups
people fought over exits

rain rain on the splintered girl
rain rain on deserted rickshaws, buicks

in certain rooms we sit
white light on our faces
objects arranged like rows of fine teeth
a man hand wrestles static hissing microphones
'today in Selma'   fire hoses
'today in Saigon'   monks soused
in certain rooms we ball our fists
in certain rooms we say   how awful
rain rain on the splintered girl
rain rain on the baby auctioneers.

Sermonette

a poet was busted by a topless judge
his friends went to morristwn nj & put
black powder on his honah's doorstep
black powder into his honah's car
black powder on his honah's briefs
tiny dolls into his honah's mind

by nightfall his honah could a go go no mo
his dog went crazy & ran into a crocodile
his widow fell from a wall &
hanged herself
his daughter was run over by a black man
cming home for the wakes the two boys
skidded into mourning
all the next of kin's teeth fell out

gimmie dat ol time
                    religion
It's good enough
          for me!

beware: do not read this poem

tonite, thriller was
abt an ol woman, so vain she
surrounded herself w/
    many mirrors

it got so bad that finally she
locked herself indoors & her

whole life became the
    mirrors

one day the villagers broke
into her house , but she was too
swift for them . she disappeared
    into a mirror
each tenant who bought the house
after that , lost a loved one to
      the ol woman in the mirror :
      first a little girl
      then a young woman
      then the young woman/s husband

the hunger of this poem is legendary
it has taken in many victims
back off from this poem
it has drawn in yr feet
back off from this poem
it has drawn in yr legs

back off from this poem
it is a greedy mirror
you are into this poem . from
    the waist down
nobody can hear you can they ?
this poem has had you up to here
    belch
this poem aint got no manners
you cant call out frm this poem
relax now & go w/ this poem

move & roll on to this poem
do not resist this poem
this poem has yr eyes
this poem has his head
this poem has his arms
this poem has his fingers
this poem has his fingertips

this poem is the reader & the
reader this poem

statistic: the us bureau of missing persons reports
        that in 1968 over 100,000 people disappeared
        leaving no solid clues
                nor trace   only
  a space
              in the lives of their friends

I Am a Cowboy in the Boat of Ra

"The devil must be forced to reveal any such physical evil (potions, charms, fetishes, etc.) still outside the body and these must be burned."—Rituale Romanum, published 1947, endorsed by the coat-of-arms and introductory letter from Francis Cardinal Spellman

I am a cowboy in the boat of Ra,
sidewinders in the saloons of fools
bit my forehead   like   O
the untrustworthiness of Egyptologists
who do not know their trips. Who was that
dog-faced man? they asked, the day I rode
from town.

School marms with halitosis cannot see
the Nefertiti fake chipped on the run by slick
germans, the hawk behind Sonny Rollins' head or
the ritual beard of his axe; a longhorn winding
its bells thru the Field of Reeds.

I am a cowboy in the boat of Ra. I bedded
down with Isis, Lady of the Boogaloo, dove
down deep in her horny, stuck up her Wells-Far-ago
in daring midday getaway. 'Start grabbing the
blue', I said from top of my double crown.

I am a cowboy in the boat of Ra. Ezzard Charles
of the Chisholm Trail. Took up the bass but they
blew off my thumb. Alchemist in ringmanship but a
sucker for the right cross.

I am a cowboy in the boat of Ra. Vamoosed from
the temple i bide my time. The price on the wanted
poster was a-going down, outlaw alias copped my stance
and moody greenhorns were making me dance; while my mouth's
shooting iron got its chambers jammed.

I am a cowboy in the boat of Ra. Boning-up in
the ol West i bide my time. You should see
me pick off these tin cans whippersnappers. I
write the motown long plays for the comeback of
Osiris. Make them up when stars stare at sleeping
steer out here near the campfire. Women arrive
on the backs of goats and throw themselves on
my Bowie.

I am a cowboy in the boat of Ra. Lord of the lash,
the Loup Garou Kid. Half breed son of Pisces and
Aquarius. I hold the souls of men in my pot. I do
the dirty boogie with scorpions. I make the bulls
keep still and was the first swinger to grape the taste.

I am a cowboy in his boat. Pope Joan of the
Ptah Ra. C/mere a minute willya doll?
Be a good girl and
bring me my Buffalo horn of black powder
bring me my headdress of black feathers
bring me my bones of Ju-Ju snake
go get my eyelids of red paint.
Hand me my shadow

I'm going into town after Set

I am a cowboy in the boat of Ra

look out Set   here i come Set
to get Set   to sunset Set
to unseat Set   to Set down Set

                 usurper of the Royal couch
                 imposter RAdio of Moses' bush
                 party pooper O hater of dance
                 vampire outlaw of the milky way

The Gangster's Death

how did he die/ O if i told you,
you would slap your hand
                          against your forehead
and say good grief/ if i gripped you
by the lapel and told how they dumped
        thalidomide hand grenades
into his blood stream and/
                          how they injected
a cyst into his spirit the size of an egg
which grew and grew until floating
        gangrene encircled the globe
and/ how guerillas dropped from trees like
mean pythons
                and squeezed out his life/
so that jungle birds fled their perches/
so that hand clapping monkeys   tumbled
        from branches and/

how twelve year olds snatched B 52's
    from the skies with their bare hands and/
how betty grable couldn't open a hershey bar
    without the wrapper exploding and/
how thin bent women wrapped bicycle chains
    around their knuckles saying
    we will fight until the last bra or/
    give us bread or shoot us/ and/
how killing him became child's play
in Danang in Mekong in Santo Domingo

      and how rigor mortis was sprinkled
in boston soups
        giving rum running families
stiff back aches
so that they were no longer able to sit
at the elbows of the president
with turkey muskets   or/ sit
on their behinds watching the boat races
off Massachusetts through field glasses but/
how they found their duck pants
    pulled off in the get-back-in-the-alleys
    of the world and/
how they were routed by the people
    spitting into their palms
    just waiting to use those lobster pinchers
    or smash that martini glass and/
how they warned him
        and gave him a chance
    with no behind the back dillinger
    killing by flat headed dicks but/
how they held megaphones
        in their fists
    saying   come out with your hands up and/
how refusing to believe the jig was up
    he accused them
        of apocalyptic barking
    saying out of the corner of his mouth
    come in and get me and/
how they snagged at his khaki legs
    until their mouths were full
    of ankles and calves and/
how they sank their teeth into his swanky jugular
    getting the sweet taste of max factor
    on their tongues and/
how his screams were so loud
    that the skins of eardrums blew off
    and blood trickled
        down the edges of mouths

and people got hip to his aliases/
                              i mean/
democracy and freedom began bouncing
all over the world
                        like bad checks
as people began scratching their heads
and stroking their chins
as his rhetoric stuck in his fat throat
                  while he quoted
men with frills on their wrists
and fake moles on their cheeks
and swans on their snuff boxes
        who sit in Gilbert Stuart's portraits
        talking like baroque clocks/
        who sit talking turkey talk
   to people who say   we don't want
                              to hear it
as they lean over their plows reading Mao
wringing the necks of turkeys
        and making turkey talk gobble
        in upon itself
in Mekong and Danang and Santo Domingo
and

Che Guevara made personal appearances everywhere

Che Guevara in Macy's putting incendiary flowers
on marked down hats   and women
scratching out each other's eyes over ambulances
Che Guevara in Congress putting tnt shavings
in the ink wells   and politicians
tripped over their jowls trying to get away
Che Guevara in small towns and hamlets
where cans jump from the hands of stock clerks
   in flaming super markets/
where skyrocketing devil's food cakes
   contain the teeth of republican bankers/
where the steer of gentleman farmers
   shoot over the moon like beefy missiles
                              while undeveloped people
stand in road shoulders saying
fly Che fly bop   a few for us
        put cement on his feet
        and take him for a ride

O Walt Whitman
visionary of leaking faucets
great grand daddy of drips
   you said I hear america singing
but/ how can you sing when your throat is slit

and O/ how can you see when your head bobs
     in a sewer
in Danang and Mekong and Santo Domingo

and look at them weep for a stiff/
                         i mean
a limp dead hood
Bishops humping their backsides/
folding their hands in front of their noses
forming a human carpet for a zombie
men and women looking like sick dust mops/
   running their busted thumbs
   across whiskey headed guitars/
weeping into the evil smelling carnations
   of Baby Face McNamara
   and Killer Rusk
whose arms are loaded with hijacked rest
in peace wreaths and/
look at them hump this stiff in harlem/
sticking out their lower lips/
and because he two timed them/
     midget manicheans shaking their fists
     in bullet proof telephone booths/
     dialing legbar on long distance
     receiving extra terrestrial sorry
                 wrong number
seeing big nosed black people land in space ships/
seeing swamp gas/
shoving inauthentic fireballs down their throats/
bursting their lungs on existentialist rope skipping/
    look at them mourn/
drop dead egalitarians and CIA polyglots
   crying into their bill folds
   we must love one another or die

while little boys wipe out whole regiments with bamboo
                                  sticks

while wrinkled face mandarins store 17 megatons in Haiku

for people have been holding his death birds
on their wrists and his death birds
make their arms sag with their filthy nests
and his death birds ate their baby's testicles
and they got sick and fed up
with those goddamn birds
and they brought their wrists together and blew/
                               i mean/
puffed their jaws and blew and shooed
   these death birds his way

and he is mourned by
drop dead egalitarians and CIA polyglots and
midget manicheans and Brooks Brothers Black People
    throwing valentines at crackers
      for a few spoons by Kirk's old Maryland engraved/
      for a look at Lassie's purple tongue/
      for a lock of roy roger's hair/
      for a Lawrence Welk champagne bubble

as for me/ like the man said
i'm always glad when the chickens come home to roost

The Feral Pioneers

For Dancer

I rise at 2 a.m. these mornings, to
polish my horns; to see if the killing
has stopped. It is still snowing outside;
it comes down in screaming white
clots.

We sleep on the floor. I popped over
the dog last night & we ate it with
roots & berries.

The night before, lights of a
wounded coyote I found in
the pass.
(The horse froze weeks ago)

Our covered wagons be trapped
in strange caverns of the world.
Our journey, an entry in the thirty-
year old Missourian's '49 Diary.
    'All along the desert road from the
    very start, even the wayside was strewed
    with dead bodies of oxen, mules & horses
    & the stench was horrible.'

America, the mirage of a
naked prospector, with sand
in the throat, crawls thru
the stink.
Will never reach the Seven Cities.
Will lie in ruins of
once great steer.

I return to the cabin's
warmest room; Pope Joan is
still asleep. I lie down, my hands
supporting my head.

In the window, an apparition,
Charles Ives:
tears have pressed white hair
to face.

Instructions to a Princess

For Tim

it is like the plot of an ol
novel. yr mother comes down
from the attic at midnite & tries
on weird hats. i sit in my study
the secret inside me. i deal it
choice pieces of my heart. down
in the village they gossip abt
the new bride.
i have been saving all this
love for you my dear. if my
house burns down, open my face
& you will be amazed.

ASKIA MUHAMMAD TOURÉ (1938–)

Floodtide

For the black tenant farmers of the South

"They carry on.
though sorrows completely
bend them down
they carry on.
though butchered
and maimed
by nature and whitefolks,
*they carry on
and sing their songs.*"

1

drought,
the river is a tricklin' stream.
drought,
dust on the dry tongues
of livestock.
drought,
tobacco leaves
droopin' in the merciless
sunlight.
clear skies, hot and dry.
haze on green mountains.

dustdevils
scaper on the blazin' wind;
drought.
(*lawd,*
we pray for warm soft rain;
for moisture in the fields,
for fat cattle.
lawd,
heah our prayer; rid us
of dis dry spell,
dis merciless heatspell,
dis drought.)

2

black clouds on the horizon.
black clouds over green mountains,
lightnin' on the hills.
baaroom, baaroom,
the rumblin' of thunder,
fills the air,
shakes the ground;
it comes:
lightnin' and thunder,
flash and crash;
it comes:
the violent spatter
of burstin'
clouds.

the rain comes
and washes the green mountains;
floods the cotton land.
the rain comes,
ruins the tobacco

kills the livestock; makin' a mock'ry
of our prayers
for rain.
the killer rain comes:
the river is a ragin' madman
the river breaks our hearts.
the killer rain comes:
the river takes our shack away.
the river breaks our hearts.
the rain;
the drippin', flooded fields.
the rain;
the dead livestock
the rain;
the rumblin' of thunder,
the green mountains,
the ragin' river,
the shack;
the killer rain,
the rain.
the killer rain,
the rain.
the killer rain.

3

silence;
gray mist and heartache,
the flooded land.
now, screams; now, crys of rage.
the wails of women
and children,
the cursin' men.
wetsmells, *deathsmells*
of cattle, pigs,
of bloated men,
of hope,
of fallen dreams.
(*lawd,*
why did yuh cuss us
wit yo' anger?
why did yuh take mah man away?
mah henry,
mah man,
oh lawd!)
churchbells,
the chirpin' of blackbirds,
the sunday air.
the sunlight on the flooded fields,
black throngs gathered,

flowers,
tears for brother henry
and others.

4

monday,
the rooster sounds
his horn:
wake up and live;
cleanup
the flooded land,
the fallen trees, the fields.
rebuild
the shattered homes,
the shattered lives,
the hopes
rebuild
your shattered dreams.

"though sorrows completely
bend them down.
though butchered and maimed
by nature and whitefolks,
they sing their songs,
they sing their songs,
they sing their songs,
and carry on."

Tauhid

For Pharaoh Sanders and the youth of the Black Nation

Reach like you never reached before past Night's somber robes
into the star-crossed plains of Destiny.
Reach with hungry Black minds towards that bright Crescent
    Moon
glowing in the depths of Malcolm's eyes.
Stranded within the coils of this most Evil of centuries,
holy with Change bursting from your spirit's loins,
reach the Sun of Nature's prophets: Ancient Magic
singing us to Love, Eternal Beauty Cosmic Rhythms flowing
in the sound of Pharaoh's horn.
Reach past the death in your mama's religion—centuries lost
in the veil of jewish eyes—into the throbbing heart of
Africa flowing into Mecca, warm undulating blood vibrating
    Truth
implanting JuJu in your mind above the plaster-death of zombies

rotting in the madhouse of the West.

Reach into the Womb of Time, past aeons of chains,
to find your Afro-Soul, that holy part of you connecting Harlem
to the roots of Timbuktu.
In this last great Voyage, walk togetha children, take my hand
Sister-Brother, take my heart my wisdom take, turn this Wheel
to Cosmic Order: Allah's Love vibrating in the Sunrise burning-
ghetto-winds-of-Freedom blowing, Angels calling *Sunrise!*
   Lovers
Warriors *Daybreak!* Dreamers, reach the mountain of your
   Rebirth
in the Whirlwind of our Rising in the West!

JuJu

For John Coltrane, Priest-prophet
of the Black Nation

The Opening
(From the Chronicle)

". . . and They were there in the City of Fire, enflamed,
Their souls burnin' and a'thirstin' for the Light—
the Rain, the Water of the Soul, extinguished by
the Long Whiplash of the Dead.
And They cried out to God to deliver them, or send
a bit of Light from Eternity to let Them know that
He really cared, still cared.
So He sent Geniuses, Magic Men of Old:
Scientists and Prophets, Scholars and Sages,
Philosophers and Myth-making Priests.
Garvey and DuBois, Langston and Booker T.,
Bessie and Satchmo, Bird and Lady Day,
Malcolm and Elijah, Otis and Aretha—
and John Coltrane.
And this Last, this is his Testament, his Requiem, his
dues-payin' Eulogy: John Coltrane . . ."

   The Pain

Tone. Blue skies and flowing fountains.
Flowering spring-trees, trees, away from here now,
this blooming inwardly as the Soul flows and grows
to newer vistas higher than before.

This journey to the Source of love, garden in the core
of life, tone, this ever-aching loneliness or need
to meet the matchless rhythms of the heart.

Take him now heart and soul of Life—essence wonder
blowing wind of love-change and sounds of Blackness
born of Mother Earth.
Tone. Brown and ebon hue shackled with the matchless
chains of Time. Born blood born tone of dripping
screaming sheets of sound, born bleeding with the
dripping wound of Lash and shrieking mindless pain
grown silent with the flow of silent years.

Down trash-blown streets among the tragic mass of shrunken
twisted shells of warriors wine-soaked, dope-bent Blackmen
once proud seed of pulsing loins thrilling to
the touch of Summer rain.

Take him! Take him! to your wombs, to your bosoms
Mothers, Harlem! Africa!—
strong and vibrant with your love.
He Priest Prophet Warrior call and Clarion Call
of essence—US, BLACKNESS—as in Eastern swan-tone
cry of pale towers falling, burning in the bitter
Fires of Change.

Or Eric in Paris, pain growing madly from his genius heart
like strange flowers of our ever-present death.
Death here, death there; they go from us, all giants:
MALCOLM! ERIC! OTIS! LANGSTON!—
now the Prophet Warrior Priest of Blackness: TRANE!
go TRANE go TRANE away in essence of blue-sky tone
hunger Black loneliness of nightdeath calling
through Eastern regions of the Heart:
                            TRANE! TRANE! TRANE!

The Joy

Down vistas of light I hear him call me, my
brother magic piper of
                    Visions of Now.
His horn cascading fountains of blood and bones and stormy
rainbows firedarts purple blue-song tear-stained
channels of love.
Past green beast-eyes and the carnal leer of lust and hate
we wander sad in our soul-song, big as life and warm
as throbbing Earth loamy in the crystal rain of Spring.

We, poet and magic myth-making Giant of Song, wander on.
Holy the bones of our ancestors wrapped in Pyramids
        resting till the end of Time.
Holy the Magi, priests and Myth-scientists of Africa
        for sending him to us.
He with Eternity upon his horn cascading diamonds of Destiny
to our blues-ridden hearts crushed against the Towers
        of the West.
O Magic! to live dynamic in the Soul against the deadly
concrete and steel blaring trumpets—Hell gazing from
        the blue killer-eyes.
Solo   Solo   Solo   for Africanic joys: rhythm thrilling from
the mobile hips of choclit mamas Bird-of-Paradise pagan colors
Joy vibrating from the rat-nests of the West.
And greens and cornbread, sweet potatoes boogalooing
        in the brilliance of his smile.

PRAISE BE TO:
                Africa, Mother of the Sphinx,
who brought our souls back from the Land
                of the Dead.

PRAISE BE TO:
                the Old Ones:
Magi in pyramidal silence who
made the JuJu in our blood outlast
the Frankenstein of the West.

PRAISE BE TO:
                Thutmose and Hermes
    Piankhi and Nefertari
                Songhai
        and Dahomey—
                    Ghana and Benin

laugh with purple gums, nigger lips, shiny teeth
at the resurrection of their seed amid
gunfire in the Harlems of the West.

PRAISE BE TO:
        ALLAH

who brought us Malcolm and Elijah
and reopened Islam like a Flaming Torch
to elevate our souls and send us
soaring to the mountains of the Black World
seeking Paradise.
And through it all the echoes of his horn
blowing Joy thrilling golden fountains Love and Beauty

I'll sink shame
& beat my wings
I've killed fear
& my soul's on fire
I confess
I am armed & prepared
to reproduce the love that made me live
I confess that this beautiful Nigguh is ready.

Initiation

For Denardo

During the season of cut organs we
shot forward like teeth spokes from runaways
a lost cargo of part flesh part ash part
copper & zinc
sucking in names like katanga
like congo
we dissolved our chains
celebrated the slit nose reality of
our severed hands and
at the base of a fifty million skull pyramid
we rehearse life
second headed face circles of
one handed life calling:
blood   blood   blood
and once again blood
where is the land for our blood that drips drips
blood
an arm for the rapist?
a leg for the servant?
No
take us to the place for the new birth blood

PRIMUS ST. JOHN (1939–)

Tyson's Corner

We were as tough as our glasses;
Wires
That bend around packages
As tight as questions;
Sometimes
Too tight, like mistakes we've made.

When the cop said:
All that blood, son, is your father,
To a boy just like us,
We looked over our rims for some mistake—
Any mistake,
But the barber didn't make one.
This time he'd cut
As deep as true feelings.

Ronnie and I were thin then . . .
And sure.
Dracula would never come for us . . .
Not us.
But we made a promise:
        For this blood
        For the whole world's

We made a promise.

The Morning Star

Rumors open up
Way down the road.
The leaves include everything
Like they're really smart.
Then there is an old car
That runs on real red smoke
When the porch goes thump.

Mr. Anderson delivers the Stars
And never has to say anything.

I vote for Mr. Anderson.

Benign Neglect / Mississippi, 1970

Suppose you were dreaming about your family,
And when you woke up
You found a man named Sonny Stanley
Had just shot you (5 times),
Or justice
Looked just like the color your blood was running—
Running wild in the world—
But the world wouldn't see.
Then
You read, somewhere

(I think it's the papers)
If it's a problem, Boy,
We don't have one, here
We don't ask a man to die
Like groceries babbling froth to flies.
But bleeding,
You watch your neighbors
Write away to their windows
       Hide!   Hide!
"He's not there, He's not there."
The last sentence?
The last sentence is your *Father*—
One of the windows . . .
"He's not there, He's not there."

    Goodbye, Johnny

Elephant Rock

We take place in what we believe.
I've memorized that
      Because
It's life
      And that
Invisible—
If you're thinking in the dark.

Take
The line we drew
Around Elephant Rock,
      A beginning
That could happen
      Any day
You put your thumb
         Down
That long block
And saw all neighbors
      As trees.

On our side
We kept these
      Possibilities;
      1. Mount up now
      2. Your ten
      3. This country is your trail too

We began to see
Near this rock

What did not look right
In our books,
        That presence
Was enough
And
Anyone who worked
Should be free
        To meet himself—
Sometime.

We called it
Cowboys and Indians
                or
The girls should stay home
It's safe that way.
But every day this
        Mythology
Grew
We'd lose time
And we'd lose.

One day, Jerry said
Believe—
        Go ahead
            Believe.

We tried—
To keep the thin trails,
Old trees,
But there's something wrong
        with America—
If you're Black

Believe—
        Go ahead,
            Believe.

These three were the most creative:
        Breno Jones
        he left five kids,
        and a thin, incredible
        wife.
        Duke
        he was never lucky,
        he just died
            &
        Jerry too,
            "O. D. 'd"
At the feet of Elephant Rock . . .

And because even this is not enough,
   Something else,
Over their heads
That still takes place
   in America.
Old walls
   &
Tall rocks
With that sign
I could never understand—

  JESUS SAVES

Lynching and Burning

Men lean toward the wood.
Hoods crease
Until they find people
Where there used to be hoods.
Instead of a story,
The whole thing becomes a scream
  then time, place, far,
  late in the country,
  alone,
  an old man's farm.
Children we used to call charcoal,
Now they smell that way—deliberately,
And the moon stares at smoke like iced tea.

Daughter,
  Once there was a place we called the earth.
  People lived there. Now we live there . . .

ED ROBERSON (1939–)

othello jones dresses for dinner

no one could have a blacker tail
or whiter tie in contrast on
than me. the face of the evening guests
is some shade earlier than darkness
which is my countenance. i bring

your daughter in the arm of midnight
she knows that i eat orchids with
my fingers. she has seen unnapkined
my whole greedy primitive body.
and she wiped it with her hair
and when i smiled she said how proud
she was that i was always dressed
for dinner. if i sneer in the sheets at night
my tie becomes crooked but do not
be alarmed i am well mannered.

poll

skin that is a closed   curtain.
it is impossible to know.   how
the light is cast.

a mark that is kept   the election determining the race
before the candidate   runs.

darkie is the night is
an old image given color.
the skin is history.the dark horse

mayday

the fly is dying hard
he is dreaming

his back has hit
the underside of heaven

he is a drill
instead of a spade

i am a monkey
man. not a babfoon

.armed for the first
time against the last

kindling floor of your dreaming

from: when thy king is a boy

III poem from benin relief

you   black   out   the   sun

tho   eye   see   clearly   you

come out your pale blue wrap

around   the sky/

so bright   a blind   spot

only the pale bottoms of your feet

whisper   where

you been walking

the clouds   in

the old grandmother's dreaming

hair/

i know where you been.

the ash of lightning shows

above the high heels   your hills

behind the thin rain of your stockings.
i find out where you been
from the shoes that forget/
the meat
of your feet   i love
you   you
been home   been home

blue horses

the cold has put blue horses where lambs were.
and quiet cows that fattened in the night
upon the grass are driven in and stones
wild veined with ice have taken over in

the fields: the moon is chewing on the snow.
and something watching from a stand of pines
has tied off screams into a hanging knot

the road has spent the night of winter clean
of passengers: the thread out of the hills
has helped the naked trees remain in love
on their bare bodies.   the decent leaves unmade.
and nothing warm has passed inside the gate
to say a word against the solid well
nor the bucket cord that does not weave its drink.

there is a man who, if he cried, the hard
rare droppings of the wolves digesting hunger
would tear his grunting eyes: who, if he spoke,
the shrill fillings of dead men's teeth could cut
his gums with silences they know, who lives
nine valleys from the sun, who if he loved—
would simply love and roll from her unnoticed
        by her arriving immigrant bees.

seventh son

those mothers down there off the hill
don't pray to the mother.
saturday is a man's day.
that's who they are.

son when you rise
don't come back here.
you are too light to make it
so dark around here.

god your father one day
or another   another day
the sunday of a friday night
that's who you are.

week without that day.
off, some mothers
has to carry evenings up the hill
to make it   dark.

if the black frog will not ring

1

if the black frog will not ring
        it's the telephone)
i promise   my fingers
for its wart garden afruit with noise
and so much touch the civilization
cannot get its thumbs into its ears.

and it is wrong to go to bed and stay
and it is wrong to stay awake and play
                        you didn't hear it so
again it is wrong
it is always wrong.

the frog's night
is the black night turned over   under covers
from the sun at both noons
the flashes before the eyes, squeezed tight,
are twenty moons   the tightness makes
the ears ring.

and it is wrong not to be home
and it is wrong to be someplace
                    else   an unreached party
or the wrong
address. me always as the wrong

2

exchange.   within the black frog's night
is the brand eyed dog
going from lance to lance to piss
upon the body

the skeletal trees   brittle reeds
the municipal legged insect
of streets   webs together

the will o' wisp of talk
pole to pole to somewhere
somewhere makes the black frog sing

JULIUS LESTER (1939–)

from: In the Time of Revolution

IV

One needs a lyric poet in these
now nights (dawns)
at 27 because revolution
is not
banners unfurling on clear
afternoons,
nor songs
(We Shall Overcome our own
inadequacies Someday,
O Lord.
Have mercy upon us.
Have Mercy upon us.)
heard in the distance.
the heartbeat of
revolution is
women
(in China and Algeria maybe it was different)
knowing that
(yes)
it must be
but in their
woman
(women)
souls
needing to ask him
(who lives only in now)
"do you think she needs a sweater today?"   "Do you
think she has a temperature?" "What's good on t.v. tonight?"
the minutiae of the day
un-
ra-
vels
(in the same way each day because God
rewinds the yarn each night and puts the neatly
wound ball back in your sewing basket each dawn)

and to keep from being
choked in its threads
the woman
(blood in the veins of poets)
needs someone to hold out their
(him)
un-
winds
because
night is
heavy
and as she lies down
it is like a
tombstone and her
bed a
grave dug by him in his
dawn
dawn
dawning of
now.

V

It cannot be
reasoned with,
revolution,
nor even
understood.
It can only be
endured.   (like labor.   Will there
ever be a Lamaze of revolution?)
Not for ideals, commitments
or any of those things
we thought
(at night, before the dawn with tea
and cigarettes and many books).
Revolution is.

VI

One needs a lyric poet in this
now
dawn (nights)
because he lives like the
hawk knowing that
what has been
will always be
and as we
(even he, too)

nail ourselves to
crosses he must be there,
pinioned,
because

atlanta, georgia
november 20, 1966

On the Birth of My Son, Malcolm Coltrane

at the time of the Newark Rebellion July 12, 1967

Even as we kill,
let us
not
forget
that it is only so we may be
more human.

Let our
exaltations not be
for the blood that
flows in the gutters,
but for the
blood that
may more freely flow through our bodies.

We must
kill
in order to live,
but let us never
enjoy the
killing
more than the
new life,
the only reason for the killing.

And if we forget,
then those who come
Afterward
will have to kill us
(will have to kill us)
for the
life that we,
in our killing,
failed
to give them.

Us

For so long
We looked into mirrors and hated what we saw
For so long
We did not dance to the rhythms of our Gods
but writhed on the cross with christ,
drank his blood and were thankful.
For so long
We proclaimed with pride "Je suis français"
Our black skins glistening
and white teeth shining.
For so long
hot combs burned our hair
and our breasts were cinched and hidden from sight.
For so long
we knew not ourselves
or each other
For so long
We saluted a flag not our own
For so long
We sang My Country 'Tis of Thee
For so long
We died in wars not our own.

But
We are reclaiming our
selves
and
Tomorrow
and
Tomorrow
and
Tomorrow
will
undulate
vibrate
and
dance
to the beat of our hearts.

If I am my   If I am my
self,   self
I have no fear.   I cannot be destroyed.

NORMAN HENRY PRITCHARD II
(1939–)

Aswelay

weary was when   coming on a stream
in hidden midst the amberadornment
of   falls   birth   here   near   edge
              aripplingsoundless
leaves   and   eddy   eyes   withtrickling
forest   thighs   in   widenings
youthful   nippling   scenic   creakless

in   this   boundlessvastly   hours   wait
in   gateless   isn't   fleshly   smelling
              muchly as a golden
on   the   crustishunderbrush   of   where
              no one walked were
unwindishrustlings   mustingthoughts
              of illtimed harvests

              and as we lay and as
              welay and as welay
                  andaswelay
              aswelay   aswelay
                  andaswelay

above a bird   watching we knew not
what cause his course of course we
      lay we lay   in the rippling
      soundlessboundlessvastly
              of a firthing
          duty leaving welay
          wanting noughtless

              and then it seemed
          as from the air he left
          the bird who watched
          what would be called
                  a dream

Self

What does the cracker
when in a barrel
>bare
>with dark
>and alone
>and
>beside it
>self

with fear
of being
>uneaten

Gyre's Galax

Sound variegated through beneath lit
Sound variegated through beneath lit
through sound beneath variegated lit
sound variegated through beneath lit

Variegated sound through beneath lit dark
Variegated sound through beneath lit dark
sound variegated through beneath lit
variegated sound through beneath lit dark

Through variegated beneath sound lit
Through variegated beneath sound lit
through beneath lit
through beneath lit
through beneath lit
Thru beneath
Thru beneath
Thru beneath
Thru beneath
Thru beneath lit

Twainly ample of amongst
Twainly ample of amongst
Twainly ample of amongst
in lit black viewly
>viewly
>in viewly
>viewly
>in viewly
>viewly
>in viewly
>viewly

in lit black viewly
in dark to stark
in dark to stark
in dark to stark
in dark to stark
in dark to stark lit

In above beneath
   above beneath lit
   above beneath
   above beneath lit
   above beneath
   above beneath
   above beneath
   above beneath
   above beneath lit

\#

Love

AL YOUNG (1939–)

For Poets

Stay beautiful
but dont stay down underground too long
Dont turn into a mole
or a worm
or a root
or a stone

Come on out into the sunlight
Breathe in trees
Knock out mountains
Commune with snakes
& be the very hero of birds

Dont forget to poke your head up
& blink
Think
Walk all around
Swim upstream

Dont forget to fly

A Dance for Militant Dilettantes

No one's going to read
or take you seriously,
a hip friend advises,
until you start coming down on them
like the black poet you truly are
& ink in lots of black in your poems
soul is not enough
you need real color
shining out of real skin
nappy snaggly afro hair
baby grow up & dig on *that*!

You got to learn to put in about
stone black fists
coming up against white jaws
& red blood splashing
down those fabled wine & urine-
stained hallways
black bombs blasting out real white estate
the sky itself black with what's to come:
final holocaust
the settling up

Dont nobody want no nice nigger no more
these honkies that put out
these books & things
they want an angry splib
a furious nigrah
they dont want no bourgeois woogie
they want them a militant nigger
in a fiji haircut
fresh out of some secret boot camp
with a bad book in one hand
& a molotov cocktail in the other
subject to turn up at one of their conferences
or soirees
& shake the shit out of them

Dance of the Infidels

In memory of Bud Powell

The smooth smell of Manhattan taxis,
Parisian taxis, it doesnt matter, it's
the feeling that modern man is all youve
laid him out to be in those tinglings & rushes;
the simple touch of your ringed fingers
against a functioning piano.

                   The winds of Brooklyn
still mean a lot to me. The way certain chicks
formed themselves & their whole lives around
a few notes, an attitude more than anything
I know about the being out of touch, bumming
nickels & dimes worth of this & that off
him & her here & there—everything but
hither & yon.

            Genius does not grow on trees.

                          I owe
you a million love dollars & so much more than
thank-you for re-writing the touch & taste & smell
of the world for me those city years when I could
very well have fasted on into oblivion.

                        Ive just
been playing the record you made in Paris with Art
Blakey & Lee Morgan. The european audience
is applauding madly. I think of what Ive heard
of Buttercup's flowering on the Left Bank & days
you had no one to speak to. Wayne Shorter is
beautifying the background of sunlight with
children playing in it & shiny convertibles
& sedans parked along the block as I blow.

                   Grass
grows. Negroes. Women walk. The world, in case
youre losing touch again, keeps wanting the same
old thing.

        You gave me some of it; beauty I sought
before I was even aware how much I needed it.

                      I know
this world is terrible & that one must, above all,
hold onto the heart & the hearts of others.

             I love *you*

The Dancer

When white people speak of being uptight
theyre talking about dissolution & deflection
but when black people say uptight
they mean everything's all right.
I'm all right.
The poem brushes gayly past me
on its way toward completion,
things exploding in the background
a new sun
in a new sky
cantaloupes & watermelon for breakfast
in the Flamingo Motel
with cousin Inez
her brown face stretching & tightening
to keep control of the situation,
pretty Indian cheeks
cold black wavelets of hair,
her boyfriend
smiling from his suit.
We discuss concentration camps
& the end of time.
My mustache
wet with cantaloupe juice
would probably singe
faster than the rest of me
like the feathers of a bird over flame
in final solution of
the Amurkan problem.

Ah, Allah,
that thou hast not forsaken me
is proven by the light
playing around the plastic slats
of half-shut venetian blinds
rattling in this room on time
in this hemisphere on fire.
The descendants of slaves
brush their teeth
adorn themselves before mirrors
speak of peace & of living kindness &
touch one another
intuitively & in open understanding.
"It could be the end of the world,"
she says, "they use to didnt be afraid
of us but now that they are

what choice do they have
but to try & kill us?"
but she laughs & I laugh & he laughs
& the calmness in their eyes
reaches me finally
as I dig my spoon into the belly of a melon

Myself When I Am Real

For Charles Mingus

The sun is shining in my backdoor
right now.
               I picture myself thru jewels
the outer brittleness gone as I
fold within always.   Melting.

Love of life is love of God
sustaining all life,
                    sustaining me
when wrong or un-self-righteous
in drunkenness & in peace.

                      He who loves me
is me. I shall return to Him always,
my heart is rain, my brain earth,
but there is only one sun & forever
it shines forth one endless poem
of which my ranting, my whole life
is but breath.

              I long to fade back
into this door of sun forever

The Move Continuing

All beginnings start right here.
The suns & moons of our spirits
keep touching.
I look out the windows at rain
& listen casually to latest developments
of the apocalypse
over the radio
barely unpacked
& hear you shuttling in the backgrounds

from one end of the new apartment
to the other
bumping into boxes of personal belongings
I can barely remember having touched 48 hours ago.
Jazz
a very ancient music
whirls beneficently
into our rented front room,
Coltrane blessing us with a loving presence.
I grow back thru years
to come upon myself
shivering
in my own presence.
That was a long time ago
when the bittersweet world
passed before
(rather than thru)
me
a vibratory collage
of delights
in supercolor.
It wasnt difficult becoming a gypsy.
At one end of the line
there was God
& at the very other end
there is God.
In between
shine all the stars of all the spaces
illuminating everything
to the two tender points
that are your eyes,
the musical instruments
of these strong but gentle black men
glowing in the dark,
the darkness of my own heart
beating its way along
thru all the evenings
that lengthen my skies,
all the stockings
that have ever been rolled down
sadly,
lover & beloved
reaching
to touch one another
at this different time
in this different place
as tho tonight were only the beginning
of all those
yester-
days

Kiss

Mayakovsky was right
the brass of my tuba does blacken
& I oompah & twist down nights
even the best female poets
couldnt brighten with song,
a quiet dog barking distantly
my only excuse for being alive
so late past 12 by taxi
horn & radio in the rain
finally having made it
to the middle of nowhere
toes aching from the walk
but fingers intact & head
quite nicely on some other planet
where there're no tempting images
to soften the Indian in me,
no sudden left turns or halts
on roads not marked for traffic,
my women human beings being human
who touch my body with a silence
more beautiful than poetry

Yes, the Secret Mind Whispers

For Bob Kaufman

Poetry's a tree
forever at your door
neither scratching nor
knocking but everywhere
eager to force its way
into the soft warm room
of your ornery old heart,
     slipping
   its fat pink tongue
      into sensitive linings
   of your weary young ear

A tree bearing blossoms, a flower
surfacing in a canal of blood,
the dream auto with dream motor
that idles eternally but has
no moving parts, no fumes just
fragrances beneficial to breathe

It breathes mystery this tree
    but no more so
  than moons over midnight seas
or the breast of a woman/child
     to whom menstruation's happening
       for the first time

It's the practice of yoga
  on rainy nights in cities,
    the sudden thought of death
     halfway thru dessert, a
  magic wafer you take
   into your mouth
      &
  swallow for dear life

Loneliness

The poet is the dreamer.
He dreams that the clock stops
& 100 angles wandering wild
drift into his chamber
where nothing has been settled

Should he get himself photographed
seated next to a mountain
like Chairman Mao
the real sun flashing golden
off his real eyes
like the light off stones
by oceans?

Give me your perfect hand
& touch me simply with a word,
one distillation of forever

Should he put his white tie on
with his black shirt
& pass himself off as a docile gangster
for the very last time?

The poet's dream is real
down to the last silver bullet

Should he slip again to Funland
in the city & throw dimes down holes
to watch hungry women flicker

one hair at a time
in kodacolor
from sad civilized boxes?

Should he practice magic
on politicians &
cause them to crack their necks
in a laughing fit?

The poet is the dreamer.
He dreams babies asleep in wombs
& counts the wasted sighs
lost in a flake of dusty semen
on a living thigh

Should he dream the end of an order,
the abolition of the slave trade,
the restoration to life
of dead millions
filing daily past time clocks
dutifully gorging themselves
on self-hatred & emptiness?

Should he even dream
an end to loneliness,
the illusion that
we can do without
& have no need
of one another?

It is true that he needs you,
I need you,
I need your pain & magic,
I need you now more than ever
in every form & attitude—
gesturing with a rifle in your hand
starving in some earthly sector
or poised in heavenly meditation
listening to the wind
with the third ear
or staring into forever
with the ever-watchful third eye,
you are needed

The poet is the dreamer &
the poet is himself the dream
& in this dream
he shares your presence

Should he smash down walls
& expose the ignorance
beneath our lying noisiness?

No! No!
the gunshot he fires
up into the silent air
is to awaken

RICHARD W. THOMAS (1939–)

The Worker

My father lies black and hushed
Beneath white hospital sheets
He collapsed at work
His iron left him
Slow and quiet he sank
Meeting the wet concrete floor on his way
The wheels were still turning—they couldn't stop
Red and yellow lights flashing
Gloved hands twisting knobs—they couldn't stop
And as they carried him out
The whirling and buzzing and humming machines
Applauded him
Lapping up his dripping iron
            They couldn't stop

Martyrdom

They've killed you
from the inside, (and.
It's   slowly spread   ing
Out our eyes
into the plates
of your. Children. They plowed
you under (sprinkled your death in)
You/ had no way of knowing.   &
when it crawl
        ed!   Up your spirit, into
your heart
and brain,   Out your mouth and eyes/
They crushed!   You to get at It.   &;
Blamed your death on (IT!

Riots and Rituals

You/
      Refuse to see. Out
eyes   huge   as planets,
heavy with   eternal winks,
                the cliffs
in the distance,
the last friday
         in centuries   of
weekends.   You grew our genocide (flavored Kool-Aid
in basements of your doorless jive)
dollar mind/
             you made
riot our ritual!   You closed the roads. Now dig it!
     Beautiful systems of silences: Millions of silences,
ears turned in, music of your fat gut
in every cat's hut. Dig yourself spreading thin

like the hymen of some pale virgin
in a black forest of her father's victims'

People,   Swelling
     cliffs, cliffs
your immoveable tomb.
& worn out brooms (nubs now)
that you sit back & dig.   Wondering

holes in your skull.   (& talking 'bout passin' a bill.
can a dying roach's spit put out the sun
can a cripple zombie laugh in a dream forgotten/huh?
or drink lightening into stomachs of putty?
Can a vaseline smear over cities
bounce back the bomb
Can we cringe pretty on
   the torture rack?
     Your agricultural cats did the planting,
We just grew/   your feelers didn't signal   you.
     (Jesus' head bashed in   Black Jesus &

your ugly gray feet
roaring gods in his part of us,
trampling daylight   under. & all your children
spilling out wide-eyed digging it!
             Baby, you're
one dumb collective cat!
You're Godless, your   whole bag. Of   wasted noise.
The Pendulum drifts in
like a bomber from   The East.

St. Coltrane
St. Langston
St. Malcolm

At the eternal   Controls.
Watch out/!
                We've got clocks on
our side   (& all the other cats that you've
pimped got clocks too!)
And photographed you
hiding the Body from
                        The Middle Cross
After you'd done
the Holy Brother in   so He
couldn't dig your funny thing (messin' us
around)

We the living! The sign on your forehead
inked in big letters on your
children's souls.   We the living!
crowds of us in every corner
of your   crime
We the living! Millions of fists cliffs wonderings.
Our rituals turned into riots
shall never be cool/
                    until
you do right.   A long while,   baby.

Amen

Night has secreted us
Out of herself
Black against black
Song against song
We travel hard upon the asphalt
Towards ourselves
Humming the tunes of our fathers
Hugging the breath
Blown forth out of our mothers' brown nostrils
We birthed ourselves
We bury ourselves
We cry and curse for selves
Beyond our birthing and burial:
Those who wear the middle skin
We live
Hour upon hour
Thump upon thump
Until we drop into space
Through the funnel of graves

To the New Annex to the Detroit County Jail

City Planners
don't eat greens &
watch the visions of their kids
go blank
                    when the
t.v. maps
don't correspond
to mainstreams of neurotic games. Story: fat men
women. Stomachs, wide eyed huge green
grapes, vines, networks of
roots artificial elevated cliffs. Blue lights
Olives
in cocktails reflect back dan
cing skeletons. Hollow hieroglyphics &
ulcers concerts   donkey?
                    struggling
to know
greens & cornbread neckbone livin'
                        Chapter 2/
                            Colonies

north east & west of the annex
eat greens.   Their kids play in
the sun &
those dirty alleys (dat the s.w. don't dig) are
strong spiritual
peninsulars: Greenhouses   tough vegetation (patrols
of thick skulls hunt from slits in smooth black pyramids)
Street ecology was explained to
anthropologist by
a mama's technological hippism in combatting
traders from the coast
wearing brighter worlds   trying to cop
her young daughters
during the puberty rites in
the hallway.

Life After Death

Everything is, once was not,
or seemed like it,
rushing to some stage of it
self   traveling for sun.
Everything's death lives in the sun

traveling is to get you there   on
time. Sun as a goal above the tree
highest building downtown   biggest pay
check   death is higher
and it lives in the sun. Everybody cries for
the   sun. It is inside, but
nobody can die that high.
We travel for it earning points
for rent on the sun.
And that is the way it suppose to
be in this house of sweat and horizons.

WELTON SMITH (1940–)

interlude

we never spent time in the mountains
planting our blood in the land planting
our blood in the dirt planting our blood
in the air   we never walked together
down Fillmore or Fifth Avenue
down Main Street together
Friend we never sat together as guests
at a friend's table   Friend
we never danced together as men
in a public park   Friend we never
spent long mornings fishing or laughed
laughed falling all down into the dirt
laughed rolling in the dirt   holding
our stomachs laughing rolling   our mouths
wide open   huge fat laughter
our black bodies shaking   Friend
we never laughed like that together

The Beast Section

i don't think it important
to say you murdered malcolm
or that you didn't murder malcolm
i find you vital and powerful
i am aware that you use me
but doesn't everyone
i am comfortable in your house
i am comfortable in your language

i know your mind   i have an interest
in your security. your civilization
compares favorably with any known
your power is incomparable
i understand why you would destroy
the world rather than pass it to lesser
people. i agree completely.
aristotle tells us in the physics
that power and existence are one
all i want is to sit quietly
and read books and earn
my right to exist. come—
i've made you a fantastic dish
you must try it, if not now
very soon.

Strategies

i

catch him coming off the thing after a state of the union
break through all his securities with aikido
aikido a language of peace when words fail me
i make circles inside the slime of his guards
the reduction
by catching him at a moment i choose
is the reduction of security to circles
circles of big black starving eyes against
the eye of the voyeur the calculating
voyeur enthralled by the sight of pain
the pain vibrating in my own eyes—
we are face to face when the guns, the claws,
the guards tear me away
and i let them.
i am a decoy. my brothers who are all dead
shall have slipped into his head and started the long march
to his heart
which they will eat
then vomit.

ii

catch him in his lust
and chop off his brain
encircle him with my dead brothers
in his primary state he is most dangerous
he is reduced to slime and lust uncontaminated
lust and noisy wolves behind his eyes.

we are quiet, do not call it caution,
we are quieted by the language of peace
which some have not forgotten.
we move with peace close to our bodies
the peace aroused by dark eyes
aware of the texture of darkness
that has no counterpart but peace
that reduces all to circles
like circles of harmony in some pieces of music
that reduce all to quiet
when words fail.

LAWRENCE McGAUGH (1940–)

Two Mornings

i

Cold morning   early.
          Blind men 'careful' into the church
                    Across my street—
Angered by the presence of flies
          I spit down a sparrow's head!
The world is so short
                    I'll make nothing of myself today.

ii

Brahms   the passive mother   wakes me.
The day is beautiful!
I'll chase buttercups
      Grow new orders of wisdom
            Relieve alcohols
                  Toast the most terrible adventures!
These people   I pick them from my neck
            Weaving them head pieces   yes . . .
And repair them more than they require!

Young Training

He tells many bad things
He hears everything . . .
Gets it backwards
Talking too much.

No sense makes him—
He doesn't act it . . .
We're not convinced.
Order the whip
He will not talk so much then
And will become wiser.

Doesn't respond to reason
Life changes one—
I've told him that.
It doesn't seem to matter much—
I try to keep him living
He resists . . .
"When shall we three meet again?"

To Children

We were alone and did your life
As close as we could get—
You are neither of us!

Small one
Things happen merely because you are so imaginative—
You shall hear me upside down . . .
Live items more possible then real.
Your cries give my escape another draw-plate
From the last known escape.

LENNOX RAPHAEL (1940–)

Mike 65

(1)

Once up u hurl a stone
            thru the window
But coming up the musulmanos laugh
            thru cactus corners

while Mike 65 looks down on sea sun and stones

            and falls upon the city

where the cacti are hungry   and mosquitoes full
        but coming up the musulmanos laugh
        and Mike 65 looks down on the city

(2)

stone upon stone upon stone the mountains are one
And the bird that dies to the loins   really dies

for the loin is   where the head is
        rested in peace

(3)

Once up yr feet sit
The wind breathes for u
The sun washes yr face

and the musulmanos come   in sandals & whistles
        begging cigarettes
to feed the mad goat   that refuses bread and apple
        as the dog turns
and the goat returns
mad as the game   that climbs mountains
        and plants flags on skeletons

while Mike 65 looks down on the city

(4)

The dead had been dead centuries
The fort never stooped to defend the truth
        the cactus was always sweet
        the children never laughed
        so openly
        and on the way down the jasmins were
        sweet
but the sea lies far and near   out of reach and love
and on the way down the jasmins were sweet

(5)

Mike 65 who cares
Not again   too much
if someone so much as mentions a castle say   SO WHAT
So what, so what!

stay away from hills
that fall upon themselves
in beautiful cities

Surprising then each time the last
But never the end of boasting boasting boasting

Mike 65 to the dozen, a dead bird, the sea, the wind

Surprising then the wind speaks every tongue
                    playing the trees to a harp
and Mike 65 to the dozen
And a bird, the sea, the stones, and the wars lost on the hill

(6)

Examine the flesh
See stone   and more stone

ask yrself: why did the goat refuse bread why the dog afraid why did the bird die
        why did the wars destroy themselves why do people go to hills of
            mourning
Tear the question from the flesh
And be fed like the rest
Tight in the city   where ruins ruin ruins
                                       and the young never grow too old
                                       to die like the yellow bird

Covered with jasmins and dew

(7)

into another sleep   another death
into the clockhand waving   you're UP
ready
And the city becomes whiter   and whiter
to the resting place of white houses & couscous daughters

And the men are hilled in their animals

And the pleasures are twofold and pleasurable

(8)

is mint sweeter than tea
on the far side of the hill
            where mountains fornicate
            and stones attend sorrow

Where Mike 65 is   scratched on the wall
Where the stone is   hurled at the city
Where the dog is   first to turn back
            smoking new dreams

(9)

The musulmanos smile at the mountains
                climbing over the weary   climbers
And the cactus becomes chumbo becomes a prick of evil
                and the stones roll up their sleeves

Where shepherds slept the musulmanos come
with staff with bag, a smile
smiling on cold rock
And dogs bark off their jaws
And children large over mountains

And when the mountain is humbled
        then shall the people pray
                and the stones will confess

And the jasmins will bloom

(10)

there is a fly on every mountain
and it romances the only jasmin   until Mike 65
Returns to the source

And thereafter
                and the fly follows the last traveler
                and takes the traveler to bed
                and seduces the traveler
With sugar and tears

(11)

coming up a stirrup in the sky
going down a dead bird
                and jasmins crisp as butterfly wings
                bathing the dead bird with sweet dreams

as the city spreads into sea river mountain and ruins at our feet

(12)

they were men once   who climbed themselves
            looking down on the city

        spread out like the beautiful lay
    and veiled by mountainous cheeks
        as the harlot returns to her tears

and a heart that like a stallion is broken several places

(13)

       Oh city yr mountains are falling

                         down
And yr dead are buried by moonlight
                            oh city
     yr cemeteries are grave mistakes
And yr houses are christian nomads
                   oh city
Are u filled every morn with the dew   that
       washes the face of the dead
Are u judge for the bird

                       that
       sits in jasmins

(14)

Some stones are firmer than the breast
Some roads shorter than the job

But Mike 65 becomes god to the ruins   and devil in time
And the musulmanos   perched on the brow of the city
              become the mouth
And speak to the bird   praising the jasmins
        and beating their chests

and the bird   seeing a stone fly
asks a lift   and is made whole
as the feet of those who danced on cacti
           and made petard of stones
           and sat in windows
           and caressed the goat
           and fed dogs
And spake to the dew with the voice of the wind
      as the wind replied
      with a mournful dirge
that goes thru one ear of the city   and become ramparts
                     and forts

       as the wind becomes silent
       as the stone that only speaks
When thrown at the dead   by the living dead
             dead as the feet of the climbers
      no longer perched on their fears
no longer at the top   no longer at the top   no longer at the now
no longer a bird   no longer a stone   no longer a voice

alone alone alone   alone as the dead

                    alone as the living dead
          whose jasmins never ripen and love
          whose eyes never see the voice of the hills
                    nor feathers on the stone
that steadies the feet   and quiets the heart
              in a cup of water
              taken with love

(15)

there are thousands of mountains in the sky
    and the mountain range is the magic darkness
and each foot that goes up is pulled down
& rushed to the dunes
dust of the magic darkness

and the falling bird
falls for the stone
and the hand used is used by the stone

and the bird that flies away
                    becomes more beautiful
and the eye that sees its flight   sees
                    everything

          and becomes the city
and as castle keeps hill   so hill keeps bird
          and each stone is smooth

                    smooth
          as the beak of the dead
                    smooth
          as the crust of jasmins

(16)

and Mike 65 is bee to hive
          as bee as honey can be

but if the castle is noised when the night is white
          say   so what
                   so what

and jasmins will never fade for love
and mountains will guard the city

and Mike 65 will be bee to the hive

and stones will not fly to sweet thrushes in the voice
and stones will not fly

JOE JOHNSON (1940–)

Judeebug's Country

Twilight glitters on the fragmented glass.
It condescends to scratch the ancient wall
Casting a fetid shadow in a hallway scented
with murmured conversations . . . loitering with broken
mailboxes ajar on expectant hinges.

The shadows are jarred by Judeebug
A black little . . . A bad little . . . motherfucka
He is the thunder splintering stairs hastening
The tenement's demurring death.
Judeebug, Judeebug, a black little, a bad little . . .
Motherfucka whose world is the block beneath unpadded
U.S. Keds, whose pants a Blumstein special, one dollar
Ninety-eight . . . a dollar ninety-eight plus taxes

      Can't jive the wind   *Can't jive the wind*

The sky a black woman's bosom bursting blues, brooding black

Caddys pass, babies cry, chicken frys
Daddy's choir sings, Michaux's flags wave

Judeebug . . . Judeebug your dreams can't jive the wind!
The sky a soiled cotton swob against indifferent grey . . . Judeebug
They cry over your vacant hands . . . They bathe your wounds
In pity's bourgeois salve
Don't pray, sit, wade, or lay-in, Don't teach him to read
The warped syntax of the white page,
Don't take the note that he holds warm in his throat,
Let him hit: "Oh say can you see" . . . Oh, say can you see!
Judeebug, a bad little, black little—motherfucka
Whose dreams won't jive the wind,
¾ man and the Parthenon is crumblin'

If I Ride This Train

If I ride this train
The long lean road
The weary road with specks of blood that punctuate
Your movement of poverty
The road of fat asses singing joyous hymns to
Life, to love, to lime, to ash
Cracked souls of pimps weep beneath the junkies jagged heel
In the night of the beginning excerpts of blood bless
The feet of the unloved
And if I ride this train when the deal goes down
The baby's pablum eyes will awake with the laughter of
Crocodiles
When the deal goes down and if I ride this train
On my nigger streets warm with neglect flowers will bloom
To greet cement pigeons
Harsh rhythms will repeat themselves to the ear of a blind
Man: Nigger boy, Nigger Man
                                Liv'in hard—Live if can!
If I ride this train I want a hotline to Jesus
I want to dance and draw blood
I want to grin and speak serpents
I want
I wanta' hiss love through my intervenous jungle
Through the trash crowded eye of my quick-soon street
In a full-lipped song
To a junkman
Cut
Cut with a razor
Bleeding tears
When the deal goes down
Black women in Hallelujah white singing blood
                                                soaked shouts
To Daddy Grace and Father "D"
And if I ride this pain
Pain will transduce this train
If I ride this train
Beyond theocratic reservations
My address will be unknown except to god and the
Boogaman.

STERLING PLUMPP (1940–)

I Told Jesus

i told jesus
don't he
be telling them
white folks
nothin (for me)
tell me
cause him
know where
i is
if him need me
i told jesus
i 'preciated
his love
his real concern
for my people
but not (for him)
to git me mad
again
by letting
white folks (tell me)
what they think
he whispered
to them
i told jesus
we black folks
been calling
him long
ain't no answers come!
so i told jesus
to fire
his white messengers
& come find out
for himself . . .

Half Black, Half Blacker

i went down to malcolmland
me come back a man.

me returned with blackness
drippin from my every breath.
i went down to malcolmland
unprepared
but him gave me a grass sack
him told me
to stuff-in all the blackness
i could
him told me
to run as fast as me could
back to blackpeople
back to blackpeople
so me wouldn't lose
all my goodies.

i went down to malcolmland
me come back a man.

me left my knees
& lifted my eyes eastward
& me ran   me ran . . .
malcolm say god black love black
man black heaven black heaven here
me made black
but me hadta run back
thru fire
with a sack of blackness
on my shoulders.
me think i all black, sometimes
me think i half black others
cause me may lose some blackness
tryin to bring it to blackpeople

i go down to malcolmland
me come back a man.

me black when
me think about malcolm, medgar, martin,
fred, bobbies, mark, lumumba . . .
me lose some blackness
when me don't do nothin
ain't me black?
ain't me black?
when
i am in malcolmland
me know me be blacker . . .

Beyond the Nigger

beyond the outstretched hands
of irrationallity
               reaching into festering
brain waves
of white america
            clapping sermons
            rise
from the soul
           sending quick(finger popping
rhythmns
      all through the syncopating
frames
   (say hallelaljah
          way out
             in black
space
free ships
   sail
        weaving
           noiselessly
              forever
untouchable
the soul holds lost keys that know
what the hand took
          and where
              the ships
are going:
      songs stolen in whip
festivities, fastened in labelled weeping,
muzzled in wrapped white death dinners.
death. white hands hide your life. break
the pale fist
      rise out the fingered grave.
get lost
   vanish
      flee
        to the clouding
        darkness. relinquish
all ties with lighted hell.
          die.
          and return
to saving blackness, multihalls hollowed
in sanctifying awareness.

                        black black black
black back back back back
                        upon the self.
the everlasting existence of me made
aware.
        blackness blinding out blue
                                artificial eyeballs
bigots' hands
            gouging out rotting images.
                                night
the black soul cracks the universe.
                        free.

The Living Truth

black history
is a banned epic

a sagasong banished
& burning in homeless homers' souls
like mastubating onions

pharoahs akan kings moslem songsters
& captured carvers whispering

black history
is a banned epic

dubois recruiting scattered dreams
arming refugees with life

wandering all over eternity
snatching still shots
dubois returning condemned lives

to pure glories . . .

ROB PENNY (1940–)

the real people loves one another

the real people loves one another
the rest bees shaming, bees walkin
backwards under the sun.

i remember how she sang

i remember how she sang
sang the blues
on east street
in opelika bama

we left
with our mother
and came to pittsburgh
to our father

blues, oh, how she sang
down in opelika

we dug socials, the turbans,
frankie lymon, the dells,
lavern baker, the el venos

east street, my, how she
could sing those blues

we learned how to snort,
to smoke reefer, to sloe
dance ("Oh, What A Night")
to play, to be slick,
to be catholics

blues, in red earth, how
she sang, gaddamn

and we never got to korea
nor to vietnam

we snort on blackness now
digs cats like malcolm leroi
jones trane stevie wonders
rob williams and sister
betty shabazz

she still sings the blues
and they go to the moon

we are evolutionary lawmakers
        and punishers

down home she steady singing
those gaddamn blues
on east street
in opelika bama

1968

be cool, baby

kneegrows niggas
coloreds coons
splibbs spades

pimp scag tracks
poor disenfranchised
vietnam rayzors

kneegrows niggas
coloreds coons
splibbs spades

baptist malnutrition
moonshine democracy
numbers hoes

kneegrows niggas
coloreds coons
splibbs spades

hate blackwomen
hate blackmen
hate thick lips
hate natural hair
you hate your self

kneegrows niggas
coloreds coons
splibbs spades

see dick, see jane
see spot can jump
syrup and bread

no ownership
no control
no resources
no blackpower, muthafucker

hill harlem hough
birthcontrol pills pig feet
no land no constitution bush

kneegrows niggas
coloreds coons
splibbs spades

be cool, baby

that's why we
ain't got nuthin

and we conquered

and we conquered
       left their tails dragen on ibm cards
           motorola showed us shooten
poison darts into their eyes
          poets in between death & dodgens recorded
  worms snappen mouth gappen creatures fleen from
      their pregnant women

             we split open their skulls & dug
        unnatural matta dissolven in the night

             cracka blood splattered against
       skyscrapers, post office boxes & mellon
         banks

             their bodies broke open with ease
     and chucken hyenas escaped from their bowels
     and the sun fried them like irish brand bacon

           our children turned to us & said

             "umph!   dig it!"

FRED JOHNSON (1940–)

Fire, Hair, Meat and Bone

it must have been a year
when you looked up
for the first time
      your eyes shielded with bone

and fur catching the rain
                         your mouth wide
watching the fiery flash
                    of lightning
the boom
          rolling up through your throat
your scream   jagged
                              shattering trees

it must have taken generations
for you to catch and hold that fire
jumping out of the sky
                    and turn
backing the shag hair
                  growing down your back
                                    to the warmth

there must have been scores of scores
                         lifting themselves
straightening their spines
whiffing the charred meat
kicked by calloused heels
                         onto a fire that spoke
somehow of power   of order
in jumping   leaping stings
that coated
          scorched their minds to reverence

and somehow
               after decades of trying
you stopped your wanderings
quieted your fears
               tamed
the wolf-wild snarling creature
hitched yourself
               to the three-toed
horse animal
found the grasses and reaped the wheat
named your world with guttural grunts
                              that spoke
sounded of years
of a mind   of a body   changing
of you-man   outgrowing caves
                         tunnels of darkness
swinging   crashing
creeping through primeval forests
rushing out
               sprawling amid sun
and rocks so hot
your image would not stand

but danced
           shimmering
your hair curling
        drawing tight
skin toughening
       darkening

it must have taken you-man
an eternity
        eons of gnawing marrow bones
eons
    learning to control your fire
it must have taken an unbroken line of fathers
                and
           fathers
        and
      fathers
  and
      fathers
        and fathers   to me

Arabesque

This is a silence
      all of flowers
      suddenly jumping
      to the futile pawings
           of a breeze
a silence
    of flowers
        moving to dryness
        in this hot breath of august
    breeze-swayed
        and bent almost to the ground
    rising in slow motion
    springing erect
        then tilting
an arabesque
     almost
a music

This is not a season for lovers
    these staccato days of heat
           push at the eyes
           thicken the mind and
           drop down to tie up arms and legs
           slow the heart
men only talk of love now
or rest from loving in this

Immobile world
        hazy-heat construction
                twisting tree   horizon
                tacking black dots of birds
                on a blue gauze sky
this world
      so still
          the shade
              of passing clouds
              crackles in the mind
these flowers
        mime of ballerinas
              silent movement
and stillness
        silent movement
              and stillness
a sudden violent shaking
          a jerking
              whipping bow
and stillness

DE LEON HARRISON (1941–)

The Seed of Nimrod

    the seed of Nimrod
brings forth matter/

    its movement
     & the void

The Room

Lines Parallel

      Traveling

at the speed of light
to disappear
         under vertical
obstacles called walls

Invisible filling (air)
              Not Restricting

My movements

Constant Molecular motion
   I am Told
To give motion to a Stillness

Creases race skyward at given points
to give definite boundaries

I leave through a tear in the Paper
so as Not to disturb the rhythm

Nor realizing that without life
there is no rhythm

Yellow

birds   &   sunlight
a piece for *bird calls , bells*   apprx. time 3 min.
       & *silence*

bells should be light tinkle or chime like to
medium ring

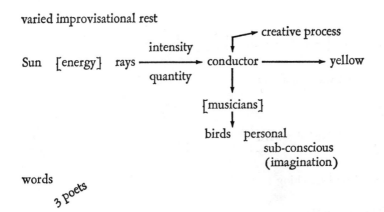

A Collage for Richard Davis—Two Short Forms

Form I

Valley Floors
                         trickling
some god cursed   to spew   slimy
                                                        mouthed
four curdling   streams   flowing   intrinsically
fast fingers
(phantom digits)
snowy pines   frozen ponds   stocking caps
laughing-moaning   building-streaking   slashing
pricking   distorting
autumn winds   browns   reds   yellows
pizzicato lines   double stopping   expiring
strumming quietly

Form II

(silence)

some days / out walking above

some days/out walking above

the sky

between blood/hurled toward
the moon

others are found searching

brighter energy levels
                natural levels
                               cosmic levels
                universal levels

CREATION

CAROL FREEMAN (1941–)

Christmas morning i

Christmas morning i
got up before the others and
ran
naked across the plank
floor into the front
room to see grandmama
sewing a new
button on my last year
ragdoll.

i saw them lynch

i saw them lynch festus whiteside and
all the limp white women with lymphatic greasy eyelids came
to watch silent silent in the dusty burning noon
shifting noiselessly from heavy foot to heavy
foot licking beast lips showing beast teeth in
anticipation of the feast
and they all plodded forward after the
lynching to grab and snatch the choice
pieces, rending them with their bloody teeth crunching on
    his hollow bones.

TOM WEATHERLY (1942–)

Canto 4

gullfish

what is black
in me is not like white
you thot enuf
to say   what we were
brought up to be

our parents we are not.

you no souf carolina gal
tell me i bring no
chocolate to an occupied town . . .
is another war i'm involved
in will do
   speak of my
   self respect
   for myself
no success, the score is
success, the ritual put down
all the blues gone west
mongers of the world unite!

Canto 5

  coon fire

the landscape was
musical cartoons.

tattoo the sound of
blood on my eardrums

taut, the tenses
i were wolfish to dance
dance the half romance
the language

& violence, music to
dance to
violate the progress:

rust at the muscle.

Canto 7

  first thesis

  for m.l.k., jr.

aim get your sights & its sound
in abstract or journal movements
to a peace settlement

old western fancy

dude shot my man

dead,
          precious lord blow off
theres no willy in th blues theres no you.

arroyo

tallest poet for his height
hang up he projectd th body
on th page. jig &
real poems unrolld off his knuckles
in tall black
neighbor hoods
faces down on him
down wif pearly
mother cohen spinning william jim crow
jane in th morning. me tarzan.

imperial thumbprint

this is a white
world dont give damn shit
to me boy. is whether live
or dead black is not
white nor is life or death

neither living nor dying
speak under breath curse the
skin you give man mother
goddamn the street full

outside where there is white
tomorrow is today the black

walk down fifth avenue, hawkbill
in my hand.

first monday scottsboro alabama

they dont hold grudges
bridges that dont know cars
are in this century.
they dont know better to

ride over wooden bridges
wagons from shotgun ridges
bridgeport, paint rock, sand mountain
they ride to county courthouse
square to honest trades of
samplers, plowshares, shotguns
bloodhounds, homebrew & gossip.
they come to buy back issues of time
from north alabama ridges
over bridges sherman didnt burn.

CONYUS (1942–)

san francisco county jail cell b-6

cold grey walls
smeared with yellow gook

damp edges of steel
that border the blackness

a shallow depth of mid night
muffling the crepe sole enforcers

the whistling
of rafters against the wind

icons of men spotting
the caged lions domain

thin shadows wandering
wandering towards the exit;

7 light beams
seen refusing hierarchy

6 popes
kneeling in reference

5 flags
waving at death

4 orderlies
performing chantries

3 nuns
studying dysgenics

2 judges
interlocking loins

1 fool

who thinks he's a poet

upon leaving the parole board hearing

deer feed on
the green slopes
in the
chestnut roam
of evening

spring again
faces me
beneath the bleeding
slash of redwood

trees in bloom
hollow bodies pendant
flowers in the moss

paths of sand
shafts of light
winding in & out
of shadows
to the summit

then descend
to the valley
like evening
ocean mist

clinging
to lost
horizons
i

six ten sixty-nine

coming from the south
pass the ships in dry dock

thick smell of oil
ash flying from the mill

weather worn shacks
filled with fat women

death lots of steel
next to the railroad

we pass through
the heart where men

stand in line
beneath the smoke

of internal social action
like casualties looking

for work in the california dusk

evening beyond the point
where the lighthouse breaks.

untitled requiem for tomorrow

for bob kaufman

there arent
any apparitions
today the room
is full of windows

i put my hand
against the pane
seven times
to touch the cool
interlude

there is
nothing
left

only lean
winds glide
through the
holes

i can see
their motion
gaunt with gestures

the hrs strained
through bone
and marrow

there is nothing
expected nor
leaving

he's doing natural life

for Roy

behind his dinner jacket
smiling at the white wait
ers

revealing his half straight
ass hair in the light so
they wldn't detect his

defection from harlem
or his blk mama

using the right spoon
& fork placing the nap
kin just so that it
caught all the garbage

waving his little finger
behind his coffee cup
like a diploma from fisk

displaying excellent ill
usions of etiquette in the
leather chair with a cigar

between his narrow mustache
& a middle class pouch
dangling over his belt

doing research for the feds
on the negro problem with
subsidized funds from blk

lynching or fumes from birming
ham churches going up in flame

like tidbits of flesh
or pink pacifiers

fed to hungry lions

or eloquent darkies

dining at the white house

DOUGHTRY LONG (1942–)

#4

Where my grandmother lived
there was always sweet potato pie
and thirds on green beans and
songs and words of how we'd
survived it all.
Blackness.
And the wind
a soft lull
in the pecan tree
whispered
Ethiopia
        Ethiopia, Ethiopia
E-th-io-piaaaaa!

Ginger Bread Mama

i love you ginger bread mama
ginger bread mama
                    all sweet and brown
love you
        more than tired boys
love collard greens and candied yams
more than new watermelons
                        do the sun.
before you,
i was older
            and owned a sky of sleep
and not even cowboy dreams
were poets enough to wish me you.

now in brownness warm
everything is everything and
our forms move in soft affirmations.
trying not to wake up the sun.

Negro Dreams

Negro dreams
　　　　in
　　　　　　pastel pants
　　and silk cadillacs
cruise the villages
　　　　　　　of my mind,
　　　　selling
leading roles in the pageants of
their madness
in Rhode Island
and split-levels
　　　　　　to shack with history
　　　　for the night.

One Time Henry Dreamed the Number

one time henry dreamed the number
but we didn't play it,
and do you know, that thing came out straight
3-67?
　　　　yes it did!
we was both sick
for a whole week,
　　　　could'a sure used
　　　　　　　　the money then too.
that was back in hoover's time
when folks was scufflin
to make ends meet.
i knock on wood though
　　　　　　we've lived through it all.
last night after we ate
the last of the meat loaf and greens
and was watching television
henry asked me if i rememberded that,
i told him yes,
　　　　we laughed
　　　　　　then went to bed
and kept each other warm.

F. J. BRYANT, JR. (1942–)

Cathexis

No thing . . .
  no-thing . . .
    nothing.
scratchy army coat, a hat, faint, on the bed end.
fire escape, itchin' chicken pox, pot,
looked in, splashed eyes, lying on couch,
blind,
hurt.

open eyes, walk to door, Mom stuttered,
raining . . .
initialed ring slips, rolls, drops, floats
on stream gurgling along curb into sewer,
gray,
hurt.

Tina, pretty Tina Miles.

venetian blinds, slat raised, David passes,
books under arm. people happy, Christmas tree,
angel hair, people happy, venetian blind, raised
slat, pale lamppost light, muddy brown snow
slushy dark, two gun holster, football helmet,
gray-silk scarf, taken, don't know
who,
hurt.

wide steps, funny smell, lady in white, needle,
funny mark on my arm. room, little
chairs and tables, glass, clay,
paint, paper, funny smell, teacher, cot room,
funny smell, graham crackers, warm milk,
uncle's dark house, riding in car, treetops
whiz, green fence, high, playground.
climb trees, funny smell, the tree top, looking
down, sandy brown color ground, falling,
arm,
hurt.

nurse pulling, arm hurting, screaming for mom,
cast itching, lost; ruler, pencil, twig,
itching,
hurt.

school, 1st grade, cast, abc's tacked on blackboard,
Mrs Hardwood, Geo. Washington's wet pants,
running, running, kissing, running.

Alberta, pretty Alberta Briggs.

school, 2nd grade, Mrs Cotton cried on Mother's Day,
we sang M-O-T-H-E-R, she cried, we
sang,
hurt.

school, 3rd grade, don't remember, why? . . .
school, 4th grade, Mrs Hall, many rulers across
my palm, long stick across backside, for my own good,
sticks,
hurt.

Mrs Land was sexy.

played war, army, baseball.
school, new school, 5th grade, played "chink" with
Leander Wilson, ring worm, Carolyn in my class, told,
talking, high hat biscuits, Sybil, pretty Sybil,
moved,
hurt.

school, new school, 6th grade, new family,
basketball, Venesa, pretty Venesa's light brown eyes,
Ivory Cohen, Stanley, big fat Joyce, big fat Joyce's
big fat family, Billie Smith's pretty sister, Catherine.
cold, safety patrol, Jewish holiday's empty school,
pretty Lois with the big eyes, Darlene, pretty skin.
"Jenny Juice."
Mike called me nigger . . .
I didn't know . . .
nigger,
hurt.

Lois' mother said not to come anymore.
Darlene's father frowned, moved away.
at corner fish store they talk different when I
walk in. playground fun, dances, *Night Owl,*
big chested Mary Jenkins, basketball, cat
family fights, Mike called me,
nigger,
hurt.

DAVID HENDERSON (1942–)

Keep on Pushing

Harlem Rebellion, Summer 1964—A Documentary

The title and excerpts are taken from a hit recording (summer, 1964) by the famous rhythm and blues trio—Curtis Mayfield and the Impressions.

I

Lenox Avenue is a big street
The sidewalks are extra wide—three and four times
   the size of a regular Fifth Avenue or East 34th
   sidewalk—and must be so to contain the
   unemployed
vigiling Negro males,
and police barricades.

The Police Commissioner can
muster five hundred cops in five minutes
He can summon extra
tear-gas bombs/guns/ammunition
within a single call
to a certain general alarm/
For Harlem
reinforcements come from the Bronx
just over the three-borough bridge/
   a shot   a cry   a rumor
can muster five hundred Negroes
from idle and strategic street corners
   bars   stoops   hallways   windows
Keep on pushing.

II

I walk Harlem
I see police eight to a corner
crude mathematics
eight to one
eight for one
I see the white storeowners and the white keepers
and I see the white police force
The white police in the white helmets
and the white proprietors in their white shirts
talk together and
look around.

I see black handymen put to work because of the riots
boarding up smashed storefronts
They use sparkling new nails
The boards are mostly fresh hewn pine
and smell rank fresh.
The pine boards are the nearest Lenox Avenue will
   ever have to trees.
    Phalanxes of police
march   up and down
They are   dispatched   and   gathered   helmet heads
Bobbing white black and blue
They walk around   squadroned and platooned
groups of   six   eight   twelve.
Even in a group
the sparse black cop walks alone
or with a singular
talkative
white buddy.
    Keep on pushing

III

I walk and the children playing frail street games seem
like no other children anywhere
they seem unpopular   foreign
as if in the midst of New York civilization existed
a crytic and closed society.
   Am I in Korea?
I keep expecting to see
companies of camouflage-khakied marines
the Eighth Army
Red Crosses—a giant convoy
Down the narrow peopled streets
jeeps with granite-face military men
marching grim champions of the Free World
Trucks dispensing Hershey bars   Pall Malls
medical equipment
nurses doctors drugs serums to treat
the diseased and the maimed
and from the Harlem River
blasting whistles horns
volleying firebombs against the clouds
the 7th Fleet . . .

    but the prowling Plymouths
   and helmeted outlaws from Queens
   persist.
    Keep On A'Pushing

IV

I see the plump pale butchers pose with their signs:
    "Hog maws 4 pounds for 1 dollar"
  "Pigs ears 7 pounds for 1 dollar"
  "Neckbones   chitterlings   6 pounds for 1"
  Nightclubs,   liquor stores   bars 3, 4, 5 to one block
3 & 4 shots for one dollar
I see police eight to one
    in its entirety Harlem's 2nd law of Thermodynamics
        Helmet
        nightsticks bullets to barehead
        black reinforced shoes to sneaker
Am I in Korea?

V

At night Harlem sings and dances
And as the newspapers say:
they also pour their whiskey on one another's heads.
They dog and slop in the bars
The children monkey in front of Zero's Records Chamber
on 116th and Lenox
They mash potatoes and madison at the Dawn Casino,
Renaissance Ballroom, Rockland Palace, and the Fifth
    Avenue Armory
on 141st and the Harlem River.

—Come out of your windows

dancehalls, bars and grills   Monkey   Dog   in the street
like Martha and the Vandellas
Dog for NBC
The Daily News and *The New York Times*
Dog for Andrew Lyndon Johnson
and shimmy a bit
for "the boys upstate"
and the ones in Mississippi
                    Cause you got soul
                    Everybody knows . . .
                    Keep on Pushin'

VI

This twilight
I sit in Baron's Fish & Chip Shack
Alfonso (the counterman) talks of ammunition
The *Journal-American* in my lap
headlines promise EXCLUSIVE BATTLE PHOTOS

by a daring young photographer they call Mel Finkelstein
through him they insure "The Face of Violence—The
    Most Striking Close-ups"/
WWRL the radio station that serves
the Negro community
tools along on its rhythm n blues vehicle
The colorful unison announcers
declare themselves "The most soulful station in the nation"
Then the lecture series on Democracy comes on
The broadcaster for this series doesn't sound soulful
    (eight to one he's white, representing management)
We Negroes are usually warned of the evils of Communism
and the fruits of Democracy/but this evening he tells us
that/in this troubled time we must keep our heads
and our Law
and our order (and he emphasizes order)
he says violence only hurts (and he emphasizes hurts)
    the cause of freedom and dignity/   He urges the troubled
restless residents of Harlem and Bedford-Stuyvesant to stay in
their homes, mark an end to the tragic and senseless violence
a pause
then he concludes
"Remember
    this is the land of the free"
and a rousing mixed chorus ends with the majestic harmony of
    "AND THE HOME OF THE BRAVE . . ."

Alfonso didn't acknowledge
he hears it every hour on the hour.
The Rhythm n Blues returns
a flaming bottle bursts on Seventh Avenue
and shimmies the fire across the white divider line
helmets
and faces white as the fluorescence of the streets
bob by
Prowl cars speeding wilding wheeling
the loony turns of the modulating demodulating sirens
climb the tenements window by window
Harlem moves in an automatic platform
The red fish lights swirl the gleaming storefronts
there will be no Passover this night
and then again the gunfire high
in the air   death static
    over everything . . .
ripped glass
shards   sirens   gunfire
down towards 116th
   as Jocko scenes radio WWRL

late at night Jocko hustles wine: Italian Swiss Colony Port
sherry and muscatel.   Gypsy Rose and Hombre "The
  Man's Adult Western Wine"
but by day and evening
his raiment for Harlem's head is different
zealous Jocko coos forward
his baroque tongue
snakes like fire

> "*Headache?*
> . . . *take Aspirin*
> *Tension?*
> . . . *take Compōz!*"

Keep on pushin'
Someway somehow
I know we can make it
With just a little bit of soul.

Walk with De Mayor of Harlem

I

enter harlem
to walk from the howling cave
called the "A" train
from columbus circle
                    (find america discovered)
all along a 66 block artillery blitz
                              to the quarter/
          nonstop
          existential TWA nightcoach
rome to auschwitz express
where multitudes vomit   pass out
witness death by many stabbings
upon pompeii/
                please close the doors please
before the madness of washington heights
          disembark   /silent moot   of black vectors
to sunder this quarter
                    thru

black mass
black land

-of rhythm n
                blues & fish of jesus frying across the boardwalk
snake dancers walk mojo along wide boulevards
sight for those
          who live away

a new land!
no dream stuff
   in dem black neon clouds of de full moon
                    to illume by sun-ra
streets just like you
                    no thinking you crazy
vertigo
        under skyscrapers/

II

where harlem lies
            find no industrial green
                                giants
only
     bojangling children in the streets
only
     the sleeping car brotherhood of underground males
only
     the knights of the mystic sea
find only
         the black sapphires
         of the beulah baptist methodist church on the
                                        mount
here
     clustered & cross-purposed

                  *you can take it where you find it
                  or you can leave it like it is*

walk with de mayor of harlem
find no   find no
                 find not
many of the millions
   of the downtown boston blackies
fancy of james bond
in psychedelic robert hall clothing
suitable drape for sawed-off
shotguns
under the trench coat

talk to me   talk to me
                    tell me like it is
the memory   of sky watch
sun dance   drum chant   body-ruba
taut are the signals thru the skin
thru bones
hard as the forgotten legions
of
the giant bushmen

O beaulah baptist in the streets/
to the paradise songs of bloodletting
the gospel singers   are   asayin/
the world is in a troubled time
when
        the knights of the mystic sea
clash
        with the sicilian asphalt paving company
a blood ruckus
                    will ensue
that night
there will be monsoon rains over harlem
black panther bonnevilles prowling
from block to block
helicopters colliding with tenements
                        in orange surprise

They Are Killing All the Young Men

To the Memory and Eternal Spirit of
Malcolm X, 1927–1965, El-Hajj Malik

Television/radio sunday benevolent sundown
malcolm x assassinated
i am watching the tennessee a&i red dog trotting team
            on network tv
and listening to the radio rock n roll
"wide world of sports" track and field event
negroes have long legs
& are accustomed to very yin jungle running/
tv shows all agony of effort
athletes at once ready
they have home worked
bright bulletin precedes event
                    precedes contagion

BULLETIN
        cbs says an unidentified reporter
        phoned in an unverified report
this is a bulletin
malcolm x shot several times in Audubon Ballroom
    (dont negroes meet in the strangest places?)

When john kennedy was iced
there was a vacancy in the air
the FCC decreed strange elevator muzak
on the total radio airwaves of america.

in the hospitals the same muzak
is piped into the rooms of critical patients

no rhythym n blues
no jass
no sass

ray wood
faceless negro cop
invisible man of the black liberation front
his photograph in the new york post
him looking militant arresting the mayor wagner
his brand new photo
back to camera
being decorated
by the new york city police chief
back to camera
page one the new york times
back to camera
so he will not be recognized
back to camera
to limit reprisals
ray wood
faceless negro cop
decorated on tv/promo rookie to lieutenant
ray wood
back to cameras and microphones
Malcolm X chest bared to the audubon ballroom
Malcolm X chest bared out front to the world

a city like new york
has very sophisticated people
many of the rulers of the world
who maintain their position
by a facelessness
an impersonalization
by a coldness
people you would never know
sophisticated men of destruction
men who dress in modern uniform
men who look like any other busy man
men who indulge in modern poisons
and who
in florid elegance
murder

we must give thanks
thank you very much
for governor george wallace
an out front man

to remind us of the north and east
that death to the natives
            (conceived in the most modern of offices)
has a long history
in the nation of america
north and south
birmingham to harlem
current and past
the first slave ship
to the last hog hearse

no jass
no sass

we give thanks
thank you very much
for george washington's birthday
the father of our country's birthday
the father of the american revolution's birthday
only we cannot recall the revolution
all we can remember about the american revolution
is that dreary sunday/monday
when there was no news about the death of our prince malcolm x
because it was the birthday
of george washington
the long weekend
the father
of silent days
of america
the news

no jass
no sass

the long weekend
when the reporters are off
the long weekend
when we can get
sunday news
saturday night

rank and file knowledge
                        Organization of Afro-American Unity
had the Black Muslims and the OAAU
infiltrated by the   fbi   cia   g-men   treasury agency   foreign legion
        as well as the new york city police department
        who took ray wood out of training
        to protect the liberty bell and the statue of liberty
america is an efficient country

if the statue of liberty was so easy to protect
then why not the life of an innocent man?
Malcolm Little, given name.
why not did all the infiltrators go to their bosses
with the news of the plot?
how much overtime pay was paid to the secret police
investigators/   agitators/   infiltrators
the weekend of Malcolm's murder?
the long weekend
of silent days & surmised news
was a sawed-off shotgun missing from the secret police arsenal?

does anyone remember Patrice Lumumba?
does anyone remember the circumstances of *his* murder?
is anyone concerned with the strange deaths of bright
young men?
Lumumba, Kennedy, Malcolm . . .
and the rest   and the rest
the rest

no jass
no sass

white faces pop up
lean with tropical sun tan oil and the decay of racist sugar
modern uniforms
the best technological equipment
sunglasses that adjust to the light
but are no good in the jungle/

the usa is becoming a land of 007s from mass clothing stores
infiltrators from monopolated gas and electric
who pollute rivers and sky with hot black ash
and bomb jungles
because they cannot see in the dark

the new york times is thin on long weekends
the new york post is thin
on george washington's birthday
their sunday editions created friday
their holiday-monday edition
skeleton crew assembled
sunday news saturday night/

the times is thin today
yet they had someone on hand
to write malcolm's obituary
(or else)
they had an obituary prepared for the occasion

one page of new york times
george washington issue

NO JASS   NO SASS

O.O.A. for Malcolm
ballroom gunshots
in neutral washington heights
broadway riverside drive   palisades view and hudson river
just below the world famous indian museum

fusillade to sawed off shotguns close to the chest
Malcolm is over backwards
brothers and sisters
wooden chairs clatter chorus
shots   arms   shouts

the police say
the police say
they are hot on the trail
of the others

today we are told
of the three black scrubwomen
put to work
on malcolm's blood
three black scrubwomen
scrubbing up blood—their blood—
in time for a brooklyn social club dance
that night
              the audubon ballroom must go on . . .

the modern men of the old confederacy
give the evening news
show
black man in black suit
back to camera
line of white collar rings his neck
ray wood
faceless negro cop
personally made detective
by commissioner of police michael murphy
back to camera
lips shut to microphone
ray wood

the secret police must go
on to higher things
white smiles

for the men who saved the statue of liberty and the liberty bell
black suit
back to camera
beaming commissioner . . . a personable man
always in the limelight
the men who murder to save us
no jass
no sass
faceless destruction
back to camera
assassin alleged
of Malcolm x
hands over face
kicked and pummeled
hands over face
kicked and pummeled
hands over face
hands over face
invisible men

winter/spring 1964
revised February 1971

Do Nothing Till You Hear from Me

For Langston Hughes

i arrive   /Langston
the new york times told me when to come
but i attended your funeral
late
by habit of colored folk
and didnt miss a thing

you lie on saint nicholas avenue
between the black ghetto & sugar hill
where slick black limousines await yr body
for the final haul
from neutral santa claus avenue
harlem usa

you are dressed sharp & dark as death
yr cowlick is smooth
like the negro gentleman
in the ebony whiskey ads/
gone is yr puff of face
yr paunch of chest
tho   yr lips are fuller now

especially
on the side
where hazard had you
                    a cigarette/

two sisters
              felines of egypt
vigil yr dead body
one is dressed in a bean picker's brown
the other is an erstwhile gown
of the harlem renaissance/
they chatter
like all the sapphires
of Kingfish's harem/
                    old sisters
                              old relations

in writing the fine details
of yr last production
you would have the black sapphires/there
guardians of yr coffin
                    yr argosy
                              in life & death
the last time blues/
                    with no hesitations . . .

day of the vernal winds/1967

white people

        white
        people
      strange customed
    clan tongued clustering
      dark peopled ports   ages of europa
    trains   boats   and planes
    dionne warwick   says
                         & in
                    new york
          fluid dark causeways
        gangplanked streets
      eerie lights of darkness

clustering natives
                tightly bundled
                europeans of the 400 millennial
                                        race war

```
              fighting peoples of clans & kabalas
axed    gunshot ancestors
stained blood fibers    of cellular centuries
some baked some fried
                         some burned
                                    some blue
```

The Louisiana Weekly #4

```
   a phone duet over the radio
the night
we got our leading lady out of jail
they were talkin about handling niggers
the white folks was
one suggestion:
                    in event of a riot
                    to flood the canals in the negro section/
they probably got the idea
from the last flood/
when the big department stores were threatened
when they had to blow the industrial canal
                                 to siphon some water off
happened to be right near black town the bombs fell
many blacks drowned
others were ferried by private boats
                         for a fee
many blacks drowned
                      the city
                 never did get
          all the names
```

DON L. LEE (1942–)

AWARENESS

```
BLACK      PEOPLE      THINK

PEOPLE     BLACK       PEOPLE

THINK      PEOPLE      THINK

BLACK      PEOPLE      THINK–

THINK      BLACK.
```

Wake-Up Niggers

you ain't part Indian

were
don eagle & gorgeous george
sisters
or did they just
    act that way—
in the ring,
in alleys,
in bedrooms of the future.
      (continuing to take yr/money)
have you ever
heard tonto say:
   "i'm part negro?"
    (in yr/moma's dreams)
the only time
tonto was hip
was when he said:
   "what you mean WE,
    gettum up scout"
& left
that mask man
burning on a stake
   crying for satchel paige
to throw his
balls
back.

&
you followed him niggers—
all of you—
   yes you did,
     i saw ya.
on yr/tip toes
with
roller skates
on yr/knees
   following Him
down the road,
    not up
following Him
that whi
te man with
that
cross on his back.

Assassination

it was wild.
the
bullet hit high.
   (the throat-neck)
& from everywhere:
   the motel, from under bushes and cars,
   from around corners and across streets,
   out of the garbage cans and from rat holes
   in the earth
they came running.
with
guns
drawn
they came running
toward the King—
    all of them
    fast and sure—
as if
the King
was going to fire back.
they came running,
fast and sure,
in the
wrong
direction.

One Sided Shoot-Out

for brothers fred hampton & mark clark, murdered
12/4/69 by chicago police at 4:30 AM while they slept

only a few will really understand:
it won't be yr/mommas or yr/brothers & sisters or even me,
we all think that we do   but we don't.
it's not *new*   and
under all the rhetoric the seriousness is still not serious.
the national rap deliberately continues, "wipe them niggers
  out."
(no talk do it, no talk do it, no talk do it, notalk notalknotalk
  do it)

& we.
running circleround getting caught in our own cobwebs,

in the same old clothes, same old words, just new adjectives.
we will order new buttons & posters with: "remember fred"
    & "rite-on mark."
& yr/pictures will be beautiful & manly with the deeplook/
    the accusing look
to remind us
to remind us that suicide is not black.

the questions will be asked & the answers will be the new
    cliches.
but maybe,
just maybe we'll finally realize that "revolution" to the real-
    world
is international 24 hours a day and that 4:30 AM is like
    12:00 noon,
it's just darker.
but the evil can be seen if u look in the right direction.
were the street lights out?
did they darken their faces in combat?
did they remove their shoes to *creep* softer?
could u not see the whi-te of their eyes,
the whi-te of their deathfaces?
didn't yr/look-out man see them coming,   coming,   coming?
or did they turn into ghostdust and join the night's fog?

it was mean.
& we continue to call them "pigs" and "muthafuckas"
    forgetting what all
black children learn very early: "sticks & stones may break
                    my bones but names can
                    never hurt me."
it was murder.
& we meet to hear the speeches/ the same, the duplicators.
they say that which is expected of them.
to be instructive or constructive is to be unpopular (like: the
    leaders only
sleep when there is a watchingeye)
but they say the right things at the right time, it's like a
    stageshow:
only the entertainers have changed.
we remember bobby hutton.   the same,   the duplicators.

the seeing eye should always see.
the night doesn't stop the stars
& our enemies scope the ways of blackness in three bad shifts
    a day.
in the AM their music becomes deadlier.
this is a game of dirt.

only blackpeople play it fair.

A Poem for A Poet

For brother Mahmood Darweesh

read yr/exile
i had a mother too,
& her death will not be
talked of around the world.
like you,
i live/walk a strange land.
my smiles are real but seldom.

our enemies eat the same bread
and their waste
(there is always waste)
is given to the pigs,
and then they consume the pigs.

Africa still has sun & moon,
has clean grass & water u can see thru;
Africa's people talk to u with their whole faces,
and their speech comes like drumbeats, comes like drumbeats.

our enemies eat the same bread
and the waste from their greed
will darken your sun and hide your moon,
will dirty your grass and mis-use your water.
your people will talk with unchanging eyes
and their speech will be slow & unsure & overquick.

Africa, be yr/own letters
or
all your people will want cars
and there are few roads.
you must eat yr/own food
and that which is left,
continue to share in earnest.

Keep your realmen; yr/sculptors
yr/poets, yr/fathers, yr/musicians, yr/sons, yr/warriors.
Keep your truemen of the darkskin,
a father guides his children,
keep them & they'll return your wisdom,
and
if you must send them,   send them
the way of the Sun
as to make them

blacker.

But He Was Cool

or: he even stopped for green lights

super-cool
ultrablack
a tan/purple
had a beautiful shade.

he had a double-natural
that wd put the sisters to shame.
his dashikis were tailor made
& his beads were imported sea shells
        (from some blk/country i never heard of)
he was triple-hip.

his tikis were hand carved
out of ivory
& came express from the motherland.
he would greet u in swahili
& say good-by in yoruba.
wooooooooooooo-jim he bes so cool & ill tel li gent
                cool-cool is so cool he was un-cooled by
                        other niggers' cool
                cool-cool ultracool was bop-cool/ice box
                        cool so cool cold cool
                his wine didn't have to be cooled, him was
                        air conditioned cool
                cool-cool/real cool made me cool—now
                        ain't that cool
                cool-cool so cool him nick-named refrig-
                        erator.

cool-cool so cool
he didn't know,

after detroit, newark, chicago &c.,
we had to hip
                cool-cool/ super-cool/ real cool
        that
to be black
is
to be
very-hot.

Positives: For Sterling Plumpp

can u walk away from ugly,
will u sample the visions of yr self,
is ugly u? it ain't yr momma, yr woman,
>   the brother who stepped on yr alligator shoes,
>   yr wig wearen believen in Jesus grandmomma, or
>   the honda ridden see-thru jump suit wearen brother.

yeah,
caught u upsidedown jay-walking across europe
to catch badness running against yr self.
didn't u know u were lost brother?
confused hair with blackness
thought u knew it before the knower did,
didn't u know u lost brother?
thought u were bad until u ran up against BAD:
Du Pont, Ford, General Motors   even the latest
Paris fashions: & u goin ta get rich off dashikis before Sears.
didn't u know u were lost brother?

beat laziness back into the outside,
run the mirror of ugliness into its inventors,
will u sample the visions of yr self?
quiet   like the way u do it soft spoken   quiet
quiet   more dangerous than danger a new   quiet
quiet   no name quiet no number quiet pure   quiet
quiet   to pure to purer.

a full-back clean-up man   a black earthmover
my main man
change yr name like the wind
blow in any direction catch righteousness,
u may have ta smile at the big preacher in town,
thats alright organize in the church washroom,
trick the brother into learning—
be as together as a 360 computer:
>   can u think as well as u talk,
>   can u read as well as u drink,
>   can u teach as well as u dress?
sample the new visions of yr work brother   & smile
we'll push DuBois like they push the racing form.

yr woman goin ta look up to u,
yr children goin ta call u hero,
u my main nigger
the somethin like the somethin
u ain't suppose   *to be.*

change-up

change-up,
let's go for ourselves
both cheeks are broken now.
change-up,
move past the corner bar,
let yr/spirit lift u above that quick high.
change-up,
that tooth pick you're sucking on was
once a log.
change-up,
and yr/children will look at u differently
than   we looked at our parents.

We Walk the Way of the New World

1.

we run the dangercourse.
the way of the stocking caps & murray's grease.
(if u is modern u used duke greaseless hair pomade)
jo jo was modern/ an international nigger
            born: jan. 1, 1863 in new york, mississippi.
his momma was mo militant than he was/is
jo jo bes no instant negro
his development took all of 106 years
& he was the first to be stamped "made in USA"
where he arrived bow-legged a curve ahead of the 20th
        century's new weapon: television.
which invented, "how to win and influence people"
& gave jo jo his how/ever look: however u want me.

we discovered that with the right brand of cigarettes
that one, with his best girl,
cd skip thru grassy fields in living color
& in slow-motion: Caution: niggers, cigarette smoking
            will kill u & yr/health.
& that the breakfast of champions is: blackeyed peas & rice.
& that God is dead & Jesus is black and last seen on 63rd
        street in a gold & black dashiki, sitting in a pink
        hog speaking swahili with a pig-latin accent.
& that integration and coalition are synonymous,
& that the only thing that really mattered was:
    who could get the highest on the least or how to expand
    & break one's mind.

in the coming world
new prizes are
to be given
we *ran* the dangercourse.
now, it's a silent walk/a careful eye
jo jo is there
to his mother he is unknown
(she accepted with a newlook: what wd u do if someone
    loved u?)
jo jo is back
& he will catch all the new jo jo's as they wander in & out
and with a fan-like whisper say: you ain't no
                      tourist
                      and Harlem ain't for
                      sight-seeing, brother.

2.

Start with the itch and there will be no scratch. Study
    yourself.
Watch yr/every movement as u skip thru-out the southside of
    chicago.
be hip to yr/actions.

our dreams are realities
traveling the nature-way.
we meet them
at the apex of their utmost
meanings/means;
we walk in cleanliness
down state st/or Fifth Ave.
& wicked apartment buildings shake
as their windows announce our presence
as we jump into the interior
& cut the day's evil away.

We walk in cleanliness
the newness of it all
becomes us
our women listen to us
and learn.
We teach our children thru
our actions.

We'll become owners of the   New World
the New World.
will run it as unowners
for
we will live in it too
& will want to be remembered
as   realpeople.

CAROLYN M. RODGERS

U Name This One

let uh revolution come. uh
state of peace is not known to me
anyway
since i grew uhround in chi town
where
howlin wolf howled in the tavern on 47th st.
and muddy waters made u cry the salty nigger blues,
    where pee wee cut lonnel fuh fuckin wid
    his sistuh and blood baptized the street
    at least twice ev'ry week and judy got
    kicked outa grammar school fuh bein pregnant
    and died tryin to ungrow the seed
        we was all up in there and
        just livin was guerilla warfare, yeah.

let uh revolution come.
couldn't be no action like what
i dun already seen.

Newark, for Now (68)

second-hand sights, like crumpled
mud-smudged postcards
buildings leaning on-towards each
and other, weight of sweat/rocked
bodies, pressing on/out/down
chips of red, blue, black & chalky
rubble that decorate the streets and
nourish hunger-dumb blacklings.

streets. splinters of pavements
lining puddles of dirt. pot-bellied
tubs like giant naked beer cans, frothy with
maggots, packed with rats dining on
last month's french fries.

Newark. 68. and a camel walking breeze
bumps the air with summer perfumes of
piss & hot dogs & eye-talian sausages. But somewhere,

from the lips of the night Sam Cooke's
sweet aria flows, "i know, I know i
know a chaaaaaaanj gonna shur-lee
cooooooom . . ."

We Dance Like Ella Riffs

the room was a
red glow, there was
a warm close pulsating.
Chairs and tables were
                    sprawled like a semi-circle
bowing to the band stand where
                            ripples of light lingered
on the silver tracings of player's
soulpieces and
brightened and glistened and
dazzjangled
like tear drops
in a corner
            suspended
and spit on by the light
                        again and again and oooooh

                        splu dah dee
                        do dah'um dah
                        spleeeeee

the dancers were
soft breezes, smooth
jerky moving
ballooon move the air
no moving was the
wrong moving
roll with the notes
sift through the beats
pause, the music
            sure carelessly careful, caresses cor-recting the air

we are music
sound & motion imitate us
each of us,
Black variations
                on a
Round theme
any one
of us—
an infinite, essential note
                sounding down this world.

Me, in Kulu Se & Karma

it's me
bathed and ashy
smelling down with
                    (revlons aquamarine)
me, with my hair black
and nappy good and rough
as the ground
me sitting in my panties
no bra sitting on my am-vets
sofa with the pillows i stuffed
the red orange gold material i bought
from the little old jew i got lost and found
in new york looking
for the garment district i never found but
found skullcaps lining up the both sides
of the street with stores that make you sneeze it's
me i bought the yellow gold and got the wrong foam
and stuffed it and sewed it but the little pieces
keep coming out but u can sit on it anyway and listen
to pharaoh ring into ur room like now, its me sitting
on the thin thin wrong pillows hearing the trills and
the honey rolling through the air and the gravel rolling and fluting and sweeet sweeeet sweeeeeet and its
me in the sky moving that way going freee where pha
raoh and trane playing in my guts and its me and my
ears forgetting how to listen and just feeling oh
yeah me i am screammmmmming into the box and the box
is screammmmmming back, is slow motion moving sound
through the spaces in the air and oh yeah its me feeling feeling rise, its rise feeling rise feeling feelings rise rise in my throat and feeling throats
my head back and feeling laughs alloverme and feeling
screams mejoy and me flies feelings wild and laugh and
its me oh yeah its me rise feeling its me being music
in kulu se & karma land

Jesus Was Crucified or: It Must Be Deep

(*an epic pome*)

i was sick
and my motha called me
tonight yeah, she did she
sd she was sorri

i was sick, but what
   she wanted tuh tell
me was that i shud pray or
have her (hunky) preacher
pray fuh me, she sd. i
had too much hate in me
she sd u know the way yuh think is
got a lots to do
wid the way u feel, and i
agreed, told her i WAS angry a lot THESE days
and maybe my insides was too and she sd
      why it's somethin wrong wid yo mind girl
that's what it is
              and i sd yes, i was aware a lot
lately and she sd if she had evah known educashun
wouda mad me crazi, she woulda neva sent me to
school (college that is)
she sd the way i worked my fingers to the bone in
this white mans factori to make u a de-cent some-
bodi and here u are actin not like decent folks
        talkin bout hatin white folks & revolution
& such and runnin round wid Negroes
      WHO CURSE IN PUBLIC!!! (she sd)
THEY COMMUNIST GIRL!!! DON'T YUH KNOW
THAT???
    DON'T YUH READ*THE NEWSPAPERS??????
                         (and i sd)
i don't believe—(and she sd) U DON'T BELIEVE IN
                 GOD NO MO DO U?????
u wudn't raised that way! U gon die and go tuh HELL
and i sd i hoped it wudn't be NO HUNKIES there
and she sd
what do u mean, there is some good white people and
some bad ones, just like there is negroes
and i says a had neva seen ONE (wite good that is) but
she sd negroes ain't redi, i knows this and
deep in yo heart you do too and i sd yes u right
negroes ain't readi and she sd
why just the utha day i was in the store and there was
uh negro packin clerk put uh colored woman's ice cream
in her grocery bag widout wun of them "don't melt" bags
    and the colored ladi sd to the colored clerk
"how do u know mah ice cream ain't gon tuh melt befo I
git home."
          clerk sd. "i don't" and took the ice cream
          back out and put it in wun of them "stay hard"
          bags
and me and that ladi sd see, ne-groes don't treat
nobody right why that clerk packin groceries was un
grown main, acted mad. white folks wudn't treat yuh that

way. why when i went tuh the BANK the otha day to de-
posit some MONEY
this white man helped me fast and nice. u gon die girl
and go tuh hell if yuh hate white folks. i sd, me and
my friends could dig it . . . hell, that is
she sd du u pray? i sd sorta when i hear Coltrane and
she sd if yuh read yuh bible it'll show u read genesis
revelation and she couldn't remember the otha chapter
i should read but she sd what was in the bible was
happnin now, fire & all and she sd just cause i didn't
      believe the bible don't make it not true
              (and i sd)
    just cause she believed the bible didn't make it true
and she sd it is it is and deep deep down
in yo heart u know it's true
              (and i sd)
  it must be deeep
she sd i gon pray fuh u tuh be saved. i sd thank yuh
    but befo she hung up my motha sd
    well girl, if yuh need me call me
i hope we don't have to straighten the truth out no mo.
i sd i hoped we didn't too
       (it was 10 P.M. when she called)
she sd, i got tuh go so i can git up early tomorrow
and go tuh the social security board to clarify my
record cause i need my money.
work hard for 30 yrs. and they don't want tuh give me
$28.00 once every two weeks.
     i sd yeah . . .
don't let em nail u wid no technicalities
     git yo checks . . . (then i sd)
   catch yuh later on Jesus, i mean motha!
     it must be
         deeeeep. . . .

EBON (DOOLEY) (1942–)

The Prophet's Warning or Shoot to Kill

it is not enough
that we sing
and dance
and smile.
it is not enough
that we proclaim our beauty . . .

for I have seen

the faces of the enemy.
and they are red,
and white,
and blue.
patriotically evil faces,
bilious
and palely foul!
I have walked the streets
at noon
in the bright glare
of their sun
and watched the dumb,
the lame,
the rich . . .
prospect for hate
in the deep black soil
of america.

and we must Be that hate,
coiled about their hearts
like a striking cobra!
black poisons to fill their veins,
bringing bullet holes
and death
and apple pie!

Query

and when
the cold white ness
is gone;
burned away . . .
leaving only
the soft black mud
of spring . . .

I wonder how will it be?

will we stop
with Love and Lush colors
only,
the sweet scented songs
of victory?

or will we dance beyond
the dream?
moved to the tune
of a different
even Blacker band . . .

The Easter Bunny Blues Or All I Want For Xmas Is The Loop

I   Crucifixion

on the first day,
malcolm
and garvey and nat;
and rufus and betty and sam;
and niehe and jomo and kofi;
and warriors
and kings
and holy men;
were martyred
and murdered
and strung,
like prayer beads,
on a hangman's rope . . .
and hung
on Calvary,
high above chicago.
where their blackest
bloods mingled;
and dripped like rain
from the sagging cross,
to feed
the angry soils below.

II   Laying dead

it was a clear day
and the morning was hot,
and the sun shone
on the cotton fields
and the rose plants
in the city park.

the ground
was still wet,
and in certain places
the steam rose
like factory smoke,
and curled
like a lazy black snake
around the roof tops.

it was the 2nd day,
and chicago was quiet . . . .

except for the sound
of children
playing in the play ground,
and the priest
praying in the attic,
and the death bird
singing in the grave yard,

where shadows and ghosts
of men and angels,
ex slaves and warriors,
were waiting
in the lord's tomb
for sundown,
and the God Child's
chant of anger . . . . .

III   Resurrection

silent rustle
of weeping leaves;
back yard ash cans;
and newspapers adrift
in the alley way;
chicago
sun rise
the morning after . . .

sewer pipes clogged
with the bodies of pale men
and aging girls.
white lice
and gangrene flesh
drifting in the scarlet waters
of the dreary lake.

it's easter sunday,
and God is pleased . . . .

with the glistening streets
and the blistered buildings,
twisted
in agonies of death
and despair;

with the candy striped bodies,
rotting
where they lie,
and laying
where they were found,
like gaily painted
easter eggs
hidden on the white house lawn;

with the gleaming shadows,
dancing in the streets
and chanting their hymns
of Peace and Joy.

it's the 3rd day,
and the Lord has risen

and struck
and claimed
his throne,
a black seat
carved
from the midnight,
and placed
above the sun.

WILLIAM J. HARRIS (1942–)

We Live in a Cage

We live in a cage.
We demand drapes.
It is a matter of our dignity.

They say they don't have any
and anyway they are not allowed.
Privacy is obsolete.

We say all right but we have the right
to answer the phone
nude. We pay our bills.

They say when we answer
the phone, we must
wear robes no shorter than 2 inches

above the knee.
It is simply
a matter of decency.

We say all right but we have the right
to make love
without the aid of the neighbors.

They say we have no rights
and threaten to take our cage
away from us.

Why Would I Want

Why would I want
to be in the distant hills
fighting in the revolution?
When I can lie
with you,
in our beautiful room.

For Bill Hawkins, a Black Militant

Night, I know you are powerful and artistic
                    in your misspellings.
How distinctively I sense your brooding,
feel your warm breath against my face,
hear your laughter—not cruel only amused
                    and arrogant: young—
insisting on my guilt.
Night, let me be part of you
                    but in my own dark way.

A Grandfather Poem

A grandfather poem
must use words of great dignity.

It can not
contain words like:
Ubangi
rolling pin
popsicle,

but words like:
Supreme Court
graceful
wise.

Practical Concerns

From a distance, I watch
a man digging a hole with a machine.
I go closer.
The hole is deep and narrow.
At the bottom is a bird.

I ask the ditchdigger if I may climb down
and ask the bird a question.
He says, why sure.

It's nice and cool in the ditch.
The bird and I talk about singing.
Very little about technique.

S. E. ANDERSON (1943–)

The Sound of Afroamerican History Chapt I

the history of blacklife is put down in the motions
of mouths and black hands with fingering lips
and puckered ravenfingers bluesing the air of
today and eeking out the workgrunts getting down
to earth the nittygritty i mean they mean:
you dig and if you don't don't you worry pretty
momma we all feel dat way anyway and sister
it's a pity whitey done this to us but I love you
and my history says whitey ain't shit and should
be flushed but poppa and momma may have the 'ligion
but god don't mean a thing baby when you got no bread
or a bed and a bad head blinding you with blackblues
of gospel bashing out of bigblack sisters' lips
spiritually into the bop and now the avantgarde jazz
of a hard shepp and backblues looking over hunched
hardworked shoulders into the sepia polyrythmic soil:
lord lord we done come far and still ain't nowhere near
even with long nappy hair and talk of rev'lution . . .

jumpin with my bro. you know out there in dolphyland
or baby maybe into that sun-ra shit/beautiful but bars
are 8 & 12 like dinah and luther king diggin malcolm
shinin in my front door sweet momma keeping kisses for
my high with fontella takin care of much business in the
rhythm of the blues

The Sound of Afroamerican History Chapt II

smith at the organ is like an anvil being
struck in time at a bach fugue at riverside
and riverside jazzsides are testimonials to other
organjazzers still leaping in black minds every day
is billy holiday: god blessin the chile dat got his
own silver and song for my fathers: du bois vesey
cinquez and garvey with ears soulfully singing from
sound of blues and rhythm of mary wells and martha
soloin with her vital vandellas subtly sayin:
remember the danger of heartbreak ahead if you are
givin more than you can get: that's why there was dancin
in the streets of ghettoes where daily black ears hear
james brown singing from somewhere on a lonely
cottonwhite plantation leaving impressions upon your mind
making you writhe to 'tunji and afrosounds that allow odetta to
meet makeba in a groovy thing that we call together and very
soulclean like mcclean and parker catchin hell in new orleans
back in the twenties when domino was not a theory but fat and
ragtime meant ragged black musicians creating the blues and
weaving a history that is so uptight and out of sight—our
black sight—that we are not hip to its beauty and weaponlike
use against the mindless monster of the european snows who
muffled jungle drums with j.c.'s holy hands and put us here
misplaced with ecumenical chants which became agonyharmony
becoming furious bitter rising up sounds

Junglegrave

Send me no flowers, for they will die before they leave America
Send me home, no matter how far strewn I am across this
rice-filled land
Send me home, man, send me home   even if I am headless
or faceless
keep my casket open and my grave uncovered
for I want to show my brothers that it is their blackskin that
stops them from being as free as whites

That whites see blackskin and say we are the fodder of America
                                                    the Libertine
Send me no flowers, for my grave that I was born in
My Mother died one more death when I was stillborn: alive & black
My Race was still and stagnant with grief of my birth.

Vietnam: land of yellow and black genocide. . . .

Send the President my flowers cremated and scented with the odors
of my brothers' napalmed flesh and my sisters' bombed out skulls

Send me no flowers, man, send me no flowers

QUINCY TROUPE (1943–)

A Sense of Coolness

For Stanley Crouch

Somewhere outside your window
the smell of voices and human love
growing up from the earths freshness;
the odor of ancestors and water
reeds bending the softness
of the blends of evening,
their shadows kissing coolly
dancing currents, the soft feathered
bellies of black swans that float
song-shadows rippling light
over waves of sparkling broken mirrors;
but the savannahs are packed with dogs
that howl at a bloody moon the snakes
have pulled down with fangs of poison

Dirge

it is the endless dance of the dead
that leads us bleeding too the weeping
songs of the living
soundless footsteps cross eons
of space resurrections
too greet you here on this funeral morning
without sun water, without life

here where the wind speaks out
but is not heard, where small flames erupt
but are not felt or seen

& the drums have been silenced but will sing
again the beat of rhythmic dancers
the conch horn does not call but will call again warriors

dancing doo-rags contemplating self murders
pimps thinking only of cadillacs & money
will die in the flames in the gutters

& there is no certainty or guarantee
no contract signed by the Magic Maker
that says
man must reach the twenty-first century

it is the endless soundless dance
of the dead that leads us bleeding
too the pitiful crimes of the living

it is the timeless footsteps
of the soundless that speaks too us
of the ruin of our heritage

In Texas Grass

all along the rail
road tracks of texas
old train cars lay
rusted & overturned
like new african governments
long forgotten by the people
who built & rode them
till they couldnt run no more,
they remind me of old race horses
who ve been put out to pasture
amongst the weeds
rain sleet & snow
till they die, rot away
like photos fading
in grandma s picture book,
of old black men in mississippi/texas
who sit on dilapidated porches,
that fall away
like dead man s skin,

like white peoples eyes,
& on the peeling photos,
old men sit sad-eyed
waiting, waiting for
worm dust, thinking of
the master & his long forgotten
promise of 40 acres & a mule,
& even now, if you pass across
this bleeding flesh ever-
changing landscape,
you will see the fruited
countryside, stretching, stretching,
old black men, & young black men,
sitting on porches
waiting, waiting for rusted
trains in texas grass

For Malcolm Who Walks
in the Eyes of Our Children

He had been coming a very long time,
had been here many times before
in the flesh of other persons
in the spirit of other gods

His eyes had seen flesh turned too stone,
had seen stone turned too flesh
had swam within the minds
of a billion great heroes,

had walked amongst builders
of nations, of the Sphinx, had built
with his own hands those nations,

had come flying across time a cosmic spirit,
an idea, a thought wave transcending
flesh fusion spirit of all centuries,
had come soaring like a sky break

above ominous clouds of sulphur
in a stride so enormous it spanned
the breadth of a peoples bloodshed,

came singing like Coltrane breathing life
into stone statues formed from lies

Malcolm, flaming cosmic spirit who walks
amongst us, we hear your voice
speaking wisdom in the wind,
we see your vision in the life/fires of men,
in our incredible young children
who watch your image
flaming in the sun

Poem for Friends

1.

the earth
is a wonderful
yet morbid place
filled with the complexities
of living
                    seeking death
we come too origins
forks which are wish/bones,
forks that are roads
of indecision
                    and we go
with foot/steps
that are either heavy
or light (depending
upon your weight,
your substance.

we go into light
or darkness (depending
upon the perception
of your vision.

we flounder
we climb, we trip
we fall, we call upon
dead prophets too help us
                            yet
they do not answer us (we hear
instead
the singing in the leaves,
the waves of the oceans pounding.

we see the sheer cliffs
of mountains polished by the storms;
sculptured too Allah's perfection.

we see the advancing age of technology;
of soul-less monsters
eating up natures perfections
we hear wails and screams
                    and sirens howling

but we hear no human voices calling

we sit at the brink of chaos laughing
we idle away time
when there is no time
left too us

we jump out of air/planes
with no parachutes
we praise the foul mad/men
of war; we are pygmalions
in love with bleak stones;

and aphrodite is not here
                    too save us

                    seeking death
we come too origins
which are shaped like wish/bones
forks that are roads
of indecision

and we go upon foot/steps
that are either heavy
or light (depending
upon your weight
your substance
                    we go
down unknown roads
seeking life in an ocean
of pure darkness

2.

journey if you can
too the far poles of the world
there you will find
flocks of sick birds
dying in the blue sea that is sky
you will find
herds of dying animals
huddled together in the snow
against the cold;

but with no touch
of each other
no knowledge of who they are
no love for their space that breathes
no love for what they can be;
they gaze each day eagerly
into seas of light
seeking darkness

3.

the mind is so wide
and wide again
so broad and deep
and deep again

far/down we go
so slow into glow
and there find knowledge;
sad songs of who we are

but go slow Effendi
go slow from here
from everywhere
go slow into sadness
of who we are
go slow into slow dance
of what you are
go slow into beauty
of space and time and distance
measure every breath
that you breathe
for it is precious
it is holy

go free into sun/lit days
fly free like the African ibis
confronting the wind
swim long in the currents of these times
like the dolphin
plunging free through blue waves

and the faces that we see
upon the curl
of the foam
of the fingered blue waters
are the faces of the world;
the sand/stones that are hourglasses
too be deposited upon these shores

they are new seeds
in need of nourishment
in search for love
in need of beauty requesting wisdom;
they are children of the universe
glissando falling
upon these death plated shores
that are reefs
that are varicose veins;
and peeping up
from the shallowness
of these churning red waters
savage rocks filled with bones
islands where all life is banned

4.

we must investigate our bodies
we must investigate our sources of beauty
we must investigate our images;
the parade of decayed heros that we see
that we help too invent
we must probe and descend into life/styles
like surgeons seeking cancer;
we must cut away
with truth's scalpel
all verbose flesh: all diseased portions;
we must fly free and weightless
like a summers breeze
too the nest of truth's sanctuary

5.

and the shell is bursting
from within from without

and in order too go out
we must come in
so come in come in
go out go out
                go out there now Effendi
too the sweet places
where the good folks gather
talk too everyone
for everyone is someone
whose life is important
too someone too everyone
whose flesh is a/part of your own

universe
for the universe
is a continual cycle
from the sun too the clouds
too the rains feeding the earth
and the green of summers forests
and the blues of the lakes
reflecting the brilliance of the sky
and the blood of the lions pouring
through the songs of man/kind
and the grass yeah the weed
lending depth too our cosmorific visions
that are all
          eye say all
a/part of you
a/part of me
and we are but extensions
of this universe's magnificent workings!
but sand/stones on the beaches of chaos
but specks—not even stars!
on the vistas of darkness!

so come in come in
go out go out
be beautiful for all peoples of this world

walk free walk proud walk tall
Effendi
walk back into streets
free streets that are ours
walk back into hours
and years of friendship

go now go now
go now Effendi
do your thang
do our thang
do the righteous thang
your own thang
          for the world
          for the world

too save the world
too save the world
too save our children

too save yourself

NIKKI GIOVANNI (1943–)

Word Poem

(Perhaps Worth Considering)

as things be/come
let's destroy
then we can destroy
what we be/come
let's build
what we become
when we dream

Knoxville, Tennessee

I always like summer
best
you can eat fresh corn
from daddy's garden
and okra
and greens
and cabbage
and lots of
barbecue
and buttermilk
and homemade ice-cream
at the church picnic
and listen to
gospel music
outside
at the church
homecoming
and go to the mountains with
your grandmother
and go barefooted
and be warm
all the time
not only when you go to bed
and sleep

Nikki-Rosa

childhood remembrances are always a drag
if you're Black
you always remember things like living in Woodlawn
with no inside toilet
and if you become famous or something
they never talk about how happy you were to have
your mother
all to yourself and
how good the water felt when you got your bath
from one of those
big tubs that folk in chicago barbecue in
and somehow when you talk about home
it never gets across how much you
understood their feelings
as the whole family attended meetings about Hollydale
and even though you remember
your biographers never understand
your father's pain as he sells his stock
and another dream goes
And though you're poor it isn't poverty that
concerns you
and though they fought a lot
it isn't your father's drinking that makes any difference
but only that everybody is together and you
and your sister have happy birthdays and very good
Christmasses
and I really hope no white person ever has cause
to write about me
because they never understand
Black love is Black wealth and they'll
probably talk about my hard childhood
and never understand that
all the while I was quite happy

The True Import of Present Dialogue, Black vs. Negro

For Peppe, Who Will Ultimately Judge Our Efforts

Nigger
Can you kill
Can you kill
Can a nigger kill
Can a nigger kill a honkie

Can a nigger kill the Man
Can you kill nigger
Huh? nigger can you
kill
Do you know how to draw blood
Can you poison
Can you stab-a-Jew
Can you kill huh? nigger
Can you kill
Can you run a protestant down with your
'68 El Dorado
(that's all they're good for anyway)
Can you kill
Can you piss on a blond head
Can you cut it off
Can you kill
A nigger can die
We ain't got to prove we can die
We got to prove we can kill
They sent us to kill
Japan and Africa
We policed europe
Can you kill
Can you kill a white man
Can you kill the nigger
in you
Can you make your nigger mind
die
Can you kill your nigger mind
And free your black hands to
strangle
Can you kill
Can a nigger kill
Can you shoot straight and
Fire for good measure
Can you splatter their brains in the street
Can you kill them
Can you lure them to bed to kill them
We kill in Viet Nam
for them
We kill for UN & NATO & SEATO & US
And everywhere for all alphabet but
BLACK
Can we learn to kill WHITE for BLACK
Learn to kill niggers
Learn to be Black men

My Poem

i am 25 years old
black female poet
wrote a poem asking
nigger can you kill
if they kill me
it won't stop
the revolution

i have been robbed
it looked like they knew
that i was to be hit
they took my tv
my two rings
my piece of african print
and my two guns
if they take my life
it won't stop
the revolution

my phone is tapped
my mail is opened
they've caused me to turn
on all my old friends
and all my new lovers
if i hate all black
people
and all negroes
it won't stop
the revolution

i'm afraid to tell
my roommate where i'm going
and scared to tell
people if i'm coming
if i sit here
for the rest
of my life
it won't stop
the revolution

if i never write
another poem
or short story
if i flunk out
of grad school

if my car is reclaimed
and my record player
won't play
and if i never see
a peaceful day
or do a meaningful
black thing
it won't stop
the revolution

the revolution
is in the streets
and if i stay on
the 5th floor
it will go on
if i never do
anything
it will go on

Dreams

in my younger years
before i learned
black people aren't
suppose to dream
i wanted to be
a raelet
and say "dr o wn d in my youn tears"
or "tal kin bout tal kin bout"
or marjorie hendricks and grind
all up against the mic
and scream
"baaaaaby nightandday
baaaaaby nightandday"
then as i grew and matured
i became more sensible
and decided i would
settle down
and just become
a sweet inspiration

Poem for Aretha

cause nobody deals with aretha—a mother with four children—having to hit the road
they always say "after she comes
home" but nobody ever says what its like
to get on a plane for a three week tour

the elation of the first couple of audiences the good
feeling of exchange the running on the high
you get from singing good
and loud and long telling the world
what's on your mind

then comes the eighth show on the sixth day the beginning
to smell like the plane or bus the if-you-forget-your toothbrush
in-one-spot-you-can't-brush-until-the-second-show the strangers
pulling at you cause they love you but you having no love
to give back
the singing the same songs night after night day after day
and if you read the gossip columns the rumors that your husband
is only after your fame
the wondering if your children will be glad to see you and maybe
the not caring if they are the scheming to get out
of just one show and go just one place where some doe-doe-dupaduke
won't say "just sing one song, please"

nobody mentions how it feels to become a freak
because you have talent and how
no one gives a damn how you feel
but only cares that aretha franklin is here like maybe that'll
stop:
                    chickens from frying
                    eggs from being laid
                    crackers from hating

and if you say you're lonely or scared or tired how they always
just say "oh come off it" or "did you see
how they loved you did you see huh did you?"
which most likely has nothing to do with you anyway
and i'm not saying aretha shouldn't have talent and i'm certainly
not saying she should quit
singing but as much as i love her i'd vote "yes" to her
doing four concerts a year and staying home or doing whatever
she wants and making records cause it's a shame
the way we are killing her
we eat up artists like there's going to be a famine at the end
of those three minutes when there are in fact an abundance
of talents just waiting lets put some
of the giants away for a while and deal with them like they have
a life to lead

aretha doesn't have to relive billie holiday's life doesn't have
to relive dinah washington's death but who will
stop the pattern

she's more important than her music—if they must be separated—
and they should be separated when she has to pass out before
anyone recognizes she needs
a rest and i say i need
aretha's music
she is undoubtedly the one person who put everyone on
notice
she revived johnny ace and remembered lil green aretha sings
"i say a little prayer" and dionne doesn't
want to hear it anymore
aretha sings "money won't change you"
but james can't sing "respect" the advent
of aretha pulled ray charles from marlboro country
and back into
the blues made nancy wilson
try one more time forced
dionne to make a choice (she opted for the movies)
and diana ross had to get an afro wig pushed every
Black singer into Blackness and negro entertainers
into negroness you couldn't jive
when she said "you make me/feel" the blazers
had to reply "gotta let a man be/a man"
aretha said "when my show was in the lost and found/you came
along to claim it" and joplin said "maybe"
there has been no musician whom her very presence hasn't
affected when humphrey wanted her to campaign she said
"woeman's only hueman"
and he pressured james brown
they removed otis cause the combination was too strong
the impressions had to say "lord have mercy/we're moving
on up"
the Black songs started coming from the singers on stage and the dancers
in the streets
aretha was the riot was the leader if she had said "come
let's do it" it would have been done
temptations say why don't we think about it
                        think about it
                        think about it

Poem for Flora

when she was little
and colored and ugly with short
straightened hair
and a very pretty smile
she went to sunday school to hear
'bout nebuchadnezzar the king
of the jews

and she would listen

shadrach, meshach and abednego in the fire

and she would learn

how god was neither north
nor south east or west
with no color but all
she remembered was that
Sheba was Black and comely

and she would think

i want to be
like that

12 Gates to the City

the white man is
nocturnal that's why
he wants to get to the moon
its his rising sign

he's a vampire see
how he strikes between
dusk and dawn preying
on us day light
comes he has to be back
in his casket or office as
they call them now but
dracula would be quite comfortable

if the cracker were natural then the by
products from his body would grow
natural plants like when we are
buried flowers grow see
the stones that spring up among
their dead

nothing violates nature all
the time and even white
people came south for warmth
when the ice age hit
europe
christians should note that
it was ice water and now
fire cause the cracker is playing
with atomic matches

allah told us all
we need to know when he called
mankind hueman beings just because
they dropped the "e" the concept remains
colored cause we recognize
if we add "s" to hisstory why we ain't
a part of it or put "n" back in
demoncracy and you'll understand
the present system war
is raw any way you look
at it even with a spanish touch
and god is a dog

when the romans started counting
they started with one and went to x
an unknown mathematically speaking
so we know they couldn't deal
with twelve zodiac signs

aquarius died when
they buried atlantis this
is the age of pisces
check it out

Poem of Angela Yvonne Davis

*i wrote this poem because i feel there are very few flowers in this field we so
dishonestly call life. and so few are involved with living but my vibrations
from this woman, angela yvonne davis, are that she wishes to live and that
desire forced her involvement to the point of death. and i listened to roberta
flack sing donny hathaway as he's never been sung saying "you were mine for
only a minute" with all the pain of understanding the minute. and this woman
brought out feelings of hope for us that no one has brought to me since i lost
someone whom i love more than . . . how can i say life when i have continued to live though he too is gone.*

*they are all only ours for a very very brief time though if we move in tune to
time and space we will become a part of them—matter being neither created
nor destroyable. and i watched the death of jimi hendricks and people trying
to say "he was not murdered" and i watched the death of a. d. king and people
trying to say "he was not murdered" and i am watching my own death and
the people saying "it is an accident" and it is, though the accident is not my
death but my life and there are too many of us who feel this way and not
enough who can do what surely must be done. our feeling is used against us all
the time and our feeling is what we must maintain. is there no way out of
this quandary?*

and i think angela yvonne has a love affair with life and she has given herself to that lover so completely that she must be consumed by her. and i thought if i talked with angela yvonne in tones other than the spirits or maybe if i tried to press her spirit between these characters from my typewriter and this paper what would it feel like. i offer in love this poem of angela yvonne davis, spoken as i think she would speak, because she's the other third of me—and some part of you.

i move on feeling and have learned to distrust those who don't
i move in time and space determined by time and space feeling
that all is natural and i am
a part of it and "how could you?" they ask you had everything
but the men who killed the children in birmingham aren't on
the most wanted list and the men who killed schwerner, chaney
and goodman aren't on the most wanted list and the list of names
unlisted could and probably would include most of our "finest
leaders" who are wanted in my estimation for at least serious
questioning so we made a list and listed it

"but you had everything," they said and i asked "quakers?" and i asked
"jews?" and i asked "being sent from home?" my mother told me the world
would one day speak my name then she recently suggested angela yvonne
why don't you take up sports like your brother and i said "i don't run
as well as he" but they told me over and over again "you can have them
all at your feet" though i knew they were at my feet when i was born
and the heavens opened up sending the same streak of lightning through
my mother as through new york when i was arrested

and i saw my sisters and brothers and i heard them tell the young
racists "you can't march with us" and i thought i can't march at all
and i looked at the woman whose face was kissed by night as she said
"angela you shall be free" and i thought i won't be free even if i'm set
loose. the game is set the tragedy written my part is captive
i thought of betty shabazz and the voices who must have said "aren't you
sort of glad its over?" with that stupidity that fails to notice
it will never be over for some of us and our children and our
grandchildren. betty can no more forget that staccato than i the pain
in johnathan's face or the love in george's letters. and i remember
the letter where i asked "why don't you write beverly axelrod and become
rich and famous" and his complete reply

i remember water and sky and paris and wanting someone to be mine
a german? but the world is in love with germans so why not? though
i being the youngest daughter of africa and the sun was rejected
and all the while them saying "isn't she beautiful?" and she being i
thinking "aren't you sick" and i remember wanting to give myself but
nothing being big enough to take me and searching for the right way
to live and seeing the answer understanding the right way to die
though death is as distasteful as the second cigarette in the morning
and don't you understand? i value my life so surely all others must value

theirs and that's the weakness the weak use against us. they so
casually make decisions like who's going to live and who's going to
starve to death and who will be happy or not and they never know
what their life means since theirs lacks meaning and they never
have to try to understand what someone else's life could mean
those guards and policemen who so casually take the only possession
worth possessing and dispense with it like an empty r.c. cola bottle
never understanding the vitality of its contents

and the white boys and girls came with their little erections and i
learned to see but not show feeling and i learned to talk while not
screaming though i would scream if anyone understands that language
and i would reach if there were a substance and Black people say
i went communist and i only and always thought i went and Black people
say "why howard johnson's" but i could think of no other place and Black
people ask 'why didn't i shoot it out?' when i thought i had. and they say
they have no responsibility and i knew they would not rest until my
body was bought out in tiny flabby pieces

the list is long and our basic christianity teaches us to sacrifice
the good to the evil and if the blood is type O positive maybe they
will be satisfied but white people are like any other gods an insatiable
appetite and as long as we sacrifice our delicate to their course we will sacrifice
i mean i started with a clear head cause i felt i should and feeling
is much more than mere emotion though that it is not to be sacrificed
and through it all i was looking for this woman angela yvonne

and i wanted to be harriet tubman who was the first WANTED Black woman
and i wanted to bring myself and us out of the fear and into the Dark
but my helpers trapped me and this i have learned of love—it is harder
to be loved than to love and the responsibilities of letting yourself
be loved are too great and perhaps i shall never love again
cause i would rather need than allow, and what i'm saying is
i have five hours of freedom when i recognized my lovers had decided
and i was free in my mind to say—whatever you do you will not know
what you have done

we walked that october afternoon among the lights and smells of autumn
people and i tried so to hold on. and as i turned 51st street and eighth
and saw, i knew there was nothing more to say so i thought
and i entered the elevator touching the insides as a woman is touched
i looked into the carpet as we were expelled
and entered the key
which would both open and close me
and i thought to them all
to myself just make it easy
on yourself

october 16, 1970

CHARLES LYNCH (1943–)

If We Cannot Live as People

If we cannot live as people,
we will at least try to die like men—*an Attica inmate*

Inspire our sons to seek their man-shadows
gauntleted, spread-eagled, mired in blood
seeping beneath walls six-feet deep
where Attica attacked no Attucks,
but nobly raging brothers
white-washed chronicles shall give
no plaque, no wreath,

no amnesty   for truth massacred
by orderlies of law slinking
along the parapets of hate,
goose-stepping to shatter flesh gasping
at the gate of non-negotiable slaughter.

Black death will not be defined by murder
(ignoble beast that charged through war-zone D).
Illicit blood sanctifies life again, again again again:
generations of Sharpeville, Orangeburg, Attica,
reckoning peoplehood,
shadowing the shadow-men.

Memo

Wednesdays at the bone orchard deliveries
are made. No spade work has to be done. That
comes later. Today we collate body parts
that have been manufractured overseas.
The right package must be sent to the home
folks. But the green plastic bags and manila
name tags are revoked here. If ears and limbs
are intact, then the package is not sealed.
If not, we slide howsoever many
parts there are into the wrapping gently
so they won't jar the hearts of the receivers.
Sometimes the contents are confused to such
an extent that the orchardeers cannot
care where they are sent. But shipment is rarely
refused (we have no bureau of complaint).

When mailings are opened the recipients
may faint and/or put the contents on display.
In a few weeks the owners are forwarded
a sum with which they can do whatever
they may choose: purchase U.S. savings bonds,
use it for a trip abroad, or erect a
memorial they could not once afford.

K. CURTIS LYLE (1944–)

Songs For the Cisco Kid

or singing for the face

we are singing for the face of cisco
and its immutable position of night and long knives
we are singing for cisco and his face
like the spirit come shrieking
                        from the sources of the world
where these eyes rotate against waves of flesh
staggering up out of an ocean, strange and mean
molded on beaches and huge islands of truth

we are singing for the face of cisco crowded
with a people's agony
lacerated beyond
lacerated into a maelstrom
of virgin blood
half-starved and lonely
crawling into a bleeding spring

Songs For the Cisco Kid

or singing

Song #2

Hugeness impressed stupor upon you
In the feral face of a sphinx
The swarming breath of life
Tragically shakes your black mane
As if you were a she-lion
And you look at the profane blond angel
Who loves you notand you love not and who suffers
Because of you and who tired kisses you.
    —"Whore With Iron Gray Eyes," *Dino Campana*

1.

this ship is the ship of butchery and increase
manned by four skid-row christians who will take the measure
of your mother with increasing butchery
who will take the measure of your mother in the morning
of increasing butchery

2.

from the leeward and the windward the cisco kid watches
the bodies of dark stinking men out of dark stinking women
out of the sky and the wind out of october sailed out
of sadness
           and huddled into a deliberate and singular congregation
cunning and climbing drunken into broken and lugubrious vessels

3.

this ship is the ship of butchery and increase
where experience is death and love is transportation
dancing to the other side of pain four dying christians
turn their blood out and spread themselves over the lampshades
of radiant crowbars
the voluntary ignorance of unwed mothers
dancing unbridled and beyond the savage motive of marrow
and red bone
beyond the thirteen bodies of poetic ash beyond the silence
of the cisco kid turning a murderer's sooty flesh
to a hero's silken blackness beyond the sixteenth note
congealing on the edge of a fragmented whore's magic mouth
beyond the sea where we dragged her and showed her the delicate
nature
        of tuna fish
and into the field
where we let her sniff the outside of the poppy

4.

i saw the cisco kid stab four skid-row-christians
and break their last composure with an army
of frenzied ukeleles and drink their blood like a rich oil
like a plum wine like a joyous paint
a transcendent tint copulating on textured canvas
and rattling his bones with youthful laughter he looms
way up high
            then higher still
far far above and beyond benevolence

Sometimes I Go to Camarillo
& Sit in the Lounge

Sometimes   I stare into an awning of spirit
and the prose of her son
burning my eye into a vacuum
of frozen blisters
Sometimes   my face hanging its tongue
half-way between mechanized jawbones
and ancient skullcaps
Sometimes   I-am-viewing the world as
yellow trumpets of starving blues
against a piece of body that used
to hold some Vietnamese mother's breast
or the ultra-high-frequency screams
of some stupid marine with his cold
fingers stumbling down past waistbands
and ending the milk of the life of some
heroic woman
Sometimes   the nature of my sickness
a driving sunflower rain of stone
and seeds onto centipedes
the choral of my brutality
pulling fifty legs from a body
maiming it for life
Sometimes   deep in the animated suspension
of my alconarcotic dreams
I am wishing for an act of holiness
and cleansing
I-am-wishing for an hour of napalm
on ALL Junior Chambers-of-Commerce
Sometimes
I go to Camarillo and sit in the lounge
fascinated
      by
incurable tics   on vacant schizoid cheeks
    I
sit and watch   spastic foam in the trenches
of madmen's mouths
the emptiness   of alienated sound   somehow
passionately colloquial like
truncated elegance   or   reams
      of   poetic potential rolling across
    asylum   floors for the dead heart
      of   emasculates
they (the inmates)   propped in gutters of cafeteria

their (funky)   bowels running thru America's
kitchen ascending minds transcending
the walls of room 305

they (the inmates)   a love conversation of sweet mangoes
to a nation of malarial armies

they (the inmates)   a continuous poem of bird-caged heads
battering-rammed against the
immobile word of corporate prophets

Sometimes   I-am-reading short stories
of Nelson Algren
       or
Pietro Di dinato
       and
ignoring whole epochs
       of
my history

my limbs   painting the grey factories
       of
the world   reds   blues   purple-blacks—
crazy colors for the fleshy segment
       of
my memory bank

my life   l o n g i n g   l o n g i n g
for the women of Dahomey . . . and . . .
their strong thighs . . . blacker . . .
than anthracite warmer than fresh
French bread

Sometimes   late morning's motioning birds
pressing tired headlines of bitter skies
into my forehead
       puritas
water flowing beneath a burning bridge
       of
snowflakes
       and
the nobility of my dead grandfathers' ash

deeper

       deeper still
         till
lost in the interior
       of
God himself

himself   an irrepressible soul-blowing
nuclear heroes
       into
the rivers of time
       and
space

Lacrimas or There Is a Need to Scream

a torrent
of cobalt bullets
smashed into the heart
of the lone ranger, heavily
damaging his dreams
and a fine marching chord
from amon ra
garroted machiavelli's mother, anonymously
dragging her voice to the other side
of her eardrum
and pushing her pupil
to the northeast corner
of her eyeball
and as we close our mouths
over these violent tears
we understand that misery
is a real language
and whether our ageless tears
are soft or loud
introjected into our body
they put us closer to the universe
than a cannabis plant being fertilized
by a soundless crystal
of cocaine

RON WELBURN (1944–)

Avoidances

avoidances
of eyes and a possible word
if we speak
it would be a diversion
of utterances
so with others we make
conversation idle
to fill the time and the place
between us in the same small room
nights fold back over the music
fold back over the dances
the scenes wonders fold back the gestures
opaque interpretations you understand
so it is I who lean against a wall

or sit at its feet
in a quiet groove
letting dense smoke sift into the music
there is a time the heart beats away wishes
before they fester on the drum.

Eulogy for Populations

Any of the several names,
who sit on the hands
they use to speak with—
the fingers' many expressions,
many carved topographies
and perspectives. They walk
into the corners of themself
when we scream . . . about
anything. One (if not the only)
beauty of their souls
is the shadow, dancing.
                              And
as though this culture had
a decrement to it, if to everything
there exists an evil half, a section
wavering like a ghoul (there is
a great possibility that the dead
will be buried with secrets
This scares me.

Cecil County

In the land of God
the dead know god
        as they are
    The Dead / dead
man's god.   Sin.

They've burned their crosses
like property (or primitive nature;
my fathers, bared from shady groved
Bible camps,
            who made then their own
Images from the flames
of crucifix in the hands of aliens;
their own musical gestures
(look at Granny run run / then
Bertha Sam & Junior too;
feelings where those songs bled from)

because of hostile breathing,
and this place crawls a poison
inside.   When you turn
back to religion it too is
now a venom they have justified.

Farmers & little girls' faces on
the roadside; (it is forever too
deeply insidious, the symbol of their worship,
too far gone. They had scared us
run us out track us down, while
our Jesus all these years
keeps them burning out their lives.

CHARLIE COBB (1944–)

Nation

I

In the furrows of the world
the paths of planting
the hoe-trails of our people

Among the cotton white
between the stalks of sticky cane
deep in sweltering diamond holes
in the wash of salty sweat

Inside:

    tobacco roads,
    the shanty towns,
    packed, in ghetto stacks

In jungle bush
and Whitey's kitchens

backs unbend
and bodies stretch

Muscles that made the world begin to flex.

We
would be
what we can do

Engaged in struggle
today and
        yesterday

a
people!
black, yellow, brown
around the world
around the golden sun
We!

can only be
do
from what we are.

II

Our hands have clenched hammers, hoes, and hope

Our backs have broken ground

around
the world

Our cries have crashed through terror
torn nights

Our bodies burnt
        the earth a bitter black

To rise

in
anger.

And I suppose
it
     will come
someday,

this thing
this black I am
that has to battle now

to
be

We will not have to say

someday,

nor fight
for what we are.

We! will be

simply
be,

We.
My children

or
  my
      children's
children

will know

We
   (are of roots
long, strong,
roots) which
grew into the world!

We!

the tree

seeds
we
spread

take root

grow

and my children shall know.

(meanwhile I) Search
words for:

Nation
Strength
People
    (now)

For Sammy Younge

Our roads are ridden
moonlight flights
alone,
       along the nights
where we run hidden
from fingers gripping
finding triggers
finding
niggers
out
of
place,
to put us back
in bleeding black
to spill among the stars;
For we the fools
who want
a place
to piss in peace
can only find
the
alley

winter 1966

To Vietnam

Carpets cover many floors where I come from
but none kiss the sky.

I have never known before
fields that filled the hungry.

I have never stood free to son,
to sun

Wind has never sung song of Nation
in my black face.

Hanoi 1967

"Containing Communism"

i

Banana leaves are burning,
not just the ones on trees;

The ones that roof the homes,
in groves, where pretty girls
giggle at guys;

where the child is cradled.

All
ash.

ii

In this wider, wetter, delta lushland

of grass house villages,

where women
till the fields
with rifles on their backs;

where everyone is children
on buffalo

What I thought was pond
was where a house was bombed
was where the rain had fell
was where the tears. . . .

7 children, 6 dead

is why the women
till the fields
with rifles on their backs
why children on the buffaloes
watch the
sky.

Thanh Hoa Province, D.R.V.
April 1967

BARBARA MAHONE (1944–)

colors for mama

when you show me
that those colors carry
special meaning in your head
i understand. there is
a sickness not your own
that makes it so. each
time you start your colortalk
you speak for me. you speak
for all of us. sanity
is colorblind.

sugarfields

treetalk and windsong are
the language of my mother
her music does not leave me.

let me taste again the cane
the syrup of the earth
sugarfields were once my home.

i would lie down in the fields
and never get up again
(treetalk and windsong
are the language of my mother
sugarfields are my home)

the leaves go on whispering secrets
as the wind blows a tune in the grass
my mother's voice is in the fields
this music cannot leave me.

a poem for positive thinkers

for the first time
i be thinkin
like i be dealin
an i be seein stuff
i didnt never see before.

like i see me
an i see
doin your own thing
is not defiance.
it aint got nothin to do with protest.
i can be me
an it dont have to mean
that i got to show somebody somehow
that im better than they think.
cause
for the first time
i be thinkin
like i be dealin
which means i can just be me.

ALICE WALKER (1944-)

from: Once

i

Green lawn
a picket fence
flowers—
My friend smiles
she had heard
that Southern
jails
were drab.

Looking up I see
a strong arm
raised
the Law
Someone in America
is being
protected
            (from me.)

In the morning
there was
a man in grey
but the sky
was blue.

v

It is true—
I've always loved
the daring
        ones
Like the black young
man
Who tried
to crash
All barriers
at once,
     wanted to
swim
At a white
beach (in Alabama)
Nude.

vii

       I
  never liked
  white folks
    really
     it
happened quite
  suddenly
    one
    day
A pair of
amber
  eyes
   I
  think
  he
  had.

In These Dissenting Times

I shall write of the old men I knew
And the young men
I loved
And of the gold toothed women
Mighty of arm
Who dragged us all
To church.

I

The Old Men Used to Sing

The old men used to sing
And lifted a brother
Carefully
Out the door
I used to think they
Were born
Knowing how to
Gently swing
A casket
They shuffled softly
Eyes dry
          More awkward
With the flowers
Than with the widow
After they'd put the
Body in
And stood around waiting
In their
Brown suits.

II

Winking at a Funeral

Those were the days
Of winking at a
Funeral
Romance blossomed
In the pews
Love signaled
Through the
Hymns
What did we know?

Who smelled the flowers
Slowly fading
Knew the arsonist
Of the church?

III

Women

They were women then
My mama's generation
Husky of voice—Stout of

Step
With fists as well as
Hands
How they battered down
Doors
And ironed
Starched white
Shirts
How they led
Armies
Headragged Generals
Across mined
Fields
Booby-trapped
Ditches
To discover books
Desks
A place for
Us
How they knew what we
Must know
Without knowing a page
Of it
Themselves.

IV

Three Dollars Cash

Three dollars cash
For a pair of catalog shoes
Was what the midwife charged
My mama
For bringing me
"We wasn't so country then," says Mom,
"You being the last one—
And we couldn't, like
We done
When she brought your
Brother
Send her out to the
Pen
And let her pick
Out
A pig."

V

You Had to Go to Funerals

You had to go to funerals
Even if you didn't know the
People
Your Mama always did
Usually your Pa.
In new patent leather shoes
It wasn't so bad
And if it rained
The graves dropped open
And if the sun was shining
You could take some of the
Flowers home
In your pocket
Book. At six and seven
The face in a gray box
Is always your daddy's
Old schoolmate
Mowed down before his
Time.
You don't even ask
After a while
What makes them lie so
Awfully straight
And still. If there's a picture of
Jesus underneath
The coffin lid
You might, during a boring sermon,
Without shouting or anything
Wonder who painted it

And how *he* would like
All eternity to stare
It down.

VI

Uncles

They had broken teeth
And billy club scars
But we didn't notice
Or mind
They were uncles.
It was their job
To come home every summer

From the North
And tell my father
He wasn't no man
And make my mother
Cry and long
For Denver, Jersey City
Philadelphia.
They were uncles.
Who noticed how
Much
They drank
And acted womanish
With they do-rags
We were nieces.
And they were almost
Always good
For a nickel
Sometimes
A dime.

VII

They Take a Little Nip

They take a little nip
Now and then
Do the old folks

Now they've moved to
Town
You'll sometimes
See them sitting
Side by side
On the porch

Straightly
As in church

Or working diligently
Their small
City stand of
Greens

Serenely pulling
Stalks and branches
Up
Leaving all
The weeds.

VIII

Sunday School, *Circa* 1950

"Who made you?" Was always
The question.
The answer was always
"God."
Well, there we stood
Three feet high
Heads bowed
Leaning into
Bosoms.

Now
I no longer recall
The Catechism
Or brood on the Genesis
Of life
No.

I ponder the exchange
Itself
And salvage mostly
The leaning.

D. L. GRAHAM (1944–1970)

tony get the boys

old man / man black man
what do you know about a
molotov cocktail
can you run / can you crawl
can you duck / can you kill
you got no gun
you'll stumble in the dark
can you kill / huh can you kill
don't want no old man going
with me—

where were you when
your daughter cried
on a piece-work-blood-stained
           pallet

were you in that same dark
shack or did you hide somewhere
                    outside

dont pray come sunday
bring bottles gas rags
& cutty sark to help our aim
yeah, help our aim old man
go home

the street lights are on /
tony get the boys

the west ridge is menthol-cool

the west ridge is an old ridge—
a cold dying place,
tired waves swirl beneath
the green torch lady
and death rides the stark gray water-birds
down by the river a cross burns
in perverted truth—
spreading its inverted light;
casting ragged shadows.
as cladded men dance jim crow jigs
amidst children standing
like small tents.

the grain has withered on its stalks—
and drooped with the oleanders—
in a mush-brown-wet-rot
pale bodies writhe in ecstasy—
unmindful of the blood-caked-mud upon their skins—
while their bastard children cower in corners—
and pray for purity to the nadinola gods—

the sands are shifting
the wind is cold today and
there's likely to be hell tomorrow for
the green lady holds only embers

all around, brothers are balled
like ebony chains
whispering truths in a black hue
the black exodus is on . . .
we are going to "step-all the way up" and out of
this menthol scented lie . . .
the cry—"uhuru"

Soul

coltrane must understand how
i feel when i hear
some un-sunned-be-bopp-jazz-man
try

to find the cause of a man's hurt

soul aint nice it's daddy's backache
the blues my mother felt when she
bore me
in a rat-infested-harlem u.s.a.

its . . .
mammas love and daddys hate—
doing it my way
survival motion set to music

LORENZO THOMAS (1944–)

The Subway Witnesses

Who are they to be in their skin,
Flags drip off them
And they appear to the mighty
In dreams of white dope.
Pictures of airplanes over
The Manchukuo hunger
Who could have done this to them
Dreams of the mighty and
Cowled hearts of the awesome
Night created now
Of handsome affairs.
Like the head of the young archery
Instructor as it marries
The fiberglass arch of his
Back; it is beautiful
Or terror to expire in tunnels.
Pick one. Ask who are you
To be frightened   who to see
Bloodshed this once and
Not to be blinded, heroic and aimlessly quick

To revenge. Revenge.
Stupid people, don't sit here
This is the throne of the
Mummy   who walks the reeling night
From front to back
Swinging between its thoughts,
Ecstasies of the dry arms
That enfold you as you stiff—
Would be caught in the new
Arms of your bodies that fear the blade
From the naked bookshops and
Stewed theaters of the approaching
Entrance we make into the
Film of our laughing endurance,
Our hands   icepicks and soft blood
Blood in our pockets.

Onion Bucket

All silence says music will follow
No one acts under any compulsion
Your story so striking and remain unspoken
Floods in the mind. Each one trying now
To instigate the flutter of light in your
Ear. The voice needling the flashy token
Your presence in some room disguised
As the summer of the leaves. Hilltops
Held by the soft words of the running
Wind. What lie do you need more than this
The normal passion. And each thing says
Destroy one another or die. Like a natural
Introducing here on this plane to Europe
The natural. A piece of furniture, smell
Taste some connection to your earth and
"Realize" nothing more than you need
Another view nothing more than you need yourself
Or that is beautiful. Or your luck that speaks.
Lifting its shoulders out the language
Of the streets. Above. The sky worried
Into its own song. Solid rhythm. She stays
Too close for a letter, scared of a telegram
The finger drum express. Impatient blues.
Anxious blues. Her chemical song loud and
Bright in his dimension. This is the world.
The vegetables are walking.

STANLEY CROUCH (1945–)

Blackie Thinks of His Brothers

They rode north
funky & uneducated
to live
& let themselves rest:

I come here
ghuddammit
to make my way,
lazy or not,
to own myself
open the touch
of my fingers

The southern twang covers
my language & I embarrass
others
I never work
but that is
of others' choice

No one knows my virtues
yet tears split
my flesh &
I say I sweat . . .
Fats Waller added
                    up everything
when the joint was jumpin
"Don't give yo
right name no
No NO"

No New Music

In Mississippi
balloons of hunger
blow themselves up
in the bellies of
children on porches
            in slat-thin houses
held up by stilts,

the teeth of mad
men turned to wood
to wood and tarpaper
and holes in the roof
                    "Holy vessel of truth
sail through the night now and save these children
these children whose legs bend bowed under the
bone-wilting fire of rickets"

Black Queen
empty as a raped peanut shell,
lie down beneath your quilt
of roaches and pray for your children
pray to the stars who
spy at night on your poverty
on your husband with his arm
across his eyes
his hands smooth with no money no work nowhere
his eyes tattooed with the
red neck and face
of the devil himself,
his eardrums playing
back the tunes of abuse
the beasts blow through
their corncob pipes . . .
                    No new music

Riding Across John Lee's Finger

For Walter Lowe

1.

The Blues meant Swiss-Up
way back when
then later it meant
another thing,
a change up of tears
from the suppressed loneliness
that glittered from our slick heads
to a more blatant tragedy:
the one we now call a natural,
the Blues billowed and sprouting
over our heads now,
nappy bent turned tears
and a scream for another place
as the maroon pants are replaced
with equally loud African clothes:
Though nobody, still, knows my name.

2.

My name is not from another place
my name is from here now
and if I am a woman
my name may be Future Mae
and if I am a man
my name may be LC or WB
whatever my name is
whatever my way is
it is not from some place else
and I know now with my gold teeth
or the meat hanging from my arms
that makes me look like a huge bird
or my bangs combed all the way to the back of my head
behind Murray's
and I know now, forty years old,
riding a bicycle decorated with roses & white dolls,
know as I do the deacon shuffle in front of the pulpit
know the slow dance, baby, know the slow dance
like a crawlin king snake
raised straight up into a giant
walkin the water if it rains
know right now, slow dance, baby,
know right now
if I stood any taller
the stars would burn my hair off
know right here that I am beautiful.
As if history didn't even exist
and don't need nothin
except how I am:
Cause that's where the future was.
Slow dance, baby:
A timeless state of mind.

Albert Ayler: Eulogy for a Decomposed Saxophone Player

(The saxophone turned into a dolphin
or a flying shark with transparent teeth of fire
behind which the shadows of ghosts could be seen dancing
or a seal spinning sound under the ice
you wore a leather suit
and the metal pipe covered with stemmed buttons
plucked the notes off the music and left the sound.
Don felt fresh wind in his face
Don Cherry did at first hearing you

when we wind back to scandinavia
and the legends begin)

1.   GHOSTS (the national anthem)

Sometimes a saxophone
is a home
twisting dead women
through the air
(You feel the hymn
the old lonely hymn
the hymn we all never would've sung)

2.   SPIRITS REJOICE

And we can step high
And we can step high
and we can high step
and walk away
And we can step high and we can step high and we can high step
                              and walk away
Don't you know that the old black men
now walk across the fields
walking slowly up their deaths
But don't you know that the old black men's
souls shout *high* across the fields

3.   EAST RIVER REFLECTION

But we could never rejoice in the river
only decompose in the dark
the flesh-ringing dumplings in the water of november.
Did the east river bite your heart,
did it bite, Albert,
while exhibitionists,
flipping themselves out,
waved from bridges?
Did the water, that wet cold fist with slobbering ripples for
                                        line of a palm,
did the water make your body look as much like a
sea horse as your saxophone looked like one—
but you though in the scales and stretches of decomposition
Mr. Albert Ayler
the old men's marcher
twisting the voices of dead women through the air
and it is the river
puzzleboard pieces of ice
and no more gray flames of drummer's howls
in the blue background

4. BELLS

> We walk
> We hum
we summon streets
we shout down the streets
we moan down the streets
we kick spit curse and sing
It is never warm now
No days

5. LAST STAND (as the flesh rises & waves away)

And the sharp nails of our notes
become burry picks with which we climb mountains.
Up that mountain of horizontal rungs of air
the chest has to be big to sing any song way up that high—up *there:*
the atmosphere thin with ghosts
weaving through saxophones
and we'll remember, Albert,
as we walk, as we hum,
that you sang up there, playing
the bells—summoning—in a ferocious, a growling,
a honking big-heartedness
before the air was greased
up under the bottom of your feet
and you fell, were pushed, accepting "the river's invitation"
and the water plucked your beard
with its filth and its cans, its garbage,
plucked your beard,
and your flesh
now a slimy brown harpsichord slapped ashore
November 25, 1970.

1970/December 24 to January 24, 1971

CAROLE GREGORY CLEMMONS (1945–)

Spring

the second man I love,
we'll find the wishbone
and make our wishes,
I won't even try for the strongest end,
because this time when the bone breaks
either way I'll be in.

Love from My Father

Left like water in glasses overnight
in a cold house,
iced children are fierce.
They see fathers slobbering, staggering
into the living room chair
and race through his pockets for nickels and quarters.
The cold gives the children pneumonia and sends
red balloons tied to hospital beds, and
a caseworker to turn the heat on.
There are many gifts,
other drunks sleep in thrown paper
and green wine bottles behind billboards
but my father brings fresh glazed donuts in a white bag.

Migration

She stood hanging wash before sun
and occasionally watched the kids
gather acorns from the trees,
and when her husband came,
complaining about the tobacco spit on him
they decided to run North.
for a free evening.
She stood hanging wash in the basement
and saw the kids sneak puffs from cigarettes,
fix steel traps with cheese
and when her husband came,
complaining of the mill's drudgery,
        she burst—
said he had no hunter's heart
beat him with a broom,
became blinded by the orange sun
racing into steel mill flames
and afterwards,
sat singing spirituals to sons.

I'm Just a Stranger Here, Heaven Is My Home

The first sign was your hair,
unstraightened, shortened from worry,
and it had only been a year since the wedding,
but you had grown older, Mama.

I felt your usual care
in the mustard greens, sweet potatoes and chicken,
yet you smelled of whiskey and prayer.
I showed you the pictures,
asked which you'd like remade
and watched you fidget, unable to see them.
Raising your arm, you spoke of your rheumatism,
it seems life left your arm first,
like crumbs given to frontyard robins.
Age and need, those simple weeds,
were gathering around and taking you away.

CALVIN FORBES (1945–)

Reading Walt Whitman

I found his wool face, I went away
A crook; there were lines I followed
When his song like a whistle led me.

Daily my wooden words fell, a parade
Of sticks, a broom bent over a thief's
Head. But then along came Langston

The proper shepherd who sat on history
Missing our music, dividing me; after
His death I rewrote, I robbed, and hid

In a foxhole until my lines were wood
On top, and soft underneath the bark.
Good Langston sat too long to lift me.

Lullaby for Ann-Lucian

My mother sliced the south for us
She divided a poison from the flesh.
And every bite made the farmer laugh.

But your golden parents are oceanic
Touching lands my mother never knew.
A lighthouse keeps you off the rocks.

Shine: though the fruit is foreign
Leave the rind. And don't swallow
The seeds, or you'll wake up a crow.

When an enemy of the harvest arrives
The country children use sling shots.
They recognize his color and his greed.

AUGUST WILSON (1945–)

Theme One: The Variations

I

Life is ours like the real
turning point the moon pointing
the sun becoming the dance
and life is ours and we breathe

lost niggers breathe again holy
niggers breathing out power
where we lie spirited again
where life is ours in our ever
moving breathing the real
in the catechism of the spirit
teaching and believing the dance
the shape the stars the real
nigger hands the real nigger
voice where it screams in life
breathing and opens
into the hands taking lives and life
from the air in harmony
with the moon pointing and
turning Eastward real nigger
hearts holy niggermen black hearts
and there is black love
again finally life is ours
making the real world breathe

II

The same darkness the shapes
you move with them—
the same and they come back
lost in the nigger's voice
in the eyes when you see them
in the holydarkness when you

are with it and love again
you open to your hands
your life running in darkness
the same the shapes the
lost nigger's live running
and you are the magic you seek
the substance and voice fire
to reshape the dance
and make holiness out of everything
and nothing and the dark

III   (Arthur Hall Dancers)

Came holy men and we sat
the body lovers in heat
and the tide the holy moon
and sun from the bodies
in heat in passion
for we came the lions mouth
open in creation the line
finished the direction pointed
to return the line to the lion's
head and we sat and they
were holy holy for what they are
to return us
eternal in the shipless night
and the star pointing
the boss creator returned
to the holy men from whom
we are lost and spinning
soundless even as we scream
and they return us to make
the scream holy and sound
brilliant starry in the universe
and our souls are stars
and visible illuminating
everything there is that is good
in the natural order of things

IIII

Ourselves and what we are
and are to be in fire
in the creator's voice
the divine and cosmic energy
where the angles cross point
and we absorb even as we move
against ourselves we absorb
and are made of the energy
the fibre and protein we seek

even in the dim world the
world lost the world sick
in their forms against love
even as we go down our
bodies which are souls
radiate the energy the force
to set the planet upright
in the Knowledge of the creator
to come as all things
into ourselves again
into the world made holy again
into the final spiritual conclusion

the lost nigger returned again
and love again again there is love

IIIII

To show what we are
is to again dance constant
in what dance is

the body moving in harmony
with the rhythms of the eternal

the body moving in dance

the body passing into the spirit
becoming visible in dance
becoming what we are
showing we are the spirit of dance
passing through bodies
into our final conclusion

the hands and voice of Allah

ALVIN SAXON (OJENKE)

Black Power

I

There shall be no more songs
of soft magnolias that blow
like aromatic winds through southern vales,
no more praises of daffodils chattering
the wind's fluttering tune—

and no eulogies of red, red roses
that fall like blood from heavy vines.

Black Orpheus calls, his lyre piercing
the dark solitude of a Hadean world:
Come O Ebony-hued Eurydice, he beckons,
he shan't look back—the lesson has
been well learned.

2

There have been despondent days
and long nights of insomnia—
but your voice, sweet Eurydice,
was like some Nigerian wind that
blew softly through the water willows,
your lips like manna—they were
good for my soul;
and your hands that caressed my
worn limbs like a profound unction
and when I laid my head, dense with
woeful memories, on your cloud breast
I slept deep and tranquil and
the day held no insurmountable fears
for me.

Watts

1

From what great sleep
lightning jumps from an amber sky
causing famine,
assassinating tin people and whole grass-blades?

Senile edifices crying like lumberjacks: "Timber!"
Streets of dwellings wrapped in cellophane
of negligence,
where old wine-winded wisemen in oversized coats
and baggy trousers soliloquize a jungle futility.
And a baby warbles a milk-dry cry
to a mother's wiry ear who sits ice-eyed
with frozen pain like icicles in her heart.

What great sleep,
resonant with nightmares,
causes a man to awaken gap-eyed?

2

Diogenes came with a burning lamp
searching for honest men, but his beautiful light
fell only upon the shadow people
and those who found meaning in the penumbral days
meted out in marijuana's fantasy
and the half-bliss of the prostitute's bed.

Socrates came with nebulous knowledge
to make a liar of the Oracle of Delphi,
but found only
schoolrooms of metal and wood carvings
and those who escape into
some kind of intoxicant—running from
some too-true truth.

Against what false fantasy
the children ball on their golden slides,
bouncing balls, and putty clay—
and Socrates, horrid-eyed, gulped the hemlock
while weeping Diogenes hurled his flame
to the barren soil.

A Poem for Integration

Votaries know
day's beginning
over the sundials
of Mecca
but I in my private death
give homage to blue-eyed lilies.

The days, the nights
come as gray continuum
(and if it were not
for cream and sugar coffee
the gray people
dining with awkward fingers
at integrated luncheons)
perhaps I feel two-dimensional—
in this three-dimensional world

I've become accustomed
to stag parties,
where after the movies
of stymie and buckwheat

we learnedly discourse
on the memoirs of Thomas Jefferson
(I smiling as if my kinsmen
too, had romped with Indians and
routed the red coats)

Africa's melodies
do not sing for me.
My feet do not burn
for the coolness of her soils,
as the songs of sweet chariots
or motherless children do.
Africa's music is a striking
of the air with fur mittens
as I sit sipping twenty years of vintage,
my hips tilted anticipating
the rose soft belly
beyond the flicker of
a puffed-out candle

MAE JACKSON (1946–)

The Blues Today

rhythm and blues
ain't what it use to be
blues done gone and got
americanize
tellin' me that i should
stay in school
get off the streets
and keep the summer cool

i says
      blues ain't nothing like it use to be
blues done gone and got
americanize

blues done gone and lost its soul
and the folks singing it
ain't singing for me
no more

For Some Poets

can—i—poet
with you roi
        can i
poet
    for
       a
        little
            while
write a poem about
The Spirit House
            can i
poet for a while?

let me
     poet
with 'cha larry
          let me
poet
    for
       a
      while
write a poem about your blackness
                    can i
poet
for
a
while.

can i
     poet
with you nikki
can i
     poet for a little taste
write a poem about your poetry
can i
just for
a day
poet
with you Marvin X
poet with you please?

i remember . . .

i remember . . .
january,
1968
it's snow,
the desire that i had to build
a black snowman
and place him upon
Malcolm's grave.

i used to wrap my white doll up in

i used to wrap my white doll up in
an old towel
and place her upon my chest
i used to sing those funny old school songs
god bless america
my country 'tis of thee
when i was young
and very colored

reincarnation

sometimes i get the feeling that i have been here before
black faces
they ain't new
plantations are still the same

                                        (jails they are now called)

sometimes i get the weirdest feeling
that nikki and i played games together
stole meat and bread from the master's house

and you know,
once when i was here before
i fell in love with don l lee
we picked cotton and stole kisses beneath the blossom trees
and marvin x and i got married
by jumping over a broom

January 3, 1970

today
i am 24
i keep trying to find a reason
to be happy
but there
is
none

slavery never did impress me

L. V. MACK (1947–)

Biafra

Biafra should be the name of a woman,
black and soft. smooth
belly,
and a heavy breast.

Biafra.
listen to the way she walks.

Biafra.
listen to the way she walks.

the black little boy
dozes in the hot sun.
Biafra.
she brings the burn of day.

Biafra. O mother, hear the growl, the night
is cold, cold, cold.

Death Songs

1. White As I See It Rising

For L.V.

it is midnite. the room is blue.
the night is a blank
like a white clock face, something
i will not remember.

i have forgotten
you,
and the blue night,
    and the morning colors: red,
white
as i see it rising
until it has blinded me
in the eyes,
                a needle of light in
        the center. of my head.
i have forgotten.
i have forgotten you.

2. The Eye Fills Itself with Light

the fragile night—a look of death might
turn it like flowers as light as snow:
through the hole
is a sleep of light, a fine dust in nothing.
sprinkle the light into the black;
in the crossing of the void,
shatter the night with fear.

3. The Eye Is a Hole in Light

do not look for me
in the night
the flowers have the look of death.
                        the eye
is a hole in light, & the night is a mirror

that the warmth of fright turns to water
chasing into nothing.

4. What Little You Know

what little you know
is not enough to live. you know everything.
you know
that you know nothing, can be sure of
nothing.
even the apparition
                    of white death
is something you do not know, that
you will forget at the instant of light (when
do you become dead?) you
never knew.
you relinquish your lover, the soft flesh,

your children, you no longer
are waiting, there is nothing
                    for you.

   5. A Flower Has a Light of Its Own

but the light—
              if you shut all the doors
there is still the light. and when the room is a black
you will still see the flowers and to shut them in
to close all the light in &
step into the night,
naked, except for the look
of fear

when the night is a flower
of white light that
the look
could turn into nothing.

you do not see the night, blinded
by the memory of everything

that you have forgotten   that
you will forget.

FELIPE LUCIANO (1947–)

You're Nothing But a Spanish Colored Kid

I see them
Puerto Ricans/Spanish niggers
Bronzed farmers look silly being doormen
Their fingers are more honest than their eyes.
Earth hands turned metallic gray
The plow rots, the mule dies, the hands rust
And the elders sit with ashes on their crowns
making fools of themselves in bars.
Those fingertips will never touch the soil again.
Those fingertips will never feel the fuzz of
small stones smoothed for centuries by the river.
Fingertips/a nigger's Mount Rushmore
Fingertips
Drunkenly wrapped around a beer can
Hatefully curled through a belt
Desperately clutching a needle

Lost their land/Losing their minds
The conga was smashed by a machine
It could always vibrate, but it couldn't move an inch.
Well, we never threatened the music teacher anyway.
Fingers frozen
No fire in the loins
Brown people look so funny in the snow.
Frostbite of the soul
Condemned to a metal existence
Rapidly becoming plastic
A little more warmth, a lot more deceptive.
The sighted blind ask where are the chains
And I run lest they hang me for showing them the cross.
Porto Ricans/Indo Afros
Grasping for the good and finding rusty machetes
Dangling from the thighs of their mothers
Waiting
Como se dice, Domino cho-cho
How do you say that chico?
Pelea, pelea, pelea
Talk that mira-mira shit now, Chico
Say it now, I'm Rican and proud
'Cause your years are numbered and daylight lasts
But so long.
Lose your color if you want to.
Me? I'm a war counselor for the Sun
From a powder puff to jitterbugging with a star.
Beware the power of chisels made of powder puffs
They're like jealous lovers
Who slash silently regardless of who started the affair.
C'mon spic.
Learn to tell time.
Your daddy was a peasant
And you're nothing but a Spanish colored kid
unless you
Get real nigger
And stop making gestures.

WAYNE MORELAND (1948–)

Sunday Morning

It is whatever day, whatever time it is,
and you are still here, next to me, with
all of this going on around us. Just you
& me, skating and bouncing funny wobble
on the sidewalks. You speak thru the things

that you have touched-thru yr rings, thru
a crumpled chewinggum wrapper, thru yr
green plants and nighttime milk containers.
We are alive and with ourselves under the
sky folding blue to grey to yellow haze,
and we are here, in the world, and the whole
day is wide before us.
Kneeling on the floor, you are making
a robe that I will wear that will tell
our story. I come in behind you, see you
there, and tell you how alive I feel and
how I love you for making things in the
morning.

PEARL CLEAGE LOMAX (1948–)

Glimpse

i saw you
on my walk last
night
you were running
between the
neatdark rows of
pine trees
behind the house
and even though
your mouth was
open
you made no sound.
your lips were stretched like
rubber
over your teeth
but your sound
was shaking inside
you
and never reached me
through the muffling skin.
i saw you
last night and
the red drops on your shirt
and the bloodprint of
your hand upon the trees.
i saw you
on my walk last
night.
Running.

CHARLES COOPER (1948–)

Rubin

his name is
       rubin
cattle man
       and animal trainer
playin' six wigs
        in his stable
deluxe
     except the black one
            with skinny legs
and the blonde one
       with stringy hair
cool
   real cool
movin' in and out
       trickin' the game
and foolin' the herd
top city athlete
      number one
         sport
a public servant
      thanks
        rubin
         for givin' us
fun

Honky

    ray john
       say
    black
     in life
is shit
so do
   charlie
     porter
   they all
      wish
   they was
white
    i say
        they is

Dreams

crooked
      beneath a denim
            blanket
lies frederick
        johnson
           the third
      he's dead
asleep
     lost in singular
          illusions
of an aging
       mind
it's
   just like being
awake
ain't it
           frederick

RICHARD E. GRANT (1949–)

Broken Heart, Broken Machine

. . . sometimes I wonder if it's really worth it (Quote from Richard Butler)

Don't worry baby.
You know they haven't seen the
Dali Christ of St. John of the Cross,
or strummed hot grease fish heads in Blauvelt, N.Y.
No
Sure it ain't never hip to be that white
like white people can get when you be
jumping on them hot subways stuck up
under the heat and schedules of all those
other faces in August, desert hot, funky slide
stick skin & certainly nobody even laughing or
five different color natural combs in yr hair
growing all over into their summer tweed Brooks
brothers, incredible nigger . . .
(I mean)
I ain't jivin , , ,
don't worry baby,

You know how it's been,
—angonna be . . . pretty much . . .
Most everybody holds their face from the
Sun & words . . .
they lean all over Camus' wobbly grave
or plain and simple
Everything comes up epics:
Young fine Kali gets blowed up and unfine , , ,
Our old friends come in from the rooftops
and disappear thru our windows
when they talk that talk about
5th avenue bread
no Body cor
nered.
Blue monday down in the soul folks . . . really
. . . next time that landlord comes around for the
bread you tell him we heard there's gonna
be a revolution
&
this is where Othello comes
back from the dead with the golden daggers
of the Black Sicilians
Yeah
that'll do him
cause (You Know Laydee Day) . . . we got all kinds
of moons that we will remember when the day
wrinkles up and pulls shabby tricks in the
guillotine hour
(don't worry baby)

VICTOR HERNANDEZ CRUZ (1949–)

CARMEN

WHY THIS GIRL HAS NO FEAR
OF NIGHT
MAYBE SHE VERY WISE
SEEN EVERYTHING
HAS BEEN THERE MORE THAN
ONCE
HAS SEEN THE REMAINS OF
THE NIGHT BEFORE
HAS LOOKED UP AT THE MOON
FROM A CROWDED STOOP
HAS SEEN THE SUN COME OUT
EARLY

THIS GIRL IS NOT AFRAID
SEEN THE CROWDED STREET
SEEN THE BLOOD
EVERYTHING TREMBLING
SHE GOES REAL SMOOTH

Energy

is
red beans
ray barretto
banging away
steam out the
radio
the five-stair
steps
is mofongo
chuchifrito stand
outside down
the avenue
that long hill
of a block
before the train
is pacheco
playing with
bleeding
blue lips

The Electric Cop

this guy on t.v.
who rob everything he got
who rob
a thief
who rob
who kill
a killer who kills
this guy on t.v.

what they say & do/captain america tears his panties
as he swings for freedom

& ch.4 where they did
the rub
the two old men

what they say
this man
who likes pig a low
on your ass
your eyes dropping blood
will sell you some
cigars of death
for you
for you

the other ch. say you
have bad breath
& yellow teeth
something about some paste
& the guy zombie looking
&
this other guy
O he could kick ass
look at him pull out his 32/bang bang bodies
crash to the ground

planes fly/fire coming out of them
people scream democrats stomp
on heads on their way to meetings
cowboys kill indians
in their soft nights
& blond angels smile gleem brith teeth
put there by plaster of paris
young white boys run the shit out of their
femalemess/pushing tootie roll thru the air
their freckles tell us stories

the parade of
colors on t.v.
from ch. to ch.
round & round
the whole dial
from vomiting shit/to more b.s./an open
window of lies
& true stories of the empire/the end for instance.

spirits

                half of his
                 body hung in
                the air
                they said it was
                magic   a secret
                between me & the man
               it was no magic that was
              in the air   it was no trick
            an old lady an old   old lady who
          saw the windows open   the wind raising the
        curtains   footsteps in an empty room
      a young man who saw a t.v. go flying into the
      air   a dying lady got up & walked & sang
     sudden loss of weight   sudden accident   a car
    rolling over a head   a building falling
   bad luck   magic.

go after them as they get lost to turn the corner & snag
one   flowers   odors   candles   light candles   morning
noise   papers flying.
                    a hand thru a wall
                    is no joke   a mind
                    going mad at a days
                    time   so wide
                    so wide spread
                    an escape
                    who escapes   who
                    runs   run where
                    from what from
                    who   a silence
                    the clouds over
                    the buildings the
                    odor in the halls
                    no one runs
                    no place to run
                    no place to hide
                    traveling   a fast
                    traveler   a signal
                    a place   the strange
                    way the walls start
                    to act   you say
                    you say you saw
                    nothing moving there
                    you deny a head
                    a head hiding   behind

the curtains   take
another look
a storm reported
only on your street
someone with grade A
health found dead of
a strange disease
a bad cold
a box found
full of nails
& flowers
names & statues
water sitting under
the beds   blood
falling out of pictures
a flower   burning under
the bed
a lady dressed in
white   flying away
from the roof
waving her hands
for you to follow
you have a bad cold

there is no medicine
there is no cure
there is only a fear
a hope   a waiting
till the spirits
come to our rescue
to your funerals

all the third world
sees spirits &
they talk to them
they are our friends.

The Story of the Zeros

zero
zero
zero

the museum of modern art/is zero ugly cans
& piles & piles that eguel anglo zeros
zero can O soup & O how wonderful the lady
said about a geometric business machine
zeroness is her/her empty zeros/the zero
film the crowd made ape sounds & vomitted

their chairs /as they spoke later about how
some zero would egual some other zero/also
others zeroness compared with another zero
ness/it was zeros talking zeros/& about other
zeros doing zero things/around zeros/things
that came from computer & IBM /zero said to
zero   what about his latest film   O its
really his best do you not think/O & she was
such a good actress/hehehehahhah   rowa ro wa
rawaraaraaaaaawaaaraaaratraooooo/the zeros
walk from can to can from zero to zero   to
zero within zero/in the zero building of zeros
& some zeros try to become $\frac{1}{2}$ but they are
the biggest zeros/within zero books/some zero
said they going to write book on zero culture/
the amount of zeroness in the modern novel/or
de developement of zeroism in poetry/or zero
play/& how zeros went to puerto rico & tried
to add up/& how zeros went to sao paulo &
tried to do the rumba/how they went to nairobi
& tried to give some rice/& to/da nang searching
for weird things to get into/but all them zeros
did was to become bigger zeros & uselessness
& de museum started raining dollars & all de
zeros tried to get one.

DJANGATOLUM
(LLOYD M. CORBIN, JR.) (1949–)

Ali

Ali
Is our prince
Regal and Black
A glass that could fall
but never break
A flower without rain
that never could die
Ali
Is our prince

Dedication to the Final Confrontation

young niggers
die old
sleep nights
in days
days in
in night
sleep niggers
sleep
until
the power
of the
night
rest
get strong
niggers
get strong
eat niggers
eat
(surplus peanut butter relief etc.)
to
do
what
others might
kill
kind
man
man-kind
white
kind
of man

LARRY THOMPSON (1950–)

Black Is Best

Black is best.
                My mother forgot to tell me.
But I told her
            that black is best.
        And she says: Boy hush your mouth
I again say:
        Black is best mamma.
            And she hit me.
    But I keep saying:
                Black is best.

ANGELO LEWIS (1950–)

America Bleeds

it does, it does, i have seen it
bleeding, brothers & sisters, i
have seen it, i have seen it,
come rushing, walk crippled,
fall flatly on tears of sad streets
where creatures fall onward with
cold eyes over them, armies on
streets over them, police on
pavements over them, tear gas
in faces over them, fires &
minds, living dreams living,
all of them innocents, yes,
yes, i have seen it, it bleeds,
it bleeds, have seen it bleed,
spill blood at my brothers,
cough no at our dignity,
i tell you, i tell you, we must,
kick on this monster, till it
dies, till it dies, dies, dies,
dies, dies, lies in the dirt
with its blood & its sickness,
head fall rolling in gutter,
red, white, & blue, flow freely,
flow freely, move over, fall down,
down, down, be finished at
last.

Clear

the children   they move   stand
  about   roam freely
    come rushing,
      their innocence
   solemn
      their grace

have you seen them have you
  seen them
can you feel   the Revolution

Clear   as the sun   that makes
                  the morning blossom
Flowing and Brilliant
            through circles & meadows
                  & on into
                        Streets . . .

ELOUISE LOFTIN (1950–)

Woman

as a child i was
constantly reminded
of the size of my eyes
or how i just saw "evahything"
and was always warned
not to look into grown folks mouths
somehow i find myself looking to
where i've been looking all the time
into folks mouths   caught in poses
that pierce all time and distances
gaping off into space
giving correction to error
and knowing that you dont realise
that i can see you from where
you cant see me
see you

Virginia

Sat in the sun
hands hung between her
legs spread wide open
and told me stories
of how she cut her
hair in the back
to make a V for
victory and when there
wasnt none for
Virginia
askin me ain't that a bitch
What do i know
i'm just a kid

when i know something
shut up you so damn grown
I remember you smokin
funny things blowin
smoke in my face
sayin soon i'd understand
Comin back a long time
after she can sew real
good now sayin she had been
to college   why does my
mother keep sayin jail
and what's the difference
I see her now still beautiful
her nose cold numb like
an old dog we use to have
scared to breathe
thinkin this may be the last time
Sitting in the sun poppin green beans
me grown
and having to understand
for real

Weeksville Women

"Old women will not enter Paradise:
they will be made young and beautiful first."—*The Prophet*

old Black ladies
carryin shopping bags
full of more shopping bags
memories and dreams
gap their legs
on buses
and say things like
"dont God work in mysterious ways, baby
sweety, yours is just startin, sugar"
old Black ladies with wise written
on their faces   youth&future
written in their eyes
spread wide open up to me
stretch out their feet
cast down on their legs
and adjust their veins
like road maps   they say
where they got on   when they got to leave
and fan fan fan
they got so much
to be hot about

JULIANNE PERRY (1952–)

to L.

you weren't even a
revolutionary
but i loved you,
didn't speak swahili
or call the brothers and sisters
brothers and sisters.
your fro was almost
nonexistent
and you missed all the
pan-african meetings
even solidarity day.
you gave 50¢ to the struggle
but you
respected me
and loved me and
you weren't even a
revolutionary but
i loved you.

no dawns

dusk,
no dawns, and silver linings
have all been melted
into half-dollars.
the sun has set
forever
over babylon.
tyrants are losing their
crowns and children.
the writing on the wall
is in blood:
the next sunrise
will be from the
east.
we await in fear
the new beginning.

Biographical Notes

NANINA ALBA (1917–1968) Born in Montgomery, Alabama. She taught English, French, and music in public schools and colleges during her long career, and was a member of the English Department of Tuskegee Institute. Her poetry was published in two volumes, *The Parchments* (1963) and *The Parchments II*. She is represented in the anthologies *For Malcolm* (1967) and *The Poetry of the Negro* (1949, 1970).

LEWIS ALEXANDER (1900–1945) Born in Washington, D.C. He was educated in the public schools of Washington, and at Howard University and the University of Pennsylvania. He was active in the theatre, as well as being a poet. His work has appeared in such collections as *The New Negro* (1925, 1968) and *The Poetry of the Negro* (1949, 1970).

SAMUEL ALLEN (PAUL VESEY) (1917–) Born in Columbus, Ohio. He studied at Fisk University and Harvard Law School. While he was attending the Sorbonne in Paris, Mr. Allen's poems were published, with the help of Richard Wright, in the French magazine *Présence Africaine*. Under the name Paul Vesey, Mr. Allen published his first book, *Elfenbein Zähne (Ivory Tusks)* (1956) in a bilingual edition in Germany. His poetry has been anthologized in *American Negro Poetry* (1963), *New Negro Poets: U.S.A.* (1964), *I Am the Darker Brother* (1968), and in many other collections and texts. He has traveled in Africa, and has worked for the United States Information Agency and the Community Relations Service of the Department of Justice. Mr. Allen has been Writer-in-Residence at Tuskegee Institute, and is Professor of English at Boston University.

JOHARI AMINI (1935–) Born in Philadelphia, educated in Chicago. Currently, she is an instructor in Black Literature and Psychology at the Kennedy-King Campus of Chicago City College. She is also a book reviewer for *Black World* magazine. Her publications include: *Images in Black* (1967); *A Folk Fable* (1969); *Let's Go Some Where* (1970); *A Hip Tale in the Death Style* (1972); and a book of essays, *Re-Definition: Concept as Being* (1972). Her work has appeared in numerous anthologies, including *Black Arts Anthology* (1969), *Spectrum in Black* (1970), *We Speak as Liberators: Young Black Poets* (1970), *Jump Bad* (1971), *The Black Poets* (1971), *Black Spirits* (1972), and in textbooks and periodicals.

S. E. ANDERSON (1943–) Born in the Bedford-Stuyvesant section of Brooklyn. He attended Pratt Institute and Lincoln University in Pennsylvania. His graduate work has been in the field of mathematics at City College and Hunter College. Currently, he is Professor of Mathematics and Black Nationalism at Old Westbury College, Long Island. Mr. Anderson's poetry has been published in such magazines as *Negro Digest/Black World* and *Liberator*, and in many collections, including *Black Fire* (1968) and *Black Spirits* (1972). He is a member of the Advisory Board of Drum and Spear Press, and is

Advisory and Contributing Editor of *Black Scholar* magazine.

RUSSELL ATKINS (1926–   ) Born in Cleveland, Ohio, where he lives at present. Mr. Atkins began his writing in the late 1940s and received encouragement from such poets as Langston Hughes, Marianne Moore, and John Ciardi. His work has appeared in a large number of periodicals, including *Free Lance, Beloit Poetry Journal,* and *Ohio Poetry Review,* as well as anthologies such as *The Poetry of the Negro* (1949, 1970) and *Sixes and Sevens* (1962). A volume of his poems, *Heretofore* (1968), was published in London. Mr. Atkins is co-editor of the magazine *Free Lance,* which he founded in 1950.

IMAMU AMIRI BARAKA (LEROI JONES) (1934–   ) Born in Newark, New Jersey, and educated at Howard and Columbia Universities and The New School. His work has been published in numerous magazines and the major poetry anthologies, and has become recognized as an important factor in the development of the Black Arts Movement since the early 1960s. His books of poetry include *Preface to a Twenty-Volume Suicide Note* (1961), *The Dead Lecturer* (1964), *Black Magic (Collected Poetry: 1961–1967)* (1969), *In Our Terribleness* (1970), and *Spirit, Reach* (1972). He is the author of *Dutchman, The Slave,* and other plays which have been produced in New York and around the world. His prose works include *Blues People* (1963), *The System of Dante's Hell* (1965), and two books of essays, *Home* (1966) and *Raise Race Rays Raze* (1971). He is the author of a book of short stories, *Tales* (1967), and co-editor, with Larry Neal, of *Black Fire* (1968), an anthology of Black American literature. Imamu Baraka was founder of the Black Arts Repertory Theatre in Harlem; Spirit House, a community organization active in the social and political life of Newark; and the Committee for a Unified Newark. He is also the publisher of Jihad Publications. Mr. Baraka is active in organizing Black political leaders from communities around the country into a cohesive force for the future.

GERALD W. BARRAX (1933–   ) Born in Attalla, Alabama. He served in the U.S. Air Force, and has an M.A. degree from the University of Pittsburgh. His poetry has appeared in such publications

as *Journal of Black Poetry* and *Poetry,* and in the anthologies *Kaleidoscope* (1967) and *The Young American Poets* (1968). A volume of his work, *Another Kind of Rain* (1970), was published by Pittsburgh University Press. Mr. Barrax is a member of the Department of English at North Carolina State University.

GWENDOLYN B. BENNETT (1902–   ) Born in Giddings, Texas, and studied at Pratt Institute and Columbia University. She has been an artist as well as poet, and has studied in Paris at the École de Pantheon. She was an art instructor at Howard University. Ms. Bennett served as a member of the editorial staff of *Opportunity* magazine, and her poetry appeared in that publication, as well as in such anthologies as *The Book of American Negro Poetry* (1922, 1931) and *The Poetry of the Negro* (1949, 1970).

LERONE BENNETT, JR. (1928–   ) Attended Morehouse College in Atlanta, became editor of the Atlanta *Daily World,* and then joined the staff of Johnson Publications. Mr. Bennett is the author of significant nonfiction works, including *Before the Mayflower* (1962), *What Manner of Man* (1964), *Black Mood* (1970), *Confrontation: Black and White* (1965), *Black Power U.S.A.: The Human Side of Reconstruction, 1867–77* (1967), *Pioneers in Protest* (1969), and *The Challenge of Blackness* (1972). He is also the author of numerous poems and stories. Mr. Bennett is Senior Editor at *Ebony* magazine, and Chairman of the Department of African American Studies at Northwestern University.

LEBERT BETHUNE (1937–   ) Born in Kingston, Jamaica, he attended New York University and the Sorbonne. His first book of poems, *A Juju of My Own,* was published in 1966. Mr. Bethune's work has appeared in the anthologies *Black Fire* (1968) and *The Poetry of the Negro* (1949, 1970), as well as in many periodicals and other collections. "Bwagamoyo," the title of one of Mr. Bethune's poems in this anthology, is the name of an ancient collection point for slaves on the Tanganyikan coast. The word "Bwagamoyo" carries the four meanings italicized in the poem.

ARNA BONTEMPS (1902–   ) Born in Alexandria, Louisiana. Educated at Pacific Union College and at the University of Chicago. His poetry appeared in magazines between 1924 and 1931 and won much critical recognition and many awards. He is the author of a number of prose works, including *Anyplace But Here, God Sends Sunday, Frederick Douglass* (1959), and *100 Years of Negro Freedom* (1961). Arna Bontemps has been co-editor, with Langston Hughes, of the influential anthology of Black American poetry *The Poetry of the Negro* (1949, 1970), as well as editor of *American Negro Poetry,* an anthology published in 1963. He was University Librarian at Fisk University for over twenty years. Since then he has been on the faculty of both the University of Illinois and Yale University.

WILLIAM STANLEY BRAITHWAITE (1878–1962) Born in Boston, Massachusetts. He was well known for his many anthologies as well as for his own writings. *Anthologies of Magazine Verse,* which appeared from 1913 through 1929, included many of the major poets of that time. Mr. Braithwaite's poetry volumes include *Lyrics of Life and Love* (1904), *The House of Falling Leaves* (1908), and *Selected Poems* (1948). He was a long-time Professor of Creative Literature at Atlanta University until his retirement in 1945.

GWENDOLYN BROOKS (1917–) Born in Topeka, Kansas, she was raised and still resides in Chicago. *A Street in Bronzeville,* published in 1945, was her first book of poetry. *Annie Allen* won the Pulitzer Prize for poetry in 1949, making her the only Black American poet to receive that award. Other books include: *Maud Martha* (1953), a novel; *Bronzeville Boys and Girls* (1956); *The Bean Eaters* (1960); *Selected Poems* (1966); and *In the Mecca* (1968). In recent years she has concentrated her efforts on support of Black community organizations, writing workshops, and Black-owned publishing ventures; with Broadside Press in Detroit she published her books *Riot* (1969), *Family Pictures* (1970), and *Aloneness* (1971), a book for children. She has edited two anthologies, *Jump Bad* (1971), and *A Broadside Treasury* (1971), and she edits *The Black Position,* a periodical. *The World of Gwendolyn Brooks,* a collection of her early poetry, was published in 1972. Gwendolyn Brooks has been active in teaching and lecturing, has been named Poet Laureate

of the State of Illinois, and has taught at the City College of New York. *To Gwen with Love: A Tribute to Gwendolyn Brooks,* containing poems in praise of the author and her support of young writers, was published in 1971. *Report from Part One: The Autobiography of Gwendolyn Brooks* was published in 1972.

STERLING A. BROWN (1901–) Born in Washington, D.C., he was educated in the schools of that city and at Williams College and Harvard University. He has had a long and distinguished career at Howard University, where he holds a professorship in English, and was selected to write a history of the University in 1961. His books include *Southern Road* (1932), a collection of his poetry, and the critical works *The Negro in American Fiction* (1937, 1969) and *Negro Poetry and Drama* (1937, 1969). Mr. Brown was senior editor of the landmark anthology of Black American literature *The Negro Caravan,* published in 1941 and reissued in 1969. His poem "An Old Woman Remembers" refers to the Atlanta Riot of 1906.

F. J. BRYANT, JR. (1942–) Born in Philadelphia, Pennsylvania. After service in the U.S. Navy he attended Lincoln University in Pennsylvania, where he was awarded the Eichelburger Prize for prose and was Poet Laureate of the school. He has had plays produced at Lincoln, and his poetry has appeared in such periodicals as *Journal of Black Poetry, Nickel Review,* and *Negro Digest/Black World.* He has been included in the anthologies *Black Fire* (1968), *The New Black Poetry* (1969), *To Gwen with Love* (1971), and *New Black Voices* (1972).

JOHN HENRIK CLARKE (1915–) Born in Union Springs, Alabama, and raised in Columbus, Georgia. He was one of the founders of the Harlem Writers' Guild and has been Associate Editor of *Freedomways* magazine since 1962. He is the author of numerous articles, stories, and poems, which have appeared in many periodicals and collections over the years. He is the editor of *Harlem U.S.A.* (1964), *American Negro Short Stories* (1966), *William Styron's "Nat Turner": Ten Black Writers Respond* (1968), and *Malcolm X* (1969), a collection of writings by and about Malcolm X.

CAROLE GREGORY CLEMMONS (1945–) Born in Youngstown, Ohio, and graduated from Youngstown State University. Her poetry has been published in such collections as *Nine Black Poets* (1968), *The New Black Poetry* (1969), *A Galaxy of Black Writing* (1970), and *To Gwen with Love* (1971). Mrs. Clemmons has worked for *Look* magazine and in educational television. She is married to François Clemmons, singer and poet.

LUCILLE CLIFTON (1936–) Born in Depew, New York. Attended Howard University and Fredonia State Teachers College. She is the author of two books of poetry, *Good Times* (1969) and *Good News About the Earth* (1972), as well as three books for children: *Some of the Days of Everett Anderson* (1970); *Black B C's* (1970); and *Everett Anderson's Christmas Coming* (1971). Her work has appeared in *Negro Digest/Black World* and *The Massachusetts Review*, among other periodicals, and she has given many readings at colleges around the country. Lucille Clifton lives in Baltimore, Maryland, with her husband, Fred Clifton, author and educator, and their six children.

CHARLIE COBB (1944–) Born in Washington, D.C., and attended Howard University. He left college to begin his association with the Student Nonviolent Coordinating Committee in Mississippi, along with many young Black students of the time. He has also worked with the Center for Black Education in Washington, D.C., and Drum and Spear Press, a Black publishing venture in that city. His books of poetry include *Furrowe* (1967) and *Everywhere Is Yours* (1971). His work has appeared in such collections as *Black Fire* (1968) and *Campfires of the Resistance: Poetry from the Movement* (1971). Mr. Cobb is active for Drum and Spear Press in Tanzania, East Africa.

CONYUS (1942–) Born in Detroit, Michigan. His work has appeared in such publications as *Ramparts, Scanlan's, The Black Scholar, Black Dialogue*, and other magazines. He is included in the anthologies *Dices or Black Bones* (1970), *Natural Process* (1970), and *New Black Voices* (1972). He makes his home in San Francisco, where he is "studying, looking, listening, and singing when there is a song, within."

CHARLES COOPER (1948–) Born in Oakland, California. He has been a drama major at California State College in Hayward. Some of his poetry has appeared in the anthologies *Nine Black Poets* (1968), *Black Out Loud* (1970), and *A Galaxy of Black Writing* (1970).

SAM CORNISH (1935–) Born in Baltimore, Maryland. He was a writing specialist with the Neighborhood Centers in that city, and is the co-editor of a collection of writings from the young people of Baltimore, *Chicory*, published in 1969. His own work has appeared in such publications as *Journal of Black Poetry, Massachusetts Review*, and *New American Review*. He is the author of a book for children, *Your Hand In Mine* (1969), and a collection of his poetry, *Generations*, was published in 1970. Mr. Cornish is a teacher of creative writing at Highland Schools in Roxbury, Massachusetts.

JAYNE CORTEZ (1938–) Born in Arizona, raised in Watts, and lives in New York City. Her poetry has appeared in *Negro Digest/Black World, Journal of Black Poetry*, and other publications. She is the author of two collections of poems, *Pissstained Stairs and the Monkey Man's Wares* (1969) and *Festivals and Funerals* (1971).

JOSEPH SEAMAN COTTER, JR. (1895–1919) Born in Louisville, Kentucky. The son of a well-known poet, Joseph Cotter had to leave Fisk University in his second year as a result of tuberculosis. In 1918 he published his only volume of poetry, *The Band of Gideon*.

STANLEY CROUCH (1945–) Born in Los Angeles, he is a musician and music critic as well as a poet. His poetry has been published in such periodicals as *Negro Digest/Black World, Liberator*, and *Black Dialogue*, and has been included in the anthologies *Black Fire* (1968), *We Speak as Liberators: Young Black Poets* (1970), and *Black Spirits* (1972). His book of poems, *Ain't No Ambulances for No Niggahs Tonight*, was published in 1972. Mr. Crouch teaches literature, Black drama, and music appreciation at the Black Studies Center of the Claremont Colleges in California. When his poem "Albert Ayler: Eulogy for a Decomposed Saxophone Player" was first published in *Negro Digest/Black World*,

Mr. Crouch included the following introductory note:

"Note on the poem: Albert Ayler, dead
like Bird at 34, a true innovator who
played with what John Lee Hooker calls
'the big feeling.' But the ugliest thing
about it is that there are chump change
slickeroo pimps running around who used
all of Albert's heart when they could and
abandoned him when they couldn't. Albert's wiped off the board now, people,
but he left something on the horn that
you'll always hear. He marched the new
music in with a joy you hear only in the
great players and he could play like a
giant snorting storm clouds. Some of the
music is on records, the best on the ESP
label and some phenomenal dates he
played with Norman Howard and Don
Cherry on foreign labels. There are all
kinds of stories about Albert's death, but
they all correspond on one fact: He is
dead and gone in the ground. Listen to
him for the music, people, don't try to use
him."

VICTOR HERNANDEZ CRUZ (1949–
—) Born in Aguas Buenas, Puerto Rico,
he came to New York City at the age of
four. He grew up in *El Barrio* (Spanish
Harlem) in New York, and attended Ben-
jamin Franklin High School. His poetry
has appeared in many recent collections,
and in such publications as *Down Here,
Evergreen Review, Ramparts, Umbra,* and
Journal of Black Poetry. Snaps, his first
volume of poetry, was published in 1969.
He has taught at the University of California, Berkeley, and is active in the San
Francisco Neighborhood Arts Program.

COUNTEE CULLEN (1903–1946) Born
in New York City, he was educated in the
public schools of that city and at New
York University. He received his master's
degree from Harvard University, and became a teacher in New York City—work
which he continued all his life. When he
was twenty-two years old his first book of
poems, *Color* (1925), was published. It
won the Harmon Gold Award for literature, and brought him immediate recognition as a significant Black American
poet. In 1927 he published *Copper Sun.*
This was followed by *The Ballad of the
Brown Girl* (1928). His other works include *The Black Christ and Other Poems*
(1929), *The Medea and Some Poems*
(1935) and *The Lost Zoo,* a book for
children published in 1940. Mr. Cullen
was the editor of an important anthology

of Black American poetry, *Caroling Dusk,*
published in 1927. *On These I Stand,* his
final collection, was published posthumously in 1947.

RAY GARFIELD DANDRIDGE (1882–
1930) Born in Cincinnati, he was educated in the schools of that city. He suffered a stroke in 1912, which left his legs
and right arm paralyzed, and thereafter
he wrote most of his poetry from his bed.
His two volumes of poems are *The Poet
and Other Poems* (1920), and *Zalka
Peetruza and Other Poems* (1928). Mr.
Dandridge's work has been included in the
anthologies *The Book of American Negro
Poetry* (1922, 1931) and *An Anthology of
Verse by American Negroes* (1924, 1968).

MARGARET DANNER Born in Pryors-
burg, Kentucky, she has won many
awards for her poetry, including a John
Hay Whitney Fellowship. She has been
editor of *Poetry* magazine, and was Poet-
in-Residence at Wayne State University
and Virginia Union State University. Ms.
Danner was a founder of Boone House
for the Arts in Detroit, and of Nolo-
gonya's in Chicago. Her published works
include *Impressions of African Art Forms
in Poetry* (1962), *To Flower* (1962),
Poem Counterpoem (1966), in collaboration with Dudley Randall, and *Iron Lace*
(1968).

FRANK MARSHALL DAVIS (1905–
—) Born in Arkansas City, Kansas, he
was educated at Kansas State College. He
had an active career as a journalist, helping to found the Atlanta *Daily World,*
and later became executive editor of the
Associated Negro Press in Chicago. Mr.
Davis has been a Rosenwald Fellow in
poetry and has published three books of
poems: *Black Man's Verse* (1935); *I Am
the American Negro* (1937); and *47th
Street* (1948). Mr. Davis now lives in
Hawaii.

CLARISSA SCOTT DELANY (1901–
1927) Born in Tuskegee Institute, Alabama. Her father was Emmett J. Scott,
the secretary to Booker T. Washington.
She grew up in Tuskegee and attended
Bradford Academy in New England and
Wellesley College in Massachusetts. She
became a teacher at Dunbar High School in
Washington, D.C., and was married to Hu-
bert Delany in 1926. Her poem "Solace"
has been included in many collections over
the years, including *The Poetry of the Ne-*

gro (1949, 1970) and *American Negro Poetry* (1963).

DJANGATOLUM (LLOYD M. CORBIN, JR.) (1949–   ) Born in New York City, he attended the public schools of that city and is a student at Brandeis University. His poems have appeared in such publications as *CAW* (Students for a Democratic Society magazine), *What's Happening, Look,* and *Black At Brandeis.* His work has been included in the anthologies *The Writers Workshop Anthology, The Me Nobody Knows* (1969), *Soulscript* (1970), and *Black Out Loud* (1970).

OWEN DODSON (1914–   ) Born in New York City. For many years he was Professor of Drama at Howard University. He is a graduate of Bates College and Yale University. Mr. Dodson has received acclaim and fellowships for his poetry and prose writings over the years, and is a longtime stage director—at Atlanta University as well as at Howard. He has toured Europe with theater groups, and his plays have been performed all over America. His poetry and stories have been included in many anthologies, and his books of poetry include *Powerful Long Ladder* (1946) and *The Confession Stone: Song Cycles* (1970). He is the author of the novels *Boy at the Window* (1951) and *When Trees Were Green.* Mr. Dodson lives in New York City, where he is an artistic consultant to the Harlem School of the Arts.

WILLIAM EDWARD BURGHARDT DU BOIS (1868–1963) Born in Great Barrington, Massachusetts. He studied at Fisk University and Harvard, where he received his Ph.D. in 1895. Dr. Du Bois was a professor of sociology, economics, and history, and an expert on Black American history. A bibliography of his writings runs well over a hundred pages, including scholarly studies in various fields as well as autobiographies, novels, and volumes of essays. His first book was *Suppression of the African Slave Trade* (1896). His *Souls of Black Folk* (1903) has had an enormous influence on Black writers and continues to be reprinted in many editions. His study of the post-Civil War period, *Black Reconstruction* (1935), remains one of the most outstanding works on that era. Dr. Du Bois was a founder of the National Association for the Advancement of Colored People

(NAACP) in 1909, and was the first editor of its magazine, *Crisis,* until 1934. He initiated Pan-African Congresses of African and American Negroes to focus attention on social and economic problems of Black people the world over. For over sixty years, through his speeches, articles, books, and poetry, Dr. Du Bois was the leading spokesman for a militant and radical attack on all forms of economic exploitation and racial discrimination. In 1961 he left the United States to live in Ghana, where he died on August 28, 1963.

ALFRED A. DUCKETT (1918–   ) Born in Brooklyn, New York, he attended the schools of that city. He was a newspaperman with the *Amsterdam News,* the New York *Age,* and the Pittsburgh *Courier.* Mr. Duckett's poetry has appeared in anthologies such as *The Poetry of the Negro* (1949, 1970) and *American Negro Poetry* (1963). In 1972 he published a book for young people on "new black politicians," entitled *Changing of the Guard.*

HENRY DUMAS (1935–1968) Born in Arkansas, he came to Harlem when he was ten years old. He attended Rutgers University and later taught at Hiram College in Ohio. He was Director of Language Workshops and Teacher-Counselor at Southern Illinois University until his death in 1968. On May 23 he was shot and killed by a white policeman on the Harlem Station platform of the New York Central Railroad. Little else is known about the circumstances surrounding his death. Mr. Dumas' work has appeared in many periodicals, and is included in the anthologies *A Galaxy of Black Writing* (1970), *Black Out Loud* (1970), and *Brothers and Sisters* (1970). In 1970, Southern Illinois University Press published *Ark of Bones and Other Stories* and *Poetry for My People,* two collections of Dumas' work edited by Hale Chatfield and Eugene Redmond.

PAUL LAURENCE DUNBAR (1872–1906) Born in Dayton, Ohio, he was the son of former slaves (his father had escaped by way of the Underground Railroad). He was unable to attend college and went to work as an elevator operator, a job he was holding when his first volume of poems, *Oak and Ivy,* was published in 1893. His second book was *Majors and Minors* (1895), and it was followed by Dunbar's highly successful

Lyrics of a Lowly Life, published in 1896. He achieved national recognition, and continued to write much poetry and prose, even though suffering from tuberculosis, which finally caused his untimely death. His *Complete Poems,* published in 1913, heralded the new era in literature that began for Black Americans in the early twentieth century.

RAY DUREM (1915–1963) Born in Seattle, Washington, he joined the U.S. Navy at fourteen and later fought as a member of the International Brigade during the Spanish Civil War. He lived for many years in Mexico, and returned to the United States for medical treatment. Mr. Durem died in Los Angeles prior to the publication of many of his poems, and has since been heralded as "the first black poet." His work has appeared in such publications as *Negro Digest/Black World* and *Umbra,* and in the anthologies *New Negro Poets: USA* (1964), and *I Am the Darker Brother* (1968). A collection of his poetry, *Take No Prisoners,* was published in 1972.

EBON (DOOLEY) (1942–   ) He has read his work in and around the Chicago area, and is discussed by Don L. Lee in his book of critical studies, *Dynamite Voices: Black Poets of the 1960's* (1971). Ebon published a volume of his poetry, *Revolution,* in 1968.

JAMES A. EMANUEL (1921–   ) Born in Nebraska, he was educated at Columbia University. He is a Professor of English at the City College of New York. Mr. Emanuel's work has appeared in many publications, including the anthologies *New Negro Poets: USA* (1964) and *The Black Poets* (1971). He is the author of two volumes of poetry, *The Treehouse and Other Poems* (1968) and *Panther Man* (1970). He is also the author of a biography of Langston Hughes and is the co-editor of *Dark Sympathy,* an anthology of Black American literature published in 1968.

MARI EVANS Born in Toledo, Ohio. She was a John Hay Whitney Fellow (1965–66) and has been a consultant for the National Endowment of the Arts. Her poetry has been used extensively in textbooks and anthologies. Producer/director of a weekly half-hour television series, "The Black Experience," she is also

Writer-in-Residence and Assistant Professor in Black Literature at Indiana University, Bloomington. Her volume of poetry, *I Am a Black Woman,* was published in 1970. It received the Black Academy of Arts and Letters Second Annual Poetry Award.

SARAH WEBSTER FABIO (1928–   ) Born in Nashville, Tennessee. She has an M.A. from San Francisco State College in California. She has taught at Merritt Junior College in Oakland and participated in the First World Festival of Negro Art, held in Dakar, Senegal, in 1966. Ms. Fabio's essays and poetry are published in such periodicals as *Negro Digest/Black World,* and she is the author of two volumes of poetry, *A Mirror: A Soul* (1969) and *Black Is a Panther Caged* (1972). She is a member of the Afro-American Studies Department of the University of California at Berkeley.

JESSIE REDMOND FAUSET (1882–1961) Born in Fredericksville, New Jersey, and educated at Cornell, the University of Pennsylvania, and the Alliance Française in Paris. She began a literary career as editor of *Crisis* magazine, but spent most of her professional life as a teacher. Her poetry appears in many magazines and anthologies. Ms. Fauset is also the author of four novels: *There Is Confusion* (1924); *Plum Bun* (1929); *The Chinaberry Tree* (1931); and *Comedy, American Style* (1933).

JULIA FIELDS (1938–   ) Born in Uniontown, Alabama, she was graduated from Knoxville College in Tennessee. Her work has appeared in numerous periodicals, including *Negro Digest/Black World, Umbra,* and the *Massachusetts Review.* She is represented in the anthologies *Beyond the Blues* (1962), *New Negro Poets: USA* (1964), *City in All Directions* (1969), and *The Poetry of the Negro* (1949, 1970).

CALVIN FORBES (1945–   ) Born in Newark, New Jersey. He attended Rutgers University, The New School, and Stanford University. His poetry has appeared in *The Yale Review* and *The American Scholar,* and in the anthology *New Black Voices* (1972). Mr. Forbes lives in Boston and teaches Afro-American and African Literature at Emerson College.

CAROL FREEMAN (1941–   ) Born in Rayville, Louisiana, she has attended Oakland City College and the University of California at Berkeley. Ms. Freeman has been described in various publications as being housewife, mother, part-time field worker and "revolutionary black nationalist." Her poetry has appeared in such collections as *Black Fire* (1968) and *The Poetry of the Negro* (1949, 1970).

HOYT W. FULLER (1928–   ) Born in Atlanta, Georgia. He is a founder of Chicago's Organization of Black American Culture, and the long-time Managing Editor of *Negro Digest/Black World* magazine. Through his work on the magazine, he has presented and encouraged hundreds of Black American writers, and played a major role in the development of contemporary Black literature. "Seravezza" appeared in *Negro Digest,* and "Lost Moment" is from the anthology *To Gwen with Love: A Tribute to Gwendolyn Brooks* (1971).

CARL GARDNER (1931–   ) Born in Washington, D.C., he writes prose as well as poetry. He was graduated from Howard University, and has had his poetry published in such periodicals as *Northwest Review, Patterns,* and *Dasein.* His work is included in such anthologies as *Beyond the Blues* (1962), *New Negro Poets: USA* (1964), and *In a Time of Revolution: Poems from Our Third World* (1969).

ZACK GILBERT (1925–   ) Born near McMullin, Missouri, he has lived in Chicago since 1943. His poetry has appeared in such periodicals as *Negro Digest/Black World* and *Liberator,* and in the anthologies *For Malcolm* (1967) and *The Poetry of the Negro* (1949, 1970). Mr. Gilbert has held a wide assortment of jobs and is employed with the B&O–C&O Railroad. He is also an editorial consultant for Path Press, a Black publishing company in Chicago. A volume of his poetry, *My Own Hallelujahs,* was published in 1971.

NIKKI GIOVANNI (1943–   ) Born in Knoxville, Tennessee, she was raised in Cincinnati, Ohio. She attended Fisk University and the University of Pennsylvania. Her work has appeared in many anthologies, magazines, textbooks, and other publications since her first books of poems, *Black Feeling, Black Talk* and *Black Judgement,* appeared in 1968. She has been active in speaking on college campuses, community-organization-sponsored programs, and television interview shows, particularly "Soul," for National Educational Television. Other publications include: two books of poetry, *Re:Creation* (1970) and *My House* (1972); a book of poems for young children, *Spin a Soft Black Song* (1971); her *Poem of Angela Yvonne Davis* (1970); and an anthology of Black women poets, *Night Comes Softly* (1970). Other works include a volume of essays, *Gemini* (1971), and a recording, *Truth Is on Its Way* (1971).

D. L. GRAHAM (1944–1970) Born in Gary, Indiana, he studied with John O. Killens and others at Fisk University. He published a small collection of his poems, *Black Song* (1966), while still a student at Fisk. Two other groups of his poems, *Soul Motion I* and *Soul Motion II,* were published through the Division of Cultural Research, Department of Art, at the University in 1969. Mr. Graham's work has appeared in *Umbra: Anthology 1967–1968,* and in the anthologies *Kaleidoscope* (1967) and *Black Fire* (1968). Donald Graham was killed in an automobile accident in the summer of 1970.

RICHARD E. GRANT (1949–   ) Born in Gary, Indiana, he attended Stanford University and entered Howard University Medical School in 1971. His work has been published in *Brilliant Corners,* a magazine of the Black Student Union of Stanford University.

ANGELINA WELD GRIMKE (1880–1958) Born in Boston, Massachusetts, she was educated in the schools of that city. She became a teacher at the Armstrong Manual Training School of Washington, D.C., and later taught English for a number of years at Dunbar High School in Washington. *Rachel,* a three-act play, was published in 1921. Her poetry has appeared in such anthologies as *The Poetry of the Negro* (1949, 1970) and *American Negro Poetry* (1963). She spent her later life in retirement in New York City.

MICHAEL S. HARPER (1938–   ) Born in Brooklyn, New York, and grew up in Los Angeles. He received a B.A. and M.A. degree from California State University in Los Angeles, and has a second M.A. from the University of Iowa. He has taught at Los Angeles City College, Contra Costa College in California, Reed College, Lewis and Clark College (where he was Poet-in-Residence), Cal State at Hayward in California, and the Center for Advanced Study, University of Illinois at Urbana. Mr. Harper is on the faculty of Brown University, Providence, Rhode Island, as Associate Professor of English. His poems have appeared in numerous publications, including *Carolina Quarterly, Southern Review, Negro Digest/Black World, Black Scholar,* and *Poetry.* He is represented in the anthologies *Natural Process* (1970) and *To Gwen with Love* (1971), among others. His books of poetry include *Dear John, Dear Coltrane* (1970) and *History Is Your Own Heartbeat* (1971). He has lectured and given readings around the country and has received fellowships from the American Academy of Arts and Letters and the Black Academy of Arts and Letters.

WILLIAM J. HARRIS (1942–   ) Born in Yellow Springs, Ohio. He was graduated from Central State University in 1968, and completed his M.A. and Ph.D. in Creative Writing at Stanford University. Mr. Harris is Professor of American Literature and Creative Writing at Cornell University. His poetry has been published in *The Antioch Review* and *The Beloit Poetry Journal,* among other periodicals, and is included in the anthologies *Nine Black Poets* (1968), *Black Out Loud* (1970), *Natural Process* (1970), *Cavalcade* (1971), and *New Black Voices* (1972).

DE LEON HARRISON (1941–   ) Born in Little Rock, Arkansas, he came to California as a young man. He is a filmmaker and painter, as well as poet, and is founder and director of Seshesh Media Workshop, and co-founder of Cinema Blackscope. His poetry has appeared in such periodicals as *Black Dialogue, Journal of Black Poetry,* and *Axolotl.* He is included in the anthology *Dices Or Black Bones* (1970). De Leon Harrison is an instructor at San José State College, teaching a survey of Afro-American music and working with Reflections, a communications workshop in the East Bay area dealing with film and videotape production.

WALTER EVERETTE HAWKINS (1883–   ) Born in Warrenton, North Carolina, he attended the public schools of that town, and was graduated from Kittrell College in 1901. He began work in the railway mail service in 1912, according to previous biographical material, and little else is available on his activities beyond the 1920s, when he resided in Washington, D.C. He published a volume of poetry, *Chords and Discords,* in 1909, which was reissued in 1920. His work has been included in *An Anthology of Verse by Negro Americans* (1924, 1968).

ROBERT HAYDEN (1913–   ) Born in Detroit, Michigan. He was educated at Wayne State University and the University of Michigan. He is the recipient of many awards, including Hopwood Awards on two occasions, and Rosenwald and Ford Foundation Fellowships. His volumes of poetry include *Heart-Shape in the Dust* (1940), *The Lion and the Archer* (1948) (a joint publication with Myron O'Higgins), *Figure of Time* (1955), *A Ballad of Remembrance* (1962), *Selected Poems* (1966), and *Words in the Mourning Time* (1971). *A Ballad of Remembrance* won the Grand Prize at the First World Festival of Negro Arts held in 1966 in Dakar, Senegal. *Words in the Mourning Time* was nominated for a National Book Award in 1972. Mr. Hayden has been a longtime member of the faculty of Fisk University and is Writer-in-Residence and Professor of English at the University of Michigan.

DONALD JEFFREY HAYES (1904–   ) Born in Raleigh, North Carolina. His early interests were in music and theater, and he studied singing and directing. He appeared in several Broadway productions during the twenties and thirties. His poetry has been published in such periodicals as *Harpers Bazaar* and *Good Housekeeping,* among others, and in the anthologies *The Poetry of the Negro* (1949, 1970) and *American Negro Poetry* (1963). He was for many years a counselor with the New Jersey State Employment Service in Atlantic City, and was a member of that city's Board of Education, serving as its president for four years. Mr. Hayes is retired and living in Raleigh, where he is writing music as well as poetry.

DAVID HENDERSON (1942–   ) Born in Harlem, he was educated in New York City at the New School, Hunter College, and Bronx Community College. He has been a teacher at Columbia University and the City College of New York, and worked with the Free Southern Theatre in New Orleans. Mr. Henderson was active in the organization of *Umbra* magazine and the *East Village Other* newspaper on the Lower East Side of New York, and was Poet-in-Residence for 1969–70 at City College. His poetry has been published in many periodicals, including *Evergreen Review, New American Review, Negro Digest/Black World, Freedomways, Journal of Black Poetry, Paris Review,* and *Essence.* His work appears in anthologies such as *Black Fire* (1968), *The New Black Poetry* (1969), *Black Out Loud* (1970), and *Black Spirits* (1972). His books include *Felix of the Silent Forest* (1967) and *De Mayor of Harlem* (1971). He lives in Berkeley, California, where he teaches, and edits *Umbra/Blackworks,* a periodical of Black American literature.

CALVIN C. HERNTON (1934–) Born in Chattanooga, Tennessee. He was educated at Fisk University and at Talladega College, where he received his M.A. in Sociology. His poetry has been published in many magazines and anthologies, both in this country and in Europe, and a volume of his poems, *The Coming of Chronos to the House of Nightsong,* appeared in 1963. His other books include *Sex and Racism in America* (1965), *White Paper for White Americans* (1966), and *Coming Together: Black Power, White Hatred and Sexual Hangups* (1971). Mr. Hernton is Associate Professor of Afro-American Studies at Oberlin College in Ohio.

LESLIE PINCKNEY HILL (1880–1960) Born in Lynchburgh, Virginia, where he was educated. He attended Harvard University and taught at Tuskegee Institute. He became the principal of the Cheyney Training School for Teachers in Pennsylvania, which later became Cheyney State College. His published works include *The Wings of Oppression* (1922) and *Toussaint L'Ouverture—A Dramatic History* (1928).

M. CARL HOLMAN (1919–) Born in Minter City, Mississippi, he was educated in the public schools of St. Louis, Missouri. He is a graduate of Lincoln University and the University of Chicago. He received the Fiske and Rosenwald poetry awards and has been a teacher at Hampton Institute in Virginia and Clark College in Atlanta. During the late 1960s Mr. Holman was a Staff Director with the United States Commission on Civil Rights, and he is a vice-president with the National Urban Coalition. Mr. Holman's poetry has been included in such anthologies as *The Poetry of the Negro* (1949, 1970), *American Negro Poetry* (1963), and *Kaleidoscope* (1967).

FRANK HORNE (1899–) Born in New York City. He was educated at the City College of New York, Columbia University, and the University of Southern California. He is a graduate of the Northern Illinois College of Ophthalmology, and practiced that profession in Chicago and New York. Mr. Horne was a teacher and worked with the United States Housing Authority in Washington, D.C. His poem series, *Letters Found Near a Suicide,* won a *Crisis* magazine award in 1925. His work has appeared in numerous magazines and anthologies. In 1963 a collection of his poetry, *Haverstraw,* was published in London.

LANGSTON HUGHES (1902–1967) Born in Joplin, Missouri, and went to school in Lawrence, Kansas, and Cleveland, Ohio. He attended Columbia University, worked at odd jobs, shipped on freighters to Africa and Europe, and returned to study at Lincoln University in Pennsylvania, from which he was graduated in 1929. He received many awards and honors, crossed the country to give public readings of his work, and was a prolific writer for over forty years. He wrote novels, books of short stories, and plays, the best-known of which is *Simply Heavenly;* newspaper columns about "Simple" and his thoughts and feelings; books for children, histories, and many volumes of poetry. They include *The Weary Blues* (1926), *The Dream Keeper* (1932), *Montage of a Dream Deferred* (1951), *Selected Poems* (1959), *Ask Your Mama* (1961), and *The Panther and the Lash,* which was published soon after his death in 1967. Mr. Hughes lived in New York City and was active in helping young writers who sought his advice. He edited the landmark volume of Black American poetry *The Poetry of the Negro* (1949, 1970), along with Arna Bontemps, and *New Negro Poets: USA* (1964), giving first recognition to many poets of the 1960s.

MAE JACKSON (1946–) Born in Earl, Arkansas. She has been active with the Student National Coordinating Committee and the H. Rap Brown Anti-Dope

Movement. Her work has been published in such periodicals as *Negro Digest/ Black World, Journal of Black Poetry, Black Creation,* and *Essence.* She is included in such anthologies as *Black Out Loud* (1970), *Night Comes Softly* (1970), and *Black Spirits* (1972). Ms. Jackson is a teacher of creative writing in Brooklyn and is the mother of Njeri Ayoka, "a beautiful daughter." A collection of her poetry, *Can I Poet with You,* was published in 1969 and won the third Conrad Kent Rivers Memorial Award of *Black World* magazine.

LANCE JEFFERS (1919–) Born in Fremont, Nebraska, "son of a farmer and grandson of a Florida slave." He was raised in Nebraska and San Francisco, served as an officer in World War II, and was graduated from Columbia University in 1951. He has taught for the past two decades and has published his poetry in numerous periodicals, including *Tamarack Review, Freedomways,* and the *DeKalb Literary Arts Journal.* His work appears in the anthologies *Beyond the Blues* (1962), *Black Voices* (1968), *Black Fire* (1968), *Nine Black Poets* (1968), *The New Black Poetry* (1969), *A Galaxy of Black Writing* (1970), *Cavalcade* (1971), *A Broadside Treasury* (1971), and *New Black Voices* (1972). Mr. Jeffers has also published fiction and literary criticism in *Black Scholar* and the *Black Seventies.* Broadside Press published a volume of his poetry, *My Blackness Is the Beauty of This Land,* in 1970. He writes: "My work reflects, I believe, the irresistible drive of the black race and the entire human race toward freedom: toward the total realization of our potentialities; toward the creation of boundaryless human harmony and the flowering of every human personality to its innate godliness."

TED JOANS (1928–) Born in Cairo, Illinois. He is a painter and jazz musician as well as poet. Although he has lived in Africa and Europe for many years, his poetry continues to be published in American magazines, anthologies, and texts. His books include *Beat, All of Ted Joans, The Hipsters,* and more recently, *Black Pow-Wow* (1969) and *Afrodisia* (1970).

FENTON JOHNSON (1888–1958) Born in Chicago, and educated in the schools of that city. He attended the University of Chicago and produced several plays at the old Pekin Theatre on South State Street. He also edited and published several literary magazines. *A Little Dreaming,* published in 1913, was his first volume of poetry. It was followed by *Visions of the Dusk* (1915) and *Songs of the Soil* (1916). He published a book of short stories, *Tales of Darkest America,* in 1920.

FRED JOHNSON (1940–) Born in Philadelphia, Pennsylvania. He was graduated from Howard University, and received an M.A. from Stanford University in their writers' program. He has taught on the high-school level in Philadelphia, and at Clarion State College in Pennsylvania. His poetry and stories have appeared in literary magazines at Howard and at Stanford. The two poems that appear in this collection are from manuscript.

GEORGIA DOUGLAS JOHNSON (1886–1966) Born in Atlanta, Georgia, she was educated at Atlanta University and Oberlin College in Ohio, where she studied musical composition. She became a teacher and moved to Washington, D.C., where she pursued that career, wrote poetry, was employed in government agencies, and was a friend to decades of young writers at her home. Her books of poetry include *The Heart of a Woman* (1918), *Bronze* (1922), and *An Autumn Love Cycle* (1928). *Share My World* was published in 1962.

HELENE JOHNSON (1907–) Born in Boston, Massachusetts, she was educated in the public schools of that city and at Boston University. She attended Columbia University in New York City in the mid-1920s and became the youngest member of that group of Black writers who comprised the "Negro Renaissance" of the Harlem of that time. Her work was published in such magazines as *Vanity Fair* and *Opportunity: A Journal of Negro Life,* and in the anthologies *The Poetry of the Negro* (1949, 1970) and *American Negro Poetry* (1963).

JAMES WELDON JOHNSON (1871–1938) Born in Jacksonville, Florida, he was educated there and at Atlanta University. He had distinguished careers as public school principal, lawyer, diplomat, executive secretary of the NAACP, and Professor of Literature at Fisk University. He and his brother J. Rosamond Johnson wrote the words and music for "Lift Every

Voice and Sing," the "national anthem" for Black people in America. He also wrote lyrics for musical shows and popular song hits. Among his many published works are *Fifty Years and Other Poems* (1917), *God's Trombones* (1927), *St. Peter Relates an Incident* (1930), and his autobiography *Along This Way* (1933). He edited *The Book of American Negro Poetry,* first issued in 1922. Mr. Johnson died in an auto accident in 1938.

JOE JOHNSON (1940–) Born in New York City. His poetry and fiction have been published in such periodicals as *Umbra, Liberator, African Revolution* and *Black Creation,* and in the anthologies *Poets of Today* (1964), *Yardbird Review* (1972), and *Dues* (1972). Mr. Johnson teaches Afro-American Literature in the School of American Studies at Ramapo College.

JUNE JORDAN (1936–) Born in Harlem and raised in the Bedford-Stuyvesant section of Brooklyn, in New York City. She attended Barnard College and the University of Chicago, and has taught at the City College of New York, Connecticut College, and Sarah Lawrence College. Her books include: *Who Look At Me* (1969), *His Own Where* (1971), and *Dry Victories* (1972), works for young people; an anthology of Black American poetry, *Soulscript* (1970); *The Voice of the Children* (1970), a collection of poetry by her students at a creative writing workshop in Brooklyn; and *Some Changes,* a volume of her poetry published in 1971.

NORMAN JORDAN (1938–) Born in Ansted, West Virginia. He is a playwright as well as poet, works with the Muntu Workshop in Cleveland, and is Playwright-in-Residence at Karamu House. His work has been published in *Free Lance, Vibrations, Cricket, Journal of Black Poetry, Negro Digest/Black World, Confrontation,* and other periodicals. He is included in the anthologies *Black Fire* (1968), *The New Black Poetry* (1969), *Black Out Loud* (1970), *The Poetry of the Negro* (1949, 1970), and *Black Spirits* (1972). His plays have been staged in New York, San Diego, and Cleveland, and his volumes of poetry include *Destination: Ashes* and *Above Maya* (1971).

BOB KAUFMAN (1935–) Born in San Francisco, he was a leading poet during the 1950s period of that city's literary

"renaissance." He was influential in the development of white "beat" poets such as Allen Ginsberg, Gregory Corso, and Lawrence Ferlinghetti. Bob Kaufman had earned great respect for his work in England and France before it became well known in this country, although he is now represented in many collections. His books of poetry include *Solitudes Crowded with Loneliness* (1965) and *Golden Sardine* (1967).

KEORAPETSE KGOSITSILE (1938–) Born in Johannesburg, South Africa, he has been in exile in the United States since 1961. His poetry has appeared in numerous periodicals, including *Journal of Black Poetry, Negro Digest/Black World, The New African, Urban Review,* and *Pan African Journal.* He is represented in the anthologies *For Malcolm* (1967), *Black Fire* (1968), *Black Arts* (1969), and *Black Spirits* (1972). His volumes of poetry include *Spirits Unchained* (1969), *For Melba* (1970), and *My Name Is Afrika* (1971). He has received the Conrad Kent Rivers Memorial Award for his poetry from *Black World* magazine.

ETHERIDGE KNIGHT (1933–) Born in Corinth, Mississippi. While he was still an inmate at Indiana State Prison, *Poems From Prison,* a volume of his poetry, was published in 1968. His work has appeared in *Negro Digest/Black World, Journal of Black Poetry,* and other periodicals. He is included in the anthologies *City in All Directions* (1969), *The New Black Poetry* (1969), *Dices or Black Bones* (1970), and *Black Out Loud* (1970), among others. He is Poetry Editor of *Motive* magazine and is married to poet Sonia Sanchez.

BETTE DARCIE LATIMER (1927–) Born in Rochester, New York, she was educated in the schools of that city and at Fisk University. She was graduated from Fisk in 1948 and did her graduate work at the University of Michigan. Her poetry has appeared in the *Fisk Herald* and in *Phylon* and *Crisis* magazines. Her poem "For William Edward Burghardt Du Bois on his Eightieth Birthday" is from *The Poetry of the Negro* (1949, 1970).

DON L. LEE (1942–) Born in Little Rock, Arkansas, he has taught Afro-American literature and history at Roosevelt University in Chicago, and at Cornell and other colleges. His volumes of poetry include *Think Black!* (1967), *Black Pride* (1968), *Don't Cry, Scream* (1969), *We Walk the Way of the New World* (1970), and *Directionscore: Selected and New Poems* (1971). He is an influential critic and essayist, as well as poet, and is the author of critical studies of Black poets of the 1960s, *Dynamite Voices*. The first volume was published in 1971, the second in 1972. Mr. Lee is an editor of the Third World Press, a Black publishing company in Chicago.

JULIUS LESTER (1939–   ) Born in St. Louis, Missouri, he has been a full-time worker for the Student Nonviolent Coordinating Committee, a folk singer, composer, and radio commentator. He has published poetry in several anthologies, including *In a Time of Revolution* (1969), *The Writing on the Wall* (1969), and *Soulscript* (1970). Since 1968 he has been a prolific author of books of social criticism, including *Look Out Whitey, Black Power's Gon' Get Your Mama* (1968), *Revolutionary Notes* (1970), and *Search for the New Land* (1969). He is the author of books for young people, including *Black Folktales* (1970) and *To Be a Slave* (1968), and has contributed many articles and reviews to such periodicals as *Liberation*, *The New York Times*, *Evergreen Review*, and *Ebony* magazine. He is editor of *The Seventh Son*, a two-volume collection of *The Thought and Writings of W.E.B. Du Bois*, published in 1971.

ANGELO LEWIS (1950–   ) Born in Oakland, California, he makes his home in Philadelphia, Pennsylvania. His poetry has been published in *Motive* magazine and in *It Is the Poem Singing Into Your Eyes: Anthology of New Young Poets* (1971). He works as a musician, travels around the country, and his main concerns are "finding the peace inside myself . . . seeing myself in others . . . finding everything in everything."

ELOUISE LOFTIN (1950–   ) Born "in the Cumberland Street Meat Market in Brooklyn. i was pretty so my mother took me home. the blessed thing that she is, she cared for me ever since." Ms. Loftin is a student at New York University and Poetry Editor of *Black Creation* magazine. Her work has been published in such periodicals as *Essence*, *Présence Africaine*, and *Confrontation*. Her first volume of poetry, *Jumbish*, was published in 1972.

PEARL CLEAGE LOMAX (1948–   ) A resident of Atlanta, Georgia, she is a playwright as well as a poet. She was a drama major at Howard University and Spelman College, and her plays have been produced at both schools. Her poetry has appeared in such periodicals as *Journal of Black Poetry*, *Poetry* magazine, *Detroit Free Press Magazine*, and *Readers and Writers* magazine. She is included in the anthologies *We Speak as Liberators* (1970) and *The Insistent Present* (1970). A volume of her poetry, *We Don't Need No Music*, was published in 1972. Mrs. Lomax writes:

"I feel that a Black writer must commit himself to exploring the various facets of the Black experience with an eye toward contributing something positive to the Liberation Struggle that Black people are engaged in. This does not mean that every poem must urge people to pick up the gun. In order to prepare for meaningful struggle, we must also have artists who reflect the beauty of Black people and begin to deal with the kinds of relationships we are building with each other. We need artists who can help us to examine ourselves carefully enough to know what is worth keeping and what must be discarded. The writer must turn his eyes inward and look at his own Black self in order to turn his eyes outward toward the needs of his people with understanding and commitment."

DOUGHTRY LONG (1942–   ) Born in Atlanta, Georgia. He has spent two years in Africa, and has traveled extensively throughout the United States and the Caribbean. His work has appeared in various periodicals and anthologies, and he has published two volumes of poetry, *Black Love, Black Hope* (1971) and *Song For Nia* (1971).

AUDRE LORDE (1934–   ) Born in New York City, she was educated at Hunter College and Columbia University. Her poetry has been published in *Journal of Black Poetry*, *Negro Digest/Black World*, *Transatlantic Review*, *Freedomways*, *Women: A Liberation Journal*, and other periodicals. She is represented in the anthologies *Beyond the Blues* (1962), *Sixes and Sevens* (1962), *New Negro Poets: USA* (1964), *The New Black Poets* (1969), and *The Black Woman* (1971). She has been a Young Adult librarian in Mount Vernon, New York, and Poet-in-Residence at Tougaloo College.

She lives in New York City, where she teaches at City and Lehman colleges of the City University. In 1963 Ms. Lorde wrote of herself: "I am Black, Woman, and Poet—all three are facts outside the realm of choice. My eyes have a part in my seeing; my breath in my breathing; and all that I am in who I am. All who I love are of my people; it is not simple." Since then she has published two books of poetry, *The First Cities* (1968) and *Cables To Rage* (1970). About her poetry, she writes: "I can only say, in regard to my work, that poets must teach what they know, or else we shall all be lost to 'thingdom,' and so share with you the beauty and the best of all I am,—which is my Fat Black self."

FELIPE LUCIANO (1947–) Born and raised on 112th Street in *El Barrio* in Manhattan, and in various ghettos in New York and Los Angeles. He attended New York City public schools and became active in the city's street life, serving time in prison for a gang fight, and coming out to join The Last Poets and co-found The Young Lords organization. He has attended Queens College and has toured The People's Republic of China. His writing has appeared in various periodicals, including *The Village Voice* in New York and *Encore* magazine. He has been published in such anthologies as *Black Spirits* (1972), in which "You're Nothing but a Spanish Colored Kid" first appeared.

K. CURTIS LYLE (1944–) Born in Los Angeles, California. He attended the University of New Mexico, was graduated from California State College in Los Angeles, and was a member of the original Watts Writers Workshop, 1966–1969. He worked in the Seattle Repertory Theatre, the Surgical Theatre and Black Arts West in Seattle, Washington, and in Theatre-in-the-Park, Cincinnati, Ohio. Mr. Lyle has been Writer-in-Residence and Professor of Black Literature at Washington University in St. Louis, Missouri, since 1969. His work has appeared in the periodicals *Journal of Black Poetry, Essence, Watts Poets and Writers, Negro-American Literary Forum, Confrontation,* and *Mundus Artium,* and in the anthology *New Black Voices* (1972).

CHARLES LYNCH (1943–) Born in Baltimore, Maryland. He is an Instructor of English at Brooklyn College, his doc-

toral dissertation focusing on the two contemporary Black poets Gwendolyn Brooks and Robert Hayden. Mr. Lynch is Poetry Editor of *Encore* magazine, and his own work has been published in *Liberator, Black Creation, Readers and Writers* magazine, *World Order,* and *Journal of Black Poetry.*

L. V. MACK (1947–) Born in Brooklyn, New York. He attended college at Tennessee A & I and has traveled to Mexico and California. His poetry has been included in the anthology *Natural Process: An Anthology of New Black Poetry* (1970).

NAOMI LONG MADGETT (1923–) Born in Norfolk, Virginia, she was educated at Virginia State College, Wayne State University, and the University of Detroit. She has lived in Detroit since 1946 and was a teacher in the public schools of that city. In 1967 she was named Distinguished English Teacher of the year. Her work has appeared in many periodicals, anthologies, and texts in this country and in Europe. She is the author of four volumes of poetry, *Songs to a Phantom Nightingale* (1941), *One and the Many* (1956), *Star by Star* (1965, 1970), and *Pink Ladies in the Afternoon* (1972). Since 1968 Mrs. Madgett has been Associate Professor of English at Eastern Michigan University in Ypsilanti.

BARBARA MAHONE (1944–) Born in Chicago, she spent most of her childhood in Alabama. She attended Fisk University and received a B.A. degree in English at Washington State University. Her poetry has appeared in the periodicals *Negro Digest/Black World, Nommo, Journal of Black Poetry,* and *Tuesday,* and in the anthology *Night Comes Softly* (1970). Barbara Mahone is the author of a volume of poetry, *Sugarfields* (1970), and lives in Chicago with her husband, artist Emmett McBain, and their four children. She writes about her work: "I write poems for my children and their children. Because I want them to know who Mama was. Mama being Black and self-conscious about her own maturation —from a child of ignorant beauty to an adult who painfully understands. It's intimate stuff, of a very fragile nature. But it's history and legend that can be built upon."

CLARENCE MAJOR (1936–) Born in Atlanta, Georgia, he grew up in Chicago. His first poems were published at eighteen. Since then he has published his poetry, fiction, and essays in numerous periodicals, including *Essence, Negro Digest/Black World, Chelsea,* and *The Literary Review.* His work appears in the anthologies *American Negro Poetry* (1963) and *Black Voices* (1968), among others. His first novel, *All-Night Visitors,* and an anthology, *The New Black Poetry,* were published in 1969. His other works include *The Dictionary of Afro-American Slang* (1970), *Swallow the Lake* (1970), *Symptoms & Madness* (1971), and *Private Line* (1971). *No,* a second novel, and *The Cotton Club,* a fourth book of poems, appeared in 1972. He received a 1970 National Council on the Arts prize and in 1971 a New York Cultural Foundation grant.

HERBERT MARTIN (1933–) Born in Birmingham, Alabama, he was raised in Toledo, Ohio. He attended the University of Toledo and the State University of New York at Buffalo, and has held scholarships at Antioch College, Bread Loaf Writer's Conference, and the University of Colorado. His poetry has appeared in such periodicals as *The Activist, Trace, Mainstream, Confrontation, Sumac,* and *Rap* magazine, and in the anthologies *The Urban Reader* (1971) and *Afro-American Literature, an Introduction* (1969). He has published a volume of his poetry, *New York the Nine Million and Other Poems* (1969), and is Assistant Professor of English at the University of Dayton.

LAWRENCE McGAUGH (1940–) Born in Newton, Kansas, he studied painting at San Francisco Art Institute and lives in Berkeley, California. *A Fifth Sunday* (1965) was his first published volume of poems, followed by *Vacuum Cantos and Other Poems* in 1969. His poetry has been included in the anthology *Black Out Loud* (1970). Mr. McGaugh has had his artwork exhibited in San Francisco, in the Oakland Museum show "New Perspectives in Black Art," and was included in *Black Artists on Art* (1969).

CLAUDE McKAY (1890–1948) Born in Jamaica, the British West Indies. He came to the United States to study at Tuskegee Institute and Kansas State University while still in his early twenties. He was active in the literary life of New York City during the 1920s and was associate editor of *Liberator* magazine. *Harlem Shadows,* a collection of his poetry, was published in 1922 and established McKay as an influential Black poet. He spent almost ten years abroad and published much prose, including *Home to Harlem* (1928), *Banjo* (1929), and *A Long Way from Home* (1937). His *Selected Poems* was published posthumously in 1953.

ADAM DAVID MILLER (1922–) Born and raised in Orangeburg, South Carolina. Of Orangeburg, he has written: "When I was young, they just ran you out of town. Today they shoot you." He has an M.A. in English from the University of California at Berkeley, and he is founding editor of *The Graduate Student Journal,* a magazine of opinion at that school. He is correspondent for *Black Theatre* and has written articles on Afro-American theatre and literature for *The Drama Review* and *The San Francisco Chronicle,* among other periodicals. Mr. Miller is the editor of *Dices or Black Bones: Black Voices of the Seventies,* an anthology published in 1970. He is a member of the English Department and head of the Tutoring Service at Laney College in Oakland, California.

WAYNE MORELAND (1948–) A former editor of *Probe* magazine. His poetry has been published in *Essence* and other periodicals. He writes of his activities: "Am working with the Rising Nation (collective in New York) developing an ideology applicable to the arts/culture/ethical structure of the rising nation. We want to be the ultimate of our aesthetic/ethnic selves, together. They are one."

PAULI MURRAY (1910–) Born in Baltimore, Maryland, attended Hunter College in New York City and Howard University School of Law. She received her LL.M from the California School of Jurisprudence in 1945, and has been a member of the bar of California and New York. While pursuing her career as a lawyer, she also received academic awards and fellowships for her writing. Her poetry has appeared in such periodicals as *Common Ground, Opportunity, Crisis,* and the *Saturday Review.* Ms. Murray published an account of her family history in 1956 entitled *Proud Shoes,* and a collection of her poetry, *Dark Testament,* was published in 1969. Pauli Murray has been a pioneer in the areas of civil rights and women's rights; she was a "freedom rider" in the 1940s to protest segregated seating on interstate buses, and she has brought actions against various universities to admit women to their graduate schools. She has taught at the Ghana School of Law and at Brandeis University in Massachusetts.

ALICE DUNBAR NELSON (1875–1935) Born in New Orleans, Louisiana, she attended public schools in that city. She became a teacher in New Orleans and in Brooklyn, New York, and married Paul Laurence Dunbar in 1898. She was a journalist, lecturer, and the author of several books of prose, including *Violets and Other Tales* (1894) and *The Goodness of St. Tocque* (1899). She edited *Masterpieces of Negro Eloquence* (1913) and *The Dunbar Speaker* (1920).

EFFIE LEE NEWSOME (1885–) Born in Philadelphia, Pennsylvania, she has spent much of her life in Wilberforce, Ohio. Most of her writing has been for children, but her poetry has also been included in anthologies such as *The Poetry of the Negro* (1949, 1970) and *American Negro Poetry* (1963). She is the author of a volume of poetry for children, *Gladiola Garden*, published in 1940.

GLORIA C. ODEN (1923–) Born in Yonkers, New York, and educated at Howard University. She has been senior editor of mathematics and science books for a major publisher and has taught at the State University of New York in Stony Brook. Her poetry has appeared in a number of anthologies and texts, including *New Negro Poets: USA* (1964) and *Blackamerican Literature* (1971). Ms. Oden teaches at the University of Maryland in Baltimore.

MYRON O'HIGGINS (1918–) Born in Chicago, he was a student of Sterling Brown at Howard University, and also attended Yale University and the University of Paris. He has received Moten and Rosenwald fellowships, and has traveled widely abroad. His poems have been published in *The Lion and the Archer*, a volume he and Robert Hayden issued privately in 1948. His work appears in many anthologies, including *The Poetry of the Negro* (1949, 1970), *American Negro Poetry* (1963), *Kaleidoscope* (1967), and *I Am the Darker Brother*

(1968). He has been on the staff of the Museum of Primitive Art in New York, and has written experimental plays.

RAYMOND R. PATTERSON (1929––) Born in New York City, he received his education at Lincoln University in Pennsylvania and at New York University. His poems have appeared in numerous anthologies, including *Sixes and Sevens* (1962), *Beyond the Blues* (1962), *For Malcolm* (1967), *I Am the Darker Brother* (1968), *Black Out Loud* (1970), and *The Poetry of the Negro* (1949, 1970). He is a teacher, edits a newsletter for poets, and participates in the New York State Council on the Arts poetry-reading project, which takes him throughout the state to schools and libraries, reading and lecturing on his work. A collection of his poetry, *26 Ways of Looking at a Black Man*, was published in 1969.

ROB PENNY (1940–) Born in Opelika, Alabama, he is married and has three sons. He is Writer-in-Residence and instructor in the Department of Black Community Education, Research, and Development at the University of Pittsburgh. Mr. Penny has had three of his plays performed by *Black Horizon Theatre* of Pittsburgh, and his poetry is included in several anthologies. A collection of his poems, *Black Tones of Truth*, was published in 1970.

JULIANNE PERRY (1952–) Born in Durham, North Carolina, she is living in New York City and attends Barnard College. Ms. Perry is a mathematics major, hopes to teach "in an elementary liberation school down South," and has published a poem, *Black Song*, in the Broadside Series during 1972. She writes: "I believe the most important thing in life is truth—that which was, is, and must be. From this element come all the flowers of the universe—love, justice, peace, and this is what we (black people) must continue to deal with."

OLIVER PITCHER (1924–) Born in Massachusetts, he is a playwright as well as poet. His poems have been published in the periodicals *The Tiger's Eye, Totem, Points of Light, Umbra*, and *Negro Digest/Black World*. His works are included in such anthologies as *Schwarzer Orpheus* (1954, 1963), *Beyond the Blues* (1962), and *Kaleidoscope* (1967). Two collections of his poetry, *Dust of Silence*

(1958) and *Prose Poems,* were published in California. The Negro Ensemble Company has presented his play, *The One,* and it is included in *Black Drama Anthology* (1971). Mr. Pitcher has taught Black Theatre at Vassar College and is Poet-in-Residence at Atlanta University Center and editor of the *Atlanta University Center Sampler.*

STERLING PLUMPP (1940–) Born in Clinton, Mississippi on a cotton farm. He has served in the armed forces, and his work has been published in various periodicals and anthologies. His books of poetry include *Portable Soul* (1969) and *Half Black, Half Blacker* (1970). He is Managing Editor of *Black Books Bulletin,* a quarterly journal of literature published by the Institute of Positive Education in Chicago.

QUANDRA PRETTYMAN Born in Baltimore, Maryland, she was graduated from Antioch College and continued her education at the University of Michigan. She has been an instructor at The New School, the New York College of Insurance, and the Summer Program at Connecticut College. Her poetry has appeared in *Negro Digest/Black World* magazine, and is included in the anthologies *I Am the Darker Brother* (1968) and *Black Out Loud* (1970). She is the editor of *The Open Boat and Other Stories by Stephen Crane* (1968). Ms. Prettyman lives in New York City with her husband and daughter, and teaches English at Barnard College.

NORMAN HENRY PRITCHARD II (1939–) Born in New York City, he was educated at New York University. His poetry has appeared in the periodicals *Umbra, Liberator, East Village Other, Poetry Northwest,* and *Eye* magazine, and in many recent anthologies. A volume of his poetry, *The Matrix: Poems 1960–1970,* was published in 1970. Mr. Pritchard teaches a poetry workshop at The New School and is Poet-in-Residence at Friends Seminary.

DUDLEY RANDALL (1914–) Born in Washington, D.C., and educated at Wayne State University and the University of Michigan. He has been a librarian at Lincoln University and Morgan State College, and has been associated with the Wayne County Public Library for many years. His poetry has been widely anthologized, and his volumes of poems include *Poem, Counterpoem* (1966) in collaboration with Margaret Danner, *Cities Burning* (1968), *Love You* (1970), and *More To Remember* (1971). He has also edited anthologies: *For Malcolm: Poems on the Life and Death of Malcolm X* (1967), in collaboration with Margaret Burroughs; *Black Poetry: A Supplement to Anthologies Which Exclude Black Poets* (1969); and *The Black Poets* (1971). Dudley Randall is the founder of Broadside Press, a pioneering Black publishing company which has presented many of the important Black poets of the 1960s. He is also Visiting Professor of Black Poetry at the University of Michigan.

LENNOX RAPHAEL (1940–) Born in Trinidad, West Indies. He was a longtime staff writer for the *East Village Other* in New York City. His work has been published in *Negro Digest/Black World, American Dialogue,* and other periodicals. He gained international attention for his controversial play *Che,* produced in New York City. His poetry has been included in the anthologies *The New Black Poetry* (1969) and *Natural Process* (1970), from which "Mike 65" is taken.

EUGENE REDMOND (1937–) Born in East St. Louis, Illinois, he attended the schools of that city. He is a graduate of Southern Illinois University and Washington University of St. Louis, Missouri. He is a journalist and editor, and is active in community organizations. His poetry has appeared in numerous periodicals, including *Black Scholar, Negro Digest/Black World, Free Lance, American Dialogue, Confrontation,* and *Journal of Black Poetry.* He is included in the anthologies *The New Black Poetry* (1969), *A Galaxy of Black Writing* (1971), and *New Black Voices* (1972). His volumes of poetry include *Sentry of the Four Golden Pillars* (1970) and *River of Bones and Flesh and Blood* (1971). Mr. Redmond is the co-editor of two books of the works of his friend Henry Dumas, and is Professor of English and Poet-in-Residence in Ethnic Studies at Sacramento State College, California.

ISHMAEL REED (1938–) Born in Chattanooga, Tennessee. He is a novelist, editor, teacher, and essayist, as well as poet. His poetry has been included in many anthologies, including *The New Black Poetry* (1969), *Dices or Black Bones* (1970), and *The Norton Anthology of Poetry* (1970). His novels include *The Free-Lance Pallbearers* (1968), *Yellow Back Radio Broke-Down* (1969), and *Mumbo Jumbo* (1972). A volume of his poems, *catechism of d neoamerican hoodoo church,* was published in 1971, and *Selected Poems* appeared in 1972. Mr. Reed is the editor of the anthology *19 Necromancers from Now* (1970) and *The Yardbird Reader, Volume I,* a semi-annual collection of Afro-American literature launched in 1972.

CONRAD KENT RIVERS (1933–1968) Born in Atlantic City, New Jersey, he was a graduate of Wilberforce University, Chicago Teachers College, and Indiana University. He was a resident of Chicago and a teacher in the Gary, Indiana, school system at the time of his sudden death. His poetry has appeared in such periodicals as *Negro Digest/Black World, Antioch Review,* and *Kenyon Review,* and in the anthologies *American Negro Poetry* (1963) and *For Malcolm* (1967). He was the author of a drama, *To Make a Poet Black,* and four volumes of poetry, *Perchance to Dream, Othello* (1959), *These Black Bodies and This Sunburnt Face* (1962), *Dusk at Selma* (1965), and *The Still Voice of Harlem* (1968). Since his death *Negro Digest/Black World* magazine has established an annual Conrad Kent Rivers Poetry Award for the best poem published in that magazine during the year. In 1962 he wrote about himself and his work:
"I write about the Negro because I am a Negro,
and I am not at peace with myself or my world.
I cannot divorce my thoughts from the absolute injustice of hate.
I cannot reckon with my color.
I am obsessed by the ludicrous and psychological behavior of hated men.
And I shall continue to write about my race—in spite of many warnings—
until I discover myself, my future, my real race.
I do not wish to capitalize on race, nor do I wish to begin a Crimean War:
I am only interested in recording the truth
squeezed from my observations and experiences.
I am tired of being misrepresented.

No white man can dare write my story for me . . . it is for me to do.
I write about color because I have no say in the matter.
My muse is blind. I am not ashamed of my flesh.
I long to be heard. I am bitter, black and tired.
And I agree with Baldwin: 'nobody knows my name.'
All the standards for which the western world has lived so long
are in the process of breakdown and revision.
And beauty, and joy, which was in the world before
and has been buried so long, has got to come back."

ED ROBERSON (1939–) Born in Pittsburgh, Pennsylvania. He attended the University of Pittsburgh, and won the *Atlantic Monthly* prize for poetry in 1963. His work has appeared in such periodicals as *New Directions 22* and the *Atlantic Monthly,* and in the anthologies *Work,* published by the Detroit Artists Workshop, and *The Poetry of the Negro* (1949, 1970). In 1970 he published a volume of his poems, *When Thy King Is a Boy.* Mr. Roberson is a member of the English Department of the University of Pittsburgh.

CAROLYN M. RODGERS Born and raised in Chicago, Illinois, she has been active in the literary life of that city. She participated in a writing workshop with Gwendolyn Brooks and a group of other active Black writers, including Don L. Lee and Johari Amini. Ms. Rodgers' poetry has been included in many anthologies: *Natural Process* (1970); *We Speak as Liberators* (1970); *Night Comes Softly* (1970); and *To Gwen with Love* (1971). Her fiction has appeared in *Negro Digest/Black World* and in *Brothers and Sisters* (1970), an anthology of stories by Black Americans. Her books of poetry include *Paper Soul* (1968), *Songs of a Blackbird* (1969), *2 Love Raps* (a broadside) (1969), and *Blues Gittin Up* (1972). Carolyn Rodgers has taught Afro-American Literature at Columbia University and at the City College of New York, and is a member of the Organization of Black American Culture in Chicago. In 1968 she was the first recipient of the Conrad Kent Rivers Memorial Award for her poetry, given by *Negro Digest/Black World.*

PRIMUS ST. JOHN (1939–   ) He lives in Tacoma, Washington, with his wife and daughter. His poems have appeared in *Poet-Lore, Poetry Northwest, Concerning Poetry,* and other periodicals, and in the collections *Poems and Perspectives* and *Agenda for Survival.* Mr. St. John has taught at Mary Holmes College in Mississippi, and has received a 1970 Discovery Award from the National Endowment for the Arts. He is Poet-in-Residence for Tacoma, Washington, public schools, and Instructor in English at the University of Utah. He says: "As a man who writes poems, I am growing to see that paper and pencil can be helpful to life if used recklessly."

SONIA SANCHEZ (1935–   ) Born in Birmingham, Alabama. Her work has been published widely and is included in many anthologies, including *Natural Process* (1970), *The Black Poets* (1971), and *New Black Voices* (1972). Ms. Sanchez has lectured at colleges throughout the country, and has read her poetry on "Soul," a National Educational Television program. She is one of the influential Black poets to emerge from the 1960s and her books of poetry include *Homecoming* (1969), *We a Baddddd Peple* (1970), *It's a New Day: Poems for Young Brothas and Sistuhs* (1971), and *Three Hundred and Sixty Degrees of Blackness Comin at You* (1972). She writes: "i'm about setting positive blk images cuz they be needed. for us, for our blk children."

ALVIN SAXON (OJENKE) A native of the Watts section of Los Angeles, California. He joined the Writers' Workshop run by Budd Schulberg at the Watts Happening Coffee House in the summer of 1966. He has attended college in Los Angeles, and his poetry has been published in the *Antioch Review* and *From the Ashes: Voices of Watts* (1969).

WELTON SMITH (1940–   ) Born in Houston, Texas, "with grave reservations." He grew up in San Francisco, has lived in New York City, and has published his poetry in numerous periodicals. His work is included in such anthologies as *Black Fire* (1968), *The New Black Poetry* (1969), *The Poetry of the Negro* (1949, 1970), and *Black Spirits* (1972). He has published a collection of his poetry, *Penetration* (1972), a play, *The Roach Riders,* and has written an unpublished volume entitled *The Art of Marihuana*

Ceremony as Performed on the Lower East Side of Manhattan, A.D. 1950–1980: A Primary Account of Ritual Among Indigenous and Emigré Potheads by a Black Nationalist of Leisure and Genius.

A. B. SPELLMAN (1935–   ) He is a jazz critic and historian as well as poet. His work has appeared in such periodicals as *Journal of Black Poetry, The Nation, The Republic, Metronome, The Liberator, Black Dialogue,* and *Umbra.* He is represented in many anthologies, including *Beyond the Blues* (1962), *New Negro Poets: USA* (1964), *Black Fire* (1968), *The New Black Poetry* (1969), and *Dices or Black Bones* (1970). He has published a volume of poetry, *The Beautiful Days* (1965), and a book of essays, *Four Lives in the Bebop Business* (1966), which concerns the careers of Ornette Coleman, Herbie Nichols, Jackie McLean, and Cecil Taylor. Mr. Spellman is an editor of *The Cricket,* a magazine of Black music, and has been Writer-in-Residence at Morehouse College and Emory University.

ANNE SPENCER (1882–   ) Born in Bramwell, West Virginia, she was educated at the Virginia Seminary in Lynchburg, Virginia, the city where she has spent most of her life. She was a longtime librarian of Dunbar High School in Lynchburg, and her poetry has appeared in such collections as *The Poetry of the Negro* (1949, 1970) and *American Negro Poetry* (1963).

SUN RA Musician, philosopher, and poet, he records and appears with his Myth Science Arkestra. He is a noted composer and has recorded on the Saturn and ESP labels. Some of his albums are *The Magic City, Planet Earth, When Sun Comes Out,* and *When Angels Speak of Love.* His poetry has appeared in *Umbra: Anthology 1967–1968,* and in the anthology *Black Fire* (1968).

LORENZO THOMAS (1944–   ) He attended Queens College and Pratt Institute in New York City. He has been published in *Art & Literature, C: A Journal of Poetry, El Corno Emplumado, The Massachusetts Review, Umbra, Liberator,* and other periodicals. His work is included in such anthologies as *Black Fire* (1968) and *New Black Voices* (1972). A volume of his poetry, *Fit Music,* was published in 1972.

RICHARD W. THOMAS (1939–)
Born in Detroit, Michigan. He served in
the United States Marine Corps, and has
a B.A. and M.A. in history from Michigan
State University. His poetry has appeared
in such periodicals as *Red Cedar Review,
Negro Digest/Black World,* and *Colloquy.*
He is included in the anthologies *Black
Fire* (1968), *Nine Black Poets* (1968), *A
Galaxy of Black Writing* (1970), *The
Poetry of the Negro* (1949, 1970), and
Black Spirits (1972). Richard Thomas is
an Instructor at the Center for Urban
Affairs at Michigan State University.

JAMES W. THOMPSON (1935–)
Born in Detroit, Michigan. During the
1960s he was "the Georgia Douglas
Johnson of First Avenue, maintaining open
house for artists in various fields: poets,
painters, dancers, choreographers, photog-
raphers, musicians and writers." He has
been a professional dancer, choreographer,
dance editor, and reviewer for *The Feet,*
a dance magazine. Mr. Thompson was
Artist-in-Residence at Antioch College,
and together with Cecil Taylor, the jazz
musician, "was involved in the creation of
The Choir of the Spoken Word in celebration of the Aframerican oral tradition."
His poetry has appeared in such periodicals as *Umbra* and *Negro Digest/Black
World.* He is included in the anthologies
Sixes and Sevens (1962), *Beyond the
Blues* (1962), and *Black Spirits* (1962).
A volume of his poetry, *First Fire: Poems
1957–1960,* was published in 1970.

LARRY THOMPSON (1950–) Born
in Seneca, South Carolina, he was raised
and educated in Harlem, New York City.
His poetry has been published in *Negro
Digest/Black World,* and in anthologies,
including *Black Out Loud* (1970) and *It
Is the Poem Singing Into Your Eyes: Anthology of New Young Poets* (1971). Mr.
Thompson is a student at Yale University
and is an editor of the Yale literary magazine.

MELVIN B. TOLSON (1898–1966)
Born in Moberly, Missouri, he attended
Lincoln University and received an M.A.
from Columbia. Mr. Tolson had a long
teaching career, first at Wiley College in
Texas, and later at Langston University in
Oklahoma and Tuskegee Institute. His
work has appeared in numerous anthologies, and in 1953 he published *Libretto
for the Republic of Liberia,* a work that
was commissioned for the Liberian Cen-

tennial celebration. His other volumes of
poetry include *Rendezvous with America*
(1944) and *Harlem Gallery: Book I, The
Curator* (1965).

JEAN TOOMER (1894–1967) Born in
Washington, D.C., he was educated at
the University of Wisconsin and at The
City College of New York. With the
publication of his first book, *Cane* (1923),
a volume of stories and poetry, he established his reputation as one of the finest
of the Harlem Renaissance writers. Mr.
Toomer went to Europe, then returned to
America to spend the rest of his life in
quiet work with the Quakers in Pennsylvania, writing very little but allowing his
early work to be included in anthologies
of Black American literature. He died
two years before *Cane* was reissued in the
paper editions that enabled a new generation to rediscover and appreciate his work.

ASKIA MUHAMMAD TOURE (1938–
—) Born in North Carolina. His work
has been published in numerous periodicals, including *Umbra, Journal of Black
Poetry, Negro Digest/Black World, Freedomways, Liberator,* and *Soulbook.* He is
included in such anthologies as *Black
Fire* (1968), *Black Arts* (1969), *Natural
Process* (1970), and *The Poetry of the
Negro* (1949, 1970). He is an Editor-at-
Large for the *Journal of Black Poetry,*
lectures widely around the country, and
has taught at Columbia University. Mr.
Touré is the author of *JuJu* (1969), a
collection of his poetry, and *Songhai!*
(1972), poetry and sketches from 1966 to
1971.

QUINCY TROUPE (1943–) Born in
New York City, raised in St. Louis, Missouri. He was educated at Grambling
College and at U.C.L.A. and was an
original member of the Watts Writers
Workshop. Mr. Troupe has taught at
U.C.L.A., U.S.C., and Ohio University,
and now teaches at Richmond College,
Staten Island, New York. He is the editor
of *Confrontation: A Journal of Third
World Literature,* a periodical he helped
found at Ohio University, and is also an
editor of *Mundus Artium,* a literature
magazine. His work has appeared in such
periodicals as *Negro Digest/Black World,
Black Review #2, Umbra, Antioch Review, Mediterranean Review, Concerning
Poetry, New York Quarterly, Black Creation, Sumac,* and *New Directions 22.* He
is included in the anthologies *The New*

Black Poetry (1969), *We Speak as Liberators* (1970), *New Black Voices* (1972), and *Black Spirits* (1972). A collection of his work, *Embryo Poems 1967–1971*, was published in 1972.

ALICE WALKER (1944–) Born in Eatonton, Georgia, she attended Spelman College and Sarah Lawrence. She has been active in welfare rights and voter registration activities in Georgia and New York, and has traveled in Kenya, Uganda, and the Soviet Union. Her work has been published in *American Scholar, Negro Digest/Black World,* and other periodicals. A novel, *The Third Life of Grange Copeland,* was published in 1971. Her two volumes of poetry are *Once* (1968) and *Revolutionary Petunias* (1973).

MARGARET WALKER (1915–) Born in Birmingham, Alabama. She received an M.A. from the University of Iowa, and has been on the faculty of Jackson State College for many years. Her first book of poetry, *For My People* (1942), won the Yale University Younger Poets competition. Her work has appeared in numerous collections, and she has received fellowships and lectured in colleges around the country. Her first novel, *Jubilee* (1966), won the Houghton-Mifflin Literary Fellowship. In 1970 she published another collection of her poetry, *Prophets for a New Day. How I Wrote Jubilee,* an account of the writing of her novel, was published in 1972, for The Institute of the Black World in Atlanta.

TOM WEATHERLY (1942–) Born in Scottsboro, Alabama. He was educated at Morehouse College and Alabama A. & M. From his poem "Autobiography," published in his collection, *Maumau American Cantos* (1970):

". . . . . had a vision
entered a.m.e. ministry
assistant pastor of saint pauls scottsboro
& next year pastor of church great grandad
pastored (bishop i.h. bonner had feel for tradition).

had a division: left god mother hooded youth &
the country for new york, lived on streets, parks, hitched the states.
                    dishwasher at hip bagel,
waiter in the mountains, cook at lion's head,
proofreading, copyediting, baking, bell-hopping,

camp counselor, dealing, fuckd up in the head.
rantd in the saint marks poetry project, ranting
now in afro-hispanic poets workshop east harlem.

HOLDER OF THE DOUBLE MOJO HAND & 13th DEGREE GRIS-GRIS BLACK BELT."

RON WELBURN (1944–) Born in Bryn Mawr, Pennsylvania, and grew up in Philadelphia. He was graduated from Lincoln University as Poet Laureate there, and editor of the newspaper and literary magazine. He has published his fiction and essays since 1963 in several periodicals and his poetry has appeared in *Journal of Black Poetry, Negro Digest/Black World, Nickel Review, Essence,* and *Umbra/Blackworks.* His work is included in such anthologies as *Black Fire* (1968) and *New Black Poetry* (1969). He is the author of three books of poems published in 1972: *Moods, Bright and Indigo, Along the Estabon Way,* and *Far Song.* He is editor-in-chief of *Dues: An Annual of New Earth Writing,* published in 1972. Mr. Welburn has been Visiting-Writer-in-Residence at Auburn Correctional Facility in Auburn, New York, and teaches creative writing and literature at Syracuse University.

JOSEPH WHITE Born in Philadelphia. His work has appeared in *Dasein, Liberator,* and other periodicals, and is included in the anthologies *Burning Spear* (1963), *Poets of Today* (1964), and *I Am the Darker Brother* (1968).

AUGUST WILSON (1945–) Lives in Pittsburgh, Pennsylvania. He is a member of Oduduwa Productions, editing and publishing Black American authors. He has been poetry editor of *Connection,* a quarterly publication of writings and art produced by that community group. His poem "Theme One: The Variations" was published in *Connection* in 1970.

BRUCE McM. WRIGHT (1918–) Born in Princeton, New Jersey. He attended Lincoln University and Fordham University School of Law. A book of his poetry, *From the Shaken Tower* (1944), was published in Wales. His poem "The African Affair" is from *The Poetry of the Negro* (1949, 1970). In recent years he has lived in New York

City where he has practiced law and continued his writing. His work has also been included in the anthologies *Beyond the Blues* (1962) and *American Negro Poetry* (1963).

JAY WRIGHT (1935–   ) Born in Albuquerque, New Mexico, he is a graduate of the University of California at Berkeley. He is a playwright as well as poet, and his plays have been produced in California and have been published. His poetry has appeared in numerous periodicals, including *New American Review, Evergreen Review, Hiram Poetry Review, The Nation,* and *Negro Digest/Black World.* He is represented in the anthologies *New Negro Poetry: USA* (1964), *For Malcolm* (1967), *31 New American Poets* (1969), and *Natural Process* (1970). A collection of his poems, *The Homecoming Singer,* was published in 1971.

RICHARD WRIGHT (1908–1960) Born on a plantation near Natchez, Mississippi. He was self-educated for the most part, and worked at many jobs in the South and later in Chicago. During the Depression he was a writer with the Federal Writers' Project, a government-sponorsed program. His first book, *Uncle Tom's Children,* a collection of short stories, was published in 1938, and in 1939 he received a Guggenheim Fellowship. His first novel, *Native Son* (1940), brought him national and international recognition. Its success was equaled in 1945 by the publication of *Black Boy,* an autobiography. In 1946 Richard Wright moved to Paris with his family, where he continued to write about life for Black Americans. In 1953 he visited the African Gold Coast, now Ghana, and wrote *Black Power,* a description of his experiences in that country. He remained an expatriate until his death in Paris.

SARAH E. WRIGHT Born in Maryland, she now lives in New York City. Her work has appeared in *Freedomways* magazine, and in the anthology *Poets of Today* (1964). She is the co-author of a collection of poems, *Give Me A Child* (1955), and a novel, *This Child's Gonna Live,* was published in 1969. Mrs. Wright was for several years the vice-president of the Harlem Writers' Guild. In an introductory note to "To Some Millions Who Survive Joseph E. Mander, Senior" she has written:

"On Sunday, May 12, 1952, in the city of Philadelphia, Joseph E. Mander, Senior, Negro, father of three small children and a fourth one on the way, died in a heroic attempt to rescue 7-year-old Paul Waxman, a white child, from death by drowning in the treacherous waters of the Schuylkill River. He was posthumously awarded the honor of 'Father of the Year' by the National Father's Day Council. The following poem was written during the first week after the tragedy, and was published in the *North Penn News,* a Philadelphia newspaper."

AL YOUNG (1939–   ) Born in Ocean Springs, Mississippi, he grew up in Detroit, Michigan. He was educated at the University of Michigan and the University of California at Berkeley. His work has appeared in numerous periodicals, including *The Massachusetts Review, Evergreen Review, Rolling Stone,* and *Journal of Black Poetry.* He is represented in many anthologies, including *The New Black Poetry* (1969), *The American Literary Anthology/3* (1970), *19 Necromancers from Now* (1970), *Natural Process* (1970), and *New Black Voices* (1972). He has published two books of poetry, *Dancing* (1969) and *The Song Turning Back Into Itself* (1971), and a novel, *Snakes* (1971). Mr. Young teaches Fiction and Poetry Writing at Stanford University.

Index